Out of the Farlans
Fresh Fields

With Best Wishes

Jean Duthie

Jean Duthie.

authorHOUSE®

AuthorHouse™ UK Ltd.
500 Avebury Boulevard
Central Milton Keynes, MK9 2BE
www.authorhouse.co.uk
Phone: 08001974150

First published by AuthorHouse   6/7/2010

ISBN: 978-1-4520-1163-9 (sc)

This book is printed on acid-free paper.

ABOUT THE AUTHOR

Jean Duthie was born to Scottish immigrants in Boston, Mass. at the peak of the Great Depression. On returning to Fraserburgh in 1932 the family suffered much during unemployment and homelessness, followed by World War 2. But difficulties were gradually resolved and the home became focused on education, literature, music and firm Christian principles.

Jean's interests lay in History and Music, particularly violin playing, which brought her into solo and orchestral work for a time. Fascination with the past led to a particularly intensive study of the preceding three generations of her ancestors and her keen observation of people nourished the very acute memory with which she had been endowed, eventually supplying the anecdotal material for "OUT OF THE FARLANS".

A graduate in English and History from Aberdeen University, she taught these subjects in the Border town of Sanquhar, later moving to Inverallochy School near Fraserburgh. Marriage and the birth of a daughter and son brought her temporarily out of teaching but eventually, they settled in the Scottish Borders, where Jean and her husband Andrew completed their years of service in Galashiels. Here with their family, they enjoyed over forty years of treasured friendships and rich experiences in the beautiful countryside.

Love of travel took the family abroad annually, camping and touring mainly in Europe until, after retiring, Jean and Andrew went further afield to the USA where she discovered the true facts of her family in that country, and this book began to formulate.

Jean now resides in Aberdeen close to her family, her Church and friends, all of whom play a vital role in her life. She and her husband still travel, storing up ideas, and ever learning about this wonderful world and the people who inhabit it.

INTRODUCTION AND ACKNOWLEDGEMENTS

It was only after my Mother, Mary Bella died in 1979 that I began to realize what an important part she had played in my life. I had lost a friend, a wise adviser, an encourager, a soul mate, all these and more, and it made me wonder what had made her so special. What influences had moulded her?

That led me to consider her parents Betsy and Alex May, her Aunt Maggie Ann and finally her Grandmother Mary May. Her experience of life with these four people had fashioned Mary Bella and now, my generation had finally reaped the benefit.

As a child often in my Mother's company, I came to know all the Aunts save Janet who died very young and, although I liked them all, Ena was my favourite. Sadly I never knew my Grandfather Alex May, or my Great Grandmother Mary May, but, when my Mother felt in a reminiscing mood, I sat for many hours listening to tales of their lives, hardships and victories.

From my childhood the names of people and places were all familiar to me and, when eventually in our retirement, my husband Andy and I visited Boston and Jamaica Plain, the Ripley homes in Newton Center and in Maine, they all became reality. For Maggie Ann and Mary Bella life with the Ripleys had really happened. Even now the family re-membered Maggie with great respect and affection. Boston and Jamaica Plain were there with all their associations and I found again my other family, Flora, Bob, Dick and Marjory, relatives I had last seen as a child of three.

All have contributed to the writing of this book and I thank them for the years of encouragement and sharing. Over the twenty years we paid three visits to the USA, each time opening up more kernels of information but there is still one more mission to fulfil; to locate the grave of my Grandfather Alex May, where he lies in Jacksonville, Florida. Then the circle will be complete. But time is catching up on me and I may have to leave that task to another.

The writing of this book has given me great pleasure but it has also been a discipline and task, which I wondered very often if I would ever complete. As most of the story is based on memories and reminiscences I had to examine the facts and verify events; a laborious task at times. But, thanks to the interest and generous efforts of many people, the research was completed and I was able to weave together the lives of my four ancestors.

In the narrative I have used the real names of family members and those of the Ripley household but, where events took the story into the realms of the imagination, I had to use fictitious names and base the characters on the qualities of people I had known and observed over the years.

If the North East dialect has presented a problem to my readers I apologise but one cannot grow up in the Broch and not speak the tongue. It is part of the local culture, sadly not so prevalent now. However, in the late 19th. Century, for most it was their only language. Perhaps the Glossary will be of some aid in translation.

I wish to pay tribute to my siblings, Alastair and Betty; to my children Ruth and David with their spouses Iain and Gillian; to my Grand daughter Shona, who, along with her parents Ruth and Iain, gave invaluable assistance in preparing the book; to the enthusiasm of my Grand children

Robert, Olivia and Melissa; to members of the Ripley family, Anne and Peter Weller, Joanne Spencer, Susan Carver, Ruth and Alison Carver; to my American family Flora, Bob, Pat, Dick, Barbara and Marjory May; and to those who researched so many details in the strangest places; Mary Findlay, Iain Clark, Lewis Ritchie Sen., Margaret Taylor, Sheila Watt Ritchie, Elizabeth and James Buchan Sen., and Mary and James Buchan.. Finally, I am indebted to the George Watt Family for permission to use copies of the paintings.

Most of all I thank my husband Andy. My patient listener, my constant encourager and enthusiast, my travelling companion, who was ever there for me. His strength and presence made the whole work possible and I am so grateful.

DEDICATION
For Mary Bella, our Mother.

Part 1
Maggie Ann 1870- 1913

Left to Right: Janet Sim holding Baby Tom Sim,
Mary May Duthie and Belsie May 1894.

Chapter 1

It had been one of those lovely, golden, October days, which happen occasionally in the northeast of Scotland. All day it had been warm, without wind, and now the sun was setting in a sky on fire with all the magnificence that the word "firmament" conjures up. Soon the coming darkness would add contrast and variety, but now the light was brilliant. Silhouetted against the sky the curving line of Broadsea Village and its fishermen's cottages showed up dark and clear. The rocky coast, dotted with pools, stretched in a wide semicircle out into the wider Firth while on the eastern side a sheer wall of basalt rock, scored here and there by long, deep crevices, gave wonderful shelter from the fury of the North Sea. And right in the deepest curve of the shore lay the reason for Broadsea Village-a natural landing and a tiny sandy beach where yawls and small sailboats were anchored or winched up above high tide level.

Scattered here and there over the yellow sand were the marks of the fishermen's trade- bits of rope, an old basket, the odd bucket, a sea boot and, where the sand met the grassy bank lay a skull, no longer used for the baited lines but maybe used as a sledge to pull gear down from the houses on the brae heads. The scene was not marred by the litter, rather it was a sign of the living, thriving community which was Broadsea

Above the broken coastline the rocks gave way to grassy slopes crowned with the fishermen's cottages, low, two-roomed, stone built houses with red tiled roofs; a few still had the original turf roofs and all of these dwellings had been in the same family for generations. The road followed the line of the bay with the houses on the seaward side built gable on to the sea for shelter and protection from the lashing of the storms. The little window set in each gable wall was the constant link with the sea, marking the mood of the restless water or the safe return of the boat as it rounded the headland, or the weather, always a topic of vital concern. Below, the grassy slopes were laced with a fine network of paths and steps, all leading to the beach and on a weekday there was the constant coming and going activity of men at work, women about their households and children at play; life was everywhere.

But not today- it was Saturday, early evening, and all that moved was the slow drift of smoke from the chimneys and the leisurely wheel of the gulls. Even the sea in the ebb was lulled, hanging on the few moments between the ebb and flow, as if the waves were resting to muster enough energy to resume the long haul back to the shore.

So thought Maggie Ann as she sat on the cliff top surveying her village, Broadsea, where she had spent most of her life. She knew all the families and as her eyes moved on from one house to the next she named them to herself. There was the Broadsea School standing taller above the houses and beyond that, she could just see the pointed gable of the village hall, 'the Hallie'. She smiled to herself as she remembered schooldays; she had been a good scholar and quiet, so the teacher had favoured her; but the children had called 'teacher's pet'. Not that it worried her as she had always been too busy at home helping with her younger brother and sisters. And the memories of Sunday school soirees and weddings in the hall were wonderful. Her eyes roved on and came to light on the green painted wrought-iron structure, just at the top of the braes opposite her grandfather's house at No.1 Main St. Old Alex Duthie had raged long about the establishing of a pisserie opposite his front door. It would cause rats to increase, smells would fill the air, water from the street well would be polluted- all sorts of arguments for and against. But the facility went up and in a strange way became a focal point. None of the fears materialised and mothers especially, were glad that men no longer went behind houses or rocks when the need arose. Maggie Ann could still hear her mother's quiet remarks about it being plain common sense to have a pisserie there right by the shore where most people worked .She could not see what all the fuss was about. They lived round the corner from No.1, on Broadsea Rd. and could watch the daily activity to and from the shore as carters came and went along the low road that led to the jetty and the curing yards on the braes.

Maggie Ann and her mother Mary May were very close in their views on life. Sentiment was strictly controlled and practicalities, honesty and self-sufficiency were diligently followed; not that Mary May was unkind, but Maggie Ann knew only too well what had moulded her mother into the woman she had become. She loved her deeply never giving any indication of her feelings of course, but above all, she respected her and admired her strength of character. Amongst all five sisters she, Maggie Ann, the eldest, most resembled Mary May both in looks and nature and now, as she sat in the evening stillness she realised that she was in fact saying goodbye to all that she had ever known-this beloved village, the people, the childhood she had loved here;

even as the thought passed through her mind she realised that this was also the moment for memorising; memories would be all she would have where she was going for the next many years.

As she sat, the peace of the scene began to act as balm on her soul and she became acutely aware of the silence as if time, like the sea, was waiting to reassert its sense of direction and come crashing in against the rocks below; but now it was full and dark and waiting. The only sound was the lonely piping of a late gull returning to its nest on the cliffs below. The gold of the sunset was casting a blush over the braes where she sat above the cliffs and Maggie Ann could pick out the patches of white gowans, now closed to the daylight, and the large purple and white clover heads, and everywhere grew that great yellow flower head that she could not name. Folks said it was a weed but she loved the bold richness of its colour. All her life the braes had been her garden, she knew every inch of them, could remember the feel of the wet grass under her feet when she had run barefoot in childhood, and the wind whipping her hair as she and her sisters had raced each other towards the high, black, rocky outcrop that was the Rummlin' Goit, the dreaded place and always forbidden to them. Maggie Ann wondered how deep it really was. Even as the sky darkened to a deep rosy pink patterned with wispy drifting grey clouds, the lights in the windows came on one by one- it seemed to bring the houses closer- and Maggie Ann realised it was time to go, but she could not drag herself away. Just then the first beam of Kinnaird lighthouse swung across the bay and the whole scene was illuminated for a few seconds setting her memories off on another tack.

Chapter 2

The road behind where she sat continued right along the braes past the Goit, then the foghorn and the bathing spot to the lighthouse and the ancient Wine Tower. Skirting the landward side of the road were the walls of the fish curing yards stretching all the way to the lighthouse and dotted here and there along the wall were wooden benches where the old men usually sat and yarned about sailing days while they smoked their pipes and kept an eye on the bay below. Sometimes on a fine day women would come out and sit there while their fingers were busy with the four needles on the everlasting knitting- pullovers, sea boot socks or the long, wheeling wool drawers their men folk wore in winter under the thick kersey trousers. There was an ethic of industry and women were never idle. "To look well to the ways of her household" was regarded as women's work and taken very seriously.

As her eyes lit on one of the benches Maggie Ann relived the most terrible night of her life. She had been eleven and because she was the eldest, she had always been given more responsibility than the others. Janet, Betsy, Bella and Alexander all played a role in the family but, because their father William was a fisherman and often away for long months deep water fishing, Maggie Ann became her mother's right hand and often the two heads would be together quietly talking while the others were asleep. Now that she was eleven Maggie Ann was contemplating leaving the Broadsea school and had given some thought about what she would do with her life- not that there was much choice at that time- it was either domestic service or fish worker. Meantime there were other things to think about as another baby was on the way, father was at sea and her mother needed all her help. They hoped for a boy but when the baby arrived after a short labour it was a tiny, doll-like girl, beautiful and perfect in every way. She was called Wilhelmina after her father- Ena for short- and from the day of her birth she became very special to Maggie Ann.

This had been such a happy short time but a few days after Ena's birth Maggie Ann began to notice a look of worry on her mother's face. Nothing was said, but then the day came when the man from the shipping office arrived to say that the boat was overdue and there was some fear about it. Three days later it was officially declared lost at sea with all hands and Mary May found herself a widow with six children, the youngest only ten days old.

For all of them that day there was a numbed silence. The routine of home went on although the children did not go to school and each was given a black armband to wear. A few neighbours called to give comfort and Aunt Annie May from Cairnbulg came in for a few hours during the afternoon. What was most vivid to Maggie Ann's memory were the long spells of silence and very little was said about her father. For them as children he was an occasional visitor who was never there long enough to get to know. There were so many questions that could not be answered and they were grieving in shock for a person who was not there.

It was a relief when bedtime came and the younger children went off through to the front room and settled for the night. Maggie Ann bathed and fed Ena and laid her in the cradle where she soon fell asleep. Then she realised her mother was not in the house which was very unusual but Maggie Ann continued being busy until another hour had gone by. She decided to go and search. Having whispered to Janet to keep an ear open for Ena's crying she wrapped a shawl round her shoulders and set off along the braes thinking that was the most likely rout her mother would have taken. It had been a damp, misty day and now in the darkness the fog had thickened and a fine rain saturated everything. Her boots slipped on the wet stones. She wished she had thought to take the lantern. As she hurried on a deep anxiety gripped her as she remembered the cliffs and the Goit and the steep slope of the braes. She pulled the shawl closer over her head and hurried on, eyes scanning everywhere in the darkness. In the distance sounded the mournful 'hooo' of the foghorn and faintly through the fog on the interval came the flash of the lighthouse. Maggie Ann was glad of it; it seemed the only kind thing on that terrifying walk. Then she heard it- a faint sobbing drew her to a corner of the curing yard wall and there she found Mary May huddled against it, lost in her grief.

Maggie Ann put her arms round her mother and drew her to the nearest bench and there they sat gripping each other in their need for comfort. Great shudders ran through Mary May's small body as the pent up grief found an outlet and Maggie Ann wept with her because she suffered for her mother. Gradually the spasms subsided and calm was restored but they still sat holding each other enfolded in the large plaid that Maggie Ann had wrapped round them both allowing the shared heat of their bodies to comfort them. Sitting under the lee of the wall they were sheltered from the cold wind and the worst of the driving rain. Maggie Ann whispered,

"Janet is watching Ena," thinking her mother would be concerned, but she took no notice, seemingly far away, lost in her own thoughts while her hands gripped the girl's like a vice.

Presently she began to speak in a whisper that Maggie Ann had to strain to hear,

"Wull wis a gweed man an weel daen an he ae lookit oot for us a'. Bit he niver kennt his ain mither an niver onner-stood fou tae treat a wife. He jist hid his faither and brithers an' didna kenn much aboot wimmen. He wis a bonny loon 'at simmer I met him in the gutten yard. I looed him an' he looed me an' I wud hae deen onything for him. We courted that simmer an' then he gaed sooth for the winter fishin' an' didna come hame for a year. You were born in July Maggie Ann an' fan he cam hame in November we got merried. My mither and Annie niver likit him an' thocht I shouldna merry him though twas an affront haen a bairn outside wedlock. But I wanted him. My faither cam tae the weddin' in the Rathen manse."

After another long pause.

"We jist had eleven years an ae fan he cam hame he wis happy tae see us a', but then he hankered efter the sea again an' went aff leaving me wi' anither bairn."

She was silent for a time during which Maggie Ann sat reeling from what she had just learned about herself. She had been a bastard child when she was born. She would not have dared say it but she knew what it meant and now she realised why there was such a close tie between herself and Granny Bellsie and Aunt Annie May in Cairnbulg. They had been the first to love this unwanted child- would have even kept her for their own in spite of the affront. It did not matter that her mother had married her father and they had become a family. She felt a cold stone- like chill settle in her body, a sense of rejection of what she was. The whole edifice of her security had disappeared and she did not know what to do or what to say.

Mary May began to whisper again,

"He's gone an' I dinna ken far an' I hinna even got his body tae bury him."

Turning she grasped Maggie Ann by the shoulders and digging her fingers in she cried like a lost creature,

"Whit am I gan tae dee wi six bairns an' nae man. Hoo can I feed them?"

Maggie Ann realised that her own grief had to be put aside as she wrapped her arms round her mother and led her gently back along the braes to their own house.

After a cup of tea Mary May lay down exhausted in the box bed in the kitchen alcove. Ena and the older children still slept and Mary May slept fitfully, rousing every now and then when a sob choked her throat. But Maggie Ann kept her vigil by her mother, staring into the fire and pondering her thoughts. About dawn her mother fell into a deep sleep and Maggie Ann slipped through to the room, undressed and lay down, spent, in the bed she shared with Janet.

When she woke next morning it was to hear the usual sounds of preparation for school, porridge on the table and children's chatter. Mary May was as normal and as they set off for school she gave Maggie Ann a nod as if to say,

"Things are alright now."

The events of that night were never referred to again. Life took up a new pattern as Mary May became breadwinner as well as mother and they all had to take on a shared responsibility in the home. Although life was to present her with sadness again, Maggie Ann carried with her always the awesome memory of that night when she felt that she had plumbed the uttermost depths of sorrow.

Chapter 3

Some significant changes took place during the following weeks after their father's death. Behind their home was a yard, cobbled all the way across. Four coal sheds, one for each of the four tenants, stood along the back wall and the communal wash house was situated in the corner farthest from the back gate leading onto the main road. In the centre of the yard rose the wooden staircase leading to the two flats upstairs and under the stairs was the shared toilet for the four families. Because they were conscientious tenants the place was immaculate, swept weekly by the neighbours in turn and every spring the whitewashing took place when toilet, walls and all outhouses received a fresh coat. Sometimes a herring net was spread over a horizontal pole hooked to the wall next the washhouse and on a fine day the women would sit and mend the net, chatting while the children played. Often cups of tea were brought out and scones with jam and there was a lovely sense of fun for the children while the mothers worked. Sometimes they fixed up a small length of net for the children to practice on and that is where Maggie Ann had her first lessons on net mending.

These were happy memories, which brought a smile to her face as the evening gathered in around her.

Throughout her short life Mary May was skilled in only two spheres, working with fish and being a good, thrifty mother and wife. Now she was no longer a wife, but she realised that she would have to support her family as she knew how. There was also in her nature a very fierce sense of independence and pride which made her refuse all offers of help, of which there were many as was the custom in village life at that time. So people learned to stand back and respect her wishes and no longer looked with pity on her plight.

Mary May's first move was to visit her neighbours in turn and to outline her plan which required their agreement. Here there was no problem as they knew her standards and they were so glad of the opportunity to help this proud woman. Then her large coalhouse was cleared, the coal was removed to a new bunker standing against the outside wall and the whole outhouse was swept, scrubbed down and whitewashed. A new padlock was screwed to the door and three empty tea chests were placed against the inner back wall; a cutting block lay on a marble topped washstand alongside a small washtub. In the corner stood an old, low kitchen chair, likewise scrubbed, and Mary May had her work place.

Being deeply involved in all the changes and developments outside provided excitement and interest for the children which played a large part in their healing from grief and shock and as Mary May pursued her plan Maggie Ann more and more took on the role of housekeeper and mother. So much so that by the end of the summer, when she was twelve, her mother applied to the school board for an exemption on the plea of hardship in the home and Maggie Ann said goodbye to her beloved school. That day in August after the summer recess when all the children went back to school she found her solace again on the braes. There she resolved that one day when her time came, she would do something with her life, have learning, and see other places. But now her mother needed her.

The weekly routine was always the same. On Monday morning the washhouse boiler was lit at five o'clock and by eight o'clock the lines were full of the family wash. The older children went off to school and Maggie Ann dressed and fed Alexander and Ena. She did any necessary housework and prepared dinner which was always mid-day and on Monday generally consisted of some sort of soup followed by a pudding. Meantime Mary May would be occupied doing her weekly stint of cleaning up the wash house, tidying the close as the yard was called, finishing with scrubbing out the toilet with the hot water remaining in the wash boiler. Then the shed was cleaned out and left ready for the work next day. During the day, as the clothes dried they were brought in and ironed on the kitchen table set ready with an old thick blanket and sheet. The four flat irons were ranged on a ledge in front of the fire and used in turn. As the day wore on a lovely smell of clean, freshly ironed clothes pervaded the kitchen as the rail below the mantelpiece was filled with the still damp garments and the clotheshorse held the rest. The children enjoyed Mondays for mother was there all day. As she worked she listened to their chatter and their questions, their arguments and grievances, putting in a word here and there, but generally observing in silence.

After school Maggie Ann and Janet's Monday task was to visit the sawmill at the top of Windmill Street to collect saw dust for Mary May. The girls loved this for the workmen were jolly, often teasing them about their boy friends, especially Janet who was taller and looked older than Maggie Ann. But the men were kind and admired the girls for their keenness to help their mother. On Mary May's strict instructions the sawdust had to be clean and dry and above all-oak dust. So during the week the sawyers would set aside the best, sometimes adding a few handfuls of fine oak chips, and save it for the girls' visit on the Monday. Often they came home with the sacks slung over their shoulders and some pan drops in their apron pockets. Mary May did not approve of the sweets but she appreciated the good sawdust.

When Tuesday and Wednesday mornings dawned Mary May, creel on back ,would be at the first fish sales in the Fraserburgh market. The line boats arrived before seven o'clock so she was there at the first bidding for haddock, cod, sole and skate. She knew what she could handle and what was in greatest demand. Her quota complete, Mary May would be seen trudging up College Bounds, her loaded creel on her back, to arrive in time for breakfast and to see the children off to school. The rest of the day was spent in gutting and cleaning the fish, filleting some on the marble block and hooking the larger haddocks to the wooden triangles fixed on the outside walls for the fish to dry in the sun and fresh air. Other haddock and cod were set aside for smoking which was a longer process, but it was a very good selling commodity. This was where the tea chests featured. A thick layer of sawdust and oak chips was spread on the bottom and a very hot metal brick or coal was placed in the sawdust. Once it began to smoulder a thick smoke was created. A thin metal rod was threaded through the lugs of the fish so that they hung down, about five fish to a rod, which in turn were laid in fours across the top of the chest suspending the fish in the oak smoke. A lid was placed on each chest, then a heavy tarpaulin to trap any smoke and the fish were left for about forty-eight hours. When they were uncovered the fish were a beautiful pale golden yellow, moist and appetising, and especially flavoured with that oaky taste.

As time went on Mary May's skills as a fish wife became known in Broadsea and folks would come to the close entrance to watch her at work in the shed and to buy fish. But this was not her main objective, she had a wider enterprise in mind. Come Thursday morning she was up at dawn; the creel was packed, dried fish on the bottom, smoked above that and the filleted white fish on top, all wrapped in spotless white cotton cloths and thin waterproof sail cloth. There was also a shallow basket holding some lemon sole and other specialities. Dressed in her warm, most decent clothes and wearing strong walking boots Mary May set off for the country. Her journey would take all day till evening and she would cover over five miles, sometimes more, going from farm to farm and being directed to others, wherever she thought there was a customer. Every Thursday she set out faithfully and her clients came to rely on her arrival. She never ate in any farmhouse although she was often invited to partake in the family meal. Rather than be beholden to anyone she carried her piece, most often cheese and oat cakes, in her apron pocket, and a masking of Macdonald's blended tea which required only a can of boiling water. Such was her sense of independence. Nothing deterred her. Even in the worst of winter weather she made her rounds and when fish was scarce she always managed to prepare something to fill the creel.

No money changed hands on these journeys for Mary May dealt on a barter basis. In exchange for fish she received the equivalent in butter and eggs and as the day went on the creel never grew any lighter. Sometimes the two older girls would walk out along the Watermill Road to meet her trudging home in the darkening and they would relieve her of the heavy basket from her arm, giving her all the news of the day and bombarding her with questions about who she had seen. Occasionally in the summer holidays one of the older girls would accompany her all the way and would see another aspect of their mother, which they remembered and spoke about later on; but usually she went alone.

Friday was another sort of day for the shed became the shop. The butter was all laid out on the scrubbed marble slab; the butter clappers were at the ready in a stone jar of cold water and the eggs were graded large and small into two baskets. All day the customers came to the close and made their purchases and by evening when all was sold, Mary May was able to work out her costs and her profit.

As the weeks went by she learned a great deal about human nature, the pinching meanness of some and the great generosity of others. She knew sometimes that the block of butter she received in payment was far larger than required but when she remonstrated no argument was accepted. She was grateful for such customers; fortunately their numbers far exceeded the other.

Saturday was the big housecleaning day. Feather mattresses were turned, rugs were carried out to the yard and beaten, the grate was blackened and polished, the floors were swept, dusting everywhere, brasses were cleaned, the front doorstep was scrubbed, windows were polished inside and out. Everyone had a task. By dinnertime there was a feeling of relief and anticipation for in the afternoon they would all set off to pay the bills and maybe have a treat. The payments were simple. At Charlotte St. corner was the grocer where Maggie Ann purchased on account anything she needed for cooking during the week. The butcher was next door into the High Street and then they set off for

Macdonald's, the large wholesale grocer on Cross Street. This shop was a magical place for them, full of wonderful smells of coffee beans, tea blending, fruit, and at the dairy counter the children watched fascinated as the assistant cut off a wedge of creamery butter from the large block. He then worked it between wet ridged wooden clappers until it was a perfect round. This was all done in mid air and he never dropped the ball once. Then he placed it on a stone slab and, taking a round metal tool with a pattern on the bottom he so carefully pressed down on the ball until it was a pat with a perfect thistle in the centre. Breathless, the children watched, utterly spellbound until the process was complete and wondered if he had other patterns and did he ever miss the centre? Shopping complete, they would set off for a walk round the harbour or climb Castle Terrace to the lighthouse to follow the road round the braes to Broadsea and home. Sometimes they just played on the shore where there was always plenty to absorb. Maggie Ann remembered the box of tiny John o' Groat shells she had sifted from the rough sand on the shore. Ena had them now. When evening came the large kettle was set on the range and preparations began for the weekly hair wash and bath. The little ones came first and one by one sitting in the big zinc bath by the fire and amid lots of splashing and laughter, they washed each other. Then there was cocoa and into a lovely soft clean bed.

There was always an atmosphere of quiet on Sunday. Sunday School was held at eleven o'clock in the Broadsea Hall and all the children trouped off to that dressed in their cleanest aprons over their best dresses. Alex wore a deep folded back white collar which he really found irksome and not to his taste, but all the other boys wore them so he conformed. After the hair washing and pleating the previous evening the combing out on Sunday was wonderful, and each girl had a most beautiful aura of crimped hair, which, caught up with a ribbon, stood out in a halo and bounced as they danced along the road. Although never a vain woman, there was a certain satisfied pride in the heart of Mary May as she waved away her little brood and came in to sit for a quiet hour. In all the week this was the time she treasured unashamedly for herself, when she took stock and played one thought against another. She would not have regarded herself as a religious person, but in the thirty odd years of her life she had experienced enough hardship and sorrow to realize that behind all her struggle there was a hidden strength, which she relied on. Many times she had called on God in her distress and whether He heard her or not she did not know, but she was conscious of her will power, her courage, her energy, her need for straightness and honesty and mercifully, her good health, and if they came from above then she was thankful and had a grateful heart. There was a certain peace underlying all the struggle and in her quiet moments she savoured that sense like a benediction.

Occasionally, in the summertime they would all set off on the long walk to Cairnbulg to visit Granny Belsie and Annie May, their only aunt. This was really an adventure, particularly if the tide was out and they could walk along the beach, which curved for two miles in a beautiful, golden sweep below the grass- topped dunes. They set off sedately enough but soon the wide-open space inspired the urge to run and the children were off, boots slung around their necks, up and down the dunes, through the mysterious paths of the bents, along the wet sand. Mary May just let them go, glad to see their joy and fitness as she strolled along steadily with Ena by the hand. The local Sunday conventions did not concern her as long as no one was being hurt. By mutual agreement they usually waited for each other in the sand hole- a large amphitheatre of towering golden sand dunes which was quite awesome if you were little and there on your own. But now it rang with the shouts of the children as they climbed and rolled down the high sweeps of sand. Sometimes she would linger behind one of the bents and, unseen, observe their joy and exuberance and her heart would lift with thankfulness. When Mary May arrived they sat down to cool off and eat the pieces, which she produced from her apron pockets. Now was the time they talked- each one trying to outdo the other; how many times they had been to the top and rolled down; how big a bunch of bluebells they had collected; what was the new flower they had found in the tall grasses; here was a tiny skull skeleton, was it a bird or a mouse? Sometimes Betsy and Bella fell out and argued; this was how it often was between these two with the clash of their temperaments and Mary May had to be peacemaker or disciplinarian. After crossing the Waters of Philorth the group moved on along the last stretch and stopped by the first rocks to tidy up and don the boots before going through the village. Mary May knew from experience how rigid the rules and conventions were in Cairnbulg. She would give no one cause to criticize her children so she had them well drilled in how they were to behave and present themselves. A very sedate little group arrived at the door of the butt and benn at No.61 and knocked before going in.

Of course the welcome was always warm although restrained on the part of the old lady, Granny Belsie who as usual, was seated in the large chair by the fire. The glowing fire relieved the gloom in the low-ceilinged room, but little light penetrated from the tiny window set high in the wall in spite of the brilliant sunshine outside. The visitors peered around until their eyes came into focus and they could see their grandmother and aunt. Because of her distant and austere expression the children were hesitant in their approach to Granny but Annie May had hugs for all and in no time they were enjoying drinks of tea or milk with scones and jam, seated on the hearth stone or the fender round the fire telling what they had found on their walk. Mary May and her mother talked quietly by themselves but there was always that restraint between them going back a long time and, through stubborn pride, never being resolved. After an hour their visit was over and with the thought of school and work tomorrow, they had to get home before too late. So sadly they took their departure promising to come back before too long; they were always reluctant to leave Aunt Annie.

Usually if they went out by the beach the return journey was by road as the tide would be coming in but that also was an adventure as each stage presented its own highlight. They cut off a good two road miles by following a well worn track behind the dunes and, once clear of the village, the children marched along in step singing at the top of their voices, Sunday School hymns like 'Onward Christian Soldiers' and 'Hold the Fort for I am Coming'. This soon brought them alongside the main road to Philorth Bridge and it was at about this point that they very often met groups of walkers, also singing, going home to Cairnbulg from the afternoon service at the Baptist Church in Fraserburgh. There was always a pause to chat and rest a little and very often a sweetie changed hands, but Mary May did not encourage too much familiarity and they were soon on their way again.

One outstanding memory stayed with Maggie Ann as the years passed. It was on one such return journey that they heard the singing a long way back and as they approached the bridge they could see crowds gathered and the singing was so wonderful. One parapet of the bridge was hidden by people looking down and when the children reached near enough to look they were amazed to see throngs of people on both sides of the river below. A service was in progress and the preacher stood in the middle of the river. It reminded Maggie Ann of the story of Jesus preaching from the boat. They could not quite hear all that was being said but shortly afterwards first one woman, dressed in a white robe went forward to the preacher who laid her in the water and then lifted her up. This happened to two other ladies and between each occasion the congregation burst into a song 'Down in the Valley with My Saviour I Would go'. Maggie Ann never forgot the atmosphere of joy and exaltation even she as a young girl recognized. All the way home they wondered and talked about it asking endless questions but all Mary May would say was that it was a group of Baptists using the river instead of the church for a baptismal service. It was a thing they did differently to other churches and if the children wished to know more they could read about it in the Bible. So that is what they did and in the quietness after supper they sat round the table with the big Bible which held all their names and, remembering the Sunday School stories, they turned to Matthew and read how Jesus had been baptised just as they had seen that afternoon. Maggie Ann felt that she personally had found a real link with Jesus that day, and although she did not yet understand the meaning and implications of it all, it was a relationship that she never lost but it stayed with her in all the years ahead. They never witnessed another baptismal service on their journeys from Cairnbulg.

Chapter 4

As she reflected on these years of childhood Maggie Ann came to the conclusion that they were the happiest years. Certainly there was very firm discipline and much responsibility on each of them as they grew older, but there was great fun in the simple things. Sharing was taken for granted and, although they quarrelled and argued as children do, there was this strong bond which held them together in a unit. This lay in the person of Mary May and as Maggie Ann pondered on these things her wonder at her mother's resilience, which knew no bounds. She was their rock, a quiet source of wisdom, strength, example and guide, and even on occasions when they rebelled against her strict regime, they knew that all their mother wished for was their safety, their well being, their advancement; the children were the focus of her life and in that lay their great sense of security and trust. Maggie Ann felt a great flood of gratitude well up inside her as she remembered, for these years were not without sorrow. When he was ten Alex had died quite suddenly of appendicitis. It had all happened so quickly, they could not believe he was not there. But again life adjusted. Perhaps the loss was made easier for them in that Alex had been such a quiet, retiring little boy who seldom asserted himself. He was often on his own reading or studying things, especially on the shore and Maggie Ann could not remember his voice ever raised in anger. Maybe he had learned this in a small house with five sisters and no father. She knew that Mary May sorrowed deeply for once again she had lost a William, the last male link with her husband.

When Janet was fourteen she left school and came into the house to share the work with Maggie Ann. The two girls house kept and cooked and shopped and all the time Maggie Ann was imparting to Janet her different ways of economising, planning the week's work, being systematic in the use of time in order to run a small house of two rooms holding six people, without chaos and misery. It was hard but Janet learned and by the time Maggie Ann was sixteen she was ready to take on work which would bring in a wage.

Maggie Ann smiled as she thought of her early dreams. She loved cooking and was a born organizer and had longed to get away to develop these talents, but at sixteen that was out of the question. Mary May would not condone the thought of her leaving home at that age so she had opted for what was available to a Broadsea girl. Not much choice was presented, and most was seasonal work. Service in the large houses of the fish curers in the south end of Fraserburgh was one option but not too attractive as the work was long, very hard and poorly paid. There was an attitude of superiority and disregard for their workers in the manners of these newly rich 'Brochers' and although they found them to be good workers, these wealthy employers looked down on the Broadsea girls. There had long been a feud between the town people and the Broadsea community and it certainly continued into the conditions of domestic service.

Then there was the fishing where women played an essential role in gutting and packing herring. This was Maggie

Ann's world for it was the only work in which she had ever seen her mother employed; and her world was the braes where most of the curing yards were situated. Although she had lived in the midst of it for most of her life she had never handled a gutting knife or a ladle of salt, but often she had stood at the farlan windows with Ena by the hand, and watched the flying fingers of the gutters and packers. She listened to the give and take of chat, and the bursts of laughter and song amongst all the movement of changing barrels and kits of fish tumbling into the farlans, men coming and going and horses pulling carts; it was all so alive! Sometimes, if there was a huge catch of herring and the curer had to work late into the night, Mary May would be called out as an extra and between eleven and twelve Maggie Ann would go along the braes with a piece and a flagon of tea for her mother. It was wonderful to stand there in the dark with the carbide lamps flaring over the workers and watch and listen. Outside the arcs of light shadowy figures carrying baskets and kits of herring moved over the cobbles, carts and hurrlies came and went, and the steam from the horses' nostrils rose into the lamplight along with the odours of dung and urine and fish. Fish scales on the sleeves caught the light as the men moved over to top up the farlans where the greeny-black oilskin aprons of the gutters stood out dark against the gleaming silvery lustre of the newly caught fish. There was a rhythm in the team-work and an exciting urgency, for the pay depended on the amount of barrels gutted and packed. Two gutters and one packer made a crew, which would share the pay. Hard, fast work was the rule of the day.

So the summer that she became sixteen Maggie Ann was presented at the ship chandler's to be fitted with an oilskin, gutting apron and to purchase her gutting knife and boots. After a great deal of thought and listening around Mary May asked John Ewen if he had an opening for Maggie Ann to start as a learner and he agreed to employ her as such whenever she was ready. Mary May approached John Ewen because he was known as a very considerate employer; he had strong Christian principles and allowed no swearing or rough talk in his yards; times when the men and young carter boys would become over explicit it would end in instant dismissal for he expected rules to be kept. Yet break times were frequent, shelter was provided in bad weather, fair pay was always on time and the yards were clean and kept in good repair. He had a few curing yards stretching along the braes and going through to Denmark Street where his huts were built. This was accommodation for the huge bands of girls from Ireland, the Western Isles and other fishing centres employed by John Ewen for the season. From June to August when the Fraserburgh fishing was at its peak, the town thronged with these itinerant workers all serving one curer or another and everywhere different dialects, even languages could be heard. In September at the end of the fishing some gutters went home for a rest but others moved south following the sail boats to the fishings at Shields and further to Yarmouth and Lowestoft. Everyone returned home for Christmas and New Year and then with the movement of herring, the seasons would begin again on the west coast, Isle of Man, the Clyde, and the Minches and then on to Shetland before Fraserburgh again. Thousands of people moved for the fishing fleets were huge, demanding all sorts of trades and work; cooks, ostlers, coopers, carters, gutters, packers, salters, net menders, yard men; there was work for all; hard work; but then everyone worked hard. To even exist required great physical effort and poverty was not uncommon. But amidst all that, as she pondered these things, Maggie Ann could honestly say she had never gone hungry, and never could she recollect when her mother had not a spare bowl of soup or round of oat cakes to give to a neighbour in need. There was a great deal of practical love shown in Broadsea –not spoken about, just practised.

Maggie Ann already knew many of the Broadsea girls. They had been at school with her and she had often seen them passing the house on the way to work along the braes. Now she was joining them and it gave her a wonderful sense of excitement that she was entering a new world, a new freedom. Not that she had ever looked on her life at home as imprisonment, but it had been restrictive, even lonely at times, and had given her little opportunity to follow her own desires or fulfilment. That first morning as Maggie Ann joined the army of gutters trudging along the braes in their heavy boots and stiff oilskin aprons she felt scared, but very resolute that she would learn fast and do well, and above all, bring home some pay at the end of the week to add to the family budget. Soon she knew how to wrap her fingers in strips of cotton to protect them from cuts and the cruel, rough salt, how to use the grind stone to sharpen her knife, how to hold the fish to slit the belly easily and to finger out the gut quickly, which fish to discard, how to stand to relieve the pressure on back and feet; such small details but all so valuable in doing an expert job of many hours' duration. It was not many days before Maggie Ann was in a team and her speed improved so much that by the third week a new team was formed consisting of Maggie Ann, Kate Stephen and Elsie Strachan.

To be partnered with Kate and Elsie was an immense new experience for Maggie Ann for there never could have been such a combination of opposites. Where Maggie Ann was small and quiet and very earnest about her work the other two were robust and loud, boisterous and very comical. At the farlans as their fingers flew they sang all sorts of songs, religious and patriotic, gave back-chat to the men and seemed to live on a plane of high spirits that never faltered. Yet in all this they were never malicious or unkind; their friendship was sincere. As the weeks passed and they grew to understand each other a deep bond was formed; Maggie Ann began to laugh more and enjoyed listening to them talking about their homes and families and about their journeys back and forth to Pitullie where they lived.

Sometimes in the early morning they had a lift on one of the wagons going to the Fraserburgh fish market and always when they worked late John Ewen saw that they were taken safely home on one of his carts. There was quite a crowd of gutters from Pitullie and some very interesting antics took place, especially when they teased the young carter in charge of the wagon. Very often these were shy young men from the country who came down to the fishing with their horses during the summer months when things were quieter on the farms. The two miles to Pitullie stretched along a lonely road close by the rocky shore and sometimes if two carts from different curers overtook each other they would race amid screams and encouragement from the passengers. Occasionally on a warm summer night if the tide was out they would stop and paddle in the rock pools to cool their aching feet, or tell ghost stories in the eeriness of the half light. Many couples began their courtship on these journeys. So there was always a stock of news and interesting gossip to regale each other in the mornings. Maggie Ann enjoyed it all although she seldom had anything to contribute to the chatter, but Kate and Elsie did not seem to notice that. It brought a whole new outlook into Maggie Ann's life and it relieved a great deal of the seriousness, which had been her lot. Because she knew how her mother would react she was very circumspect about how much she related at home to the family but in the seclusion of their own bedroom at night under the bedclothes the four sisters had many a giggle at the antics of Kate and Elsie. All that Mary May knew was that her eldest daughter was happy and doing a good job; no less than what she would have expected.

At the end of the second week Maggie Ann brought home her first pay and presented it to her mother. Mary May quietly accepted it without fuss, as was her way, but after supper when they were all round the table she brought it out, laid it before Maggie Ann and asked her to count it, which she did, quite taken aback. But Maggie Ann realized that her mother had a reason and sure enough, before the five girls , she showed them how to budget. Firstly a portion would be set aside for saving, then an amount to contribute to the household for one's keep, and lastly an allowance for personal spending such as clothing and small individual needs. She explained how one should never spend more than one earned; that was the road to disaster and poverty; one should never borrow and, no matter how little the wage was, something, be it a penny or a pound, should be set aside to save for the day of need.

Maggie Ann smiled as she remembered her mother that night. It was one of the few occasions when Mary May showed pleasure. Laying her hand on Maggie Ann's head she smiled saying,

"Ye hae deen weel lass."

Maggie Ann also recalled how her sisters Janet, Betsy and Bella had all followed her into the gutting yard and as each in turn brought home the first pay, the lecture was repeated. The girls laughed about it later, but they realised that this method led to openness within the family so that an atmosphere of mutual trust prevailed. The principle of hard work and careful living was a firm foundation, which would stand them in good stead for life. And they loved having the responsibility for personal money to spend at their own discretion. So they had grown into their teens with the feeling that things were improving. Mary May still walked her fish round on Thursdays and fulfilled her commissions, but as each daughter left her childhood she took on some more responsibility in the home and contributed to their daily needs.

During the nineteenth and well into the twentieth century most girls had a 'Hope Chest'. This was usually in the form of a wooden chest, highly polished, with the girl's name burned into the lid or, if she was well off, set in brass letters. Little girls have always had treasure boxes; a fancy toffee tin or a patterned cardboard box became the receptacle for favourite things like shells, ribbons, trinkets, picture scraps, stamps; there is no end to what children collect in the younger years but as girls grow older this treasure takes on a much deeper personal aspect and the tin becomes a larger box and eventually a chest. In the front room at No.3 Broadsea Rd. there were four such chests, one for each of the older sisters, for Ena was still very much the little one in their eyes. Two double beds, a chest of drawers and a hanging press in the wall more or less filled the room but along one wall stood two chests while the two, slightly smaller ones were kept under the bed, hidden by the deep white lace-edged bed pan or curtain. None of the chests was locked but the rule of privacy was respected and no one dared open another's chest. This was the one private area in a crowded home, as was every home in Broadsea at that time, where one could hold secrets and precious keepsakes and know that they were safe. Like all other girls as they grew older Mary May's daughters looked forward to the day when they would find someone with whom they could share their lives and so into the 'Hope Chest' went chosen doilies, ornaments, embroidered tea cloths and many other things, all with a view to home making.

Maggie Ann too had her dreams and as she listened to Kate and Elsie talk of the 'loons' they had met and how this one was great fun or another was too quiet or too keen on the drink and so on, she wondered what it would be like to have a 'lad' and she did begin to regard the boys and young men with an interested eye. Growing up in a totally feminine world had deprived her of any knowledge of the male species and being naturally reticent and shy, Maggie Ann did not find it easy to even pass the time of day with them. But intelligence taught her that she would have to hold her head up and stop being a wilting violet and respond to the lads when they talked to her. It took great effort, for Mary May's strict training in discretion and self control coupled with her own natural tendencies presented a mountain which took many weeks to conquer. But by the end of her first summer in the gutting yard she was more relaxed and responsive, could accept the kindly teasing of the men as they came and went to the farlans, would even bravely link arms with Kate and Elsie and some of the young carters for a walk along the braes if there was a short break between deliveries of herring and they had a chance to rest. This was a new Maggie Ann growing up. She was happy with herself and much more confident in company; so much so that, when the end of July came and the only topic of conversation and excitement was going south to the Yarmouth fishing, Maggie Ann began to hope that she might go too.

But when eventually she broached the subject to Mary May the response was a very firm,

"Na, na. Oot o' the question. Ye're ower young. Maybe come anither 'ear."

This was a moment when Mary May deeply regretted her isolation- that pride and fierce independence which had prevented her having close friendships or trusting relationships with others. If only she had had someone close amongst the many gutters going south to whom she could have entrusted Maggie Ann. But there was no one, so she had to refuse her daughter when so many others of her age were setting off. Maggie Ann accepted her mother's answer, without surprise, but the day the long train, crowded with fish workers, pulled out from the Broch station and wound its way slowly alongside the Links, a sad little figure stood on the Bathalonian Brae waving as the carriages passed under the bridge, hardly able to see for the tears blinding her eyes. As she walked slowly home past the fountain and along Saltoun Place she wondered despondently what she would do now till the fishing began again in the spring.

Maggie Ann seldom had occasion to visit this end of the town. Sometimes on their return journeys from Cairnbulg they would wearily come this way, heading for Cross Street and all the short routes through to the bottom of Charlotte Street and home. But generally life and interest was in Broadsea or westwards to the villages and country areas where her mother made her deliveries. Mary May would have nothing to do with the 'granders' as she called them, for they were not reliable payers and did not barter her way. So now, with time to herself, Maggie Ann strolled slowly along gazing, deeply interested, at the wonder of these tall, stone-built edifices, or so it seemed to her. She walked on the other side of the wide road, overlooking the broad Links and a magnificent view over the broad sweep of the sandy bay, one end of which was the harbour light point and the other, three miles away, the Cairnbulg Beacon. How wonderful to sit at one of these wide, high windows and look across at that wonderful view! No smells of fish or rumbles of carts. She had heard stories about these houses; the water came out of a pipe at the turn of a tap and right enough, there was no water pump on the street; the toilet was kept flushed by water coming down from a tank; and the floors were patterned with coloured tiles right to the front door; the stair cases curved round right to the top of the house. As Maggie Ann considered the height of the houses she thought about the buckets of peat and coal that someone must carry up those stairs. She had grown up carrying water from the street pump and thought the piped water must be the best advantage of all. Some houses stood alone looking very grand with gardens and railings surrounding them; others were joined together and appeared less imposing but still tall and impressive. She wondered where they kept their carriages and supposed there must be a back entrance. Her question was answered when she turned the corner into Victoria Street for there, alongside the Baptist Church, was a lane behind the houses. Indeed she could see one or two small carriages standing in the lane. Across from the Church were two very elegant, squarish houses built right on to the street and next to the Church was the most beautiful house; not tall and square as the others, only one storey high, but with pointed gables for the upper rooms. The front door was in the middle and the bay windows seemed to stretch out on either side saying," Come in". Maggie Ann felt drawn to the house and wondered who lived there. She knew her master John Ewen lived on Victoria Street and it was just the sort of house she visualized for him as he was such a kindly man. Later she was to discover her mistake; the Bruce family, also curers, lived here and John Ewen lived in the one at the top of the hill. Maggie Ann crossed over to have a clearer view of the buildings as she climbed the rising street and then at the top she turned to face the sea. Here was space! These people did not live huddled together in tiny, dark houses, back to back with the next street. Gardens were all around. The afternoon sun behind her shone down the whole street all at once, touching every wall, and standing proud on the Links was the new South Church gleaming white and so beautiful in the sunshine. For Maggie Ann it was an awakening day. She knew nothing about what lay beyond the walls of these homes but the stirrings of curiosity were rising in her mind and already she was coming to a resolve.

Returning to the Baptist Church, she read the notice at the gate and then set off along the lane towards the muddle of curing yards, houses and shops, finally reaching Manse Street and Hanover Street. Now she was on home ground and crossing College Bounds on her approach to Broadsea she was so aware of the contrast with where she had been earlier. Much as she loved her home and all associated with it she knew that it was not enough; some day she would have to leave and seek out another way. Mary May's way was what she had had to do at that time, but for her daughters, life must have something better; hopefully, as much love and consideration, but also much less of the sheer stress of practical living. So Maggie Ann decided there and then that she would seek work as a servant in one of the houses of the well off.

Once the household had settled down that night and they were all in bed, Maggie Ann and Janet, as they so often did, went over their day. At first Maggie Ann was reluctant to reveal her thinking, but she needed a confidant, and soon was pouring out all her ideas and plans. As a result of this conversation the two sisters set off together on Sunday, bonneted and gloved in their best, to the afternoon service in the Baptist Church. In the intervening days they had consulted the local paper, the Fraserburgh Herald, and asked friends about vacancies, and now they were going to have a closer look, expecting that quite a few of these rich people would be attending church. Mary May gave them solemn warnings about their reception there but did not deter them from going for from her own experience, she knew there were good and bad in every level of society. She herself had never been in a church; content with the unpretentious Gospel Services in the Broadsea Hall, which one could attend dressed ordinarily with a shawl over one's head. But she suspected the Church would be a different scene and as she waved off her two girls, one tall and handsome, the other small and neat, she realized that this was their first step into the unknown and she trembled for them.

As they stepped out together they decided they would walk the length of Charlotte Street and have a look at the new buildings being completed at the top end near the sawmill, so well known to them both. In the distance beyond, they saw the rolling farmland and crofts rising to the surrounding low hills, but when they turned the corner into Victoria Street they were at once caught up in the audacity of what they were doing. They could see people converging on the church and pausing to chat at the gate, and when they themselves approached they were met with welcoming smiles and greetings. Rather awestruck, they continued up the path to be confronted at the door by a tall, elderly gentleman who shook their hands and ushered them in. An inner door opened to reveal another gentleman holding out

red Sankey hymnbooks and beyond, a sea of faces all staring curiously at the two strangers. Somehow the girls found
themselves in a pew on their right at the back of the church,
and there they sat, numb with embarrassment. But soon
the service began and the well known hymns put them
at ease; the minister, Rev. Walter Richards, had a strong,
commanding voice which made one listen and gradually
they relaxed and entered into the spirit of the gathering. To
their surprise, amongst the young people, there were quite
a few faces that they recognised from the fisher circle, but
the older folks were stiff and austere. Indeed some of the
women looked really proud and haughty and Maggie Ann
wondered if any of these required a servant.

When in fact Maggie Ann found a domestic post it was
by word of mouth through a friend, also in service. Within
the week she rang the bell at no. 77 Saltoun Place and was
ushered into the parlour where Mrs. William Thompson
sat by the window. She was elderly and rather stout, with
a kindly face and the most beautifully piled up snow-white
hair. Maggie Ann was quite drawn to her. After the preliminary talk of references, of which there were none, Maggie
Ann explained that this was her first time in service and
her only experience had been keeping house for five years
for her family. Mrs. Thompson was quite amazed at this
fact in one so young and decided to give Maggie Ann a
month's trial. There was no live in accommodation but she
could stay at home and report for work each morning at 6
am. Her pay would be two shillings and sixpence weekly,
with her food, and she would work alternate weekends with
the other maid. Her day would end once the family dinner
was served at seven o'clock. She would have to provide her
own black dress and aprons but that could be arranged
once the month was completed, meantime she would wear

a dark dress and white overall. One other request was
that she should be called simply Maggie for easiness and
thereafter in her working capacity, Maggie she remained.
Maggie Ann returned to Broadsea, not quite sure what she
had undertaken.

Maggie left home in the half-light at 5.30 on the Monday
morning. There was a cold east wind and a fine, driving
rain so she walked by the most sheltered streets hugging
the walls for protection. Some carters were about and quite
a few girls like herself heading in the same direction so
that by the time she turned into Saltoun Place she had
passed the time of day with some known faces. No. 77 was
in darkness but Mr. Thompson opened the door for her,
murmuring something about getting her a key.

So began her education in domestic service. As time
went on she would have called it slavery; much harder than
all the hours of standing in a gutting yard. There you were
paid for the amount of work you did, but in service it was as
though the mistress could not get enough in return for the
pittance she paid. Even the kindest of employers seemed to
feel they were doing the maid a kindness by allowing her to
work there. Yes there was running water on tap, even hot
water; the food was good and the house warm; everywhere
there was comfort and no lack of materials, but the kitchen
built on at the back of the house, their main place of work,
was another matter. Had it not been for the large cooking
stove they would have frozen, for the room was virtually
a shed with no insulation against the cold. This was common to many of these large stone fronted houses; good
façade, but poor amenities where the core work went on,
and through the winter months the staff, whose only communal room was the kitchen, had to bear the stone floor
and the thin walls. Maggie Ann was thankful she could

come home at night to a warm room and welcome, though the daily long walks took their toll and as the months went by she grew very weary.

As she cleaned the door brasses in the early mornings she would watch the sun rise up over the horizon on the sea and when she cleaned the windows she enjoyed that beach view. Many things in the house pleased her. She loved to stand in the hall and look up at the graceful sweep of the oak staircase as it turned below the long stained glass, oriole window; the beautiful deep rich reds and blues of the carpets; there were the drapes on the front windows, velvets and brocades, so lovely to touch, held back during daytime by long tasselled cords; and another wonderful idea, folding out the shutters from the wall facings at night cutting off the draughts blowing in from the sea. Maggie Ann was familiar with outside shutters but to have them tucked away inside and then hidden behind drawn curtains was such an excellent plan. This was a new world for her, but the most enjoyable of all her tasks was the monthly pleasure of cleaning the contents of the cabinets. On each side of the central window in the drawing room stood a mahogany glass fronted case displaying the mistress's collection of fine porcelain and glass. Dresden, Wedgwood and Venetian were all new names to Maggie Ann but as she dusted with a fine brush under the supervision of Mrs. Thompson, she asked questions and soon was listening to the story of each piece and where it had come from. She learned what to look for to assure authenticity and what was the characteristic of the different names, how to judge what was good. The value was not discussed but Maggie Ann understood that, although this was a pursuit only for the rich, it in no way reduced the beauty of the pieces and the charm and delight they gave to the onlooker. It was given to some to possess and others to simply admire.

Most of Maggie Ann's experience in cooking had been over an open fire using three heavy iron utensils; the broth pot, the stew pan and the potato pot, which had many other uses. Often the vegetable was cooked with the potatoes, a dumpling was cooked in with the broth; simple, plain, nourishing meals, came out of these utensils; economy of space coupled with economy of heat source forced this method. Surrounding the open fire was a flat, polished metal surface and once a pan was brought to boiling point it was set aside to simmer on the hot surface while another was put to heat on the fire. Thus cooking was a slow process and often a Broadsea housewife would be heard saying,

"I'll jist get the denner on an' syne I'll see tae 'at ither job."

Adjoining the side of the fire was an oven where puddings were made, and in winter many cold toes were heated there, sitting with the door open. The fire with the black kettle on the swee, was the source of life in the home. No one could have been more proud of its shining efficiency than Maggie Ann.

So when she came to use the large cooking stove at No.77 it was a thing of real wonder with the covered fire, the dampers and draughts raising the heat and the wide hot ovens on each side of the fire. Cake making and pies opened up a new field for her, replacing the old girdle scones and oatcakes. More and more she realized that this was her ideal work and she looked with envy at the shelf of recipe books in the kitchen, longing for a moment to take them down and read.

Normally Mrs. Thompson supervised and Ellen, the cook housekeeper, prepared the meals while Maggie Ann cleaned. She had to answer to Ellen. To keep an orderly regime there were strict rules of discipline regarding standard of work and routine and at first Maggie Ann found it hard to keep up with all that was required of her. But, determined to persevere, she gradually evolved a pattern of work for herself where everything was accomplished and she could relax more, even to the point of standing back occasionally and taking pride in a shining, polished floor or a gleaming bathroom. This latter fascinated Maggie Ann for she had never seen a bathroom before. The luxury of lying in that beautiful, white, enamelled bath, soaking in scented hot water, completely private, was in sharp contrast to the weekly zinc bath before the kitchen fire; and the china wash basin and toilet with the gleaming brass taps, not her favourite job to clean; the floral patterned tiles above the dado and the lovely chain pull in the shape of a thistle. These all gave Maggie Ann great pleasure to contemplate, but also presented her with another enigma. Why should people, with a room like this only a few steps along the landing from the bedroom, require to use a chamber pot. One of her morning tasks was to empty these as she went from bedroom to bedroom. It always amazed her that the household would wish anyone, even a maid, to perform such an intimate service. In her own home a chamber pot was connected only with illness. Mary May would not have countenanced any such unnecessary luxuries. She trained them all to practice good habits and self control and during the night to use the outside toilet if they must. But Maggie Ann smiled as she recalled these pots, one in each bedside cabinet, all china, gold rimmed and patterned with flowers to match the colour of the wall paper and curtains. It would take a few half crowns to buy one of these.

When December came in and Christmas and New Year were approaching there was a changing atmosphere in the house. The family, two sons, were coming home and bringing friends so a great cleaning happened as rooms were prepared for the guests. Ellen and Maggie Ann worked well together and by the week before Christmas all was ready; even the decorations and lanterns were strung in the hall and a Christmas tree stood in the bay window. Maggie Ann was entranced with it all. But when Ellen told her she was now to work with her in the kitchen her dream was fulfilled. Hungry for knowledge, she watched and listened, fetched and carried, whisked and chopped, cracked eggs and grated and took endless delight in what came out of the ovens and the beautiful copper pans. Such smells filled the house, and the grandeur of the laid table took her breath away.

Christmas Day was for the family only so the meal was during the afternoon enabling Maggie Ann to help with the serving. Ellen gave her some tuition so that she performed without mishap and finally with the last coffee cup and piece of cake removed to the kitchen, they set to together to finish the washing up and put away the left- overs in the larder. At last when all was tidy Maggie Ann wrapped herself in her thick shawl and was very surprised when Ellen, smiling, handed her a basket covered with a white cloth.

"For you and your sisters. The mistress told me to make it up for you. You deserve it. You really worked hard."

Looking back, Maggie Ann still felt the glow of that moment. And when, just as she was leaving to go along the back lane home, Mrs. Thompson handed her a small parcel saying,

"Thank you Maggie. You have helped to make this a wonderful Christmas."

she felt that she had reached the pinnacle of all joy.

As she raced along the familiar streets to Broadsea she could hardly wait to see the pleasure on her sisters' faces, but the one lingering doubt was her mother's reaction. Would she regard it as charity and send the basket back? Maggie Ann was wondering how she would resist that, but she need not have worried; Mary May joined the girls in their joyous response to the gift as the basket revealed its wonders; the fruits, the cakes and pies that Maggie Ann had cooked herself and, crowning all, a large piece of ham set in its aspic jelly. When at last Maggie Ann turned to her own parcel she took her time opening it, savouring the moment, and was speechless to find a shining new half crown wrapped in tissue paper lying on top of a small box. Inside lay a brooch, a tiny, golden bird with a blue stone set in its eye. As Maggie Ann raised her head to look into her mother's eyes her face showed such inexpressible joy that Mary May could have wept with gratitude for this moment. Always she had had the feeling that life would be hard for this her oldest child but now, someone had appreciated her worth and Mary May was thankful. The gifts, wrappings and all, eventually went into Maggie Ann's hope chest but round the table they shared the luxuries with such delight.

At No.77 New Year's celebrations took the form of open house on Hogmanay and an afternoon New Year's Day dinner for a large company of friends. It was arranged, with Mary May's permission, for Maggie to stay overnight to help with the preparation and serving and a bed was made for her in one of the larger box rooms in the attic. Ellen's room was also on that floor so she did not feel so isolated, but it was a strange feeling sleeping alone in bed, let alone in a room by oneself. Not that they were in bed long for the party was late and had to be cleared away in readiness for the next day's feast. The hospitality was quite lavish, for Mr. Thompson was a prominent personality in the business affairs of Fraserburgh, so status was important and service at table had to be of the highest standard. When eventually all was completed and Ellen and Maggie could at last sit down in the kitchen and take a moment for themselves, they looked wearily at each other, some of the glow of achievement worn off in their tiredness, knowing that for them tomorrow would not be a day of rest, but the work would begin all over again. Service was hard and unrelenting unless one reached the higher levels of responsibility and command. As she did her daily routine Maggie Ann thought much about these things and came to the conclusion that if she was going to continue in her intention to study house keeping and cookery, she must proceed the correct way and plan.

Maggie Ann fulfilled her nine-month contract with Mrs. Thompson and left with an excellent reference, but resolved that her work meantime must be in the fishing world where, with a view to her future training, she could make more money. No.77 had given her an invaluable glimpse into another way of life, which in future years was to play an important role in her career.

As she sat on the braes remembering, Maggie Ann shook her head when she thought of what followed that time.

Chapter 5

Now that her days were her own again, Maggie Ann joined Janet in keeping house, always remembering that Janet was in charge. The whole month of April they spring cleaned, painted, renewed covers, cut up old garments in preparation for a new clicked rug for the fireside, white washed the toilet and the close walls, did out Mary May's fish house; their industry was inexhaustible and when at last they could not find another doily to wash or article to repair, their thoughts turned to farther afield.

After the restrictions of the past winter months, Maggie Ann felt she had become really cut off from the Broadsea world she loved so much. She and Janet had kept up their visits to the Sunday afternoon services in the Baptist Church and in addition had attended the evening Gospel meeting in the Hallie along with the family. But Maggie Ann needed to get back into the familiar relationships she had enjoyed before so the two girls planned their walking visits. May was a beautiful month and so, after the dinner dishes were washed, they would set off in the sunshine along Main St., stopping in at the little post office and lingering to talk. The sunshine had brought folks out to gather in groups at the doorways, with their knitting, while the children played at their feet, and so it was easy to stop here and there and join in the conversation; who was ill, who was getting married in the Hallie and what was the latest news of the

Shetland fishing. Reports were coming back that it would soon be ending as the herring were moving south. That meant great excitement anticipating the return of the workers with their presents and news, and possibly weddings; the Shetland fishing was famous for its courtships. As they walked they dropped in on some of the older folks they had known all their lives and the girls knew they would be welcome. Sitting in these shadowy rooms with signs of age all around them the girls had a sense of timelessness. The flagstone floor by the doorway, worn hollow, the soot blackened hearth, even the ancient wooden stools they sat on, reminded them that here was a home that had survived for many generations handed on from one to another. This was the timelessness of Broadsea. Many went sailing far to make a living, but always the core remained, often only the wives and the old ones, supporting each other in the struggle to hold the family together and keep the dignity and standards, which, they considered, life demanded of them. Doors were always open in Broadsea and when these old friends asked about their latest activities Janet and Maggie Ann were pleased to tell what had been happening to them. Janet was always very open and gentle in her handling of older people, finding relationships easy, but Maggie Ann had a more reserved nature and was discrete in her descriptions of her last few months in service, only relating the happy incidents.

Sometimes they did not reach very far down Main St. before it was time to return for Ena coming out of school, but other days their walk took them right down and out over the Wasten past the Baudlies to the rocky shore dominated by the gut factory where the smell of the fish processing was sometimes so strong. And then they turned up the burn at Phingask looking to see if the marsh marigolds were out. This was a great place for wild flowers. Then on to the watermill and home by the main road. That was a long walk but most often they turned in from the Wasten to Broadsea farm and home by the parks to College Bounds.

As she relived these days with Janet, Maggie Ann was so thankful for their walks. Right now she could see and hear these dear friends in their homes; Sonny Taylor, Jeannie Wattie, the Maclemans, Doddie Noble and so many more; hear their voices speaking their own broad dialect, feel the warmth of their caring; know the poverty and hardship that many of them suffered but which was covered over by a fierce pride and independence, just like her mother. The sea was a hard master and there were many Mary Mays in Broadsea, struggling to survive and rear a family. Maggie Ann did not know the source of their strength but she strongly suspected it was their faith in God. Prominent in every house was a text in the living room such as "The eternal God is thy refuge and underneath are the everlasting arms," and the big Bible lay handy for the nightly family worship. The God of all the elements was important to them and they gave Him due worship and reverence, drawing strength from His presence.

On these walks the two girls talked much about their futures. Betsy and Bella were coming up to leaving school age and Janet was anticipating the summer gutting spell. She did not for a moment consider going into service but would keep house and do the occasional line fishing work in the smoke house during the winter. Janet was very much a home lass while Maggie Ann on the other hand had every intention of following the fishings now that she was nearly seventeen. She had much saving to do to fulfil her plans and this work was her best source.

There was a joyful reunion when Kate, Elsie and Maggie Ann at last reformed their crew at John Ewen's curing yard in June 1886. Maggie Ann realized how much she had missed them as she listened to the endless tales of fun and adventure they had experienced travelling and working; the train journey south; the unusual characteristics of the English fisher folk; the landladies; the markets; the dances. Then there was the sea trip to Shetland, stormy and crowded, but so exciting. And the strange bare islands with everlasting daytime. There was no wavering in Maggie Ann's intent that she would be there next year.

This time a much more mature and self-possessed Maggie Ann tackled her work at the farlans. Now as fast as any of the gutters, she could keep up her speed to match Kate and Elsie and they were a top crew, filling the barrels steadily and diligently keeping count. Looking across at her tall sister Janet working with the learner crews Maggie Ann felt a warm sense of happiness that another of her family was here and, as her eyes roved around, now and then she spotted faces familiar from last year. There was one in particular. He was a cooper. It was just his manner that appealed to Maggie Ann. Always busy at his work he moved about the yard without fuss, going from crew to crew tapping the lids on to the topped up barrels and sealing them finally with the last iron hoop. There was such a kind, peaceful look on his face. She wondered who he was and when at last she asked Elsie the answer embarrassed her.

"O, that's Sonny Sim. Hi Sonny, Maggie Ann's sicken tae spick tae ye!"

Poor Maggie Ann was mortified and kept her head down, but when break came and they gathered on the braes to rest, Sonny made his way to their group and sat down to chat so easily. Janet was there too and with Elsie's banter

49

there was no strain. Sandy Sim was his name and he travelled in from Pitullie every day to the cooperage. He had been south to Lowestoft and also to the Shetland fishing but this next winter he planned to stay at home and set up his own cooperage business. He was twenty-one and felt he had saved enough to start. Maggie Ann was impressed by his earnestness and the frank way he spoke about his plans and as the days went by they found themselves discussing hopes and aspirations and many things with ease. No romantic element entered into their relationship, it was purely friendship, and a tremendous stimulation for Maggie Ann who never before had shared discussion on any topic with a man.

Although her education had been interrupted so early, or maybe for that very reason, Maggie Ann had an inordinate curiosity and thirst for knowledge. She read everything that came her way and regularly borrowed books from the Mid St. bookshop, which had a small lending library. One of her pleasures in service had been dusting the books in Mr. Thompson's study. All the great writers were there from Shakespeare, Gibbons, Scott and Dickens to copies of Punch. Maggie Ann wondered if Mr. Thompson ever read them; she would have given anything to have asked for that liberty but she did not dare. Just to handle them stimulated her great desire to own and read, and strengthened her resolve. What she had read needed to be discussed and she found the busy home life was not conducive to that, so now that Sandy was available and willing, Maggie Ann opened up and when they were on their own they had many a good argument on social conditions, work regulations, fair and honest pay, women's role in life. Sandy was by no means an intellectual or politically minded man but he had some very definite views on conditions of work, especially for women who, he thought were very exploited by both husbands and employers. He knew of many women who had died young in childbirth after having had a large family and women were very undervalued in the work place. Maggie Ann was extremely captivated by his views and she pondered on them.

That had been a wonderful summer. The fishing was extremely good and the sunny days just seemed to go on and on. To rise early and walk along the braes with the sun behind you, striking the opposite shore and lighting up all the greens of the slopes, the red roofs and that wonderful sheet of silvery water in the bay; and to know there would be a good day of hard work ahead, punctuated by fun and good humoured banter; knowing that friendships were strong and could be relied on. For Maggie Ann that was a good time.

As the weeks passed Elsie would tease with knowing looks that Sandy was becoming very attentive, but Maggie Ann just smiled and kept her own counsel for she too had been observing things which gave her a great sense of joy. So often now when they were on the braes , Sandy and Janet would pair off together, still in the group, but together, and although Janet was so much younger than he, it was obvious they were meant for each other. When Mary May heard the first whispers of the romance she approached Maggie Ann,

" I'm hearin' things aboot oor Janet an' 'at Pitullie loon, Sandy Sim. Is't true? Fit dae ye ken aboot him?"

Maggie Ann tried to placate her mother knowing full well how she would hate having her girls the subject of gossip.

"Mither, I think ye should jist leave Janet an' Sandy alane. Sandy 's a very good, steady man an' he'll dae the richt thing by Janet. He has plans for the future an' has lots tae dae afore gettin merried, so he'll wait for Janet. He's the kindest man an' a perfect match for her. Jist be patient an' dinna worry."

So Mary May kept her peace and Sandy was invited for a Sunday afternoon tea to be given the nod of approval. Occasionally he joined the family at the evening service in the hall and sometimes the three of them attended the Salvation Army meeting as Sandy was a Salvationist and played the cornet in the local corps band; another point in his favour. Maggie Ann was very much aware she was playing chaperone but she was only too glad to do so if it was going to enable this gentle pair to protect their happiness and future prospects. Soon she would be off to Lowestoft and they would be on their own, but by that time the courtship would be accepted. Sandy sometimes dropped in for a cup of tea when he was passing on his way home from town, and other times the girls would walk out to Pitullie to visit Elsie and they would all meet up at the harbour there.

"Such happy times," thought Maggie Ann smiling as she hugged herself. She was so glad it had all worked out for Janet and Sandy, now happily married with their little boy Tom. Sandy's plans had materialised and he now owned a house on Charlotte St. with a garden stretching back to the lane giving access to his large cooperage. Here he made his barrels in preparation for the Fraserburgh fishing and at the same time could be close to his beloved Janet and Tom. There was lots of love in that house. People liked to go there. You could feel it in their company as you intercepted the glance of trust and love that passed between the couple now and again.

Chapter 6

The Lowestoft fishing was fast approaching and Maggie Ann was excited. Mary May no longer put any objection in her way for by now she had come to know Kate and Elsie and realized that underneath their boisterous front they were two reliable, sensible girls to whom she could entrust Maggie Ann. They were just that bit older and experienced, and when she learned that the three girls could stay together with the same landlady, who had housed them in previous fishings, Mary May was content.

The kist stood in the middle of the front room, gradually being filled with all that was needed for an eight to ten week's fishing. September to October could be cold so the knitted petticoats and jumpers went in, all the underwear clean and crisp, and warm head shawls because the girls said the curing yards were down by the shore and the wind off the sea could be perishing. On top lay Maggie Ann's blue Sunday dress and bonnet to match for everyone went to church on Sunday, and at last the kist was ready to close. The gutting apron and boots were placed on top covered with a tarpaulin and then it was roped and placed at the close end ready for collecting when the curer's cart came to pick it up for transportation either by train or ship to Lowestoft.

Such a stir at the station. There seemed to be thousands of people. Standing with Ena at the corner into Broadsea,

Mary May had waved her off, but the girls had accompanied her to the station and now, looking down from the window, she had difficulty picking them out in the crowd. Shouts of good wishes, last minute instructions, laughter, banter, calls of all sorts added to the bursts of singing, and the hissing and clanking of the engines made a cacophony of sound quite overwhelming for Maggie Ann. Her eyes sparkled as she laughed and waved with the others standing in the window as the whistle blew and the long train pulled away. All along the Links and right to the Kessock bridge people lined the railway, waving and looking for their loved ones. Maggie Ann thought most of the Broch must have been there that day, and with a lump in her throat, she remembered that she had been one of them last year.

At last they turned into the compartment and settled themselves after securing the luggage on the rack above. There were eight of them and not too much room considering the length of the journey but they planned to rotate every so often to share the corner seats. Toileting was going to present a problem but the experienced travellers knew all the stations where the train would stop and warned the novices that they 'had to go' whether they needed or not. As the long train snaked its way across the flat emptiness of Buchan the excitement died down a little and the girls settled to watch for the rail junction at Maud where the Peterhead contingent would join them. While the train stood in the country station they watched the comings and goings of this busy farming centre. There was a large cattle mart here and close by, a general market, which drew the girls like a magnet, but they could not leave the train. Soon, after much shunting and jolting back and forth, the completed train with an extra engine began its journey which was to last many hours, stretching their patience to the limit, and making them increasingly aware of the restricted space and the sense of being cooped up. But they sang and told stories, teased and slept, shared their plentiful supplies of food, and gradually the hours passed. When the train drew in at the larger stations for water and refuelling, the passengers could walk on the platforms for a few minutes and purchase a cup of tea from the vendors' trolleys. Then it was back on board for the next stage.

So it went on all day and into the evening. For Maggie Ann it was a total revelation. She had read about many places and train journeys, but when her farthest destination had been the five miles to St. Combs, this experience today was out with her imagination. After their last glimpse of the sea from the cliff tops above Stonehaven, the direction changed and began the long inland route by Stirling and Perth. There was some talk of maybe going over the new Tay Bridge at Dundee, but they realized that this would not be any advantage as they would still have to go to Perth to cross the Forth. Maggie Ann listened to all this discussion and wished she had her school atlas to follow their route.

As she recalled from quite a few years on, travelling south to the fishings was greatly eased when the train did eventually cross the bridges; the Forth one opened in 1889, and, combined with the replaced Tay bridge, it meant a straight run from Aberdeen to Edinburgh and south, saving many hours.

It was a very weary, slightly dishevelled group that dismounted from the compartment long after midnight. Fortunately , it was a mild autumn night and they set off on foot together, carrying their hand luggage. The landlady's house was not too far away and they relished the freedom and fresh air after the journey. Although it was the early hours of the morning there seemed to be people everywhere and Maggie Ann began to realize just how big these fishings were. Even in her weary state she could pick out foreign tongues and she understood now that the Fraserburgh group was just one fraction of a huge operation. Boats from Isle of Mann, Cornwall and Devon, Hebrides, Wick, Lerwick and so many other ports had come with their fish workers to reap the herring harvest as the fish moved south. Yarmouth and Lowestoft had more than tripled their populations and the whole town in every sector of industry benefited from this boom time.

After the Sunday rest and settling in they were off to the yard to see what the Monday afternoon sales would bring in. The fish was so abundant and so close in shore, the herring boats were not at sea very long. After midnight on Sunday the Scottish boats were off and back by noon next day, unloading, tidying the nets and away again by four in the afternoon, to return next morning. So it went on all the week and the gutters were constantly on call to handle the catch and fill the barrels. Huge quantities of herring were gutted, packed and loaded into cargo ships from Russia, Germany and Poland especially, and the curers who seemed to have the monopoly of power and profit from the whole operation accumulated immense fortunes.

Maggie Ann soon adapted to the routine for she was strong and keen. But it did take her a while to adjust to the realization that she had no one but herself to be responsible for or answer to. For so long her life had been controlled by the needs and rules of home but now, for a time, she was her own person and working for herself. It gave her a slightly heady feeling, sometimes a little feeling of guilt, but then she looked at Kate and Elsie and observed their confidence and independence of choice and thought,

"I am my own person now. I can make my own decisions."

And although the work was long and hard, and some mornings, so cold, Maggie Ann could not get away from the sensation that this must resemble being on holiday. Indeed, when they did have their free time the girls took the brake to Norwich and Yarmouth and explored the historic wonders of the ancient city and the seaside magic. Maggie Ann was enthralled with the promenade and the pier and although autumn was well established there was still enough colour in the gardens to enable her to visualize what it must be like in summer. Some of the entertainment centres had already closed for the winter, but she was not sure that Mary May would have approved of her attending them anyway. The open markets were the greatest source of pleasure. They seemed to be in all English towns and villages. The girls spent hours lingering by the stalls, trying to restrain their inclination to buy. Now that their earnings were coming in regularly they could budget and know what they could freely spend. So every week they bought something, a present for one of the family or a special piece of linen or china for the 'hope chest.' Although she could never have dared to engage in it herself, Maggie Ann loved to watch the girls haggle over the prices, sometimes winning a real bargain.

One present gave Maggie Ann considerable thought. Ever since being widowed Mary May had worn severe black, which was the custom, and had scorned all manner of personal adornment. Being very small in stature with a pinched, careworn face and hair tightly drawn back in a bun, Mary May gave the impression of an aging woman, which concerned Maggie Ann. She knew her mother was not really old. So she wished to buy something special that would perhaps encourage her mother to ease away from the tradition. It had to be modest and sensible, and useful of course, but would give such pleasure to the wearer. At last she found it, a beautiful, hand knitted, Shetland cardigan in a deep, soft blue colour. Accompanying that was a white crepe de chine blouse with a high neck and gathered sleeves and to complete the gift, was a brooch. This comprised two entwined hearts in gold with the word 'Mizpah' set in tiny diamonds across the hearts. It would fit beautifully at the front of the blouse. Maggie Ann was aware that it was the sort of gift exchanged between courting couples, but for so long now her mother had been without any such expression of affection and Maggie Ann wanted her to have it and to know they loved her, for that was the meaning of the brooch. 'Mizpah' was a Hebrew word saying, "May the Lord watch between you and me when we are away from each other." So it was all carefully wrapped and placed in the bottom of the kist along with gifts for her sisters, Didy Alex, Granny Belsie and Aunt Annie May. One especially for her in thanks for the warm head shawls she had sent in for Maggie Ann. They had been such a boon on these cold days.

Towards the end of October there was a general feeling that the herring fishing had peaked. The sailing boats were having to go farther off. The fish were moving away south and would not appear again until the spring in the Irish Sea. One after another, as their boats sailed away north, the curing yards were packing up and closing to lie silent and ghostly till next year's influx again. There was a frantic last minute shopping in the market before the kists were finally closed and carted off for transport. The box of Yarmouth rock; pink peppermint rock with a herring motif in the centre; and the box of Fry's chocolate bars, were traditional but, in addition, having considered the matter carefully, Maggie Ann made a large purchase of wool suitable for men's socks and pullovers. She had a little plan for the winter, which she thought, might work for Janet and herself, and buying the wool here was considerably cheaper.

When the departure day came and John Ewen's group along with one or two others, were all assembled on the platform of Lowestoft station, there was an atmosphere of quiet excitement; they were all going home to their folks after a good fishing. Once settled in the train, after goodbyes to the English friends, the singers began and there was the usual banter and stories about the dramatic events of the past weeks, in many cases much exaggerated, but gradually things quietened down to a subdued murmur as the tedious journey across East Anglia went on interminably. Once Peterborough was reached and their train joined the main north line then the girls really felt they were on their way and could settle down. It had been a punishing eight weeks of long and very hard labour. Nor had their breaks been times of rest because the need for enjoyment in the young leads to long hours of dancing and partying, often returning home only to change and go out to the gutting yard in the early morning. But they had kept going, carried along by enthusiasm and good spirits fortified by the moral support they relied on from each other. It had been honest fun and the girls were all too aware that their employment depended on the approbation of John Ewen and their parents who would condone no mischief. So they talked, shared their food and, one by one, succumbed to sleep, taking up all sorts of positions in the cramped compartment. Occasionally they surfaced as the train drew in to a station, but it was not till they reached Aberdeen that the girls began to waken refreshed and, all tidy and smiling, prepared to meet their families.

Maggie Ann was just so happy to see the beloved faces again at the station. As the long line of passengers crept along to the entrance shouts of recognition echoed all around and Maggie Ann was surrounded by a great sea of smiling faces. They were all there, even Ena, and there was Mary May standing back a little, but with one of her rare smiles. That was all that Maggie Ann required. After farewells and promises to meet up again with Kate and Elsie, she set off with her excited family for the long cross-town walk to Broadsea. Here was home and when they entered the familiar kitchen and saw the table all spread ready for supper Maggie Ann felt a great choking in her throat. She was just so glad to be home.

In the following years Maggie Ann was to come back many times to this familiar scene, but none of the returnings were ever quite so poignant as this first one.

During the next afternoon the kist was delivered to the close and there was great excitement and firm instructions not to open it until the girls returned from school. Sure enough, there it was in all its pine splendour, sitting unroped in the middle of the kitchen floor and they all gathered round, eyes wide in anticipation. Lots of talk had gone on in school about what came home in the Lowestoft kists and here they were with their very own one.

First the heavy lid was lifted up, then the shallow, wooden inner tray holding all Maggie Ann's small personal things was removed and underneath lay the parcels. Each one was presented in turn, Mary May first, and then the ripping of paper began and the oohs and aahs. For Betsy and Bella, winter dresses in red wool trimmed with white lace at neck and wrist. They had to be identical otherwise the usual ructions would have occurred; and for Ena a similar one in deep blue. Janet's eyes lit up as the contents of her parcel revealed a beautiful, grey, silk shawl with a deep fringe, complete with grey silk gloves. Maggie Ann guessed what was in Janet's mind as she draped it round her shoulders with the peak falling elegantly down her back. As Janet fingered it lovingly Maggie Ann knew it would lie in the hope chest till that special day.

As the younger girls disappeared to try on their dresses, Janet and Maggie Ann turned to watch Mary May open her parcel. True to character, when she saw the contents, her first reaction was to scold Maggie Ann for wasting money in buying things for her. But when she looked into their anxious, pleading faces, she was silent, realizing that she should not wipe out the pleasure and love of this moment. Instead she ran her hand over the softness of the wool and felt the smooth silk and with a smile on her face said,

"Fan am I iver gan tae wear 'at?" and they both answered together,

"Now!" and guided her to the privacy of the box bed to try them on.

When she emerged Maggie Ann knew that she had won a battle. Mary May had donned her best black, moiré skirt and emerged complete with blouse, cardigan and brooch, which she had found in the cardigan pocket. The girls combed her hair a little more loosely round her face where it curled slightly when unrestrained, and then led her to look in the mirror on their chest of drawers. Mary May gave a little nod of satisfaction at her image, and then to the girls, and turning, headed back to the box bed. No more was said and when Mary May reappeared there was no further mention or sign of the clothing. Maggie Ann wondered if she really would wear them again, but she felt satisfied that her mother, not yet forty years old, had perhaps come to realize that there was another aspect of life to be lived, apart from the drudgery of sheer existence which had been her lot for too long. She would wait and see. Maggie Ann was aware that her gifts cost more than she should have afforded, but this was her first trip. She knew there would be others, but this time was special and the family needed that extra uplift of pleasure.

Then came the parcels of rock and chocolate and the dividing out, deciding who amongst the friends and relatives were to receive a share. It was all very exciting and when at last all had been emptied out and the bags of Maggie Ann's clothing and wool had been removed to the front room, the kist was put out to the close. It would be stored at Didy's till she required it for the Shetland fishing in the spring.

Chapter 7

That evening, after the younger ones had been settled in bed, and the three sat by the fire, Maggie Ann unfolded her plan for using the wool. After her experience of service last winter she was unwilling to return to that drudgery. Service meant cleaning and scullery work and although she felt there were still lessons she could learn in that field, her real desire was to cook and train as an assistant cook. But these posts were few and only available in very large houses, which were generally situated outside the town and meant living in. If such a post should come up she would apply, but since it was unlikely, she had opted to join Janet in the winter white fish work in the smokeries, help with the house keeping and knit. This was her reasoning.

All Broadsea women could knit. Even before going to school girls knew how to handle knitting needles and by the age of ten, had graduated to four needles, could turn a heel and shape a toe on a sock. Knowledge of varied patterns and stitches was passed on from mother to daughter; knitting never stopped; it was a totally home industry. The custom was to have an old garment for work or play, a good one for dress and one in the cupboard to bring into use when required. Whether it be jumper, cardigan, socks or under drawers, the system prevailed and a well doing housewife felt responsible for having it so. There was a certain prestige about home knitted garments and the occasional remark,

"Oh it wis jist a bocht een." indicated the attitude to factory produced goods.

Now they were all knitters in their home and if they worked hard at it, during the winter they could produce a stock of articles, especially for men, which they could then sell. Betsy and Bella would do socks, Janet and herself the jumpers and Ena would knit squares from the left over colours, which eventually would be sewn into a blanket. Mary May would be the adviser and examiner of the garments, and lend a hand with the knitting if she had time.

At first the others were a little doubtful and hesitant but gradually, with Maggie Ann's enthusiasm, they had to agree that it could be a source of income to eek out the scarce winter fishing, and a great deal better than the half crown Maggie Ann earned in service. Better to rise at five o'clock and knit rather than walk to such hard labour. The wool was such a bargain. It was a great opportunity and if they earned the cost of the wool and a fair profit for their work, then it would be worthwhile. They might even become known in Broadsea and Cairnbulg for their excellent garments. So it was decided and they began the enterprise.

Initially Betsy and Bella were rather slow in their output, but, as their expertise improved so did their enthusiasm and soon the conversation centred round how many times longer the leg would be compared to the rib; on a sock was a plain rib better then a twisted rib; could they do a pair of socks in a week? The knitting went to school with them, carried in a cotton bag, and during the recess they sat on the grass- covered rocks behind the school, fingers flying, never wasting a minute. Competition was strong between these two sisters and it was the greatest motivation. Every night Mary May examined their work looking for split loops, dropped stitches and irregular shaping and she was meticulous in her judgement. Nothing was passed unless it was the best and sometimes the girls rebelled, thinking her unfair and too fussy. But they knew she would not allow any garment to be sold if it was not of the highest quality. So they worked on and, to their great satisfaction, saw their little pile of socks grow.

For Janet and Maggie Ann the task was somewhat harder for the jumpers required more stitches and longer needles and as the garment grew it became heavy. Stitches were counted in scores on the four long needles and although it was all in one colour, they still worked in a pattern of squares containing diamonds or anchors or cables, all picked out in purl or twisted stitches. This required calculating and they would often be sitting with paper working out the division of stitches as they created the new patterns. The challenge stimulated their inventiveness for they were not satisfied with just plain knitting. Even when the stitches were picked up to knit on the sleeves and collar, the operation had to present a good pattern. To speed up the work they learned how to use a sheath; this was a leather pouch worn on a belt round the waist. It was stuffed with sawdust and pierced all over one side with small holes into which the working right hand needle was pushed for support, leaving the hands freer to control the knitting. This was a tremendous advantage as the article grew heavier. Some of the garments the girls produced were works of art and they were really pleased with the results.

Little Ena was, as ever, full of her latest ploy, making her blanket. Too young to be aware of what her older sisters were about, she was just absorbed in her blanket and carried her little bag with her wherever she went. She had such a happy nature and a bright smile, every door in Broadsea was open to her and she was often to be found in one or other of the cottages sitting on a stool, knitting at her squares and chatting like a little old person. In fact it was on one of these visits that she learned how to start a square at a corner and increase to the full size then decrease again to the opposite corner. This gave a good free edging easier for sewing together and made a fine pattern. She came home in triumph that day and requested another bag because people were giving her balls of their spare wool and she needed to carry them. Once she had completed enough squares to sew together, Ena was particular about the mixing of the colours and then when Mary May crocheted the outside edging with a bright red, she was satisfied. She gave much thought about who was to receive the blanket. After having toiled so long she had secretly come to love the feel of it and was rather sad at having to give it away. Should it go to Granny at Cairnbulg or Didy? When the older girls suggested that since it was her very first one, she should keep it and spread the cover on the kitchen bed which she shared with her mother, Ena was delighted. Childlike, she showed it off to all who came to visit and at night, curled up close to Mary May, she would finger it lovingly and plan the next one for Granny and Aunt Annie.

Christmas and New Year came and went and the knitting continued, punctuated by occasional calls from the curers to the smoke house. Mary May prepared her fish in the little hut in the close and continued her country fish round when the weather permitted. Janet and Maggie Ann rose very early to put in two hour's knitting before the household tasks of the day began and every spare minute was devoted to the work. At last, when they judged they had enough garments completed, they decided to involve

Ora's Kirsten, the Broadsea post mistress who had been a long time friend. For a small commission she agreed to display in the window a jumper and a pair of socks with a price label, "For sale." By now they knew how many hours it took to knit a jumper or a pair of socks so they could ask a fair price without overcharging. They waited. Within two days the garments were sold. They were overjoyed. They had proved that they could do it.

As long as the wool lasted they toiled on and had the satisfaction of seeing the garments sold almost as soon as they were displayed. There was very little spare money in Broadsea and most people knitted for their own families but a certain clientele from the upper class end of Fraserburgh sometimes patronised the Broadsea post office and Maggie Ann suspected that they might be the purchasers although she never enquired. Enough for Maggie Ann that they had worked and earned and, over the winter, had paid all their bills with something to spare. She was not ruling out the possibility that they might repeat the enterprise another year, now they knew what it entailed, but another fishing was ahead and a new horizon.

Chapter 8

Maggie Ann remembered that New Year especially, for another reason. Usually on New Year's Day they had held a quiet family celebration with Didy, or at Cairnbulg with Granny, and last New Year's Day Maggie Ann had been working at the Thompson's. Normally the girls had taken no part in the Broadsea Temperance Walk which was held every New Year's Day, their mother considering them to be too young, but now they were older Mary May realized she would have to allow them that freedom. So it was arranged for them to walk in a party along with others, do the itinerary by Pitullie and Rosehearty and return sometime in the afternoon for the traditional New Year's Day dinner of broth, hen, dumpling and jelly dessert.

It was still dark in the frost hung, early, wintry, morning air when Maggie Ann and Janet joined the others at the Broadsea Hall. Already a large gathering had assembled. The band of flutes was tuning up with great expertise of trills and flourishes; occasionally a daring one would sneak in and give the big drum an isolated 'boom', much to the wrath of the drummer, who would carry the drum for the most part of ten miles that day. There was such a hubbub of chatter and excitement. Some had been up all night first footing and, in spite of this being a Temperance Walk, they were still full of enthusiasm to continue the celebration and complete the round. Maybe their accumulated 'drappies' would carry them through. Drunkenness did not worry the girls as it was not uncommon in Broadsea but, remembering the firm advice of Mary May, they steered well clear of those worse the wear of alcohol and kept close to their own group.

At last the band formed, fluters in front followed by the drummer, his huge instrument strapped firmly to his chest with colourful bands crossed behind his shoulders. People steered well clear of him as he was apt to be over exuberant when he became carried away and gave his sticks an extra high flourish. Precisely on the seven thirty stroke the front line set foot and struck up the great Salvation Army marching song 'Sweeping Through the Gates of the New Jerusalem,' giving it full forte, and the drum took up the beat setting a brisk pace. Those who knew the words joined in and as she listened to the triumphant sound and watched the flickering lanterns and the joy and happiness on the surrounding faces, Maggie Ann wondered to herself,

"Will this be what it will be like when Jesus comes again to lead the believers to glory?" She had had long discussions with Sandy about this and knew he had firm convictions on the subject, but she herself still had many questions.

Linking arms, they formed up in rows behind the band and set off as the grey dawn was breaking through. Having toured the village they turned in the direction of the westward villages. They did not notice the chilly damp in the air, or the bleakness of the road as it hugged the rocky shoreline; nor did they worry about the long miles ahead before they would turn for home. All that mattered was the present company, the folks they would meet up with in the villages, the cups of tea awaiting them and the pure fun of being together.

Near the first house in Pitullie they spotted Sandy waiting to join Janet who took his arm and walked proudly alongside. They stopped off for a moment to call in on his family while the band halted and played near the school. Kate and Elsie arrived to join Maggie Ann, full of excitement as Elsie's cousin Jim Strachan had arrived from Peterhead and was going on the walk also. This was interesting news for Maggie Ann. She had heard Elsie talk of him but had always been under the impression that he worked away from home. She wondered what he would be like. The girls were anxious to show him off so they hustled her along to the end of the village to Elsie's house where her mother had tea waiting. The girls burst in but Maggie Ann followed more hesitantly, shy at meeting this stranger. But she need not have worried. The welcome was warm and sincere and soon she was seated at the table with the rest tucking in to the wonderful hot tea and abundant food. During introductions she was too embarrassed to look him full in the face, but now, sitting opposite, she liked what she saw. Occasionally their eyes met as the fun and talk went on, and Maggie Ann could see the warmth and kindness displayed on his face as he, like herself, listened quietly to the goings on. No surprise then, when they were setting off again, heading for Sandhaven then Rosehearty, that Maggie Ann found herself beside Jim at the end of the row, next the sea. Thanks to Elsie, she suspected. Elsie seemed to have some motive in mind, but Maggie Ann was just too happy to be there and would have fallen in with any plan to continue the pleasure of this day. When they all linked arms again Maggie Ann found it comforting to have the strong support between herself and the shore. The tide was high and so close to the road they felt the icy spray, especially on that bare, exposed stretch along by Breemies road. She could sense he was leaning forward to give her added protection, a new experience for her.

When the walkers reached Rosehearty some of the local Temperance Group joined with them and shared in the short service in the Square. Later a fine rain began to fall so, after a hasty cup of tea in the nearby houses, the procession set off for the long return journey to Broadsea. This time the going was made easier for the wind was behind them, buffeting them along. There was little conversation but lots of calling out to each other and joking as they sang their way home.

As they came on to College Bounds Maggie Ann ran ahead to warn Mary May that they had two extra guests for dinner. Even as she entered the kitchen she knew that Didy was there by the aroma of his tobacco, but the scene that met her eyes brought an added exultation to her happiness. She could hardly believe this was home. The table was extended and already laid for eight; the long, gleaming, white, damask cloth Maggie Ann had never seen before and the wedding china, unearthed from the back of the dresser cupboard, was now sitting sparkling and clean waiting to be used. Betsy, Bella and Ena sat primly on the bed attired in their best new Lowestoft dresses and there was a distinct conspiratorial glint in their eyes. And best of all, Mary May was there smiling, a flush on her cheeks from all her morning's exertions, and wearing her present under a large snow white apron. In her joy Maggie Ann could have wrapped her arms round her mother and hugged her, but you did not do that. Instead she just smiled widely and said,

" 'At looks grand. There'll be twa extra forby Kate an' Elsie." and turned to welcome the rest as they crowded into the close.

At first the kitchen seemed to be crammed with people but once the girls headed for the front room to tidy themselves and rest a little, the men divested themselves of their heavy coats in the little back lobby and sat down by the fire. As they were all connected with the fishing in some way the conversation was soon flowing well. Didy still had his yawl drawn up on the shore and went out line fishing when the weather was suitable Sandy was full of plans to have his own cooperage and his regular curer customers; and now Jim made his contribution from the point of view of yard manager. As she assisted her mother to prepare a cup of tea, Maggie Ann listened to the men's voices and thought how good it sounded. They had missed male voices and male conversation in the house. Didy dropped in quite often but it was not the same. She would have enjoyed just sitting down with them and listening, but there was a dinner to set on the table and she and Janet were needed. However, she did pick up little details about Jim as he and Sandy were deep in a discussion about the issues involved in setting up a cooperage. He had done his apprenticeship as a cooper and enjoyed it, but when Peter Buchan had offered him a yard manager's position it was attractive and he accepted. It brought more money and responsibility, which he enjoyed, but also meant he would have to travel more widely as the fishings followed the herring; wherever his master decided to cure. His work was to manage the yard during the curing season; oversee the carters, the gutters, and the coopers, labouring hands, salt deliveries, stables, the workers' accommodation and welfare. It was a huge coverage. The most enjoyable part was being able to know all the workers and once the yard was up and running, there was very little trouble. Two weeks before a new fishing began he would go on ahead and prepare the yard, check the huts for the girls and order any repairs and deliveries so that when the contingents arrived all was in order. He would soon be off to Isle of Mann and then, apart from the Peterhead fishing and New Year, he would be away from home most of the time. It was fine for a single young man but he supposed the day would come when he would want to settle, and then he would go back to coopering again.

A little hiatus in the scullery drew Maggie Ann away from the discussion. Mary May was concerned that the hen, sitting proudly on the ashet, would not be large enough to share round eleven people once it was carved. But Maggie Ann had another idea. If they broke it all up into reasonably sized pieces and laid it out in two sections on the dish, white meat and dark, then they could arrange some of the potatoes, carrots and mashed turnip round the dish as decoration. It would look much more copious. Mary May would serve the guests first, and then they themselves could do with very little meat as long as it was not too obvious to the visitors. Problem solved, they then set about rearranging the kitchen to afford enough seating and table space. The girls were still sitting on the bed, awestruck at the unusual happenings taking place in their kitchen, so the table was pushed up in front of them and the others sat round, managing to accommodate everyone; a little short of elbow space, but that all added to the jovial mood. Didy opted to have his meal by the fire and Mary May said she would keep him company and do the serving up.

Hungry as they were from the long walk, they waited while Mary May asked Didy to give a blessing on the food, and then they set to. The hen broth tasted wonderfully flavoursome and satisfying and second helpings were called for. Then came the mountains of mashed potatoes and turnips, glowing gold with the gleam of melted butter; the carrots lifted straight from the broth pot still held the flavour of the barley and the peas; and, last of all, Janet carried in the work of art, the hen platter. The whole presentation deserved the oohs and aahs and once the plates were filled and the rich gravy was poured over all, a silence descended for a little as each savoured the pleasure of that moment. Nods of appreciation were directed to Mary May as the mouths dealt with the matter of eating. But it was more than that. For Maggie Ann and her sisters it was a miracle because such an event had never happened before and they were seeing a new mother for the first time. For the guests it was a sense of deep well being from a sincere, warm family welcome and a bounteous sharing.

The moment of the Clootie Dumpling arrived as it was born in on its tray and set on the table. Steam issued forth and there was lots of laughter as fingers tried to untie the boiled- in knot of the cotton wrappings. At last the clootie was folded back and the dumpling lay exposed and naked, all the gooey surface releasing such odours! To many this was the best part of the dumpling and at once plates were thrust forward for a share. Then the knife was plunged in and slice after slice was shared out for all and the jug of fresh milk was passed round the table. Maggie Ann wondered,

" I winner 'at naebody's written a poem tae the Clootie Dumplin' like Burns wrote tae the Haggis."

" Maybe they're waetin for you tae dae it." teased Jim.

The back and forth fun went on until at last they were filled and when the jellies arrived all agreed they would wait a while before tackling that.

At last, with everything cleared away and the precious dishes set to soak in a bath of water, they settled down to have a little social time round the fire. Normally the dishes would have been washed but Mary May did not feel assured of their safety with so many boisterous girls around, so they were left till tomorrow for her and the older girls. Before very long Jim had his pipe going too and Ena, having recovered from her shyness, had succumbed to the excitement and was now curled up fast asleep with her head upon Jim's shoulder. The blue dress and the fair hair glowed in the firelight. Sandy being a Salvationist did not smoke, but he took out his mouth organ and soon the songs were going on demand. Didy kept time with his pipe in hand, enjoying this treat hearing the old favourites, 'Granny's Hielan' Hame,' 'The Crookit Bawbee', 'Mary Morrison', and, if the moment became too sad, Sandy would burst into a rousing chorus and have the young ones sing their own choice.

As she sat by the table looking on the group Maggie Ann was reminded again of Burns.

"I winner fit wye he's aye comin' back tae me the nicht. He jist seems tae ken fit I'm thinkin' an' has the words for it. 'From scenes like these-----' in the cottar's kitchen; it's jist fit we hae here an' I'll niver forget it. I jist wish we could stop the clock for a bit an' haud the time still."

So she pondered this moment to cherish. No one knew, but Maggie Ann was to hold that scene close to her heart for many years to come.

Then it was time for another cup of tea and a move to prepare for the next New Year's Day event—the 'Surree' in the Hallie. Fortunately they did not have far to walk and set off together well wrapped up in capes and shawls against the frosty night air. The hall was a fine sight, every window aglow with the lamps, and the doorway was resplendent with streamers and paper lanterns. Two men from the Hall Committee stood handing out bags of buns and white china cups to the arrivals and then ushers showed them to their seats in the long benches laid across the hall. Already it was well filled but they found seats, all together, about the middle and settled down to look around and wish Happy New Year to acquaintances till the program began. Maggie Ann sat between Ena and Janet with Mary May at the end next Ena and Sandy next to Janet. Then came Jim, Betsy, Bella, Kate and Elsie. This gave no one cause for speculation or gossip. The Temperance Walk and Soirée was essentially a time for courting couples and intentions were often publicly declared that day. So Maggie Ann did not wish to be the subject of discussion and took care to sit well away from Jim.

The social took its usual course; mainly a religious program with good lively hymns, pieces sung by the Mission Choir and solos from a few of the well known village singers. The speaker was amusing, stimulating some hearty laughter with a few well-told stories. During the interval tea was served along the rows from shining copper kettles specially decked for the occasion with ribbons, and the contents of the bags were enjoyed. As usual, there was a 'softie' sandwich, a German bun and a 'sair heedie', traditional New Year's Day fare. Now and again a boisterous hand would let fly a crumpled-up bag to land on a distant acquaintance, but the good humour was maintained and at the end it was considered to have been one of the best soirées.

Once the crush round the doorway had dispersed they found each other again and made their way across to the open fields by Marr's house where the Rosehearty brake was waiting. This had been specially arranged for the visitors to save the long walk home and Sandy, in the rush, had been quick to claim four seats. Once Kate and Elsie were handed up the men came over to say their farewells to the little group standing in the darkness. Holding Mary May's hand in both his own Jim said so warmly,

" Thank you for a wonderful day. It's been the best N,eer Day I've ivver had." And turning to Maggie Ann, he looked down into her face saying,

" Remember, ye've a poem to write. I'll be askin' ye aboot it fan I see ye again. That'll nae be lang. I've enjoyed y're company the day, all o' ye. Gweed nicht." And running to the brake, he jumped up and took his place beside Sandy. As the brake drew away they could make out the smiling faces and waving hands in the glow of the carriage lamps. Soon the sound of the horses' hooves faded away and the villagers turned slowly for home. Janet and the younger ones ran on ahead racing to be first to open the door, but Maggie Ann and her mother took a path between the houses, leading to the shore. The dampness had gone out of the air and now it was a clear, crisp night with a sky aglitter with stars. Between the flashing beams of the lighthouse the constellations could be clearly picked out. There was no moon, but the sky was so luminous the water seemed to reflect its own light and there was a distinct line where sea and sky met. They savoured the freshness of tangy air after the closely packed hall. Down below, the fishing boats at their moorings clanked at the rise and fall of the tide and the waves made a lazy 'sooch' as they broke on the sandy shore. Up here where they stood looking out, the lights from the windows beamed out like tiny beacons and the smoke from the chimneys drew up straight and even in the still air; always a good omen for tomorrow's weather.

" 'At Jim seems a fine chiel."

" Aye mither, he is 'at." replied Maggie Ann, trying to account for the warm, singing feeling within.

Their moment of communion over, the two women turned away home to face the normality of family life, but somehow, there was a feeling that with this New Year's Day a new chapter had begun for them; full of unknowns of course, but there were now three women in their home, all with different futures and destinies, wherever that may take them.

Chapter 9

Their busy winter passed and then spring was upon them again calling for the annual onslaught on dirt. Now that the grandparents were older and frailer, the girls adopted responsibility for these houses also; Janet went to Didy's and Maggie Ann to Cairnbulg where she decided to stay for a few days while the spring-cleaning went on. This was a new experience for her as, apart from the Lowestoft fishing sojourn, Mary May had never allowed her girls to sleep away from home. Now here she was, elevated to the honour of the bed in the benn when she would have much preferred to sleep in a shakedown under the rafters at the top of the attic ladder. But Annie May would not hear of it,

" If ye cam tae vrecht ye need yer sleep." She insisted and there was nothing more to argue.

As she lay in bed in the flickering candlelight her eyes roved around the room, this 'holy of holies' for, as children, they were forbidden to enter. To be sure, driven by curiosity, they had dared to peek in at the door, but never had the courage to walk in. Now, here she was in sole possession and she did not much enjoy the experience. The bed, usually shut away behind panelled doors, felt musty and dank and in spite of a warm stone pig at her feet, Maggie Ann shivered. Maybe it was the gallery of severe faces staring down from the walls. Didy, long dead, hung above the mantelpiece in place of honour; a big bearded man in best seaman's suit with his hand holding a cheese cutter cap resting on a stone pedestal. His judgemental eyes rested on her wherever she went in the room as did the other ancients, and now just part of her family history. She must ask Annie May who they were when they cleaned the frames tomorrow. At the end of the room stood a tall, oak sideboard covered with a snowy, lace runner and all sorts of ornaments; nothing like Mrs. Thompson's delicate porcelain, but little jugs and plates with 'Present from Yarmouth' and other places stamped on them. In pride of place were two tall glass globes containing a delicate china shepherd and shepherdess surrounded by flowers and fruit and tiny birds with lovely colourful plumage. A low kist stood in front of the window. Maggie Ann wondered what it held, and how old was the tall grandfather clock standing over by the fireside; there seemed to be a name and date on the decorated brass face; she would look tomorrow; the tick seemed to grow louder the longer she listened; what a good job the chimes had been shut off. Why did people keep a room like this? She remembered her mother telling her the last time it was used was when Didy had been laid out and the room would not be used again till Granny died. But here she was, lying in the bed, and Maggie Ann shivered. She could well understand her mother wishing to escape the brooding severity of this house, longing for the warmth of her Willem's arms. How sad it was when tradition and pride and bitterness took over one's life and people stopped showing that they loved each other. Her mother was not a demonstrative person but they all knew her love, and showed theirs in return. She decided to close the doors and shut out the condemning eyes; and she fell asleep.

During her time in the village Maggie Ann took time to visit one or two friends, particularly the Cows who lived in No. 60. There had always been a warm welcome, for their door was open to all. Jane Cow was Maggie Ann's age and the two girls had been firm friends since ever they could remember. Jane worked at the fishing too but with a different curer, and whenever they met they shared many thoughts and dreams of what they planned to do once they were old enough and had sufficient money. Both girls were practical and showed no hesitancy when it came to making their dreams materialise, so during the few days when they had time to discuss things, the matter of real training as cooks was turned over. This was something they must leave home to achieve and even leave Fraserburgh, to obtain certificates, which would gain them entry to high class work. Both were positive this was what they wished to do so they decided to research during the summer and, come to the end of the Yarmouth fishing, see what they had found out. Perhaps even next winter they could be fixed up in training service. It would all depend on their summer savings as well.

Once home in Broadsea it was time to think about the Shetland fishing and all the preparation. Maggie Ann was excited although she tried not to show it. She had heard such stories about the sail across the Firth and then the northern waters to the islands; there was also living in the 'huts' along with so many other girls sharing the facilities and 'doing' for themselves; and, although she hardly dare give it place in her hopes, would she perhaps see Jim again? It was a huge adventure, and Maggie Ann could still recall the tingle of excitement mixed with apprehension, which coursed through her mind in these weeks of preparation.

Once again the kist stood in the bedroom, lid open, ready to receive its assortment of contents. This was to be an early summer fishing so the skirts and blouses were printed cotton, dark for work but a few lighter colours for Saturday and Sunday; one or two woollens and shawls were there in case the weather was cold, and the usual underwear made up the clothing needs. Since the huts had stood empty for a year the custom was to redecorate so the girls brought their own curtains, utensils, dishes and wallpaper- all things required to create their own little home for the few weeks. Again sharing with Kate and Elsie, Maggie Ann's responsibility was to supply the wall paper, so in went four rolls of the cheapest paper- cream coloured with a little rose and leaf pattern, and a bag of flour to make the paste. Added to that was a pasting brush and her precious stone pig for she would miss sleeping with Janet. A few odd cups, saucers and plates were included along with some cutlery and a pot flower vase and lastly, over the top of all, was laid her patchwork quilt to use as a bed cover and blanket. This last was very treasured for over the years Annie May had sewn one for each of her four older nieces involving hours of cutting and hand stitching to form the diamond pattern. These diamonds were arranged in a light and dark coloured alternate design and the whole was backed with strong unbleached cotton creating a most colourful and warm quilt. Maggie Ann loved her one and normally it lay folded away in her hope chest, but now she thought it would be good to have it with her to add a touch of colour spread on her bed. At last the lid was shut, the apron and boots on top, covered over with the tarpaulin and, finally roped, the kist was stood at the close end for collection. It was to go to Baltasound by fishing boat while the workers travelled by steamer and they would find the kists waiting for them at their accommodation.

Now it was just a few days before leaving and there was such excitement amongst the girls in Broadsea. For those who had been to Shetland before there was much talk like,

"Dae ye mind fan'?" and they would go on to reminisce on some escapade. Or another would wonder,

"Dae ye think so an' so 'll be there 'es time?"

For the uninitiated it was all so exciting they could not wait; although the dread of the heaving sea and sickness gave them a little sobering thought. They all knew the sea, had lived by it and depended on it for a livelihood, understood its moods and troughs and had witnessed many storms; but they had never travelled on it, and such a long way too.

The word went round that the SS Rognvaldt was in the harbour at the steamship jetty. The ship had arrived early morning and all that day would be refuelling and laying in stores so that by evening the passengers would be called out. Groups from Ireland, Isle of Mann and Ayrshire had already boarded at Leith so when the Fraserburgh teams along with the gutters and coopers from the coastal villages arrived, the ship was really loaded to capacity. As they climbed the gangway of the great steamship under the funnel belching black smoke, there was a real holiday mood and as Maggie Ann looked down on the families and friends standing on the pier she felt a great exhilaration and excitement. This was a real adventure into the unknown.

Slowly the ship pulled away, hooting its horn in response to the cheers and farewells, and edged its way along the breakwater to the harbour mouth. Some of the well-wishers ran alongside until the ship took up speed and reached the Horn. There, with a huge lift, it ploughed into the real sea swell and made a quick turn into the German Sea heading to cross the Moray Firth to the Butt of Caithness and Wick. As the three girls watched the land receding they kept their eyes on the home villages until in the fading light only the lighthouse on Kinnaird Castle remained. Then they turned to look at their fellow passengers. Like themselves, with a view to storms and illness, all were dressed sensibly; no elegant outfits here, just warm skirts, aprons, bodices and shawls. Belongings were carried in a bag and any valuables were sewn into underwear. Finding space on the crowded ship was difficult but they finally discovered a corner in the upper deck lounge where they could rest and come and go for fresh air if the sea grew rough. At the moment it was calm and the passengers settled down to pass the time in their own diverse ways. Now and again singing would break out and some areas were noisier than others but generally folks conversed, listened to the strange dialects, or slept.

The crossing was calm and the ship made good time, arriving early in Wick harbour. The passengers were not allowed ashore as it was just a stop to collect more workers, this time from the Western Isles and Caithness. These folks had already been journeying by sea and land for over a day and here they were, still travelling on. They were a sad, weary looking group and Maggie Ann wondered at their endurance and determination. Maybe like herself, they came for the earnings; on the other hand it allowed them to see some of the world outside their islands. She had heard that the Highland men were great sailors.

Another few hours brought them past the chain of the Orkney Isles to a short stop at Kirkwall and then, some hours later, past the Fair Isle. Now began the real test of their seamanship when they crossed the Roost. Here the swell of two oceans met, the Atlantic and the German

Ocean, creating a constant turbulence of rough water. Huge waves crashed into deep troughs and cross currents were a constant drag on the ships. One was a good sailor if the Roost was crossed without seasickness and Maggie Ann felt a great sense of achievement that she was one of those. Kate and Elsie and many others were not so well off and when they came into the calmer waters in the lea of Sumburgh Head there was a great sigh of relief .

As the Rognvald sailed up the coast of the mainland of Shetland Maggie Ann could not take her eyes off the scene; long, low hills, very green, but with no sign of trees; scattered houses and occasionally soaring cliffs seemed to form a fairly barren landscape. But when they entered the bay between Bressay Isle and Lerwick the signs of a busy seaport were evident. They tied up at one of the landing stages built out in long piers into the Voe and at last the passengers were allowed ashore for an hour while the ship replenished. The girls set off to reach the town and show Maggie Ann the delights of Lerwick, and that is what they were. The busy narrow main street, still paved with ancient flagstones and cobbles, the low houses, some of them part shop selling all sorts of wares from food and sweets to china and household goods. This fascinated Maggie Ann and she would have lingered but the others hustled her away for a cup of tea before returning to the harbour. She made a mental note that here she would buy some of her gifts on their return journey.

The passengers were now aboard the Zetland Steamer which would navigate the close, shallow waters between the isles, a slow and hazardous feat; past Whalsay and later Fetlar to Unst, the northernmost island of the Shetland chain, and at last, to the long narrow Voe that was Baltasound. It was very late in the day but in that land of the midnight sun there was no gloaming or darkness and the passengers were alert and searching the closeby shore for familiar places and people. All along the margins of the Sound lay the curing yards, up and ready to be operational and Kate pointed out Ewen's place near the head of the waters. As the ship neared the landing shouts and greetings reached across the narrowing stretch and suddenly Elsie grabbed Maggie Ann's arm and pointing, called out,

"There's Jim." And so it was, waving his arms. At last, when they disembarked, he was at the foot of the gangway, smiling as he reached out to welcome them.

"My it's gran' tae see ye again. Ye've had a nae bad crossin'. The brake is ower there ready for ye. I hae tae wight for ma ain crew but a'll be oot tae see ye the morn." And with a special hug round Maggie Ann's shoulders, he saw them off and hurried back to gather his own workers.

The cart trundled along the rough, stony track by the Sound, dropping off the parties of workers at their designated curing stations until at last it came to John Ewen's yard. As she was handed down Maggie Ann's eyes were everywhere, trying to take in this strange world she had come to. She had never imagined anything like this; such desolation and yet so much activity. At the landing stretching out into the Sound there were already a few early sail boats and just up from there stood the roofed in farlans, the wooden tubs and rows of empty kits. To the right was the cooperage with stacks of barrels all ready for filling; and along the back, a little distance away, stood a long, low, wooden building with two rows of windows; the huts. Here they were to stay for at least a month and Maggie Ann wondered, would she survive? Maybe it was because she was tired and hungry, but as she followed Kate and Elsie into their allocated room and saw the three empty beds, the bare floor and table and chairs, she could have wept for home.

But Kate and Elsie would have none of it. They were delighted with their room being so near the sink and lavatory at the end of the central corridor. Their three kists were standing by the door so they would make up the beds, sort out the food left over from the journey and have a cup of tea with it. The rest could be left till tomorrow. So they did and, once in bed, hugging her warm pig under the quilt, Maggie Ann immediately dropped off to sleep.

Next day was a whirl of activity, scrubbing, papering the walls and hanging curtains. Clothes went into the wall press at one side of the stove and food and dishes into the other. Once the ornaments were out and a cloth spread on the table, the whole room was transformed and homely. Maggie Ann felt better.

The building interested her for, living at home in Broadsea, she had never needed to enter a gutter's accommodation, and so she was curious. It comprised a ground and upper floor, each with a central corridor; an outside door, an open staircase, an iron sink and a lavatory were at each end and the doors to the rooms opened off the corridors. Most rooms held the three members of a team and groups from certain areas usually preferred to be together so there would be Highland or Wick or Fife girls forming their own community of rooms. As many as a hundred people could be housed here and Maggie Ann understood why Kate was so pleased with the location of their room near the entrance. She was a bit doubtful about the dry toilet but Kate assured her it worked very well and one of the carters emptied it every few days. Built on at one end of the huts was a large cookhouse where Mrs Isabella Watt with two helpers reigned supreme. Better known as Isie Wattie, this lady became a queen indeed, for her job was to have food on hand for all John Ewen's workers at whatever time the landings of herring allowed. Of course they had regular meal times but if an afternoon landing was some hundreds of crans then work to cure the herrings while fresh went on well into the night. That meant hot food had to be available and Isie was always there with a pot of soup and tea. She had cooked in Shetland for John Ewen over many seasons and he considered her contribution as priceless. With her long association and experience of Baltasound she was a fountain of knowledge, especially for first time workers, and many a homesick gutter would weep her eyes out on Isie's shoulder and then be comforted with a cup of tea and a scone. She was the mother to them all and long years later, workers would speak of her kindness and generosity of soul which always took her the second mile. When the girls took Maggie Ann to meet Isie her first words were,

"Aye, ye're a new quinie. Fa's yer foulk? Wid I ken them?"

When Maggie Ann said her mother was Mary May Isie's face lit up.

"Fine I ken her. She's the fish wifie wi' the creel. A hard worken' gweed wifie. Keeps hersel' tae hersel', bit neen the war for 'at. So ye're Mary Maee's dochter. I ken yir granny in Belger as weel."

The family connection settled Maggie Ann felt she had now been accepted and they continued to discuss the village shop and where they could buy supplies for the many cups of tea that would be brewed in their room. Baltasound village was not far away and the one shop carried all they needed; the post was collected there and bread could be bought from the bakery set up by a Broch man who had come for the fishing to meet the huge demand of the workers.

Maggie Ann was amazed at the massive operation that comprised the Shetland fishing; how many walks of life it touched, and the immense organization behind it all.

Jim arrived on Sunday afternoon. After their two hard days of travel and settling in the girls treated themselves to a long lie on Sunday but were up and tidied by dinner-time. They decided to go for a walk in the afternoon and were just leaving when Jim walked in carrying a large fruit cake, most welcome. Seated round the table with tea and the sliced fruitcake they enjoyed exchanging news and the girls listened as Jim described his travels since Christmas; then they all set out for the walk.

As they headed for the village at the head of the loch Maggie Ann saw the emptiness of the islands; the rolling low hills still covered with the brownish shades of the winter bracken, interspersed with the light green of bog land and the outcrops of dark, brooding rock formations. Summer had not yet fully come to these northern isles and there was an empty bleakness over all. A very few scattered croft houses filtered a thin spiral of smoke and she could pick up the scent of peat in the air. What amazed her most was the vastness of the distance she could see. Maggie Ann was accustomed to the far view to the horizon across the open sea, but this was something different with the long arms of the low land splintered with sea lochs and rocky coastline, all reaching away to more land and more sea and never seeming to come to a horizon. Then there was the silence. Occasionally a whaup or a grouse, disturbed by their footsteps, would flutter out of the undergrowth; and amongst the scattered sheep a late lamb would bleat for its mother; overhead the gulls soared and keened to each other; but that was all. It was as if the world of men had not reached here and yet here they were. Jim pointed out the various curing yards as they strolled along. His own one was on the other side of the sound and was easier to reach by boat than by road. There was a similarity in the set up of each station and as she counted them Maggie Ann estimated that there must be thousands of workers at this fishing. Of course the steamers loaded with workers were arriving every day and the forest of masts across the Voe indicated the size of the fleet. Maggie Ann was thrilled to be part of it all and wished Janet could be here to share it with her.

Being Sunday the village shop was closed and not many inhabitants were visible, Sabbath rules being strictly adhered to, so the girls turned to retrace their steps and Jim made his farewells saying he would see them again next weekend. As he departed with a few cheery remarks he reminded Maggie Ann of that poem. Had she written it yet? She shook her head and the blush rose up her cheeks. He had remembered. All the way back the girls teased,

"Winner foo he's comin' again niest weeken'. He nivver cam' afore tae veesit us lik' 'at. Fa's he comin' tae see I wunner?"

Maggie Ann said nothing in reply, just laughed, but her heart sang within.

Next morning the reality broke on them. The boats had sailed in the early hours and were back, already unloading at seven o'clock. The whole building was alive with activity. Feet ran in the corridors, shouts, laughter, the odd scream and crash of china, last minute queues at the toilet, then the stream of women heading for the farlans. The coopers' hammers had already been pounding for an hour and the silence of yesterday was no more. So it began, the endless refilling of the farlan, the flying fingers gutting and sorting as the herring came; broken ones into one tub ready for the fish meal factory and good ones to be packed layer on layer in the waiting barrel. The speed of the workers was amazing and all the time the fun, the chatter and the occasional break out of song made the whole atmosphere one of energy and purpose; it was good to be here. Breaks for meals and rest eased the physical strain but by evening of their first day they were very tired. Glad to step out of the rubber boots and the stiff oilskin aprons, the three took turns using the basin to wash, and lay down till time to go for their evening meal. From then on it was at times a punishing routine till Saturday lunchtime; or when the last boat unloaded its catch and tied up for the weekend. But most of the gutters were young, and on the whole the weather was good, and counting up their barrels by the end of the week, they knew it had been worth while coming. By now the three had formed a routine of chores; dealing with and supplying the stove, bringing in the bucket of fresh water to prevent congestion at the shared sink, cleaning the room.

As the days went by new friendships were formed and, when time allowed, a good deal of socialising went on in each other's rooms. Sundays were special for then the husbands and boy friends came to visit and it became a regular event to look out for the rowing boat crossing the Sound bringing the men from the other side. Then they would disperse to their various destinations, having arranged to meet at a certain time for the return journey. Jim was always there, sometimes bringing friends who had no family connections at the fishing, and then there would be long walks over the moors and picnics. Sometimes they would borrow John Ewen's rowboat and take the girls down the Sound to Balta Isle where they explored the island climbing over what was left of the old deserted crofts and wondering at the primitive existence of these long gone days. After a picnic on the shore and singing as they rowed, they would return in time to catch the boat across the Sound. Often they just sat round the table talking over a cup of tea, having some fun and laughter, teasing each other and relaxing; often they finished the day attending the service held in the mission hall in the village.

Although the work was intense and physically hard to endure, for Maggie Ann this experience was a treasured memory. Twice more she made the journey and worked the fishing at Baltasound, also times of great joy and happiness, but this first time was special. It was like an awakening in herself to a new freedom, to an awareness of new responses; the expanses of land and sea drew out of her a desire to see more beyond; ancient ruins made her wonder about the past; she found she could laugh and tease and hold her own with the girls. But the greatest wonder of all was an awareness of her growing feelings for Jim. At that time she would not have called it 'love' as she did not know what that meant, but she realised day by day that her need to see him increased with every visit. When he was there she felt complete and although he never gave any indication of his feelings or compromised her in any way, she knew there was an understanding and sharing of soul. Just in the quiet companionship, the nod of agreement, the private smile, the touch on the shoulder, the singling out in a group. All these communicated that he felt the same way but she knew he would say nothing until he had spoken to her mother. So Maggie Ann hugged this sweet knowledge to herself and looked forward, dreaming and hoping. She noticed too that the girls had stopped teasing her about Jim, accepting him as her special lad.

Now as she sat on the Braes in the gathering darkness Maggie Ann savoured the memory of that first fishing at Baltasound. Nothing could erase the sweetness and innocent faith of these few weeks when knowledge of their feelings belonged only to the two of them and the world had not rushed in. Once in a while in later years Maggie Ann allowed herself the indulgence of dwelling on the memory, taking it out like a precious jewel and looking into its depths. No matter what happened in her life, she would always treasure and be grateful for that time.

The Shetland fishing drew to a close and once again the girls faced the long, return journey. The Lerwick stop allowed time for some purchases and then it was on to the Roost and the long haul to Wick and across the Moray Firth to their first sight of Kinnaird Head.

Chapter 10

Once home again in Broadsea, they were pitched straight into the North East fishing which brought the usual influx of workers. The town was an exciting place. Mary May, Janet and Maggie Ann were in the gutting yard every day and sometimes late into the night while Betsey and Bella looked after things at home. In all this scene of activity Maggie Ann did not imagine that Jim could possibly find time to visit. Two weeks later a letter arrived for her saying he would come on Sunday; he was looking forward to seeing her and would like to speak with her mother. When she read these words her heart gave a leap for now she knew he was serious and they could declare their love to each other and to the world. She still felt a little apprehension about her mother's reception of the news but when Maggie Ann told her, Mary May simply nodded saying,

"Aye weel, we'll hae a cup o'tay an' you an' Janet can tak the bairns for a wak."

It appeared as though this was an every day occurrence, but inwardly Mary May trembled for the happiness of her first born was of such importance to her. This child, born in so much sorrow and disgrace; who had sacrificed so much of her young life to help her; who had struggled through wind and sleet in the dark mornings to put an extra half crown on the table; and now she, Mary May, was having to face a young man who was going to ask her permission to court Maggie Ann, and she hardly knew him. As so often before, Mary May relied on her instincts. There was little doubt about Maggie Ann's feelings, judging by the light in her eyes, but how could she, her mother, judge Jim on the strength of one meeting? One thing was certain, she had to be direct and frank with him; but who was she to control the lives of two people who loved each other, when she herself had married for love against all reasoning?

What transpired during that meeting no one was ever told. When the girls returned from their walk to Watermill they found the table laid with the best china, Jim was carrying things through from the scullery and there was an air of ease and peace.

During teatime, as Maggie Ann studied the two faces most dear to her in the world, a great surge of love and thankfulness welled up inside and she said a silent prayer of gratitude. The chat ranged round the fishing and Shetland and the great changes taking place at the harbour and in the town. At last it was time for Jim to go and when they accompanied him to the close end it was the most natural thing in the world for Maggie Ann to walk away with him as he gently took her arm and linked it through his own. Nothing more needed to be said; the physical contact was enough, their feelings pulsing from one to the other, and when they reached the foot of Charlotte Street where Jim was to pick up his lift, he squeezed her hand very tightly and looking deep into her eyes, he whispered,

"Yir mam wis winnerfu. A can say fit's in ma hairt noo lass. A'll be back neist Sunday." And with that he was away.

In the ensuing weeks Jim was there most Sundays and they roamed the Braes and the shore to Pitullie, on their own or sometimes in a foursome with Janet and Sandy who were now engaged. On rainy days they stayed by the kitchen fire and enjoyed the family. It was a good time.

Then the south fishing came round and Jim was very busy organising his crew. He operated from Yarmouth while Maggie Ann was at Lowestoft, but they met each other on the occasional Sunday and wrote frequent letters.

But now it was Hogmanay with the Broadsea Walk on the morn when Sandy and Jim would accompany the girls. What an amazing year it had been since last Hogmanay. This time it was a brisk, cold, sunny, winter day with none of the drizzle of last Ne'er Day and, as they all stepped out in the dark behind the flute band to tour the village, the girls linked with their escorts and marched proudly along. Elsie and Kate met up with them at Pittulie, accompanied by their lads for the day, and then it was on to Rosehearty for the final ceremonies before the return to Broadsea. As they walked along Maggie Ann remembered the shy child she had been last Ne'er Day and wondered at the change in herself that had come about through loving someone like Jim. She felt overwhelmed, exultant, humble, motherly, all at the same time; and a little scared at the strength of her feelings and at the suddenness of it all. But one thing held fast; young as she was she knew she loved him and all she wished for was, when the time came, to be with Jim always.

Once back in Broadsea, the traditional meal was served amidst lots of laughter and teasing. There was the same table arrangement, just as last year, and the great appreciation of the good food delighted Mary May who smiled and nodded. Now that three of them were bringing in an income things were easier and she was able to add some extra luxuries to the meal; the trifle and the chocolate biscuits and, of course, a larger hen. Janet and Maggie Ann gave their mother a knowing look when she carried it in.

Before the singsong time Ena began to insist on the 'present time' for she could not wait any longer to give out her parcels. Quite on their own, Ena, Betsy and Bella had been quietly working on gifts for the family and although Mary May was aware of the whispered discussions and an air of mystery, she did not interfere with their conspiracy. Now all was revealed when the parcels, beautifully wrapped, were presented with great ceremony. Starting with Didy and Mary May, then Sandy and Jim followed by Janet and Maggie Ann they passed them out by name. It brought tears to the adults' eyes to see the beautifully knitted socks, gloves, hats and scarves; Sandy and Jim received the same, and Mary May a short dark red cape crocheted by Ena, which she wore proudly for the rest of the day. Then Janet and Maggie Ann handed out theirs, and magically, Sandy and Jim found tiny parcels in the depths of their greatcoat pockets, which delighted the girls, old and young. There had never been such a Ne'er Day as this.

Once the excitement had settled a little, Jim took out another small parcel from his inner jacket pocket and handed it quietly to Maggie Ann. All eyes were on her as she undid the red ribbon and shiny paper to reveal a small grey box. Inside, tucked into the dark red velvet, lay a gold ring set with two deep pink coral stones with a row of three seed pearls between them. Maggie Ann's hands trembled as she gazed on the lovely ring and there was a profound, waiting silence in the room. Jim quietly took the box out of her hands and looking into her face, slipped the ring on to her third finger saying,

"A hae Mary May's permeesion. Maggie Ann, wull ye be promised tae me tae be ma wife, for a loo ye wi a' ma hairt?"

Maggie Ann could simply nod, too choked to speak, and when he bent his head to kiss the ring on her finger, she laid her right hand on his head like a blessing and a pledge. At that moment she longed to draw his head to her shoulder and hold him close, but that was for a private moment. Instead, her eyes met her mother's and she saw there joy and tears and great happiness and Maggie Ann was glad to respond.

Once the moments of astonished silence had passed the girls began a bombardment of eager questions,

"Fan wull ye be getting mairit? Wull it be afore Janet?"

"Can we be best maids?"

"Foo did ye ken the size o' the ring?"

"Yir mither helpit me there. She can keep a secret." Jim answered, laughing across at Mary May.

Amidst all the fun and happy banter Maggie Ann blushed and laughed and held on tight to Jim's hand, feeling the unusual sensation of the ring on her finger. It was really a simple ring but oh, it was so precious and meant so much to her.

There was no need to plan the seating at the surree this time. Maggie Ann sat next to Jim and once the news of the betrothal went round the hall like wildfire, she was proud to show her ring to well wishers.

At the end, walking away from the lights of the hall, heading slowly for the Braes, Maggie Ann told Jim about last Ne'er Day when she had come this way with her mother, and how they had talked about him. Her mother had liked him then.

"An' fit aboot you. Fan did ye like me, Maggie Ann?"

"Mony times, but the first wis fan ye bielded ma frae the rain on the Pitullie road last year."

By now they were well over the Braes towards Kinnaird and, drawing her into the lea of the wall there, he gathered her close and held her wrapped in his arms, his head buried in her neck. As they stood bonded in their closeness, arms round each other, Jim whispered as though speaking to himself,

"It's been sae lang a've wanted tae dae this; jist tae hae ye in ma airms an' tae ken ye wis mine. A can scarce gresp et." And framing her face between his two hands he gazed down at her then gently kissed her lips. As though she suddenly came alive, Maggie Ann responded to that kiss, drawing his head back to her and yielding to his kisses in a passionate embrace. They stayed like that for some time, the floodgates of weeks of restraint let loose, and then reluctantly turned to walk back to the glow of the kitchen and the family.

When Jim had departed for his lodgings and the girls' chatter had somewhat subsided, Maggie Ann slipped away to bed for some peace, and to ponder and relive the amazing events of the day. She slipped off her ring before washing and in the doing noticed the engraving inside the band below the stones, M.A.D. and J.S. How wonderful to see the names together and how thoughtful of Jim. Before going to sleep she slipped the ring back on and, curling her fingers round it, passed over into oblivion.

Chapter 11

The following weeks of the lull between fishings passed all too quickly. During these winter days Maggie Ann took Jim to Cairnbulg to visit Granny and Annie May and all her childhood friends. They roamed over the rocks of the Rack and past the school and the church to the sand dunes on the shore path to St. Combs. Maggie Ann described to him all the adventures they had had in their childhood rambles along the sands to Cairnbulg and promised to take him to the sand hole once the summer came in. As she relived with Jim these early times, Maggie Ann realized just how wonderful her childhood had been; poverty and hardship had been ever present but had never clouded their bond of love and sense of security in their mother and in the family. Jim watched the changing emotions in her face as Maggie Ann shared these memories and he realized once again that here was someone with a deeply sensitive nature, who felt deeply, would love deeply and commit deeply, and who had, for all her years, worked out what were the true values of life and responsibility. He felt humbled and very grateful that she was his. He knew that her promise, once given, was for ever and he also realized with some trepidation that her expectations of him would demand no less.

So they studied each other and learned about each other. Jim took Maggie Ann to meet his parents in Peterhead and it was a good visit. The welcome was warm hearted and simple with no air of artificiality; so much so that when Jim was off to the west coast fishing Maggie Ann felt free to return to Peterhead on her own, or sometimes with one of her sisters, and visit Jim's parents. A warm friendship formed.

She in turn presented Jim to all her old acquaintances and friends in Broadsea, enjoying watching how easily he fitted in and became engrossed in conversation with the older men. Sea was obviously in all their blood but Jim had a great capacity for listening and there is nothing better to a storyteller than a good listener. Maggie Ann was so proud of him as he joined in the romance and laughter of the tales of the olden days. There were so many things they had to discover about each other.

The next two years passed. During the summer they had frequent meetings beginning with the idyllic Shetland time in that land of strange light and long vistas; then the home fishing, followed by Lowestoft. But after New Year there were the months of the winter fishing at the west coast and then Maggie Ann and Jim had to rely on letters. Possibly their very separation enabled them to gain a deeper insight into the minds of each other. They wrote avidly, discussing all sorts of topics and at the same time revealing the dreams and longings each had for their life together. They were saving hard and by another year Jim would set up his own cooperage. This became Maggie Ann's focus in life and, with her mother's assistance, the Hope chest was gradually added to with linen and other household effects. Janet and she were now in the same position and the two sisters would often lie in bed talking about their men and what the future would be like for them both.

Maggie Ann could not remember when she first realized that all was not right with Jim. April had brought the end of the Isle of Mann fishing and the gutters and curers were home but Jim had not contacted her. It was three weeks since he had written. She also sensed a strange silence in the company of the usually boisterous Elsie, an absence of any reference to Jim and an avoidance of eye contact. Elsie was obviously hurting over some matter. Maggie Ann put the query to her and her quiet reply,

"A think ye need tae spik wi' Jim." confirmed for Maggie Ann that the problem lay there. So she wrote asking him to meet her.

Their rendezvous was at the gate of the South Church and as Maggie Ann watched Jim come slowly round the corner of the Station Brae her heart sank at the weary expression on his face. They greeted each other formally and turned to walk away over the Links where they could talk without interruption, away from prying eyes.

Once settled on the hillock overlooking the beautiful bay with the neat cut of the railway just below them, they sat without speaking until Maggie Ann laid her hand on his arm and whispered,

"Jim, fit's wrang? Fit his happened atween us?"

Jim heaved a deep, shuddering sigh and turned to look into her face, the tears brimming in his eyes.

"Maggie Ann, a hardly ken hoo tae stert. God kens lass foo much a dinna want tae hurt ye, bit a maun tell ye the truth. A hae bin a feel an' a ken 'at, bit fit it's daen tae ye is fit maks it sae ull tae thole. Ye're wirt better nor me."

Maggie Ann simply shook her head and said,

"Stert at the affgo Jim."

"Dae ye mind a telt ye aboot a mairrage we wir a' bidden tae in Isle o' Mann? Weel, the nicht afore wis the feet washen in the lad's hoose an' we a' went, an' there wis a lot tae drink there. We were a' gey drunk an', fan we set aff tae the huts at the curin' yairds, the qwines cam wi' us for company. Een efter annither drappit aff an' there wis jist me an' es quine ca'ed Kirsty left. A dinna mind a' that happened. The nicht air seemed tae mak mi mair glaikit; a near passed oot. Fan a cam tee in the mornin' a wis lyin' across the door o' the hut, ma clyes wir a' in a mess, an' ma heed stoonin'. A didna think ony mair aboot it, jist a bad nicht, an' a hid been wrang haen sae much drink. But twa wiks afore we cam hame Kirsty cam tae say she wis in the faimly wye an' a wis the faither."

The silence that followed was profound. Maggie Ann found breathing difficult so great was the leaden weight in her chest. Waves of cold swept over her; the words she had just heard could not really have been uttered; what was she to do? Then she found her voice and asked the question that had to be posed.

"An' cud ye be the faither?"

"Maggie Ann, a dinna ken. She says a'm tae blame, bit a hae nae memory o' fit happened 'at nicht."

It took Maggie Ann a long time to comprehend the immensity of what she had just listened to. Her confused mind rushed hither and thither trying to find an outlet to the situation but, as her head sank lower, as though avoiding a physical blow, she had to come to the only conclusion possible for her.

"Jim, oor mairrage cwid nivver last kennen there wis a faitherless bairn oot there. We maun think o' 'at first. I hae something tae tell ye 'at a nivver thocht a wid hae tae tell onybody, nae even you."

And she related the story of her own birth and illegitimacy. It was not so bad for Maggie Ann as the man her mother married was her real father, but the stigma remained and her birth certificate was still stamped with 'illegitimate' in large letters. Could they do worse to this child by not granting him his real father, if Jim really was that? They both knew the answer.

After a long time of silence, sitting in a turmoil of thoughts, Maggie Ann whispered,

"A wid like tae gang hame noo, an' ye hae a train tae catch."

So they walked together, sadly; apart, but each longing to hold the other close for comfort and to give comfort. Back over the Links; and when they paused at the top of the Station Brae, Maggie Ann gave Jim a brief nod and hurried off, desperate to get away, to sort out the turmoil of her thoughts, to reach the haven of home and her mother. Maggie Ann never saw Jim again.

The next weeks were hard. Being by nature a reserved person Maggie Ann could not reveal what had happened except to tell the family that there would be no marriage. To questions she merely shook her head but within, the endless personal debate went on. Had she been too hard on Jim? Should they have waited for things to sort out? Maybe it was all a trick on the girl's part. Why should she and Jim suffer on her behalf? Was it just her own pride that had been hurt? The endless confusion went on, seeking some vestige of hope for them both. But always arose this image of the child; and she knew that a trust had been broken and the relationship could never be the same.

But Maggie Ann did suffer. It took a long time for the frozen, lost emotions to melt and ease. Sometimes at night, lying beside Janet, she could no longer bear the raging of her weeping mind and at last rose and went to her mother in the kitchen bed. Glad to feel the warmth and the comfort of her mother's arm and clasp the rough, careworn hand, she eventually fell asleep. Mary May did not ask questions. She knew that in time Maggie Ann would tell her; but she did understand the sense of loss, the grieving that her daughter was experiencing; who better. Even after ten years the wound was still raw. So they shared a silent communion, walking the Braes at times, working together; waiting for life and time to bring back some relief from the pain.

Maggie Ann went more often to Cairnbulg where she felt a peace and freedom from people. Annie May was glad of her company for Granny was becoming frail and required more care. To be needed was a great solace and one day her Aunt quietly spoke to her,

"Keep yersel thrang Maggie Ann. Time dis haill, bit there 'ull aye be a wee sair bittie left e' the middle o' yer hairt."

She felt gratitude for this quiet understanding and stayed on with her aunt, this time taking up her abode in the little room at the top of the wooden, attic stairs. Every so often Maggie Ann went home for a few days but then returned to the peace of the village, and Mary May was glad for her to have found some reason for living again.

The Shetland fishing went on without her this year and by the time the North East fishing came round Maggie Ann was engaged in another ploy.

Chapter 12

As she pondered in the darkening on these events, Maggie Ann had to agree with Annie May's words. She had recovered from the grief but the little sore bit still remained. Maybe it always would. Now she was twenty-six and, looking back, Maggie Ann reflected on the words she had heard quoted so often, 'When He closes one door God always opens another.' And it had certainly seemed so at that point in her life.

During her sojourn in Cairnbulg Maggie Ann had renewed her friendship with Jane Cow and they talked again of their girlhood dream of high class cooking. Now grown up women of twenty-one, they were excited to discover their early ambitions were as strong as ever. So they began all over again to plan. Both had some money saved and were experienced in travelling away from home for work. What was to stop them? Should they advertise or watch the city newspapers for vacant positions?

In due course Jane replied to an advertisement in the Scotsman and three weeks later they found themselves gathering their luggage off the rack as the train crawled through Princess Street Gardens and came to a halt in Waverley Station. After their slow progress through the imposing station halls and the climb up the long slope they emerged into the sunshine on Waverley Bridge. The two girls paused a moment to find their bearings and then simultaneously crossed the road.

As they leaned on the broad, stone balustrade and allowed their eyes to take in the city scene, they were silent. So many times they had wearily watched the scene from the passing train, but now they were part of it. The noise of carts, the horse smells, shouts, people, the trees turning with the first touch of autumn; away below, the flower beds and lawns of the Gardens with the railway snaking away into the distance; and on this side of the next bridge two temple-like buildings; what were they? Following the line of that bridge their eyes rose to the dome of another beautiful building and then continued along to the rise of tall houses leading to the rugged castle towering on its huge rock. It was all breath taking, and it was all there to explore and learn. Maggie Ann felt a great rush of excitement pulse through her as she surveyed it all and for the first time in many months, spoke with a lilt in her voice and a new confidence,

"Jane, we did recht comin' here."

They smiled at each other, picked up their portmanteaus and with a light, jaunty step, set off to follow their employer's written instructions to Great King Street. The temptation to linger on Princes Street was strong but they resisted, crossed between the milling confusion of cart, wagon and carriage traffic and found their way up Hanover Street to the top of the rise where it crossed George Street. And there they had another moment of joy for, away on the horizon, beyond the slope of the gracious, mansion houses, they could see the sea washing the Fife shore. Their descent through Queen Street Gardens was a little slower for now they were on Dundas Street and they realised that the house was not far away. What awaited them was all unknown and courage failed a little as the two crossed the imposing avenues of Heriot Row and Northumberland Street. The carriages drawn up before the pillared porticos; the liveried footmen rushing up and down steps; the basements below ground, all lit up and occasionally allowing a glimpse of maids moving around. As she considered the three and four storied heights of the buildings Maggie Ann again thought of the endless stairs. This was a world they had never realised existed. Could they meet the challenge? Had they been too hasty in agreeing to come before making fuller enquiries? By the look on her face it was evident Jane was having the same thoughts.

Their arrival at Great King Street dispelled all these doubts for immediately, they found their house. The one on the corner diagonally opposite bore their number. It was imposing; four stories high with rows of tall windows; there were no pillars but the entrance was wide, on a landing at the top of a flight of six steps; two large tubs of pink geraniums flanked the doorway adding a touch of brightness to the black painted door and the whole was surrounded by an elegantly carved metal railing broken only by the gateway leading down the stairs to the basement area. Because it was on the corner the tall windows faced both south and east and the front of the house was bathed in the late afternoon sun, giving it a mellow, warm, welcoming look. Even as they paused, their minds crowded with these first impressions, a carriage turned the corner and came to a halt in front of the house. The young coachman jumped down and quickly opened the door to fold out a step. The carriage swayed a little and then he handed out a well rounded, little lady dressed in a ruby outfit. He accompanied her up the steps and pulled the gleaming, brass bell by the door. Then he ran down to his horse and drove off into Dundas Street. Almost immediately the door opened and the lady disappeared inside.

There was no more time to linger. Watching their chance between the busy vehicles, they crossed over and hesitated, wondering whether to climb the steps or descend to the area. The black door was flung open and a bright faced maid smiled and called,

"Come this way please. You are the girls from the north? Mrs. Stuart saw you across the way and thought it was you. I've been watching for you."

Leaving their bags in the hallway, Jane and Maggie Ann were ushered into a smallish, square room, book lined, apart from the two tall windows. The westering sun rested on the wood panelling of the shelves and the high mantelpiece, bringing out the sheen of years of polishing, and the rose coloured drapes and chair coverings glowed in the warm light. A fire crackled in the hearth and the whole atmosphere was one of comfort and welcome. They sat together, silent, waiting, trying to control their feelings of apprehension.

At last the door opened and the maid entered bearing a wide tray laden with afternoon tea which she set on a table already prepared. At her back came Mrs. Stuart, the lady from the carriage, still in her ruby red dress, but without hat and gloves. The girls rose immediately and as they gazed at this, their new employer, they became more and more sure of the rightness of their decision. They saw a kind, interested face, not beautiful, but the candid, grey eyes and firm chin coupled with the warmth of her smile projected an integrity and sense of humour which was most attractive. Holding out her hand she said,

"Well now, here you are. You've had a long journey and must be hungry. But first of all your names. Which is Jane and which Margaret?"

As the girls identified themselves their hands were enfolded in a warm handshake and then turning, Mrs. Stuart said,

"And here is Ella who has been with us quite a few years. She is getting married shortly so is leaving soon. Ella will show you round the house and tell you all you need to know about our little ways here. But meantime I think a cup of tea and food are going to be welcome."

With a nod to the girls and a smile for the mistress, Ella left and the three settled down to the welcome tea and hot scones, which had been keeping warm under the chafing dish.

Putting the girls at ease as they ate, Mrs. Stuart chatted about her family. Her husband had been in the diplomatic service spending many years abroad, the family with him, but when he retired, being Scots, they settled in Edinburgh. The three children had finished their education at the university there and now were married and in their own homes. One son had stayed in Edinburgh and often visited with the three grandchildren. At that Mrs. Stuart, with a proud smile, pointed to a photo on the mantelpiece. Maggie Ann felt a little thrill that there were to be children about the place for she was going to miss her sisters terribly.

Mrs. Stuart went on,

"Four years ago my husband died suddenly so now I am on my own in this huge house. But I am a busy person with lots of interesting things to take me out and I entertain quite a bit and give dinner parties. But you will learn all about that in due course. What I want to know is why you have come all this way to go into service. Could you not have chosen Aberdeen?"

"We have both had a little experience of domestic service but our real wish is to become good cooks, to really study cookery in a high class way and we thought we could do that better in Edinburgh. We have wanted to do this since we were young and to do it together, and when the Scotsman advert appeared it just seemed right for us, so we replied."

Maggie Ann spoke for both while Jane nodded in agreement.

"I find that very interesting and I'm sure you have made the right choice. There are opportunities in Edinburgh for such ambitions. We shall have to search out some information sources. Now how do you come to be such close friends? Tell me about yourselves and your families and what sort of work have you done since leaving school. You start Jane."

Relaxed now, the two girls told their stories; home, families, working in the herring yards, travelling to fishings, domestic service, their interest in reading and travel and, in Maggie Ann's case, her desire to supplement her curtailed education. Once started, they spoke freely and frankly, responding to the sympathy and obvious interest of the listener. For her part, the more she heard, Mrs. Stuart realized that here were not two raw recruits to the domestic realms, but young women with a deep experience of life and hardship, particularly Margaret; such struggles she herself had never known. She listened, only prompting with an occasional question, gradually building up a picture of what sort of material had come into her hands. Here were two young people, hungry for knowledge, with the will to go out and search for it, who needed support and guidance in a way that even her own children had not required. And now in the wonderful scheme of things they had arrived under her roof. She faced the challenge. A light of enthusiasm shone from her eyes as she smiled,

"You have both been blessed with wonderful homes. I can see that from the way you speak of them. Now it is your turn to make something of yourselves and fulfil your ambitions so I have a suggestion. I shall enquire about what domestic and cookery classes are available and put you in touch with other areas for widening your education if you are willing to fit it all in with your duties here. It may mean rising earlier or working later. Your work here must not suffer, but if you are determined, you will make the sacrifice and I am very keen to help you. I have never had servants who voiced such desires. I think we must be in this together."

The following silence was profound. Then the girls looked at each other and laughed aloud. This was the first time that someone had ever volunteered them real assistance and they did not know quite how to handle it. Turning to Mrs. Stuart, the tears in their eyes, they whispered a profound,

"Thank you."

The mistress realized what Jane and Maggie Ann were feeling so she changed the subject and asked,

"Now tell me. How do you two come to use such good English? Coming from the far northeast I expected you to speak only the local Doric, but you don't. How does that come about?"

Maggie Ann replied,

"O we do speak the Doric when we are on our own, but we learned English at school and had to use it there.

Also when we went north and south to the fishings we met other dialects and the best way to understand each other was to speak English. We wouldn't speak English at home because they would think we were putting on airs. But we read a lot from the bookshop library and any magazines we could find."

"Excellent. I'm very glad you are fluent for I have a policy in this home that all speak correct English. Miss Macleod, our cook-housekeeper, whom you will meet soon, is from the Isle of Lewis and a native Gaelic speaker, but she has fluent English. Mr. Laing, our butler, is from Dumfriesshire and uses perfect English and all the people who frequent this home in whatever capacity, I insist upon using this common language. It is a medium of shared understanding and culture, and the gateway to higher learning."

The girls had a distinct impression that Mrs. Stuart had firm views on certain subjects.

"Jane, would you pull that bell by the side of the fireplace? Miss Macleod will be your immediate superior and you will answer to her in all things relating to household affairs. She and Mr. Laing run the house between them and frequently consult with me but I trust them implicitly and we work well together. We are a team here. We all need each other and I like to think we are all loyal to each other."

Following a light tap the door opened.

"Here is Miss Macleod."

A tall angular lady filled the doorway. Dressed in a full skirted, deep blue dress with neat white collar and cuffs, the housekeeper paused, waiting for Mrs. Stuart to speak. The girls gazed at the presence, for that is what it was. Maggie Ann and Jane recognized the quiet dignity of the person and were drawn to it even before they were introduced.

Chrissie Macleod had come a long way since her childhood years on the croft at Bernera away on the western shore of Lewis. The middle child in a family of nine, she had had her fair share of toil; potatoes, peat, fish farm and house chores, made all the more arduous because her mother was ill with TB and fading. The struggle that mere existence presented seemed ever present; the harshness of the climate and the merciless Atlantic storms; the rigid, repressive regime of the church; the battle to attend school, which at times seemed their only relief from the drudgery. Yes, her early years had not been kind to Chrissie but, when gradually the older ones had flown the nest and her turn came, she had gladly moved away eastwards, first to Inverness, then to Perth, and finally to Edinburgh, always gaining more experience and responsibility, until she came to Great King Street and Mrs. Stuart.

The wide angular shoulders, the large hands with broad, spatulated fingers folded at her waist band, the pronounced jaw line dominating the large flattish face; all these detracted from any claims to beauty. But the wonder of the face was the eyes. They shone a deep blue, enhanced by the shade of the dress and there was a sparkle and energy shining there that lit up the whole image.

"Yes madam, you called."

The girls picked up the soft sibilant lilt of the words, which sounded so beautiful to their ears.

"Yes Miss Macleod. I would like you to meet your new helpers, Jane and Margaret. They are keen to work hard and to learn lots of new things. They will be in your care and I think you will get along well together. You have a lot in common. Now if you show Jane and Margaret downstairs, Ella can take the girls to their rooms and guide them over the house. Be sure and introduce them to Mr. Laing. Tomorrow you can see to uniforms and work schedules."

Turning again to Jane and Maggie Ann she repeated, "Remember, we are a team here. We all need each other."

So they followed the housekeeper out into a wider hall lit up by tall, stained glass window and dominated by a wide sweeping staircase rising to the upper floors. Not lingering, Miss Macleod led them to a swing door in the back wall opening on to a stair descending to the basement. This ushered them into another world. A long passage faced them, dimly lit by the borrowed light from the glass panelled doors, and at the far end an open, outside door permitted a flood of daylight to stream in providing a terminus to the long tunnel; or so it seemed to Maggie Ann and Jane.

Half way along Miss Macleod opened a door on the right and they were ushered into the kitchen; such a room as they never could have imagined. Three tall windows draped with fine, white screening flooded the room with light. Between two windows was a cooking stove with an immense, flat, surface area. Double sinks were at one end and all round on the walls were wooden and glass fronted cupboards. Down the centre of the room stood a well scrubbed, wooden table, which could easily have accommodated twenty people, and one end was laid with a tea cloth and china for afternoon tea. Mr. Andrew Laing, the butler, was seated there and the girls were duly introduced to this solemn gentleman before Ella whisked them away, back upstairs and further on up the main staircase. This was to be their haven for the next few years. Two identical rooms; wardrobe, bed, dressing table, wash stand, table and chair and a small rocking chair; all simple furniture but with the bright curtains and matching spread and the carpet before the bed, it looked welcoming and cosy. In the corner was a small, tiled fireplace but the round chimney vent had been closed up. The wrought iron radiator on the wall by the doorway gave off a comfortable warmth. No more coal to carry up so high. The greatest delight of the room was the dormer window with its deep sill and, over the housetops, the wide distant view of the sea stretching away and away northwards. They were sure they would walk there some day.

Maggie Ann felt a little overwhelmed that this was *her* room, her very own, her place, where she could do whatever she liked; place things, read, think, sleep, and not have to share. Such luxury she had never contemplated before-hand. Her haven had always been the Braes, but now, a new era had dawned for her and her heart gave a little lift of excitement as she gazed around.

Having deposited their bags the girls followed Ella on their tour of the house. The rest of the attic floor contained Ella's room and box and storage space. The two floors below comprised mainly bedrooms for the family and visitors, but here they were shown the narrow staircase to the base-ment, which they were to use instead of the main staircase. Miss Macleod's room was also here close to the basement stairs. Continuing down they reached what was probably the most beautiful part of the house. A wide gallery ran round three sides of the stairwell and one could look up into the gracious curve of the oak banisters rising above, and down into the polished , flag stoned hall all lit up from the stained glass window. The brasses on the hallstands shone, and the glowing reds of the scattered carpets threw up their own light with the richness of the carved oak chairs placed here and there along the walls. From the gallery itself various doors opened off; the master bedroom, unused now, with its adjoining bathroom; Mrs. Stuart's room in the corner facing the street and the sun; and along from that the light shone through a set of sliding, stained glass panelled doors which, when pushed back, revealed the drawing room. Ella smiled at the silence.

"You can go in. You will be cleaning in here like everywhere else. Miss Macleod dusts all the fine china and ornaments herself but we do all the polishing and general cleaning in this room so you must not be too terrified."

The girls smiled at that, glad that Ella understood their awe. But it *was* the most beautiful room they had ever seen. The three long windows were draped in rich, soft green velvet looped back with gold tasselled cords. This toned in with the quieter grey- green carpet spread on the polished wood floor while the sofas and chairs scattered around the room and in front of the high, white marble fireplace picked up the richness with their green and gold brocade. The occasional tables of beaten brass and the elephant's foot holding the fire irons and sundry other tokens from the far east marked the family's association with the years of travel. Many gold-framed paintings hung on the walls but by far the most impressive was that of Mr. Hector Stuart which took pride of place above the fireplace. He looked very distinguished in his imposing, diplomatic finery, but it was the face that held Maggie Ann's attention. The kindly, intelligent, slightly tired looking eyes gazed down and the generous mouth with the vestige of a smile on one side made one want to smile back. Not a handsome face, but strong and purposeful.

"A fine ambassador for his country." Thought Maggie Ann.

"Mrs. Stuart and he would have been a fine couple."

Maggie Ann visualized them in this splendid room, standing together under the chandeliers greeting their guests.

Just off the corner on the opposite side of the gallery was another glass-panelled door leading to a conservatory built out over an extension at the back of the house. Here Mrs. Stuart pursued her interest in plants- particularly ferns and geraniums but, judging by the display of colour, she had ventured into other areas of flower culture and the perfume was wonderful.

Moving on downstairs they visited the dining room, morning room and office, with another bathroom in between, and then arrived back in Mrs. Stuart's own sitting room where they had been welcomed that afternoon- one of the cosiest rooms in the whole house.

Finally they descended to the basement where another world awaited them. Here was a whole self-contained apartment with its own front and back doors and its own hall way with rooms opening off. On one wall of the long corridor doors led to rooms facing the street while the other wall housed storage cupboards for all sorts of household requirements. Mr. Laing had one of the bedrooms, Arthur Douglas, the coach handyman, another, and Miss Macleod had a small private sitting room/office there. Adjoining the kitchen at the rear end of the house was a scullery and a laundry complete with tubs, pulleys and irons and close by was the staff bathroom, just inside the back door. This entrance led out into a small garden, mainly for vegetables, and at the end of the path a gate in the high wall opened into a very wide, cobbled area, shared with the neighbouring houses where coaches and horses were accommodated in a long series of sheds and stables. The entry to this was reached from a lane opening off Cumberland Street.

Their tour finished, they returned to the kitchen and to Miss Macleod who, now enveloped in a capacious white overall, was standing over the stove stirring something. She turned smiling to greet them, her broad face rosy from the heat, and cheerily beckoned to a pile of garments on the table.

"I've looked out some dresses and aprons for you. Take them to your rooms and try them for fit. You will need two dresses and four aprons and caps for each of you. Come down after you have unpacked and dinner for us all will be at six thirty. The family dines at eight. There will be two guests tonight so we are a little busy here just now."

On their own at last, Maggie Ann and Jane climbed the stairs and were glad to close the door of Jane's room behind them, just to find a moment to draw breath and digest all that was happening to them.

"Div ye think we'll manage it?" whispered Jane, a tremble in her voice.

"Aye, we hiv tae manage. We're here noo an' they're gweed foulk. A wid say we wir fortnet. It cud hae bin gey different for us, comin' here ootlins. Noo lat's try on the goons."

Maggie Ann's chin was set firm as she spoke a little brusquely, covering up her own feeling of being overwhelmed. They set to and found the blue dresses fitted perfectly and, complete with apron and cap, they surveyed each other, smiling and liking what they saw.

Once unpacked- their heavy luggage would arrive by station carrier on Monday- Maggie Ann sat down in the rocking chair for a little, her hands idle in her lap, just going over all she had seen and done since getting on the train that morning in Fraserburgh. She felt a great sense of gratitude that they had come to this house. Mrs. Stuart especially had struck a chord in heart. Maggie Ann said a quiet prayer of thanks for God's leading and there and then committed herself to proving worthy of the service He had laid on her. After the struggle of the past months she was beginning to see some purpose and direction in her life again. She felt at peace.

Back in the kitchen the scene had changed again. Gas lamps shed a warm glow over the room and wooden shutters had been folded across the windows shutting out prying eyes. To and fro activity from stove to table, to ovens, to sink, was going non- stop. Suddenly a bell rang overhead. On the lengthy row on the wall one was swinging on its spring.

"That's the mistress. Come with me Jane and we'll see what she needs."

So Jane was ushered into the intricacies of lady's maid, an occupation she was to follow for the rest of her time in Edinburgh. Maggie Ann, on the other hand, became Miss Macleod's shadow, keen to absorb all she could about cooking, and managing a great house like this.

But on this their first evening, Maggie Ann and Jane were just happy to be part of the family atmosphere round the table, all six of them. As they ate and listened the girls formed their first impressions of their companions. Mr. Laing, slightly dogmatic, had certain strong views on city affairs, especially the new public trolley transport. Arthur was a comedian, full of chat about the other horse handlers and what went on in the yard behind the house. Upon this Ella intervened and Mr. Laing frowned.

"Not at the table Arthur."

This from Miss Macleod who presided at the top. In her soft but firm flow of conversation one could recognise that she was in charge, ruling with firm control and dignity. She seemed like a ship on even keel and Maggie Ann appreciated that. It reminded her of the same quality in her mother, Mary May, and already there was a feeling of bonding with this lady. The talk flowed on. At one point the girls were asked about the new Forth Railway Bridge, which they had crossed for the first time. And then it was time to tidy up and prepare to serve the dinner upstairs.

Arthur departed to replenish the fires in the various rooms, Ethel to give a final check on the dinner table, Mr. Laing to see that the wine was at the correct temperature after decanting, and to hover, white gloves donned, to answer the front door bell, and Miss Macleod began to arrange the warming plates, ready to load the dumb waiter when the correct moment arrived. It seemed like a military operation and Maggie Ann and Jane would have liked to linger in the kitchen to watch it all happening, but they were assigned to the scullery to deal with the washing up after their own meal. Here they stayed, continuing to wash dishes as they were brought down from upstairs, until the last coffee cup was dried. Later, Arthur joined them in the scullery and he cleaned the larger cooking pans, adding a bit of laughter to the labour.

By nine thirty it was all over, the breakfast set for morning and Mrs. Stuart's tray laid ready. Six stone pigs were filled and gradually, one after the other, the workers departed carrying their hot water bottles. Mr. Laing sat down by the fire with his pipe to await the summons of the departing guests and Miss Macleod sat in the rocker keeping him company as together they shared a sherry nightcap. They seemed to enjoy a close relationship and understanding.

Very weary, the girls climbed upwards and with a quiet,

"Gweed nicht," they parted at their doorways, too tired even to chat.

"Once undressed and with the alarm set for morning, Maggie Ann stood a moment by the window looking away across the darkness to the Fife coast and the sea. Scattered lights twinkled and she knew that away, away northward beyond was that little group of loved ones so dear to her heart. She could see them all, knew exactly what they would be doing at this moment, preparing for Sunday, bathing, readying for bed, and likely Betsy and Bella would be arguing. Maggie Ann smiled, but how she missed them all. As she lay down the longing was like a heavy ache under her ribs, but soon oblivion overruled and she slept.

Chapter 13

During the following days and weeks the girls learned the parameters of their tasks and there were many surprises for them. As their expertise progressed each found her niche and began to really feel part of the family. They did indeed work as a team, each with a role to play, working carefully and diligently for the good of not only Mrs. Stuart, but for the whole household. There was no duplication of work, no unnecessary cleaning or drudgery, things flowed calmly and without harassment. There was an orderliness about the system. When the girls went to clean the fireplaces in the mornings, Arthur had been there before them, removing the cold ashes and replenishing the logs and coal scuttles; when they went to polish the brass work at the front door he had already swept the landing and the flight of steps to the pavement.

Maggie Ann and Jane often wondered when Arthur's day began for another of his tasks was to keep the furnace running, controlling the gauges and refuelling periodically throughout the day. The two horses in the stable had to be fed and groomed and the carriage kept shining. Certainly, on the afternoons when Mrs. Stuart did not require his services as coachman, he would disappear for an hour or two, but he was always back for the meal at six. Since neither of the girls had grown up with a brother they loved his laughter and his teasing, and possibly that more than anything else, helped them to settle in to the discipline of service.

Miss Macleod ran a firm and very regulated regime. It was the only way to manage the welfare of the household, care for the large building and satisfy her mistress who was a generous person but who maintained high standards and expected her staff to do likewise. So, over the years, Miss Macleod had developed a system of planning work; seasonal, monthly, weekly, daily tasks; with the result that things ran like clockwork. There was never the annual up-heaval of "spring cleaning" to disrupt the peace. Everyone was involved in the care of the house and contents; there was a loving protectiveness in the handling of the articles be it china, carpets, books or upholstery, and each had his or her specific role to play. On the wall behind the kitch-en door was a chart enumerating the various tasks and Maggie Ann and Jane were allocated their areas of work daily, weekly and monthly, sometimes working together and sometimes separately. This inspired a sense of responsibil-ity and a challenge to maintain a high standard. Maggie Ann thoroughly approved of this system of planning. It was something that was attuned to her temperament and to her own early training of not wasting anything- food, money, skills, time. Mary May's example had borne fruit and the discipline of the fishing industry enabled them to appreciate the value of the scheme. Maggie Ann noted that the Christmas puddings, the cakes, the mincemeat and the chutneys scheduled for October were already ticked off- completed, and no doubt stored away. She was sorry she had missed that.

Nellie Scott always arrived early on Monday mornings and took up her abode in the laundry where she could be heard singing at the top of her voice as she swung her tubs about and worked the mangle. A jolly, cheery person with a strong, lilting Border accent, Nellie was a widow having lost her husband in the Crimean War. Now, with her five children all grown up and married, here she was in her fifties, able to go out to work and enjoy for herself the fruits of her labour. Nellie was good. The way she achieved that fine, glazed, calendared finish on table linen was truly remarkable and her gentle touch on the mistress' fine, lawn underwear, lace edged and beribboned, was pure art. Her presence brought warmth and fun to the rather serious little group round the dinner table and even Mr. Laing would smile when she told some of her Border stories, or swing his foot in time when she broke out into one of the ballads; and she could sing; knew them all by heart, word perfect.

Sometimes, if there was an unusually large dinner party Nellie would come in and provide an extra pair of hands in the scullery, leaving the two maids to assist in serving. When the work was finished and Nellie set off for the Cannon Mills where she had her two-roomed flat, Maggie Ann and Jane offered to accompany her, as it was dark and so late. But Nellie gave them a big hug, laughing heartily,

"Wheest ye lassies. Whae's gaun tae gang efter an auld yin lik me? A'll jist gie thim a sang an' they'll a' rin awa. Dinna ye worry. A'll gang the straicht wye doon i' the lichts. A'll be a' richt."

And so she was. During all those years in Great King Street Maggie Ann never remembered Nellie missing the Monday and Tuesday laundry. When the girls asked her why she was always so cheery and happy she looked surprised and answered,

"Whit wye wad a no be happy? A've ma werk, ma hoose, guid freens lik yersels, a kin sing, ma waens 're weel an' happy. Whit mair cwid a need? A'm niver alane for a hae Jesus in ma hairt an' the Gweed Maister up there tae guide mi."

Chapter 14

The house fascinated Maggie Ann. She never quite lost her sense of privilege in living there and being part of it and its household. She loved her own little domain and the privacy and seclusion it provided- her special place- away at the top. But there was also so much about the house that intrigued her; its layout and history; the position in the New Town; the comparisons with the other Regency houses in the various streets. She asked so many questions that eventually Mrs. Stuart called her into the library and handed her a book outlining the plans and development of the New Town. Many famous names were mentioned in connection with the various locations and Maggie Ann developed a thirst for the history of Edinburgh and then for the wider Scottish scene. So much of Scotland's story emanated from Edinburgh and as she delved, Maggie Ann realized an awareness that she was not just a 'Bredsea Quine', but also a Scot, with a growing sense of pride in her country and its achievements on the world scene.

Because the house stood on a corner, the entrance area to the basement reaching round the two walls was more extensive than usual. In the early morning it was flooded with sunlight, greatly enhanced by the white washed walls below the street and stair railings. This, coupled with the tubs of red geraniums scattered on the well-scrubbed flagstones, made the whole area bright and welcoming. It reminded

Maggie Ann of the close in Broadsea where her mother prepared her fish and, as she scrubbed the steps, or polished
the windows, swept, or just sat on the low bench beside the
door, quite oblivious to the hustle and noise of people and
traffic passing above, she could almost smell the smoked
fish and hear the voices she had grown up with. Often in
the early days, as she worked in the area, that great choking of homesickness came over her, but it grew easier, and
the work in this particular spot became Maggie Ann's own
responsibility. Sometimes, when she had a moment, she
would slip out and linger, just taking pleasure in looking
at the bright, neat and tidy scene.

Opposite the main basement doorway two entrances
gave access to two large stores built in under the street
itself. These cellars were brick lined and spacious. The
one on the left housed ladders, shovels, a few pieces of
wooden tubs and other discarded articles, while a chute to
a metal-covered opening on the pavement above connected
the right hand cellar. Here, without great effort, the coal
man delivered the coal and then Arthur would sweep up
the dust and replace the heavy lid. Maggie Ann thought
this was the peak of efficiency, especially since the door
to the furnace cellar was situated on the opposite wall, so
handy to the fuel.

Maggie Ann continued to make discoveries. At the back
of the house six rows of windows puzzled her until she
worked out that since the house was built on a slope there
must be another lower basement. Here the staff had been
housed until the Stuarts came in the seventies when they
had modernised with central heating and the new gas lighting. The servants' quarters had been relocated at the top
of the house and a new staff stairway installed to connect
with the basement. The lower basement was now the wine

cellar and store, but Maggie Ann was so thankful she had her own high room which caught the first sun rays and the late afternoon sunsets, instead of living submerged between high walls where the sun never penetrated. But some houses still maintained the old system.

One such was the house further down the hill on the corner of Dundas and Cumberland Streets. It was a single, ground floor house complete with basement and sub-basement, and here lived John Wyllie with his wife Kirsten and grown up daughter Sarah. As had happened with so many similar owners in Dundas Street, the basement had been developed as a business concern and John Wyllie operated a very successful wine and spirit shop under his home. He was also well acclaimed as a tea blender and clients came from all across Edinburgh to purchase this expensive commodity.

Ella had first introduced the girls to the Wyllies when they shopped for Mrs. Stuart's special tea. Mrs.Wyllie, who had been hovering at the back of the shop, came forward whenever she heard Maggie Ann speak.

"Noo, yon's a real north tongue. Far are ye frae ma lass?"

Maggie Ann's surprise overcame her shyness as she answered,

"Fraserburgh." Mrs. Wyllie gave a delighted laugh.

"I kent it."

She went on to tell Maggie Ann that she herself had come from Macduff many years ago and had never lost her ear for the dialect though she seldom spoke it, her husband being from Edinburgh

From that meeting a warm friendship developed and sometimes, if there was time, Maggie Ann was invited to climb the stairs into the imposing flat for a cup of tea and an opportunity to chat in their own tongue- a rare treat for Mrs. Wyllie.

Here was another gracious home, perhaps less ornate than Great King Street, but with the same lofty ceilings, tall windows and flag stoned hallway. The hall was lit from the stained glass window overlooking Cumberland Street, and the stairs from the shop came up into the hall by the dining room doorway. As she passed the half open doors Maggie Ann caught only a glimpse of the comfort and elegance of the rooms. Entertaining was always in the drawing room, a room dominated by the beautiful, marble fireplace with the wide guilt edged mirror above. The reflection seemed to enlarge the space. A huge fire always blazed in the deep hearth. Although she came from the north, Kirsten Wyllie suffered greatly from the cold, northeast wind that blew across Edinburgh, right into the front door, chilling the house whenever the door was opened. So she insisted on her fire and her place of comfort, and spent most of her time there working on her tapestry or knitting, talking with her friends and enjoying a rather pleasantly comfortable life. Maggie Ann was included in the homely atmosphere and she always knew there was a welcome. Although they pursued a life style of elegance with a certain amount of grandeur, as befitted a successful man of business, the Wyllies maintained a simple, honest approach to people. There was none of the snobbery that often tainted the 'nouveau riche' in the New Town and all who frequented the shop responded to the friendliness and willingness to help and advise.

The staff consisted of two middle-aged ladies who lived in the sub-basement. One served in the shop and the other helped Mrs. Wyllie in the home upstairs. It was a very happy household and Maggie Ann appreciated being counted one of their friends.

During the remaining few weeks before her marriage Ella took care to acquaint Maggie Ann and Jane with all their regular shopping areas. Rose Street and Thistle Street were the main locations and certain stalls at the Grassmarket or Cannonmills market. Miss Macleod was very particular about quality and insisted on the correct supplier. When the fishwife from Newhaven called and unpacked her creel Maggie Ann thought about her mother. One day she told Miss Macleod that that was how her mother earned her livelihood for her family, which set them to sharing memories of childhood and fishing. Maggie Ann began to realize that this lady had experienced a childhood similar to her own, in fact maybe harder. It only increased her admiration for the housekeeper and spurred on her own ambition to succeed.

By Christmas the girls had adapted to the new way of life. It was hard and the hours were long, the discipline was strict and the expected standards were high. But Maggie Ann and Jane did not regard it as a hardship; rather, they felt they had found themselves in a privileged position. The work was full of variety, the mistress could not have been more kind and encouraging and all the staff worked hard.

Chapter 15

Sitting here in the almost dark evening quiet of the Braes Maggie Ann now felt a great wave of nostalgia sweep over her. They had been such a wonderful five years. How she had loved the city. Saturday afternoon was their free time and they explored, sometimes together and occasionally alone. Mrs.Stuart presented them regularly with a list of famous and historical places accompanied by some short background information and every now and then she checked up that they had fulfilled the visit. Maggie Ann and Jane appreciated her interest and were glad to expand their knowledge. But they also discovered their own favourite haunts and walks. On a good day they set off immediately after lunch, crossed over Princes Street, down into the gardens and round the base of the castle rock into the Grassmarket where they caught the last hour of the stalls. Then they wandered through the streets of the old town and eventually reached the Mound and down past the art galleries to cross over into Hanover Street and home. The old town fascinated them.

On other good days, and if they thought they could afford it, they caught the horse drawn tram in Princes Street and travelled all the way down to Leith where they wandered along the shore and smelled again the tang of the fishing boats tied up at the pier for the weekend. It was at such times that Maggie Ann and Jane realized how much they missed their direct contact with the sea and all it meant to them. Newhaven was further along the shore but they seldom had long enough time to go there to watch the fish workers and smell the kippering kilns. Sometimes they took the long walk home by the Water of Leith until they had to branch off and cut through by Cannonmills to Dundas Street. It did not take them long to learn the geography of the city and, provided they were together and walked briskly, they never had any fear of being molested.

Occasionally they donned their Sunday best and treated themselves to afternoon tea at Mackie's on Princes Street. They felt quite daring the first time, fearing they had been rash in crossing the social line, but they came to realize that afternoon tea in a restaurant was different to that in a drawing room. Here social distinctions were not so finely drawn and they could sit by the window at ease, nibbling the famous shortbread and watching Edinburgh's world go by. Princes Street was an amazing place. The first of the New Town boulevards to be built, in its magnificent setting, it had been the pride of Edinburgh's Council, but once commerce caught hold and business enterprises added shop premises to the elegant facades of the houses, then the whole atmosphere of the street changed. But with all that, there was still the beauty of the monuments, the art galleries, the sweep of the Mound and the wonderful skyline of the Bank of Scotland, the Assembly Halls and the Old Town, culminating in the ancient Castle on its rock high above the Gardens. Now that they knew what all these places were, the girls, more and more, appreciated their life here and, sitting in the tearoom window, observing, they felt very much a part of it all.

Another precious memory was the Sunday afternoon visits of the children. After attending church the family usually returned with Mrs. Stuart and stayed for a late lunch, often extending the visit into teatime. In her wisdom Mrs. Stuart insisted that Sunday meals should be simple, easy to serve and suitable for children as well as adults. Miss Macleod had her afternoon off on Sunday when she attended the Gaelic service at the Free Church and then went home with friends for tea. So it was left to the rest of the staff to deal with the meals. These were generally prepared on Saturday and kept in the cool larder in readiness. Often soup, shepherd's pie, a hotpot or, in summer, a salad with cold meat or chicken – easy to heat and serve, was on the menu. There was never any fuss on Sunday and the staff appreciated the consideration of their mistress.

Often after lunch the elders would settle for a nap and the three children, John, Kenneth and Emily were permitted to go to the top floor to play hide and go seek under the supervision of Jane or Maggie Ann. Their own nanny had her day off on Sunday so Jane and Maggie Ann had the children to themselves, and they revelled in it. If the weather was good they were given the key to the gardens in Queen Street and set out with the children to walk there, returning in time for afternoon tea. Sometimes, on a wet, winter Sunday, with Mrs. Stuart's permission, they descended to the kitchen, donned aprons and with much laughter and scattering of flour they created scones or biscuits, which were proudly presented for tea. Mr. Laing never complained about the noise and the mess. He just quietly retired to his room, trusting the girls to be in control. Arthur frequently joined them too. When the laden tray was carried in for tea, the children, all clean and tidy again, joined the elders and sat waiting for the words of approval and praise, which they knew would come from Granny. If she had not remarked by the third mouthful, Emily would burst out,

"Don't you like our scones Granny?"

"They are the best yet. Did you make those? They are so good I thought Margaret had made them."

Then they all beamed at each other, content.

Many times the grownups must have been grateful for the presence of Jane and Maggie Ann, for it made these Sunday visits a pleasure instead of a duty and relieved the burden of three bored children. It was during these times that Maggie Ann first realized that she was being called Maggie. It was little Emily who began it one day walking in the gardens when she slipped her hand into Maggie Ann's and looked up smiling,

"My Maggie." And that was it. She was Margaret in the parlour but Maggie with the children, and she rather liked it.

As the months went by and they gradually made the acquaintance of the servants in neighbouring houses, Jane and Maggie Ann came to realize that they themselves worked in a very privileged situation. They experienced none of the drudgery, unreasonable discipline and lack of human respect that were practised in some homes. Not that they gossiped, but little remarks here and there made them aware of what went on and they just felt all the more loyal and dedicated to the household of Mrs. Stuart and the wise authority of Miss Macleod and Mr. Laing.

Chapter 16

The Christmas festive time was beyond anything they had ever dreamed of. Maggie Ann and Jane had seen pictures in books of how the rich celebrated, but here they were, living in the midst of it. They felt quite overwhelmed, first by the wonder of it all, and secondly by the work it entailed. Even though Nellie Scott came in for the whole week to help in the kitchen, everyone was working at fever pitch; long hours and hard. Mr. Laing and Arthur hung festoons of holly in the hall and on the stairs, then the huge tree was placed in the hall just inside the front door and when the children arrived on Sunday, they helped to decorate it amid great laughter and a few little accidents.

A special moment was the setting out of the Crib on one of the hall tables. As Maggie Ann lifted each figure out of the box and dusted gently with a soft cloth the children told her,

"Granny and Grandpa brought them from Switzerland from a place called Brienz. They saw them being carved. Every time they went back to Switzerland they brought home some more so now there are lots of animals and people. Look, there's the stable to start with and then the baby in the crib goes next, and then Mary and Joseph and the donkey------."

Even now Maggie Ann could still hear the children's voices as they told the Christmas story while so carefully placing the figures. The meaning of it all came home to her in such a real way and, day-by-day, as she handled the beautiful wood while dusting, she pondered about the miracle and the immensity of what God had done for mankind in the sending of the Christ Child. Tears came into her eyes as she thought about these three young ones. What joy they had brought to her life in Edinburgh, and how hard it had been to part from them.

It seemed to Maggie Ann that the major part of Christmas was involved with food- planning, cooking and serving. Her long ago experience over New Year at Mrs. Thompson's in Fraserburgh paled into insignificance in comparison to Christmas week in Great King Street. Mrs. Stuart loved entertaining and giving hospitality was one of her pleasures in life so always on Christmas Eve she held a dinner party for ten of her associates in the various charities she supported. This was followed on Christmas Day by a full-scale dinner for the family, including relatives who were on their own, about twenty in all.

Then on Boxing Day eight children from a city orphanage arrived for afternoon tea. To make them feel more at home they were served in Mrs. Stuart's own sitting room where a table was laid with the goodies that children would enjoy, and they came and went with their plates. She really enjoyed children, was good with them and knew how to chat at their level, so the visit went off well. After the meal they donned their coats again and Arthur lead them downstairs where they explored the kitchens and other areas then out into the garden and yard to the stables. Jenny, the mare was a little excited with the children milling around her, but Arthur soon had them piled into the carriage, four facing four, supervised by Jane on one side and Maggie Ann on the other. The day was fine enough so they had the open carriage and soon the faces were rosy as they jogged through the New Town to Leith Walk then up the hill to Princes Street. The drive took them all the way down past the gardens to the west end where they turned into Charlotte Square and home to the mews. The children had lived an hour of pure joy and their faces registered that as they went in to say, "Thank you." When they left Mrs. Stuart handed each one a little parcel done up in coloured paper and tied with a ribbon. It must be wonderful to be in a position to provide such joy for others.

That Christmas Day was a revelation to the girls. Now they saw the teamwork in operation and appreciated its value. Necessary household cleaning was quickly dealt with and then all six assembled in the kitchen for a cup of tea. Afterwards there was a separation when Mr. Laing, Jane and Arthur disappeared upstairs to begin the preparation of the dining room- table setting, china, crystal, flowers, and all the necessary utensils required in the butler's pantry next to the dining room. Everything was meticulous to the last half inch. Mr. Laing demanded the highest standards and permitted no fault.

Meantime, in the kitchen, Miss Macleod, Maggie Ann and Nellie set themselves to the task of preparing food. Much had been readied well in advance and now lay in the cold storage on the shelves of the lower basement, but vegetables, meat and poultry had to be prepared fresh. It was on her journeys, fetching and carrying, that Maggie Ann realized just what an artist the housekeeper was. Out of the store came all varieties of delicacies- sauces, stuffings, chutneys, preserves, jellies, glace fruits, crystallized fruits- each one labelled and dated. And when she saw the final presentation of the food on the silver serving dishes arrayed along the table in readiness for the dumb waiter,

Maggie Ann was thrilled that she had participated in the creation of it all. Here was where she really belonged and where her fulfilment lay.

The dumb waiter was a wonderful invention. It consisted of a large zinc lined box, suspended by weights and pulleys. It travelled inside a wall cavity between the kitchen and the butler's pantry immediately above, bringing food piping hot to the dining room and returning the stacks of used cutlery and dishes to the kitchen. Alongside the waiter was a speaking tube enabling communication between the two floors so that course followed course without a hitch. Running up and down stairs carrying laden trays was avoided and the whole operation ran like clockwork. The girls had never seen such a machine before and they just thought the whole mechanism was wonderful.

So the winter weeks slipped by and the girls were glad of their head shawls and warm plaids, which they had brought from home. The north wind, straight off the sea, whistled up Dundas Street and cut to the bone so that they did not linger long outside. Once Christmas and the much more modest New Year festivities were over, the house was cleaned from top to bottom, all the china and silver was checked and counted and the basement stores were reviewed for replenishment. Mr. Laing made a list for wine replacements in his cellar and had his annual discussion with Mrs. Stuart on the subject of any decorating or repairs necessary in the house. There was an air of companionable industry and, now that they all knew each other better, a greater freedom for conversation and laughter. Maggie Ann and Jane could honestly say they were happy.

Chapter 17

One day towards the end of March, Maggie Ann and Jane received a summons to Mrs. Stuart's sitting room. Once again they sat side by side on the sofa across the fireside from Mrs. Stuart and wondered what the occasion was going to present to them. She began right away,

"You will both be pleased to hear that Miss Macleod has given me an excellent report on your time here over the past six months. You have learned fast and have given a very good standard of work and Miss Macleod is most satisfied. I wanted to tell you that first of all because very often credits and appreciation are missed out and I do not think that fair as every one has a part to play in a home like this. In addition, I would like to express my appreciation for the way you devote your time to the children on Sundays. I know that it is an extra task you have willingly taken on yourselves and that you obviously enjoy it, but you do have a way with children and have proved yourselves resourceful and trustworthy. I want you to know that it has been observed and I join my son and his wife in thanking you both most sincerely. Now there is another matter to be considered."

Turning to the side table she lifted a few leaflets and passing them across to the girls she continued.

"I have not forgotten my promise about your studies, but I decided to wait to give you time to settle in to the ways of the household and indeed, to the newness of city life. It has all been quite a change for you, I'm sure. But now I know that you are happy, we can go ahead and I'll tell you the results of my enquiries.

"The Edinburgh School of Cookery in Atholl Crescent presents courses at various levels. I have discussed this with Miss Macleod and I would like you to talk it over with her for I'm sure she would give you the best advice. She is willing to arrange times for you to be out of the house, but insists that you will complete your allotted tasks here, which means you may have to rise earlier or work later. But you can come to some arrangement between you. I understand you have enough money to cover the fees? The classes don't start till October, but I have been told there is a great demand for places, so the sooner your applications go in the better. Once you have decided, let me know and I shall make the place requests on your behalf. I have some influence here. Meantime, you can be collecting your study books and reading as widely as possible because you will be mixing with all levels of society. I'm sure you will hold your own and it will be worthwhile to gain your certificates."

With that she rose and gave each a warm handshake. The two went out, carefully holding the leaflets and once the door was closed they fell upon each other with an ecstatic hug. At last, it had happened.

Miss Macleod was a great support and after considering their choice of High Class Cookery, Plain Cookery and Cheap Cookery, they accepted her wise council to start with the Practical Course in Plain Cookery which was offered on Wednesday and Thursday mornings from 10 till 12.30. This would allow time to deal with home tasks and the quite long walk to the College on Atholl Crescent. It was decided that Maggie Ann would go on Wednesday and Jane on Thursday.

Within weeks, and thanks to Mrs. Stuart's strong recommendation, the girls were accepted and enrolled for the courses at the College. It gave an unbelievable thrill to enter this place of learning along with all the other young ladies and to embark on a study course. For Maggie Ann, looking back now, it was one huge step in the fulfilment of her dream. Just to be recognised in her own right, regardless of origin or background, and to be given the opportunity to prove her ability. Failure did not enter her thoughts.

It was difficult to be patient during the summer months but they continued their historical visits, read extensively among the classical authors, both poetry and prose; many from a reading list that Mrs. Stuart recommended to them, and, because they read together, the girls could discuss and share opinions. They made many visits to Thin's bookshop and, once the reading list for study was available, they purchased their books. It was with a real sense of pride that they set up the little array of books along the wall at the back of the tables in their rooms.

One other achievement that first summer was learning to ride a bicycle. Arthur knew that there was an old bicycle, very dilapidated and rusty, lying at the back of the carriage house, so one day he pulled it out to discover it was a man's cycle. When he asked Mr. Laing where it had come from he was told,

"I don't know lad. It was there before my time, even before the family came to this house. Why do you ask?"

"O, I thought I could do it up and maybe sell it. It's doing no good lying there. What do you think?"

"Well, you have my permission and I'm sure Mrs. Stuart would agree. Go ahead. See what you can do."

So Arthur quietly got on with it. He scraped, rubbed down, painted, polished, oiled, added a few new parts here and there and eventually, asked Mr. Laing to come and inspect. The latter was very impressed and complimented Arthur on the finished work saying he was sure he would make a good price on it. Arthur thanked him and began his rounds of cycle shops and second hand dealers.

Then came the Saturday lunchtime when Arthur asked Maggie Ann and Jane to join him in the yard. He wished to show them something. There, propped against the garage wall, stood a gleaming lady's bicycle, and Arthur beaming from ear to ear.

"It's for you," was all he said, "but you have to learn to ride it first. It will take you back and fore to the college and save a long walk. Lots of ladies ride a bicycle these days so why not you?"

The girls were speechless. Such a wonderful thing! Of course they would learn! But when they heard the whole story from Mr. Laing, how the first bicycle had been prepared to exchange for the lady's cycle, they were silent in the face of such kindness and thoughtfulness. All they could do was quietly thank Arthur and voice their appreciation for all he had done for them. His reward came when he could stand at the end of Cumberland Street and watch, first one and then the other, riding along confidently over the cobbles. Worth it all.

Such moments came back to Maggie Ann as she allowed her memories to run free. The cycle had been a boon, saving them many miles of walking, and once they had learned the short cuts and back ways to Shandwick Place and

Atholl Crescent, they managed to avoid the heavy traffic on the main streets. It was wonderful to speed along with the wind in your face and enjoy the sense of getting somewhere without the effort of always walking.

At last the momentous day dawned and Maggie Ann arrived at the college in good time, complete with a snow white overall and a frilled cap to confine her hair- college regulations. In spite of the crowds of students milling around she had never felt so alone and nervous, terribly strange and inadequate. If only Jane had been with her. But no, she had to do it herself, and with a straightening of her shoulders- even now she could still almost feel the physical effort that took- she stood a moment to take in the scene and realized that signs and arrows on the wall directed the students to the various class locations. So Maggie Ann joined the group following "Plain Cookery B 10am." along the corridors till they reached a vast room laid out like a kitchen. An extremely long stove filled one side of the room and well scrubbed tables stretched down the centre while the other side was laid out in rows of seats with desks, providing lecture facilities. Shelves under the tables held pans, bowls and jugs in various sizes and in the centre of each table stood an earthenware pot containing an assortment of utensils. Here was the arena where she was to prove herself; not that she felt much like a gladiator that day, but, ever practical and purposeful, Maggie Ann was fully determined to succeed. It was a miracle that she was actually here and now she was learning in areas beyond her wildest dreams. She had to give her best.

Every detail of the following five years stayed with her vividly. Such busy years- too busy sometimes to fit in all that was required of her. The work at Great King Street went on unchanged, but the college demanded more and

more of her time and concentration. It was not only a practical education but the related theory and science had to be
studied in tandem and for Maggie Ann, without any earlier
experience of study, this came hard. She sat up long hours
preparing her essays and presentations, determined not to
give less than her best. She had never been one to shirk
hardship and firmly believed that one could overcome any
difficulty if one had the will to do so. Again she could see
her mother in herself. And she won through.

A smile crossed her face as she thought of the four
certificates in her top drawer; three with a 'Merit' seal
and one with a red 'Distinction', her proudest possessions,
along with her letters of reference and commendation from
Mrs. Stuart and Miss Macleod. More treasured still was
the memory of the proud smiles of the family, Mrs. Stuart,
Mr. Laing and Miss Macleod when she showed them her
certificates. They appreciated what it had cost her in time
and effort, and rejoiced with her.

Chapter 18

Right from their first meeting Jane and Mrs. Stuart had formed a close relationship. There was a quiet winsomeness about Jane, which inspired confidence and trust and, more and more, as the months went by, Mrs. Stuart came to rely on her for personal assistance and companionship. When she required help with dressing, or a companion while shopping, or someone to help with her vast correspondence, it was always Jane she turned to. So much so that, after the first year, she became Mrs. Stuart's personal maid and a daily help was employed to undertake Jane's tasks.

After her first session at the College Jane realized that this course was not for her. Much as she had loved cooking and housekeeping, its appeal did not draw her as it did Maggie Ann. The role of lady's personal maid was much more attractive. Jane loved the feel of fine silk and beautiful clothes but, above all, she had developed a real affection for Mrs. Stuart and found the greatest enjoyment in caring for her needs and making life easier for the old lady.

Maggie Ann chuckled to herself as she remembered the times she had teased Jane about taking the easy way out, but there was never any resentment in the banter as each respected the other's value. However, just after their third Christmas when Mrs. Stuart suffered a slight stroke, Jane's role changed dramatically and her work became much more demanding. The mistress made a good recovery and, in most respects, returned to normal, but there remained a weakness in her left leg and arm, which reduced her confidence and curtailed her old freedoms. No longer could she set off on her charitable and committee work without the arm of Jane or Arthur on one side and her cane in the other hand. This frustrated her immensely and, gradually, these activities diminished until she became almost house bound. Reading, corresponding with her many friends, and her grandchildren became her life, and of course, the welfare of her immediate household. She was inordinately proud of Maggie Ann's success; basking a little in the credit her own part had played in that. And she loved Jane like the daughter she had never borne. But it was hard on Jane. Many evenings as she sat late studying, Maggie Ann would hear Jane's quiet step passing the door as she returned yet again from a visit downstairs to Mrs. Stuart. Her patience was infinite. This experience confirmed where her real aptitude lay and Jane knew that the role of companion-lady's maid was where her future rested.

They continued their walks. Every Saturday, rain or shine, they set off together, if only for an hour, so that they could enjoy the fresh air and relax in each other's company. As time went on it became vital for Jane in her present role to escape for a little into the real world, so they occasionally attended a concert or lecture and, more often, the Saturday evening gathering in Carrubber's Close Mission. Here there was a great atmosphere of warmth and friendship, the singing from the Sankey and Moody Songs was hearty and there was always a good encouraging message from the speaker for that evening. Later, a cup of tea drew people together and the girls formed many friendships amongst these warm hearted Christian folks. Carrubber's became their church for these Edinburgh years. As she remembered, Maggie Ann reflected to herself that much of their strengthening and encouragement had come from these evenings at the Mission. The teaching they had received had been inspirational, beyond anything they had heard before, bringing them face to face with their commitment to God, to Jesus and to their fellow men. Deep subjects, which they had to discuss and come to some decision. They found their answers. Not all at once, but gradually an awareness of a personal relationship with God and his son, Jesus Christ, became a reality, vital to both as they toiled with the demands of their daily living. They learned to lean on that Presence.

Chapter 19

But the Edinburgh years came to an end. Nothing stayed the same forever. Looking back on the events of that time Maggie Ann could see how all the indications came together and the next step in their lives was mapped out for them.

For some time after Maggie Ann finished her final domestic course they had talked about their need to move on. Here they were, both in their twenties, and, unless they sought promotion, they would be domestics for the rest of their lives. Jane could see that Mrs. Stuart was failing and would ultimately require more nursing care than she could give. The third factor was a letter from Jane's mother passing on news from her cousin Leebie Stephen in Boston. She was remarking on the fact that so many Scots lassies were arriving in Boston and finding good positions with the rich families there. Maggie Ann and Jane hesitated, mainly out of loyalty to the household and to Mrs. Stuart who had been their wonderful mentor and who needed them more than ever now.

However, the decision was taken out of their hands. Their mistress suffered a second stroke. After some days it became apparent that recovery had been partial and she would require constant nursing care. The household was shaken. Although Mr. David Stuart, her son, assured them that nothing would change immediately, they all knew that things could not go on as before. Eventually, Mrs. Stuart was moved to her son's home in Morningside where she could be nursed and enjoy being close to her family. The house in Great King Street was to be kept on until the family could decide about its future, but only a reduced staff would be required.

This finally prompted Maggie Ann and Jane to set about realizing their plans. Within a few weeks they had their passports. Letters of introduction to the States came from Jane's cousin Leebie Stephen who vouched for them and pledged responsibility for their residency. With these in hand they travelled to Glasgow to the offices of the Allen Line Shipping Service, which had been recommended to them, and booked their second class passages to Boston, sailing on the S.S.Nestorian on 14th. October 1895. How excited they were; but without any doubt about the wisdom of their move. When they told Miss Macleod and Mr. Laing they, in turn, imparted their own surprising news. They had decided to marry and take up a shared care taking-companion post in a little town called Sanquhar in the border country. It would suit them as they grew older and now was the time to do it. Maggie Ann and Jane were not really surprised. For a long time they had suspected a closeness and companionship between the two. They were just so happy for them both.

Arthur decided to stay on as caretaker, keeping an eye on things and tending to the horses, while Nellie would come in and do any necessary cleaning. It seemed a good arrangement until such time as the house was put up for sale. It was a sad six weeks for all, breaking up this little group of strangers who had become a close family. Hard too were the final goodbyes and, especially for Maggie Ann, closing the door on her attic haven where so much had been achieved.

Chapter 20

Once more they were in the train, heading north this time, with yet another ordeal to face. How to tell the family? It would be difficult. Edinburgh was one thing, only a few hours away, but America was far, with an ocean between, and these goodbyes would be for a long time.

They were all there on the platform as the train rolled into the Broch station. Jane's mother and younger brother, Ena hardly able to contain her excitement, and Janet smiling, proudly holding on to the high pram, ready to present baby Tom, now six months old. This was Maggie Ann's first meeting with her nephew and as she looked at the sleeping baby and at his smiling mother and father she thought, "This is just right, just as I imagined it would be for them. May it always be so. They deserve such happiness."

After waving Jane and her family on to the St. Combs train they set off on the long walk across town to Broadsea. Maggie Ann had the honour of pushing the pram while Ena poured out all the family news. Sandy, thoughtful as ever, followed pushing his small hurly, which he had brought along for the hand luggage. Being the peak of the herring fishing Betsy and Bella were still in the gutting yard. The fishing was huge this year and they were hardly at home to sleep. Even Mary May was called out sometimes but today she was at home getting the supper ready. They were all eating together. So the news went on until they reached

College Bounds and turned the corner into Broadsea Road. There at No.3, the door stood wide open, an unheard of occurrence, for the front lobby served as a spare area or box room and the front door was never open. But today was special, the passage was cleared, and Mary May, in her best, stood framed in the doorway. As usual her greeting was brief and unemotional, but the smile was real and from deep in her eyes. As she turned to look at her grandchild her grasp on Maggie Ann's hand lingered and they leaned against each other slightly as they admired the child.

Suppertime was a really wonderful event. Didy, very old now, was in his usual place by the fire. Betsy and Bella returned from the gutting yard and, although washed, still smelled a little of herring, but no one minded for that was what it was like during the fishing. Mary May plied them with food while Ena, quite carried away with all the excitement, kept the news going, telling all sorts of stories and information about what was going on in the village and yes, even in their own house; this with meaningful glances at Betsy and Bella who looked threateningly at her. But she was so full of fun and showed no guile in her hints. The company had to go along with her laughter and high spirits.

Once the meal was over and Janet and Sandy made a move to go home to Charlotte Street with the baby, Maggie Ann spoke quietly,

"Wad ye bide a wee filie langer? A hae something tae say an' a wid like ye a' here thegither. It's nae easy sae a'll mak it short. Jane an' masel hae decided tae emigrate an' we're gan tae Boston tae work. We sail on the fourteenth o' October."

From the profound silence and shocked faces Maggie Ann could feel the enormity of the blow she had just dealt them all. She knew it was a cruel thing to do after such a time of happiness and fun, but it was best done early and the idea would grow to be accepted in the coming three months. She saw it that way and there was no easy solution to the problem.

As she slowly unfolded all the events of the past few weeks in Edinburgh and the need for Jane and herself to move on to pastures new, Maggie Ann could feel the love and understanding coming back into the circle. When they asked,

"Why Boston, fit wye dae ye hae tae gang sae far awa as America?" she replied

"We jist want tae gang there. There's wark an' we hae aye winted tae traivel an' see ither places. Noo is oor chance fan we are young aneuch an' able. Jane's cousin Leebie, is in Boston an' we'll bide wi' her till we get sorted oot in a place. Bit there's three months yet afore we gang an' we'll jist enjoy bein' here thegither an' getting' ready for Betsy's big day. Fan am a gaun tae meet this lad Alex? Ena says he's winnerfu."

With that the subject moved away from Boston to the coming wedding and, amid much teasing and laughter, they parted company- Didy accompanied by Ena round the corner to his own house in Main Street, and Janet and Sandy with the pram to Charlotte Street, not far away.

Once the kitchen was tidy again Mary May and Maggie Ann set off for a quiet hour on the Braes. All was silent there, now that today's catch had been dealt with and the gutting yards were empty, waiting for tomorrow's landing. Here and there a yardman was hosing down, and a cooper was hammering on a last hoop. The cry of the gulls hovering above and the sea crashing on the rocks below the cliffs were like music to Maggie Ann. The white carpet of gowans mingled with purple clover and yellow flags; the green of the grassy slopes peeping between the dark rock piles and crowned with the low, red tiled houses; this she would always carry in her memory.

This warm summer evening they walked farther than usual, past the end of the curing yards, and eventually sat down in the lee of the lighthouse wall. There, her mother listening in silence, Maggie Ann related the story of her life in Edinburgh; the staff family closeness; the house and life style in Great King Street; the children; the wonderful opportunities they had been given; the wonders of the city discovered during their walks; the Mission and their deeper Christian understanding; the sadness of their mistress' illness and finally, the events leading up to their decision to emigrate. At last her story ended. It was as though Maggie Ann had been trying to persuade her mother of the rightness of her decision, and wanted her blessing.

They sat a while, letting the calm subdue the emotions they were both experiencing and then Mary May spoke quietly,

"A ken ma lass fit ye're sayin' an a oonerstan. A've aye kent ye had a plan for yir life, an' a wudna be able tae keep ye here wi me for iver. A kent fan ye gaed awa tae Edinburgh 'at it wis only the first step tae something farrer. Noo it's cam an' a'm gled for ye. Ye've aye hid a mind o' yir ain an' gweed gumption an' a've nae fear 'at ye'll tak care in faat's aheid. Ye're a growen umman noo an' hae a recht tae mak yir ain deceesions. Ye hae deen weel wi yir studies. A'm prood o' ye an' ye hae ma blessin' on a' ye plan."

Maggie felt at peace as she took and squeezed her mother's hand. This was the approval that mattered. The others in the house would marry and stay, or go, even emigrate like herself, but Mary May was the rock and life source who had given them her all and she had a right to be taken into their confidence.

By Monday Maggie Ann had signed on again with John Mc.Ewen and acquired some borrowed gear for gutting. The last few weeks of the fishing saw her at the farlans again, renewing old acquaintances and realizing the passage of time as she teamed up with young women who had been children six years ago. The rich fishing continued into early September and Maggie Ann was glad of the money, enabling her to contribute to the family budget and also, she hoped, to gather a little nest egg to leave with her mother.

Chapter 21

Maggie Ann shivered a little. The evening damp was gathering around her. She could feel it on her skin and she knew she should go back. It was so difficult to pull herself away from her reverie and this hour with all the years of her past. As she drew her shawl round her shoulders and made to rise, her hand brushed against the green ribbon tied round her left arm. Maggie Ann smiled as she thought,

"That's twice I've been the older sister bridesmaid; but I won't be Bella's one. I wonder when this Green Garter Custom began?"

As she hurried along now Maggie Ann pondered how easy it would have been if Betsy had followed Janet's example and had her wedding in the old fashioned way in the Broadsea Hall. The friends who had been visited and personally invited, came to the hall on the wedding day, complete with all the catering- food, dishes and cutlery- such an abundance and variety; and everything gifted out of love and respect. The wedding dance that followed had gone on for hours until finally, after the brake took Sandy's older family home to Pitullie, all the young folks with much boisterous teasing, accompanied Janet and Sandy to their front door on Charlotte Street. Such a happy day!

But Betsy was different. She had planned on a modern wedding and Mary May, who always wanted the best for her girls, did not dispute the matter. So the wedding was held in the Dalrymple Café across the road from the station with catering laid on by the big bakery on Cross Street. Because of the seating capacity the guests were restricted to the two families and only the closest friends so that it was a rather subdued gathering. The meal was good and afterwards there were some games and music, but the fun and high spirits were lacking. It was a very dignified event, which suited Betsy for she was inclined to want to climb socially and shake off her Broadsea background. There was no doubt Betsy was the beauty of the family and she and Alex made a handsome couple. She had been fortunate for he was a very fine looking, tall fisherman with a kindly and intelligent manner. Maggie Ann liked him from the start and took comfort that she would be leaving her mother with two fine sons-in-law to help her if the need arose.

Now she was running along the Braes, conscious that she was going to miss the end of the wedding and she still had a last visit to make.

The kitchen was dark with only the glow of the dying fire giving her a focal point. Maggie Ann lit the lamp on the table and drew the kettle forward over the fire to bring up the water to boiling; then she set the three stone pigs to warm in the oven. She waited, taking a little time to survey this familiar place where so much of her life had been lived. Ena's crocheted blanket still held pride of place on the box bed; Maggie Ann rested her hand on the brass rail over the fireplace where she had hung so much of the weekly ironing; she fingered the lace edging of the mantelpiece and studied her father's photo that always stood there. He was a good-looking man, fine featured; Betsy and Janet resembled him; the rest of them were small, and favoured Mary May. She filled the three pigs and carried them to the beds- her mother's, and Bella's and her own in the front room. Now, after Monday, there would just be one occupant, and after Bella was gone, nobody. She was sure Ena would not sleep here on her own. Strange to think of the room standing empty, after all the years of fun and quarrels and secrets. Maggie Ann refilled the kettle and set it over the fire, which she banked up with a shovel of small coal, then she turned down the lamp and made her way to the door pulling her shawl round her shoulders. As she drew the door closed behind her Maggie Ann's hand brushed against the creel hanging high up on the door, the snow white scrubbed band dangling loose below. Maggie Ann choked back a great sob as she laid her cheek on the rough webbing- this symbol of her mother's years of toil and their own livelihood.

Then she ran all the way across town to the bottom of Station Brae, arriving at the Café door just in time to join the end of the wedding procession accompanying the bride and groom to their new home on Shore Street.

Maggie Ann had seen Betsy's house last night when she had helped to carry the presents and other household goods to Shore Street. Alex had rented two rooms just a few doors up from his own parents at No.65. They were connecting, one to the back and the other facing the front, looking straight across the harbour, and he with Betsy had spent a great deal of effort papering and painting and making them really comfortable. Alex had done well during his few years of fishing and was able to furnish according to Betsy's wishes and taste so, in Maggie Ann's view, they were beginning married life very well set up. At the end of the communal lobby were a sink on one side and a toilet on the other, to be shared by two families, so there would be no need to carry water from the street pump.

Maggie Ann was fascinated by the view across the harbour. She could have sat there for hours, just looking. Being Friday night the fishing fleet was still gathering to tie up for the weekend. Although the summer fishing was now well past, many of the boats still went after white fish and came in at all hours before the Sunday. The huge forest of masts stretching from side to side of the harbour excited her imagination. She had seen many great fleets in her years at the fishing, but had never quite appreciated the magnitude of this fleet tied up in her own town. Seeing the boats in array, each alongside the other, named and numbered with its own characteristic colour and sign. Here was a sight she had not taken in before, and a memory to be added to her store.

Later that evening they had all moved along to Alex's home where his parents held the traditional pre-wedding "Feet Washing". The bride and groom, usually in hiding, were captured and forced to have their feet washed in a shared tub. A feast and a time of fun and games followed this. Mary Masson, Alex's mother, and her lively, young family, put on a great party. For the three sisters next in age to Alex there seemed to be no limit to their energy, especially Nellie, and the fun spilled over into the street when the neighbours gathered to wish the young couple happiness. Mary May, sitting by the fire, looked on with her usual serious expression, but there was an air of contentment about her, only shadowed by the thought of Maggie Ann's departure so near. Every now and again Maggie Ann drew near her mother and touched her shoulder as much as to say,

"I'm still here."

In the darkness, lit up by the harbour lamps along the pier, the wedding procession followed the shore road until

Betsy and Alex paused by their close end, refusing to allow their supporters any further entry. Amidst all the banter and joking they stood laughing, Betsy looking so beautiful in her blue wedding finery and Alex taking a firm stand by his bride. Finally, they went in and closed the door and the guests, with a few encouraging words of advice, slowly parted company as they took their way up High Street towards Broadsea. The younger ones hurried on ahead to change out of their wedding finery while Mary May and Maggie Ann climbed Duke Brae and North Street, heading for the Braes and their own way home. Maggie Ann said nothing about being here earlier in the evening. She knew that her mother would have guessed what she was doing and why she had slipped away from the wedding.

Chapter 22

Maggie Ann worried about Sunday, her last day. There had been so many goodbyes in their way of life, but not like this one, and she dreaded emotional scenes. However, she need not have worried for all day, friends and neighbours 'cried in' just to wish her the best. Endless cups of tea were drunk and most of the talk was about the wedding with only passing reference to Maggie Ann's departure next day. She was surprised that so many people cared to come, but that was how it was in Broadsea, and she was one of their own. It gave her a warm feeling and relieved a little of the small niggle of guilt she was experiencing at leaving them all.

Greatest surprise was the arrival of Aunt Annie May from Cairnbulg, just before dinnertime. This wee woman in her fifties, indomitable as ever, decided that she would make one of her rare trips to the Broch that day. The occasion merited it. Maggie Ann's last day, and she had a special mission to perform. It was Sunday and no trains, but she would walk. And here she was, complete with her basket and contribution to the day's fare, scones and a jar of home made strawberry jam. Her way was never to go anywhere empty handed.

Having settled herself into Didy's chair by the fire, she looked at them one by one, then nodded,

"Aye, yir a' growen up. Seen there'll jist be you an' me Mary Mey. A ken ye cam oot tae see me i' the train last wik, bit a jist thocht a wid like tae spen some o' the last day wi ye Maggie Ann. Ye wir aye the een a cwid lippen on fan granny wis here an ye hiv aye been a gryte stey tae me fan a socht help. So a jist got up an' set oot tae waak. It wis sic a bonny mornin'; the birds wir a' singin' their hairts oot an' a jist felt it wis really the Lord's Day. A got aboot tae the Philorth Briggie fan Jeemsie Buchan stoppet an' gaed mi a hurle tae Victoria Street. He wis gawn tae the kirk, an' a've tae meet him again at fower, aifter the service, tae gang hame again. A wis gled an' a' for a wis a wee bittie dylt efter the mairritch yestreen. It a' gaed weel though an' Betsy made a bonny bride. She'll be a' recht wi Alex Mey ; he's come o' fine foulk. An' fit aboot you Bella? They tell me 'at yir walken oot as weel. Is he frae the Broch or Braidsea?"

Bella's reply came quite shyly,

"He's frae Braidsea. He's Willie Taylor an' his folk bide on Main Street."

"An fit dis he dae for a livin'?"

"Willie's a sail maker an' he works in the chandler's on Shore Street."

"Weel 'at soons a recht. It's fine tae hae fand a gweed man. Yir quinies hae deen weel Mary Mey. 'At jist leaves oor bonny Ena, bit ye'll hae her a fylie langer yet."

Mary May glanced at Ena and, in her usual dry manner, replied,

"A wid think sae."

Bella gave a little smile to herself as she remembered the times she and Betsy had slipped out of the house on a Friday night and attended the dances in the School Street hall. But that had all come to an end the night Mary May arrived at the hall door and firmly withdrew her daughters from the dancers. She marched them home, scolding all the way, affronted that her family should consort with people in such places. The girls were angry and embarrassed, suspecting that Ena had let slip where they were, but they also knew that Mary May was very concerned about their safety and their good name. Respectability was high on her agenda for herself and for her family and she would go to any lengths to maintain it.

Annie May withdrew a little cloth bag from her skirt pocket and passed it to Maggie Ann.

"Es is for you, seeing as ye're the aldest. It's granny's waddin' ring an' a thocht ye shud hae it afore ye gang awa."

Maggie Ann accepted the ring, remembering another such moment, and passed the broad gold band round for all to see. Then she laid it with her other treasures in her open case.

Annie May left soon after and, once the tea was past, they joined Janet and baby Tom for the service in the Broadsea Hall. Sandy was on the platform with the Salvation Army group leading the meeting and they settled into the back row where the baby would not cause too much distraction. It was good to sit here quietly and gather her thoughts and, as she responded to the warm smiles and greetings from the gathering congregation, Maggie Ann realized how much these people meant to her, and how they had played such a large part of her life. And she was leaving them all. She was sure she would never meet any finer.

After the service they all strolled down to the shore be-hind the houses, Mary May carrying Tom close wrapped to her in a plaid. They stood a few moments in the soft evening air, looking across the familiar scene, before they turned back to number three for a last cup of tea.

Chapter 23

They were all up early on Monday morning, Mary May to light the washhouse fire, and Bella and Ena to accompany Maggie Ann to the station for the seven o'clock train. Breakfast was quiet, each one maintaining a steely control and concentrating on the moments ahead as they watched the clock speeding on. Sandy's arrival with the hurly broke the tension and now it was all hustle to get away, for the walk to the station would take some time. He knew the hurly was unnecessary but Sandy had an understanding for these situations and felt the humour of the moment might ease the partings. As he loaded on the hand luggage he told Mary May that Janet would be down with the baby later to help her hang out the washing on the Braes, and with that he, along with Bella and Ena, set off along College Bounds towards Charlotte Street where they would call on Janet for a moment.

Mary May and Maggie Ann lingered a little at the close end. All that was necessary had already been said, but Mary May put her hands on Maggie Ann's shoulders and looked deep into her face as though she would keep the imprint forever.

"Tak care o' yirsel lass. Keep yirsel stracht an' dee fit's recht," she whispered.

With that she turned away to the wash house to rinse out the whites which she had set to soak two hours previously.

Maggie Ann hurried after the others to catch up with them at Janet's for another difficult farewell.

The station was milling with people. A Yarmouth train was leaving this morning carrying south the last contingent of fish workers, and the station hall was a scene of excitement and confusion till the passengers were sorted out and finally queued up to board the long train. Betsy and Alex were travelling together, the herring drifter having gone on ahead to allow the couple time for their wedding. Alex would join his boat at Lowestoft and Betsy was going to gut with a team there. Maggie Ann and Jane joined them in their compartment to go as far as Aberdeen where they would change to the Glasgow train.

At last the train slowly drew out, away from the platform and the final wavings, gradually taking up speed as it passed the Links and the sweep of the beach. The girls lingered at the open window until the branch line went off to Cairnbulg and the train turned inland to the south. Then they took their seats with the others to listen quietly to the chatter going on around them. A little pang of envy went through Maggie Ann as she looked at Betsy and Alex sitting opposite. How happy and complete they were, how at one with each other, and how handsome. She was so glad for them and prayed it would always be so.

Chapter 24

The train sped westwards and Maggie Ann and Jane were glad to sit in their corners facing each other and saying nothing; just allowing the sense of freedom to envelop them. The emotion and restraints of the past few days had been exhausting and after the last farewells at Aberdeen, they had stood on the platform weeping as the Yarmouth train pulled out. But now that was all past, and they could freely put their minds to what lay ahead. The old sense of excitement and adventure came back and, as they anticipated their arrival in St. Enoch's Station and the hotel they had booked into, their enthusiasm increased.

It was darkening when the train arrived and they emerged from the noisy, grimy station into the milling crowds of Glasgow's teatime rush. They thought their years in Edinburgh had prepared them for city life, but not for this; so many people all thrusting past; so much noise; the clanking trams, the wagons, the carriages, all horse drawn, rumbling over the cobbles. And the smells; the acrid smoke from the many fires and factory chimneys; horse manure and urine, refuse lying around and the human smells as people pressed close by. Against the street gas lamps they could see a fine haze of fog hanging over all and carrying the suffocating odours. Clutching their portmanteaus, they drew back into the lea of the entrance till they found their bearings and the courage to step out into the melee.

How they blessed the booking clerk at the shipping office who had advised them so wisely. Just a few steps to the right of the station was the imposing entrance to their destination, the St. Enoch Hotel, and as Maggie Ann and Jane mounted the steps between the marble pillars and saw the opulence and grandeur within, their cheeks flushed with excitement at this immense step of extravagance. Although the clerk had booked them the cheapest room possible, they were still within this place of elegance and they were going to make the most of their one night here.

The footman who accompanied them to their room on the second floor seemed to sense their newness to hotel life and explained as they walked along together. Breakfast times extended over a few hours, rooms were never left unlocked and the best time to have a bath was late evening when the preparation for dinner rush was over. He would be on call all evening and if they required assistance, just to ring the bell by the two single beds. With that he left them with a cheery smile. Maggie Ann and Jane felt they had really been made welcome.

As they unpacked their necessities for the night they laughed at each other, realizing they had been whispering, not talking. Once tidy, they set out for the dining room, conscious of their hunger after a long day. How wonderful to sit in a beautiful room and be served so graciously. They could choose from a menu, which had caused them no labour, and afterwards, rise and walk away without any responsibility for clearing the table. This was how the other half lived and, whatever lay ahead of them, they would never forget this night. Later, they took turns to luxuriate in the bathroom along the corridor, allowing the heat to ease the fatigue, and bring a glow of well being in preparation for sleep. Their room faced the back of the hotel so they slept long and deep, undisturbed by the early morning traffic on the street outside.

Over breakfast they sat and planned their day. Boarding was from noon onwards as the Nestorian would sail with the tide on Wednesday morning. So they decided to follow the advice of a helpful concierge, leave their luggage in the hotel, and take an hour to find their way to the docks. There was no time to sight see in Glasgow, much to their regret, but their route took them a little way along Argyll Street, much quieter now, and Jamaica Street, leading down to the bridge spanning the great river Clyde. As they stood on the bridge looking first east, then west, and watched the movement of huge ships, the towering masts and funnels belching smoke, and all the wharves and jetties below, milling with people and horses and carts, and mountains of bales, and casks of tallow, or whisky, or whatever, they were awestruck. Not even the largest fleet they had ever seen in Lowestoft could come near the magnitude of activity in this port at Glasgow.

Chapter 25

They were early for it was not an enormous journey to bring their luggage down to the Broomielaw where the Nestorian lay at anchor. To be early was important. Maggie Ann and Jane were determined to miss nothing and, perched on two bales of wool, they watched enthralled, as the loading of supplies went on at a gangway positioned at the stern of the ship. Another gangway linked to an open doorway in the mid ships was closed off with a barrier. Smoke poured from one funnel causing the occasional black speck to fall on them. A tea vendor called from his booth just along the quay and the commotion went on unceasing. Gazing up at the ship towering above them they felt quite dwarfed. Somewhere amongst all these many rows of portholes was their cabin, forward or aft? How would they be able to find their way about this vast vessel? Plenty others had gone before so they too would manage. From their vantage point they watched and pondered, afraid of so many unknowns, but at the same time, excited, and so glad they were together and not travelling alone. They sipped hot tea from the vendor's stall and enjoyed a buttered roll, all the time keeping an eye on the gangway and conscious of the throng growing around them. Elegant carriages deposited rich passengers with what seemed mountains of hand luggage. Many like themselves in neat, modest outfits and looking just as nervous, stood in little groups quietly talking. But the passengers who most held Maggie Ann's attention were the migrant families, so many of them. By their language they were mainly from the Highlands. They stood or sat in groups, parents holding close their numerous children, many barefoot, with their possessions tied in a large plaid. Their poverty was apparent, but there was hope in their eyes. They had courage to face a new future, whatever the hardships, for nothing could surpass the misery, degradation and disillusionment they had already suffered at the hands of landlords and mine and factory owners. Maggie Ann had heard of these cruelties and was now seeing at first hand.

The hour soon passed and the time for boarding approached. All around many farewell tears were being shed and Maggie Ann and Jane were thankful that all that was behind them. Two signs were posted at the top of each gangway and the crowds began to filter into their respective queues. Maggie Ann and Jane joined the long line for the centre gangway marked first and second class, but by far the longest queue, tailing and curving away back along the wharf, formed up for the steerage entry which had formerly been used for loading supplies. The barriers were removed and two officers took up position at the foot of each gangway. Passengers, clutching sailing tickets and passports, passed up in a steady stream, halting at the top where other officers again examined their papers and ticked their names against a passenger list. Maggie Ann and Jane were given their cabin number and directed aft where another seaman accompanied them to their deck level and cabin. After a few brief instructions he rushed away to attend to other passengers and Maggie Ann and Jane were left alone.

Their cabin was diminutive, a miracle of compactness. Two bunk beds, one above the other, filled one wall behind the door, and a washbasin with a mirror, a chair and a short hanging rail comprised the rest of the furnishings. At least they would have their privacy. Again their thoughts turned gratefully to the shipping clerk who had strongly advised them against the discomforts of communal living in steerage in the bowels of the ship. The eight pounds charge for a cabin was worth it.

Maggie Ann and Jane did not linger long, but soon were on their way back up to their own deck, following a plan of the ship which they had found on a chair in one of the main hallways. Each class had its own deck, the second- class one being immediately below the first. They were made aware of the segregation when they came on a little metal stairway with a chain across and a notice saying "No entry. First class only."

Most of that afternoon they spent, leaning on the rail, gazing down on the Broomielaw. The activity continued and carriages depositing passengers came and went; the long line of emigrants seemed to stretch on, never growing less. From their perch, high up at the ship's rail, they had an overall view of the proceedings and the scene affected them in so many ways; the excitement and daring in what they were facing; apprehension; sorrow watching so many tears of parting; amazement at the size of the ship and the seeming multitude at work all over her; curiosity as they watched fellow travellers climbing the gangway; what would it feel like on the high seas for so long; would they be sea sick like crossing the Roost?

As the afternoon wore on the first and second-class queue grew shorter and thinned out and only one officer was required at the bottom of the gangway. The wharf became gradually less busy, friends and relatives filtered away and so did the passengers to their cabins. A cool wind came up off the river and, after a few turns round their deck to bring back the circulation to their cold feet and legs, Maggie Ann and Jane decided to go exploring to find their dining room and other important places of interest to them.

Back in their cabin, they tidied themselves and, refreshed, lay down to rest for a little before the dinner call. Resting itself came as a novelty to them and, as they luxuriated in it, Maggie Ann and Jane began to think these next ten days were going to be the most amazing holiday they could ever have dreamed of. And that is how it was.

Chapter 26

They approached the dining room a little apprehensively. So many unknowns, which they were just having to master as they went along. There was the question of dress; their meagre wardrobes would not allow them to change regularly for dinner; should they wear a hat? Would they find conversation convivial and easy? And who would join them at their table? Once allocated their places, Maggie Ann and Jane sat and waited, delighted with the fine table linen and gleaming cutlery, content to sit and watch amidst the soft hubbub of conversation as others found their seats. Like themselves, most people were strangers having to open up new avenues of communication and friendships.

At last they were joined by first one couple in their mid forties, and then by a very elderly husband and wife. After the preliminary smiles and greetings they sat a few moments before the waiter came for their orders. This took some time as the older couple had a language problem and required a little assistance in translation, which the other gentleman could offer. Now that the ice was broken the conversation opened up.

"Since we are going to share meals together for so long I think we should introduce ourselves and get to know each other. Do you agree? I am Rob Lennox and this is my wife Bess. We come from York, but we have been living in Galashiels in Scotland where I was a schoolmaster for over ten years. We're going to Boston first and then plan to go inland to open a school in a new settlement where we are needed."

That would explain the fine homespun tweed suit that he wore and his healthy, ruddy complexion. His wife Bess in her quiet, grey dress had a sweet, sad expression in her eyes as she smiled and looked from one to the other. Her really outstanding feature was the shining, red hair piled high above her forehead, making a glowing contrast to the pale grey below. Maggie Ann and Jane felt there was a tragic story lying somewhere behind that smile.

They in turn, told a little about themselves, that they were going to relatives in Boston with the intention of finding posts as cook and lady's maid.

Joseph Cohen and his wife Marta, in very halting English, between them managed to tell an amazing story. They were tailors in Aix-en-Provence and, after their two sons with their families emigrated to America, they missed their children and grandchildren so much, they decided to uproot and join them. But, since they would not ever be back in Europe, they planned to make a detour, travel north to Paris, then across to London and on up to the woollen towns of Yorkshire and the Scottish Borders to see the famous textile world which had produced so much of the materials they had used. Now at last, they had come on the final lap to take up their cabin on the Nestorian. They had been on the journey for three months and any English they possessed had been acquired during that time. Such courage!

Later, Maggie Ann and Jane stood again at the rails, intently watching the final departure activities. They saw the last of the steerage emigrants hastening on before the gangway was drawn up, and the now empty wharf lay quiet for a few hours. The hazy air carried a whiff of oil and smoke and that peculiar odour that comes from creosoted timber that is always damp, a smell familiar to both. Today had been wonderful, especially round the dinner table, and they looked forward to further conversations. At last they went below to lie awake for a while, listening to the gentle throb of the ship's engines before they fell asleep.

The early dawn light was just breaking when they were awakened by a sudden change in rhythm of the engines. They must be leaving. Anxious not to miss any of the departure Maggie Ann and Jane quickly dressed and, wrapped in warm plaids, made their way up to the deck to find a place at the rail. Rob and Bess Lennox were already there and made room for them along side. The hawsers had been loosened and now they could feel the gentle roll of the great ship as it freed itself from the restraints. Slowly it drew away from the quay amid many cries and shouts, and the horn sounding its long, low, resonant note, seemed to be making its own sad farewell. Maggie Ann felt a lump come into her throat. She could not have spoken at that moment. The distance from home and Broadsea was suddenly becoming very wide. She felt like reaching out her two arms to clutch on to the receding land and hold them all close for just a little longer; but the moment passed. The vessel swung into midstream and headed slowly down river. There was a long way to go before they would meet the ocean.

For the next hour they watched as the great liner nosed its way between the arrays of steam ships, cargo boats, tenders, every kind of ship used in the business of a great seaport. Most were moored at the quays along the waterfront while behind, great, sloping, shipbuilding yards provided an immense backdrop. World famous names like Fairfield, Mc.Intyre, Ferguson, Abercorn and many more, declared their presence in huge letters above their slipways. Here and there a near complete ship towered aloft with men like ants clambering all over, and always the clang of hammers pounding rivets echoed from all sides. Bonded warehouses competed with tobacco stores and locomotive yards and, even at this early hour, people were everywhere so busy. As they watched, the passengers could see where the wealth of Scotland lay.

There was much to speak about at breakfast and then they returned to the deck. By now the river was widening out and they were able to see the panorama of mountains and sea inlets opening before them. Away to the north Ben Lomond was visible and, in between, rolled a seeming endless array of mountains, glorious in the greens, and golds, and browns of autumn. They sparkled in the brilliant morning sunshine, the distant ones tinged a misty purple, but as they came closer, the hues glowed more distinct and vivid in contrast to the green, grassy lower slopes, and the blue of the sea. The passengers had not anticipated the beauty of Argyll as they gazed spellbound.

Soon the Nestorian rounded Gourock Point with the Cloch lighthouse high above on the hill, and veered south into the Kyles of Bute. Shipping was busy here. All along the coasts on both sides, small ports provided havens for all sorts of trade and passenger services. Navigation was not easy, but once past the humps of the Greater and Lesser Cumbrais and on to Arran, the channels opened out into the real Firth of Clyde and Nestorian picked up speed as she headed for the tip of Kintyre and the Irish coast.

Once the ship had moved out of the sheltered Firth into the open Atlantic, circumstances changed and the Nestorian reacted to the head wind and the swell. More than a few passengers disappeared below, but Maggie Ann and Jane knew from past experience where to go for most comfort. Late afternoon found them, wrapped in their plaids, seated in the stern of the ship close by the funnel where they were sheltered from the wind and could gain warmth from the engine room ventilators. They sat in companionable silence watching their beautiful land slip slowly out of sight, regretting that there was so much of it they had not yet seen. But they would return. They were sure of that. Here they were, sailing into the sunset, not knowing what lay ahead, but they promised themselves they would come back.

As they rounded the north west corner of Ireland darkness fell, hiding the mountains of Donegal and shrouding the low, grassy slopes and long beaches of Sligo. Sometime during the night the ship would drop anchor in Galway Bay to take on her final complement of passengers and cargo, but now there was no more to be seen so Maggie Ann and Jane returned to their cabin. The dining room was quiet that evening. Conversation round the table was spasmodic, each one overwhelmed with thoughts of home and concerns for the future, not least being the long sea crossing. The Atlantic looked very vast.

Chapter 27

Once again the Nestorian was on her way, following closely the navigation channel into the deep water of the wider Galway Bay. Once past the Aran Islands, the ship entered the real Atlantic and the serious journey had begun. A damp sea mist hung everywhere, shrouding the scenery and the disappearing land in a grey mantle, and laying down a film of wet over everything; rails, seats, clothing. In a short time the decks were deserted and passengers returned below to the comfort of the spacious lounges or their cabins. Maggie Ann and Jane hesitated inside the swing doors of the lounge, shy before the sea of people, when they heard a known voice hailing them from the nearby corner,

"Ha my little Scottish friends. Come and join us."

There was Mr. and Mrs. Cohen seated in an alcove, accompanied by another couple who, by their appearance, were also of Jewish origin.

"We make room for you both. I would like you to meet my friends Jacob and Rachel Hartzmann from Glasgow. Fancy, they came from France two years ago and now, like us, are going to Boston. Is that not wonderful? We speak the same language, we go to the same city, we worship together and, just listen to this, we are both tailors! What do you think of that? Is our Jahweh not a good God?"

Amid the laughter Maggie Ann and Jane settled themselves into the little group, glad to enjoy the welcome and the obvious warmth of the old people. Joseph was exuberant; his flow of English heavily punctuated with French when he was at a loss for the correct word, but the meaning was clear and the girls appreciated that he included them by trying to converse in English.

The Harzmanns had been Parisians and the conversation to start with was mainly centred round that beautiful city. They too were emigrating to join their family, but they had many nostalgic thoughts about their life in the Rue des Rosiers where they had lived in an apartment above their tailoring business. Like the Cohens, they had grown fearful of the situation of Jews in Europe and longed for the freedom from restrictions and prejudice. But it had been a huge decision. The wrench was hard. Leaving lifelong friends, familiar ways, a city of such beauty, a comfortable livelihood; that had taken great courage. And their sojourn in Glasgow had not proved satisfactory. Now, much cheered on by the presence of Josef, they were looking forward to Boston and the reunion with their family.

For a while they sat silent with their own thoughts of home, then Josef again,

"You know, I am wondering how it will be living in a new city like Boston. It has a history no longer than just over two hundred years. We have come from Aix, which was a city over two thousand years ago, with an ancient university and such a culture of learning and art long established. Shall we find anything to compare with that? We shall miss the mellow, old houses and our little squares round the fountains and the tall plantane trees. You know, in every little square with a tree you would find a café with people sitting in the shade. And the markets! Every day the fruit and vegetable and flower markets in the Place Hotel de Ville, and we sat there by the Tour d' Horloge under the tree, coffee drinking. Just round the corner in the Place des Cardeurs was the Jewish market. We shopped there and met our friends, and most evenings sat and chatted. Our home was only a step away in the Rue des Cordeliers and often our friends gathered with us on Friday for Shabbat. They will be gathering tomorrow for Shabbat. I wonder, will they remember us on the Sabbath when they gather in the Synagogue? Will they still be remembering us after all this time?"

"Josef, forgive me. I must interrupt you."

This from Jacob Hartzmann,

"It is good to look back and appreciate the past, but one must not live there. Our prophets teach us that we must move forward. What would have happened if Abram had stayed at Urr and not moved on to fulfil the Promise? We have lived most of our lives and now must go on to see the fulfilment in our children and our children's children. Is that not a wonderful future? Places do not really matter, it is people that count. These two young ones here are full of hope and purpose. They go to the unknown, but we go to our own families and we must find joy in that. Do we not?"

"You are so right Jacob. Thank you. I think we have been travelling too long, Marta and I. It is time we reached our Promised Land. Now what about some of that coffee I can smell?"

And so the moment passed. But Maggie Ann and Jane were given much to discuss in the privacy of their own cabin. They knew all the Old Testament stories of Abraham, Isaac, Jacob and Moses and the Exodus, but had not really appreciated the reality these exercised in the life of the present day Jew. In fact they had not ever spoken with a Jew before and their curiosity was aroused to find out more about 'abiding in the teachings of the Book'. Maybe they would hear more.

The days passed swiftly and, thankfully, the autumn crossing was smooth. A regular pattern developed; meal times, walking the deck for exercise, resting in the fresh, sea air, wrapped in their plaids, reading, conversing occasionally, filled their days which were passing all too quickly. Later, they remembered their first Atlantic crossing as, not just a doorway to a new life, but it had introduced them to a wider understanding of people, and customs, and places they had never imagined. They felt it had in some way prepared them for what lay ahead.

Meal times were always diverting. With two such travelled and intellectually stimulating men, conversation moved over many subjects, very often relating to work and experiences. The four women were content to listen and follow, but occasionally, Maggie Ann and Jane joined in when reference was made to Scottish affairs and the fisher way of life, which was unknown to the rest of the group. They listened wrapped, as Maggie Ann or Jane described the sheer physical toil on the part of the women and the huge organization involved in moving all the related trades from fishing to fishing. They described life in the remoteness of the Shetland Isles and the fish workers who travelled from the west, the north and the east coasts to provide a work force in the great East Anglian fishings. When Maggie Ann told of her mother, a widow with five children, bringing up her family alone, as a fishwife, her hearers were visibly moved. She did not dwell on the hardships, but more emphasised the courage and resourcefulness of such women, of whom there were many. She was glad to give voice to her admiration for her mother, Mary May. Sharing her deepest feelings did not come easily to Maggie Ann. It was a thing she seldom did, but with the open interest and understanding of her hearers she felt at liberty to speak freely. This led on to a discussion on the very positive role and rights of women in the modern world and Maggie Ann, remembering her long ago discussions with Sandy on the subject, thought,

"Yes, things have changed. Here we are, six of us, discussing this very same subject. I wonder if women in the States feel any more valued."

Chapter 28

After a perfect, calm crossing without any untoward incident, the SS Nestorian came in sight of land and began the slow approach to the Charles River. On every deck the rails were crowded with silent watchers, eager for a glimpse of this new land, and the faces registered such a variety of emotions-excitement, apprehension, joy, doubt, resolution, relief. It was all there in this motley group. Every single one was fleeing from some situation and seeking a solution in a new environment and a new regime of life. Would they all succeed? Probably not. But at this moment the focus was on arriving and emotions were high.

Standing arm in arm close to their friends, Maggie Ann and Jane felt the thrill and a quiet satisfaction that their first achievement had been accomplished- they had made the crossing and would soon arrive at the next stage. After all the years of hardship and waiting, it was happening. As they turned to each other there was a glint of resolve in their eyes and a smile of happiness on their faces. They made a bonny pair. Rested and well nourished after their ten days on ship, their faces glowed with health and fresh air, and they had a new air of confidence and maturity. This was due in no little measure to the stimulating company of their fellow travellers and the long discussions that had transpired. Maggie Ann and Jane were grateful that they had been blessed with such travelling companions who had opened their eyes and minds to the wider horizons of history, religion, race, travel, indeed the world. The two young women realized how little they did know.

All through the night while the ship nosed its way slowly up the river Maggie Ann and Jane slept fitfully, concerned about what lay ahead; the landing arrangements; finding Leebie in the crowds of people; were their documents all in order; how hard it was going to be to say goodbye to their travelling friends. But when daylight came they were up and packed and ready for their last breakfast together on board ship. They kept the conversation light and cheerful and when at last the word came that the Nestorian was approaching the harbour, they assembled at the rails again to watch the docking.

As in Glasgow, Boston harbour seemed right in the heart of the bustling city. Many wharves stretched along both sides of the wide river and all the hustle and thronging activity sent out the same cacophony of sounds. As she edged in to the pier the ship's propellers thrashed far below and then the engines stopped and the hawsers were thrown to the waiting dockside men stationed by the bollards. Maggie Ann had seen this happening many times, but never on this scale.

The pier and all the area beyond was thronged with waiting people, so many that it was like a sea of faces, indistinguishable in the distance; families, parents, husbands, relatives of all sorts come to claim a loved one. Both on the ship and on the pier someone was looking for someone and every now and again came a victorious shout,

"There she is! I see her! Look, up there!"

Josef spotted his son and was upset when he lost him again in the milling crowds. But he was comforted when he realized he would be seen when his turn came to disembark on the gangway. Jane was anxiously looking for Teenie. It was almost impossible to single out one individual.

The disembarkation took such a long time, even after the long gangways were rolled out. Each class had its own gangway manned at the top by an officer with the passenger list in hand and as they slowly moved forward the passenger's names were ticked off and they were assisted on to the steeply sloping walkway. Maggie Ann and Jane watched the Cohens as they moved hesitantly down and heard the great shout of joy when they spotted their family waiting at the bottom. Such a glad reunion when they stepped on to the pier. But then the checking officer, who directed them to move along to the immigration hall, interrupted them and they passed out of sight into the long waiting queue.

Now it was their turn to pass through the check and move down the gangway to their new life. It passed through Maggie Ann's thoughts that it was like walking the plank to enter the new country. Once again they checked through and there was Teenie, standing behind the officer, waiting to escort them through immigration. When they entered the huge hall thronging with people it felt quite frightening and totally confusing, but officers guided them along into the correct line and instructed them to have passports ready with the immigration fee and all other important documents like letters of introduction from residents and their planned address in Boston. If there was any hitch they were thankful that Teenie was there waiting at the barrier. But after a long wait, all went well and they were through.

Knowing how exhausted with excitement and emotion they must feel, Teenie quickly ushered Maggie Ann and Jane out of the harbour area and along to the station to catch the train home to Jamaica Plain. Once they were seated they could relax and catch up on home news. It had been a long, very hard day. For Teenie also. She was a quiet person, not fond of crowds, and she had had the added dread that she might miss her visitors in the throngs of people. At last they came to 27 Sheridan Street and so began the new chapter in their lives.

Chapter 29

Teenie made them so welcome. Over the next few days while they waited for their trunks to arrive from the shipping line, Maggie Ann and Jane were subject to an amazing array of first impressions. There was the street of wooden houses, all-alike, with the veranda, or stoop as they learned to call it, before the front door. Some houses had been converted into two apartments, but Teenie's one was a whole house and their room was upstairs overlooking the street. Then there were the sounds of living in a wooden house with wooden floors and all the rooms linking without dividing walls; indeed the front door opened directly into the sitting room. This was much more communal living than they had ever known. And in the warm October evenings, when neighbours gathered on their porches to enjoy a leisure hour with the newspaper, they spoke across words of greeting to the strangers and made them feel welcome. There was a real sense of community.

Teenie had lived there for fifteen years and knew most of her neighbours very well. Over time she had watched them arrive, many from foreign countries, feeling strange, lost and lonely at first. And then, employment for the father, school for the children, a church fellowship and a domestic routine for the mother set in motion a stable way of life and the family settled. Teenie had been a good neighbour to them all, principally by just being there to encourage and lend a helping hand with wise understanding.

She too had arrived, a stranger, with her young husband John Stephen, and their first years had been successful enough for them both to find good employment and, eventually, to buy and furnish their own house. Sadly, they had no children, but their home became a gathering place for all new comers and they always felt they had many 'children'. The tragic blow came to Teenie one day when the police arrived to tell her that John had suffered a fatal accident at Reidville's car firm where he was an engineer. He had been in the path of a falling metal beam and died instantly. The crushing desolation and emptiness overwhelmed her at first and her immediate instinct was to take refuge in Scotland, at home with her own folk in Cairnbulg. But then she realized that all that she and John had planned and worked for lay here in the States; she must go on and make a life for herself and fulfil their dream. Here in Jamaica Plain he never seemed far away from her. Thus her home became a haven and a gathering place for all new arrivals. Her optimism and courage was an inspiration in their adjustment to this new life.

Chapter 30

Maggie Ann and Jane felt strangely at home in Boston. Perhaps it was the wide, grassy Common stretching away up to the skyline of the old houses on Beacon Hill and reaching out to the imposing, golden dome of the State House behind. To stand on Tremont Street and look across at the rising, green sward was as if they were back on Princes Street. Teenie escorted them for a day or two and then they explored on their own, anxious to get the feel of the city and to decide where to look for work.

They walked everywhere, to the harbour area, to the old historical part round the Faneuil Hall, and Copley Square with the beautiful new library and the old Trinity Church. They enjoyed the sense of history, the compactness of the city and how accessible it all was. After a day exploring they would catch the train back to Jamaica Plain to find Teenie's house full of visitors come to see the new arrivals. This suburb was a mecca for Scottish immigrants, particularly from the North East, and they were all anxious to hear news from home. Maggie Ann and Jane knew the families of quite a few of them from Broadsea and Cairnbulg and it was good to sit and chat in their own dialect and be nostalgic. Like Maggie Ann and Jane, some of the visitors were recent arrivals, settling in and looking for work, and they had all sorts of advice to give. But Maggie Ann and Jane had already decided that they would study the newspaper ads. and visit an employment agency in town. It was time to start work and face the fact of their possible separation.

Jane's work would be quite straight forward. Being a lady's maid was a universal role, but cooking in a strange country was another matter and Maggie Ann realized that she would require some tuition in basic American dishes and the terminology of the same. So Maggie Ann researched hotels and restaurants requiring assistant cooks while Jane concentrated on the Beacon Hill area and before many days they were settled in employment.

In a high, old, brown-stone house, just behind the brow of Boston Common, Jane found her family. It was the third vacancy for which she had applied and as she climbed the worn steps and pulled the decorated iron bell, she felt that this would be it. The pots of flowers on the steps and the bright window boxes, the shining brass knocker in a thistle head shape, and the sound of music coming up from the cellar windows spoke of cheer and happiness. Mrs. Kincaid herself was warm and bright and, as they sat opposite and talked, Jane sensed a strong affinity between them. The fact that she was a Scott and Edinburgh trained with excellent references really decided the matter. The Kincaids were second-generation immigrants from the Isle of Skye and held on fiercely to their heritage. They had prospered, John Kincaid becoming a respected lawyer in the Back Bay, and Mrs. Kincaid held posts on committees for welfare societies, entertained often, and required help with correspondence and management of her wardrobe. Once the appointment was decided the two relaxed and shared some information about their families and backgrounds. Jane felt a slight choking as she spoke of home and the village, but Edinburgh days were easy as she spoke with enthusiasm of Mrs. Stuart and their lives in that city. Mrs. Kincaid was entranced by the lilting Scots accent and thought she would keep Jane for that factor alone although the Gaelic would have been an added attraction.

So it was settled. As Mrs. Kincaid was without a maid at this moment, Jane would take up her appointment on the following Saturday and have the weekend to settle in to her new accommodation. Then she would have a chance to meet the family. Alastair and Hamish, the twins, were both law students at Harvard, preparing to enter the family business in due course. Mahri, married to a Presbyterian minister, Rev. Kenneth Macdonald, lived not far away in Lexington and frequently visited with her husband and small daughter Fiona, the apple of her grandmother's eyes. This was so reminiscent of the Stuart family in Edinburgh. Jane could hardly wait to tell the story to Maggie Ann and Teenie over tea that night.

Things did not work out so comfortably for Maggie Ann. Since Jamaica Plain was so far away from the centre of Boston she realized that restaurant work was out of the question. She required live in employment and that could only mean hotel life, which would not have been her first choice. But how else could she learn? A small family run hotel on Beacon Street required an assistant cook and Maggie Ann was engaged, but right from the start she had her doubts about it. It would be a beginning. However, once she settled in to her room, high up in the attic, and saw the view across the Charles River to the college buildings of the M.I.T.,and all the surrounding rich green recreation grounds of the students, Maggie Ann thought she could survive it for a while. As it turned out, the owner and staff were very friendly and, although they called her "The Scots lassie with the Scots tongue", she learned to laugh with them.

Chapter 31

As time went on Maggie Ann discovered quite a few new facets in her personality. For the first time in her life she found she was responsible for no one but herself. Yes, she thought often of her mother and sisters in Fraserburgh and regularly sent gifts of money, but they were no longer her immediate care. The disciplined training of Edinburgh, much as she had loved it, was over, and she had her diplomas as evidence of her success. Yes, she was responsible to her employer here, but this was different. Apart from her work, her time was her own. She could explore, shop, read, visit, attend concerts, study. It took Maggie Ann a little time to come into the full realization of this new freedom, but as the months passed she developed a poise and dignity, which was to remain with her for the rest of her life. She learned to value and appreciate so many things, which had been omitted from her early years.

Although never one to follow fashion, she studied the young women of Boston and eventually found the style she enjoyed wearing and took a careful pride in her neat turnout. The shock of her first summer in the city drove her to Filene's basement for the lightest cottons. The winter she found easier to contend with – more like Scotland, but longer lasting and more severe.

Mornings began early with the preparation of all the food for the lunch and dinner menus and it was hard work.

But, once lunchtime came, Maggie Ann was free till five o'clock and she always had a plan. Sometimes, if Jane had her afternoon off, they would walk on the rolling Common or by the river, explore the shops or visit the library on Copley Square. But the favourite was Quincy Market. Here the atmosphere and bustle was so exciting. They could sample new dishes and savour the delicious odours of the spices and herbs of the multitude of immigrant restaurateurs. The variety of languages and skin colours amazed them. From their memories of the fishing days they could recognize the Irish, English and Highland tongues, but there was so much more- all the world seemed to be in Boston. They would sit and analyse the food, trying to work out the ingredients and Maggie Ann had no hesitation in asking the waiter for information regarding a particular dish. Food was her main interest and over the months she acquired a great knowledge of methods of cooking and best ingredients. Once he realized her enthusiasm, Mr. Kunst, the head chef, encouraged her and involved her in all aspects of his repertoire of food. Maggie Ann, in return, initiated him into some of her own Scottish specialities such as Cullen Skink, Stovies, Haggis, and he was thrilled to add them to his menu.

She remained with her employers for two years and, by that time, was beginning to feel confident about seeking the employment she really desired. Maggie Ann needed to belong to someone, a family perhaps, in a good home where she could hold a position of some value; cook, housekeeper, a practical role. She was now nearing thirty years of age- nearly half her life gone- and a new century not far away. What would it hold for her? Time to settle.

Chapter 32

The trolley bus slowly made its way through the suburbs to the outskirts of Boston and Maggie Ann, sitting near the front, looked forward to a pleasant afternoon with Teenie and Jane too. Very often their days off coincided and Teenie's was always their home from home- full of brightness and warmth, and usually other lassies were there with all the "home" news. It would have been a perfect outing but for a slight niggle of worry which cast a little shadow over Maggie Ann's happiness.

That morning a letter had arrived from Betsy. It came as a surprise for Betsy seldom wrote, leaving these family contacts to Janet or Ena. But the letter was full of cheerful news of the family- Mary May was well, but not very pleased that Ena was walking out with George Noble. She did not think much of the Gundie (nickname) family. But then, no one would be good enough for her Ena. Baby Tom was quite a little boy now and loved his wee brother Willie. Janet had hoped for a little girl this time but it was another boy, a lovely baby with reddish hair like Sandy. Bella and Willie Taylor had settled down at 21 Charlotte Street and were both working hard to make a nice home. They had installed an inside toilet and built on a scullery at the back. Bella had great ideas and had Willie well in hand. Betsy thought it would be a long time before any babies would be there.

It was that last remark that worried Maggie Ann. Betsy made no comment about her own marriage with Alex, how they were developing their lives or their home. It was nearly four years since their marriage and still no children, but that did not really surprise Maggie Ann. From an early age she had recognized in Betsy a certain will of iron and a determination to have her own way. Coupled with her style and truly good looks, Betsy would insist on having everything right before she would have children. Maggie Ann just hoped they would not wait too long. She remembered the way they looked that last glimpse she had of them in the train at Aberdeen station. So happy together and such a handsome couple. Alex was the finest of men. She hoped Betsy appreciated the fact and did not keep him waiting too long.

So her thoughts ran on as the bus trundled out Center Street and, at last, she alighted to walk down the hill to Teenie's house on Sheridan Street. As expected, there was the usual gathering of visitors, all seated round the wide kitchen table, chatting and drinking tea.

"Come awa ben. I jist thocht ye wad be here the day. Jane's comen an a so we'll hae a gweed news."

Teenie's welcome was warm and she was so delighted with the short bread that Maggie Ann handed to her.

With Jane's arrival they all settled again to hear news from home and also to share their own activities with each other. One or two of the girls had been travelling with their employers; others enjoyed the social whirl as personal maids, moving in the world of high society; some even in the political and academic world; one or two enjoyed hotel work, but as she listened to their talk, Teenie could not help noticing how the different environments rubbed off on the girls' language and thought processes, how knowledgeable they had become, how confident and self assured . This pleased her immensely.

Maggie Ann, in her quiet way, was content to listen as the talk flowed, but when she heard a passing remark about a housekeeper vacancy near Boston, she was at once interested. One of the girls had heard it being discussed in the home of the lecturer where she was nanny and vouched that the information was true. A new Professor Ripley had come to the Massachusetts Institute of Technology and had settled in Newton Center with his family. They were looking for a housekeeper, but beyond that there were no more details. Maggie Ann noted the name and thought it may be just what she was looking for. After some enquiries she had all her details and set off early one evening to find the address.

Chapter 33

As she sat in the train heading west out of Boston, Maggie Ann felt a bit nervous and questioned her actions. Should she have written to make an appointment? What if no one was at home, or it was inconvenient to see her? Had she dressed properly? Maybe she should have waited for her day off and come in the afternoon. But she decided to follow her instincts and put these thoughts aside, and calmed herself. As they left the city behind she sat back to enjoy the spring scenery. She would follow out her plan and at least see where the family lived.

At Newton Center station Maggie Ann enquired of a porter where Bracebridge Road was situated and he pointed her in the right direction. At the end of her road she paused a little to enjoy the pleasure of what she was looking at. It rose in a gentle curve to the left, quite wide and not very well surfaced, the rain rivulets having left their ridges in the loose gravel. The sidewalks were very wide, extending into the verges. There were no fences or gates, but trees and bushes grew everywhere, fresh and green in their spring mantle and, as she climbed, Maggie Ann caught glimpses of large houses scattered without any seeming order or boundaries. How would she find No. 38? But as she followed the road round, there was a metal box on a post with the number painted on it, and Maggie Ann felt a moment of excitement. There it was.

True to her way, she stood and looked, allowing first impressions to take effect. It was a large, white timbered house, three storeys high with dormer windows in the top floor. A deep, pillared veranda sheltered the front door, and another, overhanging the cellar and basement doors, ran along the side of the house. It sat comfortably, surrounded by green lawns and tall, shading trees. A winding, crazy-paved pathway led between the lawns to the flight of stairs at the front door, which stood wide open behind the screen. Here and there under the trees bulbs were in bloom and shrubs in small beds were planted close to the house. One outstanding feature was the cream, stone built chimneystack, which climbed up the centre of the gable wall right to the top of the chimney. It gave the residence a solid, rocklike air and spoke of warmth and homeliness. Another path wound to the rear of the house and Maggie Ann decided that must be her route.

Having knocked at the door, she composed herself, checked her appearance in the glass door and waited. Soon a smiling maid appeared, looking rather surprised to find a visitor at the kitchen door, and at that early evening hour.

"Good evening?"

"Good evening. I have called to see Mrs. Ripley. I don't have an appointment, but I wonder if she would be available just now?"

"Please come in. I think she is saying goodnight to the children, but I'll tell her you are here."

Maggie Ann was shown into a small, back hall leading to the central area of the house and, looking around, she liked the feeling of a family; a doll lay in the basket, rocking chair and a small pair of boots stood by the wide stove, glimpsed through the open kitchen door. There was a good smell hanging in the air; freshly cooked food, roast beef maybe, and also an odour of baking. Soon she heard footsteps on the wooden floor and Mrs. Ripley appeared in the hallway.

Chapter 34

Many years later, when Ruth, the eldest of the children, asked Maggie Ann how they had come to meet, she smiled and answered in her simple, direct way,

"I was hunting for a position and as I had many Scottish friends who were working in Boston, I was advised of your mother who needed a housekeeper. I came out on the train from Boston one evening. Your Mother was preparing for a dinner party and when she was aware of my presence, she came out into the little back hallway to confer with me. I remember how beautiful she looked with her dark hair coiled back, and she wore a yellow, silk evening gown, which shone in the light. We took to each other at once and after inspecting the kitchen and all its equipment, especially the Fuller Brushes, I was quite captivated."

Their meeting that evening was the beginning of an association that was to have lasting and far- reaching results for many people.

In Mrs. Ripley, Maggie Ann saw a very beautiful woman of her own age; not tall, but dignified and very erect. She had a friendly, intelligent face and carried an air of quiet confidence and assurance of who she was. There was an ease in how she related to people and Maggie Ann responded to her directness. Here was the Mother of a real, young family and Maggie Ann felt she could share that task with her.

For her part, Mrs. Ripley liked what she saw in the quiet, navy clad figure standing before her. Not very tall, about her own height, but ramrod straight. She noted the immaculate white gloves, the shining toecaps peeping below the hem and the hair tightly drawn back into a bun under the small hat. The face, round with a slightly tight mouth above a firm chin, and a short straight nose, had a fresh, healthy complexion and told of experience and firmness. But the eyes spoke of honesty, patience, wisdom and candidness, which appealed very much to Mrs. Ripley. She knew she had found her housekeeper.

It was arranged that the following week on her free afternoon, Maggie Ann would return to Newton Center to meet the children and the rest of the staff. Professor Ripley was away, but would be home by then. It would also give her on opportunity to see over the house and something of what the position entailed. That evening Maggie Ann travelled back to Boston with a deep sense of thankfulness and a peace within. Whatever lay ahead, she felt she had been preparing for it all these years and was ready now to meet the challenge. To be involved in the life of a family her own age presented an exciting future- who knew where it would lead? She must write Jane and Teenie.

Chapter 35

The closely shaven lawn sloped away down to disappear under the thick, green foliage of the trees in full leaf. All around, the house was wrapped in greenery- dark evergreens mingled with the broad-leaved, lighter varieties-giving that blessed shade, so welcome in these sweltering July days. Through the trees the neighbouring Burnham's house could just be glimpsed. Maggie enjoyed what she saw.

She was having a quiet time, sitting by her upstairs window and reflecting on the new life that had become hers. She had just waved goodbye to Mrs. Ripley and the children with their nursemaid, Anna. They were on their way to spend a few weeks with Grandma Davis and to escape the summer heat of the city. Andrew, the coachman, was driving them to the station and it would be some time before he returned. The previous week Professor Ripley had departed on a tour of Europe to research more of his subject, Sociology and the European Races. So now the household would just be Emma the maid, Andrew the steady Scot like herself and Maggie, the housekeeper in charge. It still startled her to think of the trust and responsibility that had been given to her. In the previous four months of familiarising and adjusting there had been little time to sit and reflect, but this moment was here and she could indulge herself.

The two children were delightful, and so well managed by their Nanny, Anna, an immigrant from Sweden. Ruth was almost five and already able to have quite an interesting conversation with elders. She could read and bore quite a proprietary attitude towards her baby brother Davis. He was just one year old, such a happy, contented child and both children were well adjusted and obedient. When the question of her name came up, Maggie Ann told Mrs. Ripley the story of Emily in Edinburgh and how the children had chosen the name Maggie for simplicity. So Maggie she had become, and to every one. Seldom was she called Miss Duthie.

Professor Ripley was a charming man. Just a few years older than Maggie, he was young to hold the role of Professor, and to be so widely known and respected for his teaching and publications. His research often sent him travelling to Europe and then closeted him for hours every day in his study. But then he would emerge to romp with the children, garden hard with Andrew, play golf, which he loved, or hammer at some construction he was creating in the basement- a very practical man as well as an academic. He was a large, courteous gentleman, handsome in a craggy sort of way, who treated all as his friends, regardless of background or status in life. Maggie liked him. The house seemed to vibrate when he was at home.

Maggie had never met anyone like Mrs. Ripley. She was the rare combination of quiet elegance, beauty, intelligence and adventure. She was wonderful with the children, but was clearly an adult's person and loved nothing better than engaging in lively conversation with guests round the dinner table. She spent hours with newspapers every day, keeping up with current affairs and she had a real concern for the work conditions of women and children in the factories. Although she had a medical degree, Mrs. Ripley had never practised as a doctor, but had built up a huge bank of knowledge about Women's Suffrage and Rights. Now knowing a bit about Maggie's background, she frequently asked about life for the working classes in Scotland. It was a revelation to learn that the problem of poverty and hardship for women was world wide and insidious as prosperity increased. America's problems had developed with immigration and the growth of industry, but Europe's problems were ancient, arising from a class-ridden society and an accepted oppression of the poor.

Maggie enjoyed these occasional discussions, pleased to have found someone who cared enough to tackle the subject, and it made her role as housekeeper all the more worth while. Mrs. Ripley's interests clearly lay in humanitarian and social work areas, and if Maggie could relieve her of some of the load of domesticity, then she felt that was her contribution to the task. It also left Maggie with a greater freedom to put into practice all that she had learned from Chrissie Macleod in Great King Street. How often in the past months she had blessed that disciplined training.

Now that the house was empty, she planned to clean throughout, check linen, china and silver and go through the store cupboards to see where replenishments were necessary. The wood floors could be done last after the chair covers and furniture were freshened up. Yes, Maggie had her plan of action set up, just waiting till Andrew returned. They would have a cup of tea then set to work.

It was an easy house to manage. Having only recently moved to Boston, the young family had not yet accumulated the usual clutter. In fact the bedrooms were quite sparsely furnished with the simple necessities. But the sitting rooms were very comfortable. The staff one, overlooking a small veranda, led off the back hall and this room was their own domain, fully equipped with comfortable chairs and a cosy fireplace for winter; a restful room when tired feet called for a footstool.

Maggie had always been an early riser, something she had learned from Mary May and her years in the gutting yard and in domestic service. She was at her best in the early mornings and now, as housekeeper, she considered it right that she should be up first to cast a quick glance over the rooms and breakfast table before Emma and the family stirred. But if truth were told, Maggie treasured these quiet moments of solitude as her own special time of the day. Now she was in command of herself, her thoughts, her memories, reaching out to her family. When she opened the front door and stepped out on to the stoop, she leaned on the railing and drew in great breaths of the morning air. The scene always pleasured and satisfied her senses. If only her mother and sisters could have shared in the beauty that surrounded her.

The early morning dew made a carpet of silver on the lawns and glistened like gems on the dripping trees. Where it clung to the spiders' webs in the eaves, varied patterns formed, not two alike. Bird song was everywhere, birds, which Maggie had never known existed; squirrels scurried about up and down the branches making a great fuss, and very occasionally, a shy, little chipmunk would pause on a flat stone, resting motionless for a few moments before hurrying off again in its searching. She could smell the strong, earthy scent of the damp soil, mingled with the perfume of the flowers below and the piny evergreens. Soon the hot sun would absorb it all but for now, nature was being refreshed.

So it was with Maggie. Always a very private person, she did not often reveal her thoughts about God and her faith, but these morning moments were her times of communion when she remembered all those closest to her, so far away. Now she had this new family calling for her loyalty, wisdom and service and she prayed that she might fulfil all that was required of her. Lastly, she gave thanks for where God had taken her over the years. God had been very good.

As she stepped back into the house Maggie always paused in the doorway to enjoy the scene. On the right the sitting room stretched the whole depth of the house, the farthest end with its large table providing a handy family dining room. The front area was dominated by the huge, stone built fireplace surrounded by brightly covered, easy chairs and sofas calling on one to relax. Colourful rugs were scattered over the polished wood floors, and mementos of travel and family portraits were mounted here and there, particularly on the piano and the mantelpiece. Books were every where- in two tall bookcases against the walls on either side of the fire place- but also on occasional tables alongside the chairs. Large, log baskets, always replenished by Andrew, flanked the hearth and the brass fire irons gleamed. Flowers filled the opening in summer but, in fall and winter, the warmth of the fire and the wood burning, resinous odour pervaded the whole house. Windows in the three outer walls allowed the sun to shine in for most of the day, enhancing the brightness of the colours and the gleam of the polish. It was a used, family room, the hub of the house and a welcoming place for all who crossed the threshold.

The formal dining room for special occasions was situated to the left of the main doorway and, beyond that, the house stretched away to a library study for the Professor, a study for Mrs. Ripley and Maggie's own sitting room. In the centre of the house, straight ahead of the entrance and appearing to rise out of the sitting room, was a wide, open, oak staircase leading to the upper floor. A broad, surrounding gallery gave access to the main bedrooms and the two nurseries at the far end. The whole plan gave an impression of space and light, which never ceased to thrill and amaze Maggie. This was her home too. And as the weeks went by she was growing more and more conscious of how she was becoming a major part of this family's life. It gave her a glad feeling of belonging.

Andrew had returned. It was time to cease her reverie and start work.

Chapter 36

The months sped past and Maggie had been a year with the Ripley family. Much had happened in that time. The home had settled into a smoothly organized routine which suited all and made life comfortable. On Monday mornings she had her short planning session with Mrs. Ripley when they discussed menus and arrangements for any dinner parties during the week. They also talked over household issues and best shopping sources. It was really a matter of exploring as both women were strangers to the area. Maggie favoured the markets till she found her way around the best retailers. Being a thrifty Scot, she was anxious to find the best value for the money she had been granted as a weekly, housekeeping allowance. Not that money was scarce. The Ripleys were well to do, but they did not live a lavish life style. Generous hospitality was high on their list, and they were convinced of the need to invest in education and social welfare for all. As a result, many interesting people frequented the house; some from the Professor's academic circle and others from the welfare committees of which Mrs. Ripley was a member. As Maggie came and went to the dining room with the various courses, she could not help but absorb some of the conversation and it gave her much food for thought. Somehow, she could not imagine a similar discussion going on round Mrs. Stuart's table in Great King Street. Yes, that lady did her good deeds, but, in retrospect, it seemed to be a patronising sort of generosity to help the poor with a Christmas party. Very much a class distinction affair. But here there seemed to be an absence of class division and a real desire to help the down trodden, especially women, to organise themselves into some sort of active movement. To be in service in Britain was to be in a subservient position, but in the States a servant was regarded as an essential part of the household and was respected and valued as such. At least in the Ripley home it was so. The team worked very well.

Maggie kept meticulous household accounts and once a month, met with the Professor in the library to go over the details. He appreciated her exactness and, being an economist by profession, he was interested in her views on cost of living and where in the home one could make savings. Maggie was a great believer in home producing. Why buy when one could make it from pure ingredients at much less than half the cost?

"I think you need to expand on this a bit more Maggie. I find this most interesting. I have never followed this line of thought. In the country's economics yes, but not in the home."

"I would like to show you something Sir, if you have time to come with me to the basement."

So, together they descended the stairs and took pleasure in switching on the newly installed electric light. The farthest and coolest end of the large area had been partitioned off forming a separate room, fully shelved.

"This area was not being used except for discarded furniture and rubbish so Andrew helped me clear it out. Then he built the wall across and we whitewashed it all before he shelved it. Perhaps we should have consulted you beforehand Sir, but it did not interfere with the workshop or the carriage area."

"Maggie, it was an excellent idea to clear it out. I am just so curious to see what is in here."

Professor Ripley was silent as he went from shelf to shelf reading the labels all neatly named and dated. One side contained sealed jars of marmalades and jams of all varieties; then came the chutneys, squashes and sauces, bottled fruit and tomatoes; finally smaller jars of fish. On the third wall were small bottles of mixtures for cleaning-vinegar and lemon, various salts, borax and crystals, and in a wooden box underneath the bench lay long bars of household soap.

"Maggie when did you do all this and where did you learn how to do it? This is amazing."

Maggie gave a little smile; gratified that Professor Ripley was pleased.

"I learned thrift early from my mother. She had little to feed five of us. But my greatest teacher was Miss Macleod who I worked with in Edinburgh. She was a wonderful housekeeper and taught me the skills of bottling and vacuum preserving. You set up with the proper jars and equipment and then follow the year through; buy when the fruit and vegetables are in season and cheap, and follow the process. Mrs. Ripley gave me permission to purchase the jars from the housekeeping money and they will last for many years. By next year most of this will be used up but the jars will be refilled in season. This is something I believe in. Why pay others to do things you are capable of doing yourself?"

Maggie was suddenly silent, embarrassed that she had said too much. But she need not have worried. The

Professor continued to survey the shelves then, looking down into her face,

"Maggie, I can simply say Thank you for the many skills and for the order and harmony you have brought to our home. You have my blessing on all that you do."

Chapter 37

The news from Fraserburgh continued to be good. This last letter was from Ena, her first since her marriage to George Noble, and she was still full of the joy of her new status and the wonderful qualities of her husband. They had found their first home in a house on Broadsea Road at the corner just opposite Mary May and Ena was glad to be so near her mother to keep an eye on her. They shared the house with Polly Noble, an old friend of Mary May and their nearness went a good way to consoling her mother when Ena and George had run off to get married in Aberdeen. An unheard of deed. Mary May was shocked.

A few months ago Betsy and Alex had adopted a baby girl. This child had been born out of wedlock to one of Alex's relatives and they decided to give the baby a real home since there was no sign of any family for them. She was called Jane and was the most beautiful baby, just like a doll. Betsy just adored her. But Mary May did not approve of the adoption.

"Na, na. Tacken on ither foulks' problems like 'at can lead tae sair hairts in later days."

Ena wondered if her mother may be right as Janet had a strong suspicion that Betsy was now expecting. What would happen if it was true?

The others of the family were fine. The fishings were keeping up well which meant that all the men folk were very busy and prosperous. The town was growing out to the westward and new roads were opening up. There was a new infant school near the sawmill on Windmill Street, now called Albert Street after Prince Albert. Big changes since Maggie Ann went away.

Maggie always felt a little down after a letter from home. She had a concern for Betsy and Alex, wondering if they had been rash, but time would tell. She was glad it had worked out for Ena and George and Mary May. Some day she would take a trip back to Broadsea to see them all, but not yet. Too much was happening here where she was needed.

The new century came in with some celebration and people became accustomed to the new dating. Maggie, by now, was well established in her work and could honestly say she was happy and content. She had a deep admiration and respect for Professor and Mrs. Ripley. The contact she had with them in their home seemed to satisfy her own innate desire for learning and gave stimulus to her thinking and interests. Mary May's early teaching on behaviour and self control was now bearing fruit and Maggie was developing into a calm, dignified and very capable housekeeper with a widening range of interests.

Along with Jane, she had become a member of the Scottish Charitable Association and attended the meetings regularly. She admired the work they carried out among the poor and especially among the unfortunate, Scottish immigrants who arrived without such help as Jane and she had experienced. Of course there were the annual events like Burns' Night, and Scottish plays, and programs with readings from famous Scottish authors such as Burns,

Scott, James Hogg and George Macdonald. She loved the story of Sir Gibbie. These readings sent her back to the library to find the books for herself and her reading list expanded widely into both British and American authors. She never felt too old for Louisa M Alcott and the March family and, although her days were busy, Maggie always found time to do some reading before going to sleep.

Another source of inspiration was watching Mrs. Ripley sharing books with Ruth and Davis, young though he was. The three would snuggle up on the sofa, one on each side, and Mrs. Ripley would read, Ruth listening intently and Davis pointing to the pictures as the story unfolded. Aesop's Fables was a favourite and Davis loved the animal pictures. These children would never know a world without books, which made Maggie ponder and recall her own hunger for learning in the early days when she frequented Trail's Book Shop library to borrow books at a penny a time. Yet, they did have family times round the table with Mary May reading the Bible stories. They were very well versed in these. Wealth was not the only factor in a privileged home; to grow up in an atmosphere where truth, humanity and knowledge were valued was a far greater inheritance.

Chapter 38

The year 1901 brought some exciting changes to the Ripley family. After six years as Professor of Sociology at the Massachusetts Institute of Technology, Professor Ripley began his career at Harvard University, which eventually led to his appointment as Professor of Political Economy. In the fast growing prosperity of the early twentieth century his interest in economics and sociology directed the Professor to play an active role in improving labour standards and transportation. He became a recognised authority on railway and shipping economics and produced publications on many allied subjects. To belong to the staff of America's oldest university and to mingle with the intellectuals of such an elite body, gave the Professor great satisfaction and he entered his new role with energy and enthusiasm. His new sphere of work brought a further circle of colleagues and friends, some of whom he held valued for the rest of his life. This brought many new faces to the dining table and lively conversation, even argument, ranged over many topics. The household, enjoying some of the reflected glory, was very proud of their Professor.

That same year, Mrs. Ripley confided to Maggie that another baby was on the way and, in due course, William arrived. He was born at home without complication and from the start was known as Billy. Within a few days Mrs. Ripley was up and going about her affairs and Billy was installed in the safe hands of Anna. Although disappointed that he was not the much-desired sister, Ruth soon adopted the role of assistant nanny and undertook the care of Davis. The two were often seen together playing in the garden or on the stairs with a book. Because of the age gap, Ruth had quite a motherly manner towards her young brothers and treated them like a little grown up. She was a thoughtful child with a very definite artistic talent and Maggie found her a very satisfying companion when she wandered into the kitchen and sat down at the table to talk. Now that she had started elementary school she had much to chat about and Maggie was always there to listen.

Another letter, from Janet this time, brought news that the longed for baby had arrived for Betsy and Alex. It was a little girl, very dark haired and the image of her father. Alex was totally thrilled with her. She was called Mary Bella after Mary May, and Bella because Alex had a great liking for his sister in law. Betsy had her hands full now with two babies under a year. It was a good thing the children were so different. Jane was still the pretty one and so dainty, but time would tell how Mary Bella would turn out. Mary May was delighted with her first grand daughter, as she insisted on calling the new baby.

Once Billy was settled into his routine of feeding and sleeping and the new nursery maid, Emma, had proved a satisfactory assistant to Anna, Mrs. Ripley began again to pick up the threads of her political and social work. Committee meetings resumed in the dining room and Maggie had always to see that the cigarette box was replenished as many of the ladies, including Mrs. Ripley, smoked. Indeed, when she brought in the tea trolley, Maggie was rather repulsed by the haze of smoke and the unpleasant atmosphere. Smoking was a fashion of the day and very popular, but Maggie did not like the residual effect on curtains and upholstery. She had the windows open as soon as possible and burned scented candles.

Mrs. Ripley came and went. Sometimes it was to a factory to observe women's work conditions; other occasions it was to attend a demonstration for Women's Suffrage; child labour was a deep concern, and reform in women's prisons was her life long work. Over the years Mrs. Ripley's energy never allowed her to turn away from the needs of workingwomen and she always had some cause in hand. Often, research on the subject took her abroad, sometimes in a group, but often on her own. She had great courage and was very unconventional in travelling alone, which she enjoyed immensely, and did not consider that she was outré in her actions.

The three children grew up with the knowledge that mother disappeared occasionally and they accepted it as a way of life. When she was home they loved the fun she brought, the book readings, the play in the garden and the planting of the beds. Mrs. Ripley loved gardening and encouraged all three to enjoy it too. And then when she went away, there was always Maggie to love them and Anna to read and play with them. Professor Ripley played his part too but, like every young man in a new position of responsibility, he found little time for anything other than work or research. He too was often abroad on research missions and sometimes these coincided with Mrs. Ripley's journeys so that Maggie was left in sole charge of the family and home.

As they grew older and their sense of awareness developed, the children would sometimes voice their discontent.

"Why do Mamma and Papa have to go away so much? Why can they not be like other parents and stay at home with us?"

This from Ruth, usually the spokesperson.

Then Maggie would have to gently explain,

"Your mother and father are very special people with important work to do and that is what takes them so far away to Europe. Some day you will know more about it and probably sail away with them too, but now we have to stay here and work hard and wait. That is how we can best help them. And isn't it always wonderful when we get everything ready for them and they arrive home? Now I think we should have a look in the atlas and see where the last post card came from. That will bring them closer."

And so Maggie soothed the moment of ruffled feathers, but she could see that she would have to make Mrs. Ripley aware of the children's reactions.

Chapter 39

The question of summer vacation had been under discussion for some time

The annual month with Grandma Davis was proving difficult. She was becoming too old for the upheaval. Professor and Mrs. Ripley were coming to realize that the children required a definite period when they could be together as a real family. So, following the recommendations of some of his colleagues, Professor Ripley came up with the suggestion that they should rent a house in Maine and all move there for three months, June to September. There they would have the sea, fresh air and be totally away from work, meetings and travelling, and just be a family. The long university vacation would allow the time, and most organizations and committees ran a looser schedule during the hot months, which would enable both parents to adopt the plan.

Towards the end of May, Professor and Mrs. Ripley along with a very happy and proud Ruth, set off on the long journey to Maine. They were responding to the longstanding, warm invitation of the Macdougalls to visit them. Mr. Macdougall was a close colleague at Harvard and Maine had been the family second home since they had inherited the house near East Edgecomb on the Damariscotta River. The plan was for Professor and Mrs. Ripley to stay a week in order to find a house to rent for the summer months and to explore the possibilities of purchasing something suitable for a more permanent base.

Finding a house large enough to accommodate the whole household was not easy, but by the end of the week and with the aid of their friends and the local estate office, a house was found quite near East Edgecomb and not too far from the river and the little fishing town of Boothby. To reach there would mean train, ferry, river, steamboat and finally cart travel, but the rewards were great and the Professor felt it was the complete answer to the vacation problem. At least it was worth a trial.

That week was like a dream for Ruth. The first time away on her own with both parents, and on such a journey, to such a wonderful place. The little girl was transported. She never forgot that first trip to Maine, which was to colour her life in all the years ahead.

"Maggie, it was so wonderful. We were right at the sea and I wanted to step into it but Papa said it would be too cold just now. The river Damariscotta is so wide we could hardly see the other side. And Maggie, the woods! The trees were everywhere and so huge. And I never saw so many birds, all colours and the sound they made! Papa took me for a walk very early one morning and we listened. They were everywhere, flying around with moss and anything for nest building in their mouths; or food for their babies. Maggie it was amazing. I can't wait to get back to see it all.

"Maggie have you ever seen fishing boats landing lobsters and clams and all the other shell fish? Well, we actually stood on the pier so near the boats we could have touched them and we saw the lobsters alive crawling around in the baskets. It was so busy with horses and carts and the smells! I used to like clam chowder but I'm not so sure any more."

Maggie enjoyed her excitement and did not try to answer the child's questions, even if she had been given the opportunity. It was enough to listen and enjoy her enthusiasm and to remember the familiar harbour scenes from her own childhood. Now she was seeing them through the eyes of a city child and was enjoying the thrill of discovery.

"And Maggie, we are all going together. You and Anna and all of us. It will be so wonderful!"

Maggie said nothing, disregarding the child's remark, but when Mrs. Ripley sat down with her for a heart to heart, Maggie had already given the matter much thought and was ready with her suggestions and her plan of action. She needed to know about kitchen facilities and utensils, as far as Mrs. Ripley could describe for her, and about supply sources for food. How much would they need to transport from home and how was it all to travel?

"Maggie, we shall take the minimum of everything-food, clothing and whatever else. This is a trial experience and if we run short, we shall just buy what we need. It's a great adventure- a holiday for us all and we will help each other to share the work."

Maggie was not too sure about the last few statements. It conflicted with her natural taste for order. So, during the next three weeks, she quietly packed a few boxes with favourites from her store cupboard, one or two of her essential cooking pans and some cleaning materials. These boxes were stacked along with the valises, baskets of books and toys, golf clubs and fishing rods, and made quite an array in the hallway. Professor Ripley arranged for the luggage to be collected on the Friday and then on the last

Saturday in June they all set off at 7am. for Andrew to drive them to the North Station in Boston.

Davis and Billy were fully mobile by now and it took all Anna's and their parents' attention to keep them under control on that long journey. It was all so new. The throngs of people in the stations and the noise and rushing of the trains as they sped along crossing bridges over huge rivers, running along by the sea and then through the dark forests. Now and again Maggie produced little mystery parcels, which became a guessing game and usually revealed something nice to eat. Occasionally the train stopped long enough for everyone to get off to have a little walk along the platform before the whistle blew again. Portland was one of these. But at last the train drew in to Newcastle and the next stage of the adventure began.

The little group stood with other crowding passengers anxiously watching their luggage being stacked on to the waiting wagons which would convey them across town to the steamer, scheduled to take them down river to East Edgecomb This was the Damariscotta River making the last stretch of its journey to the sea, widening out as it did so and leaving little bays and islets all along the way. By now children and adults were happy just to sit quietly on deck watching the passing glimpses of villages and homesteads until they reached East Edgecomb and Poole's landing. As the steamer edged nearer to the wooden pier hawsers were thrown and the ship was drawn slowly closer till a thud told them they were attached. The smell of the seaweed clinging to the old wooden piles of the landing stage and the crust of barnacles, layer upon layer, clinging to the ancient timbers touched Maggie with a sense of coming home. All around were banks of tall pine trees, right down to the water's edge in places, and, winding away from the jetty, was the road leading to the cluster of village which was East Edgecomb.

While Professor Ripley supervised the luggage the other adults, with a child each, negotiated the steep gangplank and landed thankfully. There, meeting them with a warm welcome, were the Macdougals and nearby stood a cart waiting to transport them to their holiday home. Once the luggage was loaded they all piled in and set off at the horse's slow pace winding along the riverside road till he turned off into a sloping drive way. They had arrived and there was the holiday house, standing clear of the backdrop of pines and looking away down over the meadows to the Damariscotta. A beautiful setting.

Everything about that first summer in Maine was a marvellous adventure. The Professor taught the children to swim and, dressed in the simplest clothes, they rambled and picnicked everywhere. The multitude of birds fascinated them so bird books were bought to study their names and habits, Meal times were erratic and Maggie found herself cooking the simplest of meals that could be prepared well in advance and eaten al fresco. Every day the sun seemed to shine hot and always the soft, cooling, sea breeze filtered up river to bring comfort and freshness. The house was spacious and accommodated them all comfortably, and at the end of another good day they would gather in the large living room or on the stoop to play a game or listen to Mrs. Ripley reading aloud from one of their favourite books. Maggie with her knitting, Anna in the rocking chair with a sleepy Billy on her knee, the Professor in the deep basket chair, long legs stretched out, relaxing, and Ruth and Davis on the steps watching the dusk falling and counting the fire flies as they darted over the gardens.

Day by day the children appeared rosier and more confident and the adults felt restored and ready for the busyness awaiting them back in Boston. It was a perfect time. The first of the many annual vacations in Maine. In fact the sojourn in Maine became the focal point of the year. Christmas in Newton Centre and summer in Maine was how the children thought.

Maggie Duthie with Betty Ripley (Child) 1914

Chapter 40

In her life with the Ripleys Maggie's greatest asset was probably her organizational skills. From childhood, as the oldest of six children, and living in such cramped accommodation with scant means of survival, she had learned to manage time and resources to the best advantage. Even in Edinburgh, to cope with work and study, time had been at a premium. So now, here, in this busy household, it was inevitable that a large burden of care and responsibility fell on Maggie's shoulders and once again she had to rely on her talent for managing. In her quiet, dignified way she proceeded from challenge to challenge, never showing signs of panic or anxiety.

Her slightly austere expression could have given the impression of an aloof attitude but Maggie was far from cold and distant. It was just that life had taught her that she must be in control of herself and must weigh and evaluate before making choices or decisions. Underneath burned a kind and loving heart, full of compassion and care, especially for her own relatives in Scotland and now, here in Boston, for this little family which was becoming day by day more precious to her.

It was always a great source of happiness for Maggie that the Professor and Mrs. Ripley were near her own age and thus she could appreciate the children almost as another parent. So, once again, when Mrs. Ripley confided that another baby was due in a few months' time, Maggie looked forward with anticipation. After five years with the household, she felt at ease and relaxed in her role and could now really welcome this baby's arrival, especially if it was a girl, the long awaited sister for Ruth.

On the day of the birth, when Mrs. Ripley retired to her room and the midwife arrived, everyone went into a state of waiting. After supper the little boys were put to bed but Ruth, now ten, was allowed to stay up, and waited with her father in the sitting room, pretending to read but listening to every move. Once breakfast was laid and next day's preparations completed, Maggie, knitting in hand, sat down also. She had been through this situation so often in her youth. Her role had always been to keep the other children out of the way till they heard the first cry. Now, this time it was different and she had the freedom to indulge in her own feeling of excitement about this new child.

At last there was a thin wail and Professor Ripley bounded from his chair and rushed upstairs to the bedroom. Ruth sat on the stairs gripping her knees and Maggie joined her to put a comforting arm around her shoulders. It seemed such a long time. But then the Professor appeared at the top of the stairs, carrying a little shawl wrapped bundle and his face was alight with emotion and joy.

"Ruth, here is Bettina, your very little sister." And sitting down beside her, he placed the baby in Ruth's arms. For a long moment she studied the baby, touching the fair downy hair and the soft skin of her cheek and when the little fingers curled round her own finger she breathed,

"Papa, she is so beautiful and so tiny, and I just love her."

Then it was Maggie's turn to hold the baby. When she felt the little body between her hands and drew the child close, Maggie experienced such a surge of emotion welling up inside her. It was Ena's birth all over again, but this time it was a moment of shere joy and exultation. Here was her own special child, free from the hardship of want and poverty, a child she would love and devote her life to as long as she could. As she handed the baby back to the Professor he could read in her face the deep experience she had felt and he was glad for his little girl that she had such a guardian.

Mrs. Ripley recovered well and soon returned to being mother at home and carer in the wider world. The baby, known to all as Betty, thrived and her ready smiles and happy nature brought sunshine to the whole household. Nanny found her an easy child to handle and the boys, Davis and Billy, took delight in making her laugh and giggle when they pulled faces or pushed her fast in her baby carriage round the garden. Ruth, being older, found a different relationship with Betty. It would be some years before they would be friends and companions, but meantime Ruth just wanted to love and cherish this lovely little person. She passed many hours sitting watching the baby and quietly telling her stories. It did not matter that Betty did not understand, as long as her eyes followed Ruth and she appeared happy listening to the voice and gripping Ruth's finger.

As Betty grew older and the other children were at school, Maggie was her most frequent companion. She loved to be involved and followed Maggie wherever she went- holding up the pegs for the washing; manoeuvring the basement stairs to the store room; sitting in a high chair at the kitchen table mixing dough with a wooden spoon. Maggie had infinite patience with her and considered all these activities were good for Betty's progress. But the greatest joy for Maggie was just having the child there and sharing in her pleasure.

Toad Hall, East Edgecombe, Maine

Chapter 41

Every year in June the pilgrimage to Maine took place and always the conversation revolved around finding 'our house'. This debate had continued for some years but now, with the developing family and an enlarged household of ten people, the rented house could not comfortably accommodate them all. So much equipment had to be hired in Boothby whereas, if they had their own house, bicycles, boats, fishing gear, books and all sorts of needful equipment, even clothes, could be left from year to year and the journey would be so much easier. They could have two homes set up. It made sense. This time they would not allow the holiday activities to overrule their purpose and they *would* find that house, hopefully in the East Edgecomb area, which they had all come to know and love so much.

As it turned out, it was accomplished more easily than expected. On the first day of their holiday Professor and Mrs. Ripley visited the land agent, Mr. Hamor, whom they had come to know well over the years. He greeted them with a broad smile as they shook hands.

"Good to see you again. I heard you had arrived. How are you both? I'm glad you called right away. I think I have something you may be interested in."

Finding it hard to contain their excitement, Professor and Mrs. Ripley settled themselves to listen.

"This house has just come on the market and it looks rather an attractive purchase- just what you are looking for I think. It is within walking distance of East Edgecomb and stands back from the river on higher ground. The views are wonderful. Access from the road is by a curving driveway and a good stand of elm and pine trees on that side preserves the privacy. I have been out once to see the property and I was very impressed.

"The house has belonged to one family over many years, but now the younger generation has scattered and the last resident found it too large to maintain for herself. It appears to me that the original house has been extended at some point in time, giving it an unusual shape, but the Deeds would be able to clarify all these details. Do you wish to research it further with me?"

Without hesitation the answer was,

"Yes," and an afternoon visit was arranged for that very day.

It was an unusual building, not the traditional Maine house with pointed gables, but, noting the washing lines and the kitchen entry, they realized it was the back of the house they were seeing. An unusual, wide archway, leading from back to front, hollowed out one end of the house and gave access to the kitchen areas and to an inside stairway.

When they passed through the arch to explore the other side nothing prepared them for the scene, which met their eyes. Sloping away from the house a beautifully kept lawn stretched down to a long, curving garden, bright with lupins, hollyhocks and pink mallows, sheltering against a rustic, dry, stone wall. A gate, flanked by two tall, poplar trees, led down a few steps into a wild flower meadow, a sea of blue and yellow, and there the land fell away and away to the distant river glimpsed between small plantations of trees. Far to the left grew a more dense forest, providing shelter and endless interest to the nature lover. Drawn forward to the gate, they stood, silently drinking in the beauty and the wonderful sense of space. Then they turned to look at the house. It stood long and rambling, two storeys high, with an ivy covered porch over the main entrance, and a further trellised extension at the end provided an upper floor veranda. It seemed to have been waiting there a very long time and looked very comfortable against the sheltering trees, almost saying,

"Come and live in me. You will be happy here."

"Let's go inside Bill," Mrs. Ripley whispered, quite moved by the loveliness of the place.

And it was just as they hoped it would be. Large public rooms led off the main, central hall, which was the spine of the house and upstairs the bedrooms followed the same plan. There was comfortably room for all, family and staff, each in their own areas, and that archway would accommodate a great deal of equipment. Throughout the empty house there was an atmosphere of loving care; the wooden floors and walls glowed and the scent of beeswax and flowers lingered there.

"Bill, we must have it. It's perfect. Don't you think?"

The Professor nodded in agreement.

"Yes, it looks pretty good. I think we should think about it tonight and then bring the children and Maggie to see it tomorrow, if that is convenient for you Mr. Hamor?"

Next afternoon, a very tightly packed trap followed the River Road. The whole family was there, including Maggie with Betty and excitement was high. Although Mrs. Ripley tried to calm them down, already the conversation was about 'our house' and, when at last they reached the bottom of the drive and the Professor dismounted with the children to ease the pony's load, they ran on ahead and their shouts of delight filled the air. The elders smiled at each other. This was confirmation.

The rest of the afternoon was spent in exploring. First the surroundings, which appeared even more beautiful than on the previous day, and then the interior, when Ruth and the two boys decided which would be 'their rooms'. The Professor went off with Mr. Hamor to examine the heating plant and any necessary repairs while Mrs. Ripley wandered from room to room visualizing furnishings needed to keep this a simple home for a simple lifestyle.

Maggie departed to the kitchen and storerooms and was very gratified to find a good wood-burning stove, which provided a hot water supply and gave ample cooking surface for her pans. The adjacent stores were cool with stone shelves running round the walls and there was a cellar, dark and cold even in the height of summer. Here she could lay away preserves from year to year and save a great deal of transporting goods. Maggie also delighted in the fact that the kitchen opened straight on to the archway and on to the grass where there was an inviting bench against the wall and the washing lines were so handy. She could see days of sitting there in the sun, shelling peas and preparing vegetables. Yes, Maggie approved of the house, especially the layout, where the domestic end was quite separate from the family living area.

So at last, they had their summer home. After a month of preparation, cleaning and repairs, and wonderful pleasure in going round sales rooms looking for the bare necessities, they left the rented accommodation and moved in.

At first it was quite Spartan but, week by week, they added what was needed for the remaining vacation, knowing they would be fully equipped next summer.

Too soon September came again and they had to say goodbye to their new home. As they pulled away from the landing at East Edgecomb and sailed up river to Newcastle, they knew they would be coming back to their own place, 'Ripley's Place', and they began counting the months.

Chapter 42

In the Ripley home one of the favourite evening pastimes was reading aloud with the family. The love of books was fostered from a very early age and story telling went on even before the children were old enough to understand. Mrs. Ripley in particular, taught the children to treasure books and to handle them with care, firmly believing that the mind and memory were enriched and so developed as the imagination was stimulated. As a result, many characters such as Peter Rabbit, Jo's Boys, Tom Sawyer with Huck, and Freckles, became old friends and in their play, the children often adopted the character roles. The animal stories of Aesop, Beatrix Potter and Uncle Remus were greatly valued. Mrs. Ripley believed the talking animals portrayed human values, good and bad, and thus were much more readily understood by the children than by instruction from adults. Children related to animals, had fun with them loved them, imitated them and grew to understand and value the environment in which they all lived. When Mrs. Ripley obtained a copy of the Wind In the Willows, a new book by a Scottish author, Kenneth Grahame, it became a firm favourite. Individually the animals had strong characters and provided great laughter and endless discussion on why they should be so headstrong, reckless, wise, respected, patient- all different, and yet all relying on each other for support and guidance. A good reflection on human nature. As they talked it through, Ruth voiced her thoughts,

"You know, we have a river for Mr. Rat, a meadow for Mr. Mole and a forest for Mr. Badger, but we have nothing for Mr. Toad. Now Papa is always telling people about his wonderful house in Maine, just like Mr. Toad, so why could we not call our house Toad Hall?"

And so, with unanimous agreement, the house was renamed Toad Hall and over the years became a place of welcome, hospitality and retreat for all who wished to come there.

Maggie was not so sure she approved of the name taken from a children's book. She seldom used it, thinking something more dignified, more in keeping with the other mansions in the area, would have been suitable. But Toad Hall it remained, a home loved by all.

Chapter 43

The ensuing years for Maggie were busy, full of interest and totally fulfilling. The winter months in Newton Centre were quiet and settled, the children busy with study and the parents with their various academic and social work ploys. Maggie kept the house running on an even keel, always there to listen and to give a wise word of encouragement, and, as she followed their studies, Maggie too was learning in fields of knowledge she had never met.

The children were growing up healthy and strong and, as she watched them develop their individual characters, she took pleasure in knowing she had played such a vital role in their well-being. They were all different. Ruth, so much older, had a propriatorial attitude to her younger siblings and, with her very real artistic ability, sometimes retreated into her own teenage world. Davis was quiet and thoughtful for others while Billy was active and practical like his father, always doing things. Betty at that point was a bundle of joy, making her presence felt wherever she went and filling the old house with happy laughter.

Thanksgiving, Christmas and the occasional dinner party were the winter highlights at Newton Centre; wonderful family events, when Maggie and her team of Emma, Anna, who had joined them when Betty was born, and Andrew rose to the occasion and excelled themselves. When the deep, Boston winter turned the landscape into a wonderland and the lawns became smooth slopes of white, and when the branches of the evergreen trees, draped in snow and frost, almost touched the ground, then it was time for skating and toboggan parties. Maggie prepared the baskets of hot coffee and sandwiches for Andrew to load in the trap. She enjoyed seeing them off with their friends, indulging in good healthy sport and when they returned, rosy and happily tired, there was always a bowl of hot soup waiting.

The months at East Edgecomb were very different. From the moment they stepped off the steamer at Poole's landing there was an immense sense of freedom. Young and old felt it. Immediately, when they set foot on firm ground, too impatient to wait for the adults, the children were speeding off on their own following the well trodden river path to home. Meanwhile, the adults saw to loading the wagon with all the supplies from Boston and they followed by road at a more sedate pace. It was the same every year- an immense impatience to be there, to get settled in and to start this wonderful time of 'being in Maine' and all the pleasures and adventures that entailed.

Will Poole was always waiting for them, fires on and the house aired, and within a few hours Maggie had unpacked the necessities and a simple meal was on the table. Then they could settle in, wander at will round the old house and garden, smell the piny air, or just sit and look into the distance. The friends would soon come about the house, but the first day was for the family.

Hospitality being a strong characteristic of this family, it was not long before the guest list was extensive. Relatives came and went regularly and some came for the whole summer. Mr.and Mrs. Philip Marden, cousins of Professor Ripley were such. At times accommodation became an issue until the Professor put his design skills to work and, with the help of Will Poole and some local builders, the Cabin was built in the grounds of Toad Hall. Over the years it proved its worth when the children brought friends from school and college, and relatives and colleagues joined the family.

Many local friends visited Toad Hall on a regular basis; Saturday night picnics followed by folk songs and Sunday night hymn singing round the piano were favourite times, drawing neighbours such as Professor Walter Hall, the Macdougals, the Neilsons and many others from both sides of River Road. Feeding large groups became normal for Maggie. She seldom had to cater for just the family but, with the help of Annie and Hannah and good planning, she somehow managed.

In addition, as the berries ripened in the woods and in the garden, Maggie filled her preserving jars with jams and chutneys. Will Poole brought her fresh cod from Boothbay harbour and she filleted and dried them on frames just as her mother had done. This was the basis for her fish pies and potato mash back in Newton Centre. Occasionally Maggie set up her smoke box to prepare smoked haddock for Cullen Skink and other tasty Scottish dishes. The family relished Maggie's cooking and when Davis and Billy brought friends to Toad Hall, Maggie's pantry was always a Mecca for their taste buds and the boys surreptitiously helped themselves to the cookies.

Chapter 44

Maggie's life was full and satisfying and very much in America. The twelve years had passed almost unnoticed and she had remained healthy and strong, enabling her to handle whatever responsibilities were presented to her. She wrote regularly to her mother, sending her financial support, but it was only when the very occasional letter arrived from Scotland that Maggie experienced the old longings to see them all again.

The year was now 1912 and certain pivotal events were happening in Fraserburgh, which gave Maggie cause for serious thought. Mary May was now over sixty and growing frail so she had moved to live permanently with Ena. She and George had built a house at the top of Charlotte Street and now had more room for Granny. Betsy's husband, after years of success, had to give up the sea because of illness and was now emigrating to Florida, wisely or not. The sisters were all well and happy with their families and Maggie realized that there was a whole generation of nieces and nephews she had never seen.

It looked as if this was the time for a return visit to Scotland and Maggie decided to approach Mrs. Ripley to discuss the matter. She would go in the fall when they returned from East Edgecomb and the children were settled into school. If she went next October, then she would be back in time for Thanksgiving and Christmas. So ran

Maggie's thoughts and planning until the day the telegram arrived and her life took on a completely new focus. Now there was no question of what she must do. Betsy needed her and she must go to her. What could have happened in Florida?

"Alex died . ret. Fr. Arr. NY. Gran. Cent. 18/10/12. 20.15hrs."

Professor Ripley offered to accompany her to New York but no, she would manage the journey alone and be able, with a few days' leave, to be with Betsy and the children until the boat sailed for Scotland. It was going to be a heartbreaking reunion, but Maggie was glad she was here in the States. She would be the first of the family that Betsy had to face in her terrible grief. She would stay calm and practical where possible. The four children would need helping and probably, taking care of them allowing her to rest, would be the best help for Betsy. Maggie pondered what lay ahead as she sat through her train journey to New York.

Chapter 45

Grand Central was magnificent and awesome in its grandeur. As ever it was crowded, but Maggie was in good time for the arrival of the train from Jacksonville. It was easy to single out the tall, beautiful, pale woman in black, accompanied by the four children, one a baby in arms. Maggie quietly approached Betsy, lifted the little boy out of her arms and, tucking her hand into Betsy's elbow, gave it a squeeze as she smiled at the three sad looking older children.

"I've got a taxi waiting for us and an address of a hotel if you don't have one Betsy?"

"That was a' organised for us and I hae it here. The ship sails on the 21st. so we hae two days in New York. Can ye bide that lang Maggie Ann?"

"As long as you need me. Now let's get settled in and then we can talk."

The hotel was plain but comfortable and they had two adjoining rooms, the children in one with a cot for Norman, and Maggie and Betsy in the other. It was obvious that Betsy was drained and exhausted so, after supper, Maggie sent her off to bed and went in with the children to put Norman to sleep in his cot. The older children concerned Maggie. Jane, small and dainty and thirteen years old, talked constantly and fussed about this and that concerning her clothing, always calling for her mother's attention. Even in their short acquaintance Maggie could see a problem there. On the other hand, Mary Bella was like a person in shock. She was a tall, slim, dark haired girl, very like her father as Maggie remembered him, and her only concern at the moment seemed to be to relieve her mother of the care of Norman and to look after the others. Alex was ten and, like Mary Bella, resembled his father. He too seemed to be shocked into a profound sadness, which made him silent and downcast. Maggie could feel their lostness and, as they prepared for bed, she quietly talked about New York and her plan for the next day. They were too tired to really take in what she was saying but the calming effect of her voice and her presence reassured them and allowed them to relax and to fall asleep at last.

Maggie sat a long time just watching the sleeping children and wondering about them. Jane, even in sleep, had a peevish droop to her mouth, and the other three so resembled Alex, even baby Norman. Strange how none of Betsy's children resembled her- maybe that would change as they grew older. Mary Bella interested Maggie especially. The thick mass of black hair framing her face spread out on the pillow and the brow was high and intelligent. Faint scatterings of freckles covered her whole face and neck and were not unattractive on the pink cheeks of the sleeping child. Her nose was slightly on the long side and the mouth and chin were firm, showing resolve. There was character imprinted here and Maggie felt an affinity for Mary Bella, believing she would grow into an interesting woman. Time would prove her potential, but now they all needed love and care and Maggie lowered the light and slipped through to the still sleeping Betsy. Her sleep that night was fitful and shallow, constantly aware of the children in the next room and of the bereft sister lying beside her. Dawn was breaking when Betsy began to speak softly and Maggie heard the story of the past four weeks.

It was a normal day. Alex went off to work about 7am. when it was still cool. He walked to the bus stop to travel across town to the carpenter's yard, which he shared with Billy Noble, his brother in law. He enjoyed the work and had invested much in the business, which was growing. That day Alex never arrived for work and he did not return home at night. Alex was missing for three days and then the police arrived with news. He had been found dead of a heart attack on the street with no identification on his clothing and the police could not trace him. Eventually they discovered his Masonic fob on his watch chain and traced him through his Lodge. From then on the Masons had taken over the funeral, had made and paid for their travel arrangements back to Fraserburgh, and notified the family in Fraserburgh about the situation.

"I couldna hae deen it masel. We had nae money. Alex had put it a' intae Billy's firm an' they were partners. But the business couldna spare ony money an' I was gled o' the offer fae the Masons. Alex' sister Jessie and Billy were very kind, but I couldna bide there; I jist needed ma ain foulk an' I'll mak a new life for the bairns an' me in the Broch. We should niver hae gone tae Florida. We realized that fan it was ower late. It broke ma hert tae leave him there, but there wis naething mair I could dae. He had a bonny funeral. He was weel likeit an' got tae ken lots o' foulk through the business, but at the end he wis all alain an' that's how I mind on him, alain in his grave without me an' the bairns."

In the long silence that followed Maggie could feel Betsy's release as her body relaxed and she fell into a deep sleep.

But Maggie lay and sorrowed for her sister, remembering the terrible loneliness and hurt after the loss of a loved one. She doubted that Betsy would ever talk to her again on the subject of Alex. Betsy was strong willed and proud and, once back in Fraserburgh, Maggie was sure, Betsy would find her way, but it would be hard for a while when the children were still young. The greatest solace for her would be the support of her mother and sisters.

Everyone woke refreshed and hungry and, during breakfast, Maggie outlined for them what she had planned for their day. They just had the one as tomorrow would be taken up with the great ship and sailing away. The excitement in the children's eyes was wonderful to see and Maggie enjoyed being in total charge of the arrangements. This was to be a special day they would all remember. When he understood the circumstances, the hotel manager had been more than helpful and met with all Maggie's requests so that when they assembled in the reception area, a folding pushchair awaited Norman and a horse drawn open carriage was ready for them at the front door. Waved off by the smiling doorman, they drove away into the spring sunshine with such happiness. Betsy and Maggie smiled to each other seeing those delighted faces.

They had the carriage till midday and as the hotel location was in central Manhattan, they had not far to go to reach the river where they could see the East River docks along South Street. Following round to the Hudson, Maggie explained that they were on an island between the two rivers and they were in the centre of New York. Across the wide expanse of water they could see the Statue of Liberty and Maggie told them its story. The good-natured cabby drove slowly from Broadway into Fifth Avenue, pointing out the huge shops and buildings and mentioning the famous people connected with them, like Rockerfeller. As they progressed slowly up the Avenue the children laughed and chatted with each other and waved to pedestrians who waved and cheered back. It was wonderful to see them so carefree.

At last they arrived at the entrance to Central Park where they saw other carriages drawn up waiting for customers. However, their cabby did not stop but continued through the wrought iron gates and, setting the horses to a light trot, he took them on a circuit of part of the huge park, slowing every now and then to draw their attention to a special place or statue or tree; there was so much to take in.

At a signal from Maggie, the cabby finally drew in to a small café and it was time to leave their carriage and say goodbye to their driver. Maggie paid and thanked him for his kindness and they shook hands all round before he drove off, returning their waves and smiling over his shoulder.

Round the table the happy chatter continued as they enjoyed sandwiches and doughnuts along with coffee and milk. And then they were off again, Norman smiling, esconced in his pushchair, and the older children taking turns to push him. They would have rushed on ahead but Maggie explained that in a park this size with so many branching paths, it was easy to become lost so they must stay in sight. They paid heed to that and Betsy and Maggie at a steady pace, kept an eye on them. The exercise did them all good- they would sleep well tonight.

Once outside the Park, the group negotiated the busy afternoon traffic and reached 7th. Avenue. Very much subdued by the rushing throng of people and firmly holding on to each other, they at last reached the subway station. They descended the darkening stairway, Maggie helping Betsy with the pushchair, and waited on the gloomy platform. This was such a thrill; riding on a train underground. Maggie had experienced it many times in Boston but, for the others, it was wonderful, fearful and exciting all at once. When they eventually reached their destination and emerged into the daylight, it was to find themselves quite near the hotel and they set off walking once again. All were hungry and Norman needed his afternoon sleep; in fact they were all tired so it was good to arrive 'home'. No sooner had they settled than afternoon tea arrived and the trolley was wheeled into Betsy's room. The children's eyes were wide as they looked at the laden trolley and then at Maggie,

"Yes, it's all for us, but you must start with the scones and sandwiches on the bottom tier before you move up to the cakes. There is tea for your mother and me, but you can have milk or some of this lemonade if you wish."

It was a long leisurely meal. The children relaxed and endlessly discussed what they had seen, what they had liked best, the cabby, the horses, the people--. Betsy and Maggie were quite quiet as they listened, each with her own thoughts; Maggie thankful that the day had been the success she had hoped for, and Betsy, that today she had caught a glimpse of the joy that she could still have in her children in the days ahead. She was so grateful to Maggie for having the wisdom and forethought to plan it all and to be so caring. Today could have been so different.

After dinner when the children were all asleep, worn out but happy, Betsy and Maggie sat and talked for a long time, mainly about Mary May and the sisters. It was only six months since Betsy had left Fraserburgh so her news was fairly recent and she confirmed Maggie's fears for her mother. Mary May was growing old too soon, but after the hard life she had sustained, it was not surprising. Ena cared for her very well but it was not easy with Mary May's determined natured and strong will. They had had to hide her creel to prevent her going off into the countryside on her fish round. The story of Ena and George's elopement was the talk of Broadsea but they seemed very happy. Janet and Sandy were just the same- very contented and hard working. Sandy was doing well in the cooperage and, of course, the arrival of Netta, the precious daughter after two boys and a long wait; that was perfect. Bella and Willie were very well off with a home in Hartlepool where Willie had a good job in the shipyards. They came to Fraserburgh every summer with the two girls, Chrissie and Maisie, and spent a whole month in their house on Charlotte Street. The house, No. 21, was normally let but Bella kept three rooms for their own use at holiday time.

As she listened to it all, Maggie realized that her treasured image of the cosy, little family in Broadsea Road would have to change. These days were past, gone forever, a precious memory. Time and life had scattered them all and now a new generation had arrived. It excited Maggie to think of it; at the same time, facing this new scene, she felt a touch of apprehension. Seventeen years had wrought many changes.

As the Scotia would sail with the tide in late afternoon, boarding was scheduled from eleven o'clock onwards. Betsy, Maggie and the children joined the queue at the second-class gangway in good time, relieved to have arrived intact with their hand luggage. Norman was restless, always tugging at his reins, but they did not have to wait long as the column gradually moved along and upwards. The great Cunnarder towered above, immense and gleaming and there was an air of excitement all around. The children debated, would they have a cabin for themselves like last time or would they be all in together? As Maggie listened she thought,

"How children adapt. How much in the present they live!"

As they were checked through the boarding officer's list, Maggie was welcomed as a visitor, and they mounted the long gangway to be met at the top by a young sailor who escorted them below to their cabin. They were all in together with four berths. There followed a short dispute about who was to have the two upper bunks but Betsy soon settled that. She and Norman would have the two lower beds and the other three would take turns on the top. Whoever had the lower berth would share with Norman. Maggie was impressed with Betsy's firm handling and the children's obedience. They *would* make it together through the next few weeks and months.

For a few hours they explored the 2nd.class facilities and decks, had a light lunch in the dining area and, from the rail, watched the passengers still arriving. Maggie remembered her own long ago departure from Glasgow. Here today, there was no sign of the poverty-stricken, steerage class families she had seen leaving Scotland.

Eventually, the announcement came for visitors to leave the ship and it was time to say goodbye. Not wishing to prolong the parting, Maggie gave each child a warm hug then turned to Betsy, who gripped Maggie in a close embrace,

"Maggie Ann, I'll niver forget whit ye hae deen for us these twa days. Ye hae geen us back oor strength an' noo we can gang aheed. God bless ye."

Maggie found it hard to speak but just gripped Betsy long and hard,

"I'll be with you soon in the Broch." she whispered, and turned away.

It was nearly an hour before the great ship sailed, but Maggie waited on the quay along with hundreds of others. They waved to each other until the liner swung round into the sea channel and they were lost to view. Maggie, very tired and emotionally spent, turned to find a taxi to the railway station.

Chapter 46

Glad to be back in Newton Centre after her New York journey, Maggie took up the reins of the household again. The warmth of her welcome home gladdened her heart and did much to soothe the melancholy that remained with her. But she was troubled and felt the old load of responsibility that had burdened her teenage years in Broadsea. She knew she should not feel this way as all her sisters but Betsy, were now comfortably married with husbands to look after them and Mary May was safe with Ena. It was Betsy's four children that caused her deep concern. Baby Norman would never remember his father but the grief of the three older children was so evident, especially in the case of Mary Bella and Alex. She would long remember these sad, lost faces as they came off the train in New York. Betsy was strong and would remake her life in Fraserburgh, but Maggie wondered about the children; what lay ahead of them? Somehow, she must find a way to assist in shaping their futures.

A long conversation with Mrs. Ripley did much to strengthen her resolve. For Maggie, her employer had also become her friend and mentor and both women had a deep respect for the other's views and opinions. Maggie knew that Mrs. Ripley would understand the depth of her concern and as she related the events of the days in New York, Mrs. Ripley listened and silently sympathised.

"Maggie, you did well. Struck the right note to relieve their sadness. But you are right. It is time for you to go back to your own family. And soon."

"I thought it might be best to wait till April and I would be back in time for Maine. The children will still be in school and I would return here in plenty time to prepare for the holiday. If I could have the month of April that would be quite sufficient. Between now and then Betsy would have had time to get settled and her children would be back in school again. Meantime I could book my passage. I shall have to discuss my financial state with the Professor. He sees to all my affairs. Thank you Mrs. Ripley for being so understanding."

"Maggie, it is we who have been remiss and very selfish. We should have sent you home to visit your family long before this, but we just came to need you so much in our own family circle. You do know that you are part of our family? Yes by all means have the month of April. It's a good time to travel, in the spring.

The matter decided, Maggie felt much more energised and set about giving the house a most thorough cleaning. She would be absent from it for virtually five weeks and she wished to leave everything pristine and in order. Store cupboards and larders were reviewed and lists of contents revised, and Anna was strictly tutored in keeping accounts and records. It resembled a military operation, but Maggie found this a balm for her anxieties. She was excited about the trip, but quietly dreaded the parting from her children. Nothing was to be said until the end of the Easter holiday and then Maggie would go at the beginning of April, sailing from Boston to Glasgow on the SS. Caledonia. Ocean travel featured so largely these days. The tragedy of the sinking of the Titanic had made travellers acutely aware of the hazards of sea travel in the spring. Hopefully, there would be no icebergs next April.

Part 2
Betsy 1895-1916

Chapter 1

The closing years of the nineteenth century were exciting times for Fraserburgh, particularly so for the fishing community. It was a boom time. Huge shoals of herring moved round the coasts, bringing the fleets of sail boats from far and near. These were followed by teams of fish workers who in turn required accommodation and supplies. Shipbuilding increased dramatically and even the smallest coastal village, if it possessed a jetty, had its own fleet of `zullus' and `fifies', small boats catching the in shore fish. Ships following the fishings used the larger harbours as ports and anchorages and this gave rise to accommodation problems. Dramatic extensions for Fraserburgh harbour, involving great expense, were debated, opposed, argued and eventually decided on, and new basins were created. But a new difficulty arose with the building of steam- powered drifters, which required greater depth of water and the great debate went on for some time before deep-water basins were provided. Dry dock facilities and repair areas were other major issues and as the new century opened there was already competition between larger ports such as Buckle, Fraserburgh and Peterhead, each vying with the other for improving port facilities and the revenue it created.

It was into this scene that Betsy and Alex began their married life. It was a happy marriage; their love for each other was evident to all and Mary May was very pleased with the character and qualities of her son-in-law. Alex was a thoughtful and courteous man, quiet, but with firm views and principles. He had a real ambition to make a good future for himself and Betsy and for their family in the years ahead.

Alex was the eldest of seven children, four sisters and two very much younger brothers, so he was his father's right hand man. They worked well together and young Alex, under his father's tuition, studied and attained his skipper's certificate at an early age. Also in the crew was John Masson, Alex's cousin, and the two young men were very close friends, like brothers. They shared a similar ambition and knew that some day they would launch out on their own and together, build the most up to date herring boat in the fleet. In all the debates and discussions going on in the 1890s the two young men played a very active role and were respected for their wise suggestions and common sense outlook regarding the harbour developments and the future prosperity of the town. When Betsy and Alex were married John was their best man and, although his home was in Cairnbulg, all through their married years he played a large part in their family life.

Betsy got on well with her in-laws and became very close to Alex's sisters Helen (Nellie) and Jessie who were near her own age; Nellie in particular as she had a keen sense of humour which Betsy, a fun loving person herself, could relate to. There was always laughter when the two were together and Alex enjoyed listening to and watching the two girls. Betsy found the free, easy life style of Alex's family so different to her own upbringing under the stern eye of Mary May. She blossomed and her personality expanded into the joyful, generous, outgoing young woman whom friends and neighbours could call upon for help at any time. Betsy was popular.

In the early years of their marriage she worked hard with Alex. Building up resources for the purchase of his own boat was their main ambition and Betsy never missed a fishing, going as a gutter or packer, from the Shetlands all the way down the East coast to Lowestoft or Yarmouth. When the fishing was centred at Fraserburgh they lived in their own home but, wherever it moved, Alex would rent a room so they could live as a couple whenever the irregular hours of herring landings made it possible. These were their harvest years. They knew it could not continue when the babies arrived, but now was their time to work together and save.

With all the huge building operations going on at the harbour Shore Street was becoming a very unpleasant and unhealthy place to live. Several families moved away and Betsy also began to contemplate a move. Their present home was so convenient to the harbour but she did long for sink and toilet conveniences of their own. Eventually, they found a three roomed upper flat to rent at 51 School Street. It had three apartments, a small scullery, a toilet, and they were completely selfcontained. It felt such luxury to climb their outside, stone staircase, go in and close the door of their own home. After decorating, and furnishing a little more extravagantly than previously, they took up the work routine again. The third room became their net and gear store and there Betsy mended the torn nets ready to change over for the next fishing. It was a good life. Janet and her family lived just round the corner in Charlotte Street, and Mary May in Broadsea was less than five minutes away. Ena and Bella, soon to marry Willie Taylor, were still with Mary May and when they were not travelling with the fishings,

the sisters were often together sharing news and supporting Mary May. She was beginning to find her country fish
round a little long and her creel a little too heavy. The girls
encouraged her to stop the country itinerary and deal with
the fish at home but her reply was always,

"Na. They fermen foulk hae been gweed tae me an' a
canna lat them doon. A'll gang on a wee fylie yet, maybe
till next winter draws in."

But she did not stop, promising to do so after Bella's
wedding was past and there was just Ena and herself to
provide for.

Chapter 2

The first three years of marriage had been so happy and satisfying. Betsy and Alex made a good team and their prosperity showed the results of their labour. They had total confidence in each other, Alex admiring Betsy's skills in the home and her willingness to toil with her share of the fishing work. For her part, Betsy was proud of Alex for the position of respect he held amongst his fellow seamen. His quiet manner and wise counsel encouraged people to listen to him, as she herself did. He was probably the only person in her life that Betsy did not try to dominate for she had a very strong will and did not receive advice willingly. There was harmony in their home but there was also a shadow.

Usually by this time after nearly four years of marriage, most couples had one, even two children, but Betsy was childless and it hurt to see Janet with her two boys. She was too proud to discuss the matter, even with Alex, but she did wonder if anything was wrong. One afternoon while they were walking on the Braes, Mary May brought up the question,

"Betsy, is onything wrang wi ye? Ye seem sae dooncast. Hae ye onything on yir mind? Are ye weel eneuch?"

It was a relief to open up to her Mother.

"A'm worried we winna hae ony bairns. We hae been merried near fower years noo an nae sign. Alex an' me, we are fine thegither but naething comes o' it."

"A thocht it wis somethin' like 'at." Mary May paused a moment.

"Ye see, maist couples get merried an a' the wife thinks aboot is her man, her hame and haen bairns, bit ye wisna like 'at. Ye wanted the comforts an' the share i' the boat first, an' fan a'thing wis recht ye wid hae the bairns. Bit it disna aye work lik 'at. Fyles it's ower late an the early keenness is gone. Jist hae patience. Tell Alex foo ye feel aboot it a', an stop worryin'."

But Betsy was not consoled, even when she spoke to Alex about it. He laughed and gave her a warm hug saying,

"We need a holiday. We'll gang up the Firth tae Lossie an' hae a wee fylie there afore the Sheetlan' fishing. An' ye must stop a' this hard work for a fyle. We'll get somebody in tae help wi the nets an there'll be nae guttin' at Sheetlan' or Yarmouth this year. Ye can jist come an' look efter me!" He added with his warm smile as he rested his hand on her shoulder.

However, that did not take place. Betsy had another idea, which she pursued headlong, taking no one's advice of caution, not even Alex's. She wanted a child so badly and she knew where to get one.

Alex's distant cousin Bella in Cairnbulg was pregnant and having her child out of wedlock. It was a sad situation as no one wanted the baby, the Mother was too young and the family could not tolerate the disgrace. The baby would be put in a children's home if no one could be found to adopt it. This was Betsy's solution. They would adopt the baby. That would keep it in the family, it would be loved and Bella and her family would know that the baby was safely cared for.

When she broached the subject to Alex he sat silent for a long time, turning over the suggestion in his mind. He knew Betsy and how impetuous she was. He also realized how much a child would mean to her; he could see the longing in her face. And, being a man of compassion and strong Christian principles, he saw this child as a human being whom they could help by giving it a good home and a loving upbringing. But, he had reservations. It was a huge decision to make and it would greatly change their lives, especially Betsy's.

"Ye've thocht this through Betsy? Ye ken yir life wid be changed vastly? And foo div ye ken the baby wid be a' recht fan it's born? If ye commit tae adopt ye hae te tak it good or bad. Wid it nae be better te had aff a bit langer, maybe anither year, an see fit happens?"

But Betsy shook her head.

"Alex, we couldna hae a real hame withoot bairns an' if we did wyte an' adopt later it wad be a stranger an' we wad ken naething aboot its background. This baby is pairt o' yir faimly an' we ken a' aboot it. I jist think it wis meant for us."

Alex was not so sure but he did suggest that Betsy should discuss the question of adoption with Mary May and listen to her opinion from her wider knowledge. Betsy was not too happy about this. She was fairly sure she knew what her Mother's thoughts would be, and she was right.

"Na,na. Hae naething tae dee wi adoption. Ye maun jist wyte, you an' Alex an' ye *wull* hae yir ain bairns yet. Taaken on somebody else's mistaks is nae the road tae gang. Bad bleed wull oot. The years aheed' ll prove 'at. Jist you hae patience an' wyte for yir ain bairnies."

However, in the end, Alex and Betsy decided they would take the baby if the Mother, Bella agreed and Betsy began quietly to prepare. She and Alex visited the family in Cairnbulg and put their offer of parenthood to Bella who was relieved above every other emotion. Free of the baby, she could leave Cairnbulg and make a new start somewhere else where people did not know her, all the happier knowing the baby was in good hands and would be cherished. There were tears of relief and gratitude from the parents. The baby would be born in August and, until then, Betsy and Alex insisted on silence. No one was to know of the plan, especially in Cairnbulg where rumour ran like wildfire, and Betsy and Alex would not come again until the day after the birth when they would collect the baby. After that, adoption moves would proceed.

So they went home to wait. Betsy quietly sewed and knitted and, to her family, looked much more relaxed and happy. The Shetland fishing took them north in April and then they sailed home again for the east coast fishing in June. Great catches of herring were landed and every aspect of town life benefited. Betsy gutted when called on and Alex fished and then at the end of the Fraserburgh fishing they worked together mending the nets in preparation for Yarmouth. For the first time since marriage Alex would go south on his own and live in the boat with the crew. Already changes were happening to them.

Late one afternoon at the beginning of August a young lad arrived at their door to hand in a letter. This was the long awaited message and Betsy, in her excitement could hardly open it.

"Baby arrived safely. Bonny little girl; six and a half pounds. Will expect you tomorrow."

Now that the baby was here the dream for Betsy had become a reality and she could hardly contain her impatience. The fact that it was not her own child did not worry her; the longing to hold the baby in her arms and hug it close to herself was overwhelming. That was a very long night for Betsy. Alex too was affected. He had very mixed feelings about the adoption. He felt guilt that he had not Betsy's enthusiasm and could not support her wholeheartedly. Also as a Christian, he felt he was falling short in having these reservations about opening his heart to the child. At the same time he had a curious sense of excitement as they sat in the Cairnbulg train the next morning. Betsy had her basket of baby clothes and shawl and a plaid to wrap the baby for she was very young to make such a journey. For the young mother's sake it was imperative that the transfer was quick so, shortly after they reached Cairnbulg, they were back in the train complete with their baby. Legal arrangements would be made once the baby was settled, and the adoption process would begin. Her name was to be Jane May.

True to their mutual agreement of silence, none of the families on either side knew of the baby's presence so Betsy and Alex decided to invite the Mothers to be the first to see the baby. After that, the sisters could be visited and they would meet their new niece then. Betsy knew this was going to be a delicate matter, for illegitimacy was very much frowned upon and, as far as she knew, neither family had ever experienced such a situation before.

Once they were sat down and settled to chat Betsy told them her news and then proceded to bring forward the cradle with the sleeping child. After the initial, shocked silence both Mothers shook their heads in disbelief.

"She's a bonny bairn bit I hope ye ken fit ye are tacken on Betsy. Div ye ken a' aboot her foulk an' far she cam fae? It's an afa big step ye are tacken an ye are still sae young. Ye cud hae yir ain faimly yet lass."

This from Mary Masson, Alex's Mother. As she spoke, the deep concern showed **on** her face.

"Ye ken fit I think aboot a' this. A'm surprised Alex lat ye dae it. Ye are in far ower big a hurry. I jist hope ye dinna rue the day ye took her in. Fit's in wull oot. Bit it's on yir ain shooders an' time'll tell."

Mary May shook her head and, after a quick glance into the cradle, she gathered her shawl about her and made for the door, intent on going home. She would not linger for a cup of tea but set off down the stairs and Betsy could imagine her going to Janet's to relieve her feelings. Over the tea cups Betsy allayed her Mother-in-law's fears about Jane's pedigree and they agreed that, for everyone's sake, it should be kept private.

So the news was broken and, in time, everyone saw the baby and gradually accepted her presence. She was the most beautiful child, small and dainty with a perfect baby face and a mop of dark hair, which curled as it grew in. Betsy adored her and there was not a more perfect baby outfit and perambulator in Fraserburgh than her one. She spent hours over the baby and, once Alex had sailed away with the fleet to Yarmouth, Betsy made the baby her sole interest day and night, never allowing her to cry. Betsy was in her element- this was her world now and she felt so happy and complete.

Her new role changed her. Instead of being the boisterious, rather domineering young woman, her gentler side emerged, making her more patient and considerate for others. Watching her handling the baby with such love left one in no doubt that Betsy had matured and blossomed with motherhood. When Alex returned in late November he found a new Betsy, one that he liked even more than previously; still fun loving and beautiful, but oh so much softer and more relaxed. He fell in love with his wife all over again. It was a wonderful reunion, to be together again. Alex was now satisfied that the coming of the baby into their world had been a good thing for them and he felt glad that his earlier misgivings had been proved wrong. Seeing Betsy's devotion to the baby, he could now look on Jane as his own. There was great joy as they looked forward as a family to the New Year celebrations.

Chapter 3

Before then there was much to be done. The usual presents from Yarmouth had to be sorted and distributed and Alex, being the only fisherman in Betsy's family, had remembered them all, along with his own. The barrels of apples and grapes and the boxes of rock and chocolate were shared all round and Betsy was delighted with her sealskin jacket. After a short few days, Alex and the crew were back in the boat 'redding' the nets, spreading them to dry on the Links behind the beach, and then scrubbing the boat end to end before touching up any paint work. This was the time of year for the boat's once-over and any repairs had to be completed before the next fishing on the west coast at the end of January.

Betsy also had her part to play. Alex's straw filled mattress had to be renewed, and the mended nets waiting in the store had to be made ready for the barking yard before the boat set sail again. The dried nets from the Links were gathered and brought into the store ready for Betsy's winter work. And then there was Alex's kist to prepare; to cover the possible weeks away, six changes of heavy winter underclothing and a 'go ashore' suit for Sundays, as many socks, long and short, and woolen jerseys, wherever she could push them in. The knitting needles had never been idle while Alex was away and Betsy had always a stock of newly knits to draw from. It was the way of the fisherman's wife. As she packed these personal things and laid in his Bible and writing paper, and the favourite liquorice allsorts, Betsy could not help shedding a tear that Alex was going away again without her beside him. Perhaps, when the weather was better and Jane was a little older, they could accompany him to Shetland. Last of all to be packed were the two large slabs of rich dark fruitcake, four dozen soda scones and two deep tins of oatcakes, all freshly baked in the last few days.

The west coast fishing out of Mallaig, Ullapool and Stornoway was hard and dangerous. The herrings were plump and plentiful but the winds and seas were treacherous and harsh. Not willing to risk these hazards, some fishermen kept their boats in Fraserburgh and sailed daily to supply the white fish market, but this was not as profitable as the herring fishing on the west coast. Aberdeen had taken on the monopoly of the white fish market. Alex's father was keen to harvest the rich herring pickings and so the crew agreed, knowing they would all be home again before the spring and the annual migration to Shetland. There was a certain relationship between the men of the crew. Several of them had sailed together for many seasons and knew each other well. When one faces such harsh, natural elements there has to be an understanding and complete trust in each other, and that was the case in the Hopeful. When a new crewmember was signed on he was usually a son or nephew of the crew and that gave more cause for care and concern. The Hopeful was recognized as a 'good' boat and the crewmembers were highly respected for their personal qualities and their seamanship.

The families were all down on the point of the north breakwater to wave them off and, as the Hopeful rounded the Golden Horn and disappeared from sight into the full flowing sea, each mother and wife offered a silent prayer for their well being and safe return. For as often as their men folk sailed away, the parting was never any easier for the women left behind. They knew what a fickle and unpredict- able mistress the sea could be and, as they walked away along the pier and round the harbour heading for home, they made a quiet little group, each with her own thoughts. Betsy joined her mother- in -law, Mary Masson, and they spent the afternoon together, giving mutual comfort and encouragement. Of course, Baby Jane was their greatest comfort.

Chapter 4

Time passed quickly for Betsy. A house- proud woman with a baby is never idle. In addition, she had her net mending to deal with. In a few weeks the nets would be collected for barking and redrying in readiness for the return of the Hopeful. Ena, drawn by the baby, was often with Betsy and her sunny nature was a constant source of pleasure. They had many laughs together and shared views on Mary May's strictness with Ena, and, indeed, all the sisters, even though they were married. She told Betsy of her secret romance with George and how she felt like a caged bird never being allowed out on her own in the evenings, even though she was nearly twenty.

"It's afa bein' the youngest an' bein' left allain at hame. It'll be war eence Bella is merried. I'll jist hae tae come here an' nurse this bonnie wee cretur. Isn't `at recht ma bonnie lass?" as she hugged the baby.

There was no doubt Ena was a boon to Betsy in those early days of Jane's life. Such a strong bond grew between Ena and Jane, and Betsy could hand over her care to Ena at any time.

Occasionally during the next few weeks Betsy began to wonder if she was having signs of pregnancy. She could hardly believe it was true after waiting all this time and she was not sure she was happy about it now that she had Jane. It was too soon to care for a second baby and it would interfere with Jane's development and the pleasure she was having in watching that. However, Janet in her wisdom soon opened Betsy's eyes to the situation.

"It's nae unusual tae fa wi a bairn efter adoptin'. They ca it mother love an' it rouses yir maternal instincts. I've read aboot it. Ye shud be real gled Betsy tae hae yir ain bairn. An' think o' Alex. It micht be a loonie an' he wad be sae prood o' that. Jane'll be fine an' she'll jist learn wi' the ithers tae tak her share o' yir time. Fa kens, ye'll maybe hae half a dizzen bairns yet Betsy."

Not too comforted by Janet's words, Betsy faced the next months before Alex's return, feeling at times sad and unwell and at others, guilty both towards Jane and the new baby, still unborn. As time went on she came to realize that what really bothered her was the upsetting of her planned life. This new child would interfere with that, and the old domineering Betsy did not enjoy being thwarted. But she realized there was nothing she could do about it. The situation was here now. By the time the Hopeful berthed again in the Balaclava Basin, Betsy was ready to meet Alex with a glad smile.

When she broke the news to him that evening in the peace of their own fireside, Alex's joy was unfeigned.

"Lass, it's winnerfu. Jist imagine. Oor ain baby. I can hardly gresp it. Fan wull it be born? Dae ye think ye can manage wi twa babies?"

Betsy enjoyed his excitement and allayed his fears as she told him about Janet's knowledge and advice. It also comforted her when Alex remarked, "So we cud say that haein' Jane made this possible for us. That's amazin'."

"I'll manage fine. Ena comes here aften an' taks Jane oot. In fact, she is jist like a mither wi' her. An' since it's oor ain bairn, my mither wull be on han' tae help. The baby wull come in July fan you are here at hame fishin' so it wis weel timed. But we micht be a wee bit short o' room here. Maybe we cud think aboot anither net store an' extra help wi the mendin' yince the baby is born. That wad gie us a bedroom for the bairns."

Alex soon found a net store at the back of a house in North Street, very handy to the harbour, and he employed an experienced net mender to take over Betsy's share of the repairs. Members of the crew who owned nets were responsible for their upkeep and usually the wives shared the mending with their husbands. But often, when the husbands were at sea, the load fell on the women and Alex, very aware of this, was quick to relieve Betsy of the responsibility. Nothing must be allowed to harm this pregnancy and, although Alex, a true man of his time, considered babies and birth as women's world, he could not help being anxious and concerned for Betsy's well being and, of course, for the baby, by some miracle, growing inside her.

Alex was a man of strong Christian faith and since their marriage Betsy and he had regularly attended the Baptist Church. Betsy became a member of the Women's Meeting and she enjoyed the friendship and the various activities in which the women were involved. Mission work played a large part and there was a constant call for knitted garments and money raised from sales of work, to supply the needs of the hospitals, especially in India, where the B.M.S. had a huge work in hand. Betsy believed in practical Christianity and, as her knitting needles flew on, she often pictured the dark skinned nurses and children who would wear this garment in her hands. Ena too joined her in this work and the two sisters became life members of the Baptist Women's work party.

Now that she had Jane and was pregnant, Betsy's church work was somewhat curtailed but Alex in his role of prospective father, had a growing sense of God and his need of a greater power than his own. What was happening to Betsy had to do with him also and he just felt a great need to commit her to God for protection and strength. He became very aware of a deep spiritual hunger and found fulfilment in his faith, in prayer and in reading his Bible. The hardest trial was leaving her to go off to the Shetlands but Betsy assured him it happened all the time to fishermen's wives and she would be well looked after with all their sisters coming and going.

And that is what happened. Having had a wonderfully productive fishing, Alex returned to find Betsy blooming. When the settling up was completed the whole crew celebrated and each man banked a healthy amount.

"That's aye a bittie closer tae the new boat Alex." Betsy remarked as they talked over the fishing success.

"Aye, maybe. Bit I'm nae in a big hurry for that. The Hopeful is a good boat an' we are dain' weel. Father is still an able skipper an' I think I wid wyte till young Charlie comes aboard afore I made a move. He'll seen be saxteen, nearly able tae tak a man's place."

Alex had another project in mind but that would rest in abeyance until after the baby's arrival

Chapter 5

It was a warm afternoon in July when Betsy went into labour and the midwife, Mrs. Wilson was sent for. Ena came to take care of Jane and removed her to Janet's home. But Mary May was there, determined to be present at the birth of Betsy's first child. Her denial of Jane was still there; a strange sort of dislike and resentment had built up in her mind over the year causing her to ignore the beautiful child. For Mary May the pure bloodline was important and she abhorred any pretence and illegitimacy.

Being strongly built and healthy and having had no complications during the pregnancy, Betsy did well and the birth was not prolonged. She did want the baby to be a boy, especially for Alex's sake, and also a boy would be one of each, just in case they were not able to have more children. But Janet, the fount of all knowledge, warned her that it could well be a girl as she and Alex had so many sisters, eight in all, and only three brothers.

It was late evening when the first baby cry was heard. Alex and Mary May, waiting in the kitchen, gazed anxiously at the bedroom door, impatient to go in. When Mrs. Wilson finally appeared she looked a little upset.

"It's a fine wee girl. Ye can gang in noo. Betsy is afa tired an' a bittie weepie so dinna bide ower lang. I'll jist clear up the gear."

Betsy's first glimpse of her baby came as a shock. She had been built up on a chubby, baby- like, little boy, a pink and white baby as Jane had been, but instead, the nurse was holding out to her a strange little person. The baby was thin faced with a longish nose and a shock of straight dark hair growing low on her forehead. The long thin arms and legs were flailing everywhere, and, above all, it was a girl. Betsy burst into tears of disappointment. After she had calmed her down the nurse brought Alex and Mary May into the room and placed the baby in her father's arms.

The look of pure joy and love on Alex's face as he held his daughter close, more than anything else, settled Betsy and dispelled her hurt and fear. It brought tears of fulfilment to her eyes and even Mary May, usually so self-contained and unemotional, felt her heart stirring and a smile came on her face.

"Whit a wonder. Oor ain little quinie. My bit ye are bonnie."

As he gazed into her face the grey eyes opened and seemed to focus deeply into his, almost as though an understanding had already formed between these two. Alex could hardly part with her until he turned to Mary May,

"Here, gang tae yir Granny for a haud an' I'll see tae yir Mammy. Here Granny, yir grand dother, Mary Bella."

Mary May looked startled at the name but delight was on her face.

"Aye, she's cad efter you, an' I've aye had a warm feelin' for Bella so she has that name tae. She'll be cad Mary Bella, the hale name."

Mary May nodded and cradled the baby to her.

"Ma first grand dother, an' she's ca'd efter me. I'm that prood. Ye've deen weel Betsy. She's a fine bairnie an' a jist ken she'll bring ye baith great joy."

With that she handed the baby back to Betsy, laid her hand briefly on the mother's head, as if in benediction and turned away to go home. As she walked away her heart was quietly singing with joy and thankfulness over the coming of this child. Setting aside all her previous feelings of antagonism, Mary May could now see Alex and Betsy and their children as a real family. She had noted the bonding moment between Alex and Mary Bella and just felt deep in her heart that the day would come when this child would be special to her parents, to herself Mary May, and to the many others in her life.

Once Betsy was up and about, the family settled into its own routine. Jane toddled about, delighted to watch her little sister but truly puzzled as to why there should be another little person for her mother to cuddle and play with. As Betsy was well able to feed her Mary Bella thrived and she was a good, contented baby. Alex came and went and treasured his home time with his little family. Betsy was happy, well in control of her babies and her home, and she was still able to knit for Alex and the children. When the Hopeful sailed away a large contribution of home bakes was always sent on board. Betsy managed everything well. Some days when she pushed her perambulator along and looked at her children, one at each end, she reflected that it was good they were so different in looks, Jane so pretty and fair skinned, and Mary Bella so dark and elfin like. They would never be in competition with each other or jealous.

Chapter 6

Time brings change and that was true in the fishing world. The old, sail boat days were going. Once the whole fleet had been sail and wind powered, making a magnificent scene as the boats entered the harbour one by one and manoeuvered into the basins to tie up. They needed space for this operation and the harbour was adequate for all. Weather controlled most activities and the pace of work; if the herrings were there and the weather reasonable, then all operations went ahead fishing, landing, gutting, curing, and exporting. It meant a good livelihood, work for all and prosperity for the town. But it could not remain so. Steam power had arrived. Fishing boats became more manoeuvrable. They could go further off shore and return quicker to catch the early markets and higher prices. Many of these new, larger, steam drifters deserted the smaller anchorages around the north east coast and the main harbours became overcrowded.

Alex and John had many discussions about the need to go with the times and have a steam-powered drifter. They were young and the thought of handling a steam drifter was exciting and challenging. Alex would be skipper and John the mate. But Alex had a strong sense of loyalty to his father who had only ever been skipper of a sail- boat and was now too old to change. Perhaps in another few years he would retire and then they could make the move. Meantime, they could wait and save.

In their months at home during the annual fishing from Fraserburgh, the two young men continued to muster activity on behalf of the fishermen. They rallied support for attending public meetings and were recognized as very able spokesmen when it came to putting forward the requirements of the fishermen. Lack of anchorage and overcrowding was now a major problem and the constant fear of the inevitable disasters that would arise with boats having to anchor outside the harbour and being exposed to the elements of the open North Sea. It was well into the first decade before the arguments and disputes were settled and the harbour was expanded and deepened.

Chapter 7

The sisters were often together, especially Janet and Betsy with their children, and most often it was at Janet's home. The long garden behind the house had been divided up so that Sandy had the end half for his cooperage and work yard. A back gate opened into an access lane and lorries came and went without interfering with the home. Near the kitchen door a wide area of lawn had been fenced in and there the children could play safely while the mothers talked. Further along Janet had blackcurrant and gooseberry bushes and then beds of vegetables and flowers. Janet loved her garden and folks enjoyed going there. The atmosphere of harmony and contentment was so prevalent it was like a sweet taste of paradise. Betsy envied Janet a little, having Sandy working so near. Everything in their lives was so closely connected; husband, work, children, garden, house, all within the boundaries of home. How she longed that Alex could be more with them to share their daily lives.

Betsy's cup of joy overflowed when baby Alex was born two years after Mary Bella. Here at last was the son for Alex and Betsy was so thankful that all her early fears of barrenness had been proved wrong. She had her hands full with three babies, for Jane was still only four, but Betsy managed and Mary May was always at her hand to help out with 'oor ain bairns'.

There was a great difference between the three children. Jane remained dainty and doll like, always clean, and fussy about sticky hands. She preferred to sit and watch while the others played and she was never very happy in the rough and tumble of Janet's boys, Tom and Willie. Mary Bella, on the other hand, for all her two years, was on the move as soon as she could crawl and was into all sorts of fun and mischief. From babyhood she remained a tomboy and Mary May, her grandmother, recognized the energy and initiative in the child and simply adored her. As Alex grew he too entered the world of make believe and adventure, taking his cue from Mary Bella, whom he followed faithfully. Betsy often watched them at play, amused by their ability to communicate in baby language, and it was then that she realized that Mary Bella had given herself another name, 'Balla'. Her whole name was too difficult to say so Balla she had become, and remained so to all her close relatives for the rest of her life.

Now their little house was becoming too small, especially when father was at home. They needed space for the children to play safely and Alex wished to give Betsy the things he knew she longed for. She often spoke of Janet's home and garden and all the modern conveniences being installed into new houses. He too for some time had been thinking along these lines but, with the birth of Alex, it became a serious matter and he came to a decision. They would build a new house and he knew exactly where he wanted it to be. When Alex shared his plan with Betsy her immediate reaction was,

"Bit fit aboot the new boat? We've planned and saved for that a' this time. We could manage here for a fylie langer, until the bairns are alder."

"Betsy it's noo that they need the space. Somewhere that they can rin and play on grass, nae in a cobbled yard like we hae jist noo. The boat can wyte a year or twa. Things are aye developing an we *wull* hae the maist up tae date steam drifter. We can manage baith hoose an' boat, dinna worry."

Then Alex described to her the dream he had carried since soon after they were married. On one of their distant, spring fishings on the west coast of Ireland the Hopeful had followed a huge shoal of herrings and they had shot the nets close in shore on the Kerry coast. It was dawn when the crew was called out to haul in the catch and the men stood ready at the winch, their bodies taut against the cold, damp, morning air. Suddenly, the grey mist cleared and in the east, breasting the undulating meadows, a sunrise burst through, lighting up a whole world of the most wonderful green Alex had ever seen. As the curling wisps rolled off the pastures scattered cottages appeared, and people, stirring to their daily tasks. A dog ran barking from a doorway, followed by two boys, all bounding over the fresh, dewy grass. Such freedom. And that was what Alex wanted for his family; a good house, a garden and plenty open space for the bairns to play.

"An' faar wull ye find that in the Broch Alex?"

"I ken exactly faar. The Council is opening up Albert Street for new house building; jist opposite the windmill an'ahin the new school at the tap o' Charlotte Street. We could get a plot o' land i' the park that rins along Albert Street. It wud be near the Infant School an' the Public School for the bairns, an' nae ower far fae Braidsea, an' Charlotte Street roon the corner. It's a bittie fae the hairber bit at'll nae be a problem wi' the hurley tae cairry the gear. I can jist see the bairns rinnin' an' rollin' doon on the grassy braes in the park."

Betsy could see he had it all thought out and she felt a surge of excitement stir. Now that Alex had assured her that they could afford it, Betsy too began to allow herself to dream. Together they planned and discussed, visited the land office to acquire the plot, found their architect and builder, and by the time Alex was ready for the south fishing in September, the foundations had been laid and the house was under way. Now, it was up to Betsy to oversee progress in the next few months.

Most days she was to be seen pushing her pram up Charlotte Street, past the new Public School, round by the West Parish Church to Albert Street and `their house'. She became intensely interested in how the plans developed into reality and, as long as the children's patience allowed, she would stand and watch the stonemasons, the joiners, and all the activity involved in making a house. How could this scene of chaos become their dream house? Betsy knew it would, but she had never imagined what was entailed in creating such a building. Many letters reporting regular progress were dispatched to Alex and, by the time he returned, the house was almost complete. Only the garden walls and paths remained to be finished and the name, Barskimming House, to be painted on the fanlight above the front door. The name was a reminder of Alex's dream, the village by the green fields of Ireland. Betsy thought it sounded really grand.

Chapter 8

It was a beautiful house. The dressed granite blocks sparkled in the sun, and the proportions gave it a solid, comfortable appearance. Standing back from the street, it had a front garden, and a lane ran up the left side to the back of the house and the rear entrances. Following the modern style, the building housed two families in separate apartments. Down stairs consisted of three rooms and a kitchenette with the entry coming from the side of the house into the lane. The tenant would inhabit it.

Betsy and Alex, the owners, would have the larger, up-stairs flat of four rooms, kitchenette and bathroom and the great advantage of extensive attics. Alex had planned a proper inside stairway to the attic areas, which were divided into, at one end, an extra room with a fireplace, and a net store at the other. A small window in the outside wall provided light for the mender and access where the nets could be hoisted up without trailing through the house. For convenience, a toilet and gas lighting had also been installed in the attic so the upper residence was a fairly substantial house.

The door at the front of the house was the main upstairs entrance. It gave access to a shallow, curving staircase rising to the wide hallway and the four rooms; a back sitting room or kitchen, two bedrooms and the large front room or parlour The attic stairs continued up, slightly more steeply, and it was Betsy's delight to stand here between the two and look up and down at the lovely sweep of the stairs and the glowing mahogany woodwork everywhere. Alex had spared no expense. The ceilings throughout were high, corniced in the parlour, and here also was installed a beautiful, polished steel fireplace inset with floral patterned tiles. The kitchen range heated the water and provided Betsy with her ovens, and the scullery extension kept all the sinks and washing out of the living areas. From the scullery on one side, a door led to a small toilet and bathroom and opposite that an outer door gave access to a wooden landing and stairs descending to the back garden.

The row of outhouses comprised the downstairs lavatory, two coal houses and the shared washhouse complete with boiler and washtubs. The rest of the walled garden would have a shared drying green and growing areas for both houses, the downstairs managing the front garden and the back plot nearest the house, while upstairs would have the top end of the garden. Betsy visualised a hen run and fruit and vegetables, and maybe an apple tree or two against the sunny walls.

Alex was at home during the final weeks of house preparation and Betsy and he spent many hours debating, deciding, even arguing, about furnishings, floor coverings, curtains and all the extras required for a larger house. In their present home they had owned very little, just enough for two adults and some babies. But now, they were five people with larger rooms to furnish and equip and this was going to be their own home for as long as they could foresee. They wanted it just right.

Over the New Year period the temptation was to move in before the holiday, but they resisted. Better to enjoy New Year's Day with Alex's folks as usual, and then the following week have all the excitement of the flitting. And that was how it happened. Ena arrived with her baby, Nellie, just a few weeks older than little Alex, and took all the children home with her to Broadsea where Mary May was waiting. Fortunately it was a dry, January day and Alex, John and the younger brothers, Charlie and Doddie soon had the house emptied and the lorry loaded. Betsy, Janet and Alex's sister Nellie, remained behind to scrub out and leave the old house clean and the men drove off to set up the new home. By afternoon all was accomplished and they sat round the table in their new kitchen to enjoy Betsy's broth and Pirie the baker's pies. The new range was burning well, sending a warm glow to permeate the room, and for Alex and Betsy enjoying their first meal in their own home with the family, it was a wonderful moment of happiness.

That evening, after the children were settled in bed, Alex and Betsy stood together on the back stair landing, his arm around her shoulders. The frosty, night air seemed to make the stars twinkle more brightly, lighting up the great expanse of sky and the rolling landscape before them. Beyond the roofs of the new Infant School across the lane nothing impeded their view. Away to the left rose the outline of the hill at Dennyduff and the lights of Fatson's farm stood out against the dark blue of the night sky, and following on, the land continued climbing until it reached Gallow Hill before it sank down to the rocky shore level, just out of sight. For Alex, it was just as if he was standing in the bow of the boat as he pointed out the well- known stars to Betsy. There was the North Star, Orion's Belt, the Plough, and how you could find the North Star by taking a line from one of that group. Betsy treasured these moments, feeling she had briefly shared in Alex's work, carried out so far away from her world. Closer in was the great sweep of open fields.

Just what Alex dreamed. And their back gate opened right into it. There the children could run and play among the buttercups in summer and the hens could range and peck freely. Alex's heart was full of emotion and gratitude for the blessing of hopes fulfilled. As he gripped Betsy's shoulder he whispered,

"Aye lass, we hae deen it. We're here. Isn't it winnerfu'? Afore us, the hills an' the sky. Jist whit we wanted. Nae doot, come time, there'll be streets an' hooses built ower there, but noo we hae it a' for oorsels an' the ither folk on oor street. This has been a special day."

Chapter 9

Too soon it was time for Alex to go again. The west coast fishing could not wait and, in these less plentiful herring times, every penny was important to the crew.

Once the Hopeful had sailed for Mallaig, Betsy set about her planning for the garden. It was still winter but she felt if the outside was organized, it would be ready for the planting and sowing in spring. Fencing off would also prevent the children bringing in muddy shoes and dirtying the house. So Sandy was employed and every day, weather permitting, he was there to fence off the downstairs back garden, edge the planned lawn and paths between the vegetable and flower gardens, and finally the hen house with wire caging was erected in the space between the wash house and the end of the garden. Here the back gate opened directly into the field and Betsy anticipated her hens having access and freely coming and going. She had long talks with Janet on the subject of seed sowing and the choice of fruit trees and bushes. Betsy, who had no experience, considered Janet the fountain of all gardening knowledge, but, one day, Janet took her to Derbyhall Croft on the Strichen Road and introduced Betsy to real gardening knowledge. From then, Betsy was determined that all vegetables and fruit for jam making would be their own produce. She also rented two drills for potatoes at Lochpots Farm and they would be planted in the spring, hopefully when Alex was home.

If she could grow their own food, now was her opportunity to play her part in saving for the boat.

Betsy loved her house. Sometimes when the children were in bed and all was quiet, she would take the lamp and slowly go from room to room, just savouring the beauty of it all, moving an ornament here, adjusting a drape there, having a seat on the parlour sofa, resting and enjoying. She had always counted her blessings and felt so thankful now for all of this that had come to them. This was her palace to care for and make into a happy, loving home for Alex and the family. That was the only miss. Alex was not here. But, in a few weeks he would be back and they would get on with the garden. Soon the nets would arrive for the attic and the mending would begin, but now in the evenings Betsy sat in the rocking chair by the range, knitting or mending and thinking, planning ahead in her ever-restless mind. The hens must come soon and she would need advice on that matter. Perhaps Mary May knew some good farmers who would sell pullets.

Chapter 10

Great changes were happening on Albert Street. Almost every month foundations for new houses were being taken out. They all followed a similar pattern, two flatted, but some, following the rising ground of the site, were more elevated above the street. Mostly the owners came from the villages, Cairnbulg and Inverallochy but some were Broadsea folks whom Betsy had known since childhood. Once the flitting was in Betsy always made it her habit to call on the new folks with a bowl of soup or a baking of scones, just to say hello and welcome and to show neighbourliness. That was what happened in Broadsea in the old days and Betsy wanted to continue the custom. She believed in the `open door' and she liked people. Betsy became known for her friendliness and sense of humour and many spoke of her kindness, quietly shown amongst her neighbours when need arose. She gradually won the respect and affection as well as the admiration of all for Betsy was a handsome woman. Tall and elegant with a pleasant smiling face, there was no one to match her when she walked out with her husband and three children on Sunday to attend church. She had a style of quiet dress sense to be admired but never gave the impression of being proud or overbearing. She was a truly happy woman, above all, secure in her husband's love and that of her family.

Perhaps Betsy's sisters were slightly in awe of her but at the same time, admired her energy and her ability to accomplish feats they would not attempt. After their second winter in Barskimming House Betsy thought the back stairs looked shabby and in need of painting so she just set about it and for a few days, entry to the house was by front door only, shoes removed at the foot of the stairs of course, while Betsy painted. She did not attempt the under side which would have required a ladder, but the steps, railings and landing were refreshed with a fine shade of green. Mary May, who came to keep an eye on the children during the operation, fully approved of Betsy's work and, although she would never have voiced her admiration and pride in her daughter, she was so thankful that the stormy child had grown into such a fine woman.

"Aye, it's a bonny job. Alex 'ull be gey pleased tae see `at."

And then, there was always the mending. Once a fishing was past the nets were landed, cleaned and dried and then Alex's nets were delivered to Barskimming House for mending. Now that the children were older and the facilities had been set up in their home, Betsy resumed the task, glad to find another avenue of saving.

Once the nets were in the attic the house was cleaned from end to end and every door closed. The family then moved into the attic room and set up home there. With the fire blazing and the cosiness of all being together with the two beds, the rockers and the Tilley lamp, which they preferred to the peeping gas light, the children loved the move and would have wanted this all the time. In the evening, when they were asleep, Betsy would slip down to the kitchen and prepare soup and food for the next day before going to her bed, sharing with one of the children. They had a rota to sleep with mother. Many stories were told these evenings, games were played and dolls were rocked to sleep; wonderful memories which the children carried throughout their lives.

Most of the mending was done in the daylight by the gable window while the children played beside her but every afternoon, weather permitting, Betsy took them out for a walk up Dennyduff or to Broadsea to Granny's and along the shore. On the long walk home up Charlotte Street, they could call in on Bella or Janet or now, Ena, who had moved to her new home beyond the school near the top of the street. By this time more cousins had arrived. Bella had Chrissie, `Tina', Janet still had her two boys and Ena had Nellie. Many afternoons during the spring and summer days they would all gather for a picnic in the field on Albert Street or at the Broadsea Shore. The boys would climb into the yawls drawn up on the sand and sail away, always to the fishing, with the girls as crew members. Or sometimes if the tide was out, they bathed in the rock pools or caught crabs. These were such happy times and Mary May, sitting listening to the talk, felt so thankful and blessed that she had them all so close with their children. If only Maggie Ann could have been nearer. How she missed her. Every day she thought about her eldest child, so far away amongst strangers in a far land. No matter how reassuring the letters sounded, Mary May grieved for Maggie Ann's absence and wondered if she would ever see her again.

Chapter 11

Jane became five in August and the question of school arose. Which one should she attend? Being Broadsea folk, the old loyalties to the Broadsea School were strong but, on the other hand, there was a brand new school, wonderfully equipped, on their doorstep. How could they miss out on the conveniences of that? In fact, all the schooling, right to teenage, was round about their home and this had been an added factor in Alex' mind when he chose Albert Street. Some reports of favouritism and snobbery had been launched against the Infant school but Betsy and Alex believed their children could hold their own. And so, on opening day of the new session, Jane and Betsy joined the other parents for the enrolling.

As they sat waiting their turn in the large central hall with the ten classrooms opening off, they could hear the voices of the teachers, and occasionally children. They were not always pleasant, happy sounds and Jane, always a clinging child, became more and more nervous as she listened. Betsy had known that leaving her would create a problem, on both their parts, but when their turn came to enter the long, narrow office in the corner, she had to almost carry Jane. The head teacher took all the particulars and Jane was then ushered into the classroom to face over fifty pupils. Before Betsy could say goodbye, the teacher had Jane by the hand and the door was closed behind her.

Betsy felt bereft. On her short journey home she tried to stifle the sobs by recalling what she had seen in her brief glimpse of the classroom. There was a large, brown, rocking horse by the doorway and in front of the class stood a great iron stove with a fire guard round it. But it was the height of the floor holding the desks that alarmed Betsy. It seemed to go right to the ceiling, rising in tiers, about six of them, each with a steep step, and a row of desks and seats on each level. Jane was quite a small child and Betsy pondered how her short legs would negotiate such stairs. She could hardly wait till dinnertime to see how she had got on.

Jane's school years did not flow easily. No doubt Betsy's indulgence had something to do with it for there was no question but that Jane was the preferred child. In Betsy's eyes Jane was perfection, while the other two were lively, adventurous, sometimes dirty children. In fact Mary Bella dirtied out the pinafores that came off Jane the previous day and that angered Mary May who adored her 'Balla'. Jane played on her mother's affection and some of the innate deceitfulness came out in her tales from school and in her association with the other children. For the first time Jane met firm discipline and it was to be an ongoing problem for most of her young life, and for the family members who had to contend with it.

The following summer, Mary Bella was enrolled and from the start she enjoyed it all. Her friends called for her every morning and they set out happily for school, but Jane insisted that Betsy accompany her. Sometimes at interval Betsy would slip along to the railings and surreptitiously watch them at play. Jane would be sitting quietly in a corner with another pupil or playing one to one with a ball while her tall, leggy sister, Balla, would be in a skipping team or a tag game, racing all over the play ground. Such was the difference, but Betsy had recognized that from their infant days.

When Alex eventually joined the girls at school he too fully entered into the pleasures of the company, enjoying being with the boys and the rather more rough and tumble than he had experienced with his sisters. The school activities spilled over into the evenings and during the spring and summer the groups of children, mostly friends from school and the street, would play in the field, sending reassuring shouts of fun and laughter to the parents' ears. It was a joy to watch them safely at play. Since the building development began, the farmer had long ago given up grazing his cows there and so the grass was clean and rich and the buttercups grew in profusion. Albert Street was a happy community for both young and old and it was very satisfying to be part of it all.

Chapter 12

So Betsy had her busy life shaped out. Her children, Alex, when he was at home, the house and garden, her mother and the wider family, her mending and knitting, the hens and the neighbourly visits she made with a few eggs or baking, to hand in to some invalid or elderly person; Betsy was never at a loss for something to do.

Now that the children were older, one activity she resumed was her church work for the women's missionary outreach. Ena and Betsy together became members of the committee and added their skills to a very active and imaginative group of women. Their field of work was wide but there was a particular interest in the plight of women and children in India. The Baptist Missionary Society under William Carey had set up hospitals and schools there and an enthusiastic following from Scottish and English churches sent out huge support in money and clothing. The Fraserburgh Baptist Church adopted the hospital at Behwani and the Sunday school pupils maintained a child's bed in that hospital, which all served to increase interest and generosity.

But, the committee had a problem. The local church required hall space in order to provide storage for the goods produced, and to hold sales of the work, which the women made. With the growing numbers of children in the Sunday school space was at a premium and the church had no safe catering facilities whatever. At a social, the water for the tea had to be boiled on a gas ring in the small hall, which served as vestry, kitchen, meeting room and church overflow. The church owned land behind the building into which it could extend. The only missing factor was the will to take the step and set up a Hall Fund. Eventually, Betsy, Ena, Mrs. Catherine Buchan, Mrs A. Buchan from St. Combs and one or two other ladies approached the Minister, Rev. Mitchell Hughes, and his deaconate with a proposal to inaugurate a Hall Fund for the further good and extension of Baptist Church work and outreach of the Gospel. It would be an initiative of the Women's Meeting but all efforts would be under Church Supervision and approval. The leadership accepted the plan and the Fund was established.

Great enthusiasm followed and all sorts of events were created to make money for the Fund. Church socials, regular retiring offerings, shilling teas in individual homes where church ladies brought their friends and were sumptuously fed on home bakes while listening to a reading or some sort of wholesome talk. These friendship afternoons brought an outreach element into the women's work and the numbers grew. All the time they had to be careful that the Hall Fund did not rise at the expense of the India project and so a Missionary Committee was formed to work alongside the Hall Committee in order to keep a balance. Betsy and Ena were on the Hall Committee and, with the others, worked hard for the Church, but neither foresaw the years that would go by before their dream would be realized. Two world wars and a long depression in the country, fluctuating prosperity and a new generation were to come and go before the hall foundation was laid, but, in their time, their vision was real and possible and that was all that mattered. Betsy revelled in activity and gave her time and energies unstintingly to her community and Church.

Chapter 13

It was 1906 and, when she was in the presence of Alex and John Mason, Betsy was aware of some new plans afoot. Old Alex was ailing and there was some concern for his health, so the future of the Hopeful had become a question. Alex could have skippered it for his father but he was aware that, if he undertook the role, he would be responsible to the crew, and the dream of his own steam drifter would slip further away. Then there was Doddie and Charlie as well as John to think about. They discussed at length and eventually Father Alex retired, Doddie and Charlie decided to find land work as fish salesmen and, for the rest of the hands, employment in other boats. The Hopeful would be sold and with their shares of the old boat, Alex and John could become the main owners of their new steam drifter. They found a designer and builder at Sandhaven, J&G Forbes, who had a reputation for excellent work and their order was recorded by the end of the summer; a steam drifter to be called 'The Anchorof Hope'. This one would join the succession of steam drifters coming off theslipways in increasing numbers all along the coast.

Excitement ran high in Barskimming House. Father's new boat was the topic and so many questions were asked. Eventually, Alex promised to take them to see the keel laid and, when it was ready, they would see the launching, probably in the spring. Then the engine would be installed and trial trips would be carried out along the coast.

"An' I'm sure ye wull get a sail in her then."

So they had to be content with that promise. But Alex and Betsy felt a great sense of achievement and pride that they would now possess their own boat. This was the peak of their ambition and they felt well satisfied and blessed.

For the day of the launching, 20th. March 1907, Alex hired a large brake to take the whole family, old and young, to see the event in Sandhaven. Betsy, resplendent in a new blue outfit, was to perform the ceremony and then afterwards the company was to sit down to a meal provided by the builder. It was such a special day and most exciting. Once it struck the water there was a moment of silence and then a great cheer went up as the ship righted itself and floated out into the dock. Just the shell of a boat as it had no engines yet, but beautiful in its lines and proportions. Betsy, with tears in her eyes, watched the pride in Alex's face and she quietly slipped her arm into his and hugged him.

The Hopeful continued with them till the end of the Shetland fishing and then Alex came ashore to oversee the last details of outfitting the new Anchor of Hope. The trial runs that summer were exciting, especially for the children, on holiday from school. But more so for Alex and John when the new boat reached the highest record for any steam drifter, up till that time, 10.5 knots. The Anchor of Hope continued to work well and, during the second half of the north east fishing, was rated amongst the highest listed for record landings.

Then it was Yarmouth time again and Betsy settled down to the routine of knitting, preparing Alex's kist and baking for the crew, so happy that Alex was sailing south in a new, clean, modern boat that was not totally subject to the whims of the waves and the winds. Now Alex could control the movements of the boat and use his own initiative for speedy return to port if necessary. That brought her great peace of mind.

Chapter 14

Holidays were a most unusual occurrence in Fraserburgh and Broadsea. Only the gentry and rich, businessmen and fish curers could take the time off, and afford to do so. Amongst the fisher folk it was out of the question and not even considered. For most of them life was a struggle and, even if you were a boat owner, thrift was all important because running a boat and crew was a costly business and the moving shoals of herring were so erratic and unpredictable. It was a good skipper who could read the signs and follow the fish but he always had the elements to contend with.

The fishing crews and the gutting teams had the excitement and diversion of moving from location to location, Isle of Man, Shetland, Shields, East Anglia, and the changing scenes brought a holiday atmosphere although the workers all toiled so hard. But the wives left at home were often under great hardship from loneliness, and having to be both mother and father. Lack of money to hand was a problem. Only if the fishing was good did settling up time clear the debts. So most wives tried to have a sideline income such as knitting, domestic cleaning and fish working, just to keep the family going without running up debts. Betsy by nature was thrifty, thanks to Mary May's early training and she had her own means of income from the eggs and the vegetables she produced every year.

Having good neighbours and her sisters with their families close by, she was never lonely and was quite content with having New Year's Day in Aberdeen with Alex's family, and the annual two days' outing in October with the children at the potato picking. That had a holiday excitement, going out to Lochpots on the horse drawn cart, all of them together with Alex if he was home from Yarmouth in time. And then, coming home with the sacks of potatoes to store in the attic for the winter. The school had a regular two days holiday for that event.

But Betsy had another idea, which flew into her mind as she stood waving off the Anchor of Hope on its way to Yarmouth. What an adventure it would be if they could all sail away together in that boat! She would wait for a good moment and suggest it to Alex.

The outcome was that when the SS Magnus, the regular supply ship, sailed for Shetland in May, Betsy and the children were on board. She had arranged with the teacher to take school work with them for the last few weeks of term, Janet would look after the garden and Mary May agreed to stay in the house and look after the hens. Alex would meet them at Lerwick and escort them to the cottage on Bressay Isle and he would join them when he was ashore at the weekends. Then, at the end of the fishing, they would all come home together in the Anchor of Hope.

All their lives the children remembered that summer on Bressay. It was an idyllic time of sun, space, sea and running free. Their cottage was part of a croft with a few cows, pigs and hens, but the main work was the sheep, grazing freely on the moors. Lambing was nearly past but there were still the few lambs, which had lost their mothers and needed to be hand reared. So the children took on that task, thrilled to be involved. When Alex joined them they would roam the shores along the Voe or cross the moors carrying a picnic, endlessly talking, questioning and laughing. Everything was so different from the well-controlled life at home. Here they rose with the sun and went to bed with the sun, or so it seemed. Their complexions and the sparkle in their eyes told their own story. It was a wonderful time.

After four weeks they sailed home in their own boat, so proud and excited to sleep in the fishermen's bunks round the central table, and to be served newly baked, buttery rolls with huge mugs of tea for breakfast. There was one additional passenger, one of the motherless lambs they had helped to rear. Seeing their sadness at leaving their babies, the crofter's wife insisted that the children should take their favourite lamb home with them. Since they were travelling in their father's boat and also had a field at home for it to graze in, she could see no problem. Alex and Betsy had to agree. So 'Bressay' was their pet for quite a few months and, tethered on a long rope, she became the centre of attraction in the field at Albert Street.

Looking back on their trip to Shetland, Betsy realized how privileged she had been in Alex's cooperation. Lots of women went to Shetland to work, but none that she knew went for a holiday. It was a daring thing to do and some, she knew, would criticize her for being different in attempting such a project, but Betsy did not worry about that. Home life took up its usual pattern and they all felt the richer in every way from having been to Bressay Isle.

Chapter 15

The Anchor of Hope continued to do well, always listed amongst the top boats for landings and annual income. Exciting developments were going on at the harbour, deepening basins, extending berthing areas and dry dock facilities. Slowly but surely things were improving and Alex and John were two very effective spokesmen when it came to expressing the views and advice of the fishermen. Fraserburgh was becoming a foremost herring port and cargo ships were arriving from many Baltic ports, laden with salt to exchange for barrels of cured herring.

After their holiday, things on Albert Street had settled down again and now they were awaiting the return of Father from Yarmouth. Anticipation of presents and the usual fruit, rock and Fry's cream chocolate was the main topic of conversation and the family could hardly wait for the message from the agent's office that the Anchor of Hope was in the bay. That was the signal for Mary Bella and Alex to take off at top speed to be there when the boat tied up, and to be first to see Father.

Betsy and Jane waited quietly at home till the hurly sounded in the lane and then they had their moment of welcome. Betsy, in particular, was excited for she had special news for Alex. After eight years she was pregnant again and a new baby was due in the spring. She could hardly believe it. It was as though their cup of happiness was overflowing.

Norman was born in the spring of 1910 and the family, two girls and two boys, was complete. Mary May's little brood of grandchildren had increased, for Janet now had her little girl Netta, Bella had a second daughter Maisie, and Ena, like Betsy after a long gap, gave birth to Wilfred a few weeks before Norman's arrival. Mary May now had eleven grandchildren,

"Ten o' wir ain," as she was prone to remind one, and sometimes, when they were all around her, she would think of the long ago days of hardship and struggle and the overwhelming weariness. She would nod her head and say,

"Aye, things are better noo. Hae'n yir man at yir side maks a' the difference."

But things were not to remain so good. When the Anchor of Hope returned from the Yarmouth fishing that year, Betsy saw a very changed Alex. He seemed to have aged and had the grey look of a tired, old man. John Mason was very worried about him and explained to Betsy that Alex had persevered for the sake of the boat and crew, but he really needed a doctor. He felt something serious was wrong.

Alex was diagnosed with rheumatic fever and so began a long period of pain and weakness, going through many weeks of nursing and convalescence while he lay in the front bedroom. His joy in baby Norman was tempered by his weakness and despondency, and the weeks of inactivity and debility for this energetic man were so hard to bear. Betsy was patient, always positive, but, at times, the strain of the children and the long hours of nursing almost broke her. As the weeks went by, had it not been for the help of

Alex's and her own sisters, she would have given way to the worry. This is where her iron will and her naturally healthy stamina stood her in good stead.

Gradually the pain and the weakness receded and Alex was able to join them in the family circle. But a change had taken place. He was no longer a man interested in the world he knew, the various fishings, the landings, the harbour developments, all that had been his life. Especially the Anchor of Hope. In vain John and others tried to stimulate his interest until they realized that that part of his life had gone. Alex in thought had moved away and only time would resolve the question of his future.

But Alex was very aware of his problem. As soon as he began to recover he realized that his eyesight had been affected by the illness. Without perfect eyesight he could not skipper his Anchor of Hope and he would not sail in her in any other capacity . The share of the boat must go and, like his brothers, he must find work ashore. But could he do that after all these years on the sea, which he loved? Could he live by the sea and not be part of the life on it? It was so hard to accept.

At last he spoke with Betsy who had been aware of his worry for some time, and together they came to the decision to meantime sell his share of the Anchor of Hope to John, and wait till he was fully recovered before deciding on a new career. If it meant moving away from their beloved home, so be it. As long as they were all together. That was the main thing.

Chapter 16

Betsy and Alex May 1912

The answer came from a most unexpected source. One morning a letter postmarked Florida arrived from Alex's sister Jessie and her husband Bill Noble. A few years previously, they had emigrated to Jacksonville and now had a carpenter's business set up there. They heard of Alex's illness and were suggesting that the family should come out and join them. Possibly Alex could join Bill in the business.

Such a huge proposition. At first unthinkable. It would entail so many changes. It would mean selling their home, leaving parents and family, new schools for the children, the church friends, the neighbours, the garden, the hens, the field behind. They all passed before them as they talked and Betsy shed some bitter tears. But, at the same time, there was a tingle of excitement at the thought of a new start, an adventure together, out into the totally unknown. The unexpectedness of the proposition, coming when it did, gave Betsy and Alex the feeling that there was something of God's planning in this. Much thought and agonizing went on for some weeks. At last they made the decision to go and wired Billy to that effect.

What followed was hard. The families on both sides, especially the grandmothers, could not understand why they had to take such a drastic step. Likely for them, it would mean saying goodbye forever. Mary May was heartbroken at losing her Balla and little Alex. As the parting approached, Betsy and her sisters shed many tears together, realizing now just how precious they had all been to each other.

But events rolled on. Barskimming House was sold, complete with furnishings, and the new owner was happy to allow the family to stay there until their departure for Florida.

Alex decided that he should go out first. On his own he would better see what lay before them and find accommodation for the family. Then Betsy could follow with the children. At that time many people were emigrating from the North East so, most likely, she would find company for the long journey, and Jane and Mary Bella were old enough now to help with Norman.

They had their last New Year celebrations together with the families and these were followed by several other farewell gatherings at the church and amongst the fishing and harbour colleagues, all expressing their sorrow at their going, but also wishing them Godspeed in their new life.

Alex was to sail from Liverpool on board the SS Campania on Saturday 1st. February. So, once again, it was a farewell scene, but at the station this time, and Betsy went home with the children to wait for the promised telegram. She worried about Alex's health, going so far on his own. And the long winter crossing on the Atlantic, the icebergs and other sea hazards worried her. Although Alex knew the sea, this was the Atlantic Ocean, far from land.

During his leave takings, many tributes were paid to Alex, but one in particular gave Betsy much gratification. The publication of the Fraserburgh Herald on the week following his departure, announced his sailing and the following,

"Mr. May was one of our best known and most respected fishermen and his many friends wish him the best of luck in the land of his adoption "

Betsy cut out the excerpt and laid it away amongst her treasures to show Alex when they were together again.

After an anxious two weeks, a telegram arrived saying all was well, and Betsy went ahead with her arrangements. She and the children were to sail on March 3rd.. on the SS California and Ena's George would accompany them to Glasgow and see them on board. When Alex's letter followed she felt much more relieved to hear that he was happy with Jessie and Bill and he felt sure he would enjoy working in the carpentry business. He also had a house or two for them to choose from when Betsy arrived.

Chapter 17

At last they were on their way, able to sit quietly in their compartment and review the last trauma of saying good-bye. Mary May had not come to the station. After their last visit to Broadsea she had just waved from the close end and gone in and closed the door. For the children's sake Betsy was glad she was not there with the others. Watching the children's excitement, their heightened colour and their delight in their new outfits, one would imagine they thought they were going on another holiday to Bressay. But Betsy could see the deep hurt and sadness in the eyes of Mary Bella and Alex. They were old enough to realize that they might never see their beloved Granny again, she who had been such a rock in their young lives. Betsy shared their deep sorrow.

As the miles from Fraserburgh disappeared behind them spirits rose and the talk turned to the hotel, the ship and what would Jacksonville be like, and their new school. But, above all, seeing Father again. Betsy could say 'Amen' to that. She could hardly contain her longing for him, a desire tinged with anxiety for she was still worried about his state of health. Her old Alex had never quite come back after the fever.

George had booked them into an hotel near the docks. It was adequate for their needs and allowed them to reach the quay in plenty of time for the morning boarding at eleven.

With George carrying Norman they made an excited little family as they passed the boarding officer and climbed the gangway, George being allowed to pass as a visitor. They were travelling second class so the cabins were small, two adjoining with two bunks in each. The girls claimed one and Betsy with Alex and Norman were in the other. It was all so exciting for the children, and so different from the SS Magnus going to Shetland. From the quayside the SS California looked immense as it towered above them, but now, inside, it appeared like a maze. It would be so easy to get lost in the endless passages and stairways.

By sailing time George had located some North East country folks immigrating to Pennsylvania where they hoped to farm along with relatives. On this vast ship they were only too glad to join up with people who spoke their own Doric language. Betsy was thankful to have them by her for their cabins were near, on the same deck.

It was time for George to leave the ship. He had a train to catch for Aberdeen. It was so hard to let him go, their last link with Fraserburgh, and he had been so good.

"I canna thank ye enough George for a' ye hae deen for us. Ye hae been a real blessing. Tell them a' at hame I'll write aboot fit happens. Bit I'll miss ye a' sae much." Betsy ended on a sob.

For a minute George hugged her hard then turned away to hide his tears. Little did she realize just how much they at home would miss her. She had been the one to bring colour and drama into all their lives. There was always fun when Betsy was around and her energy and initiative had been their inspiration. Life was going to be much quieter and duller without her presence.

The week passed quickly. It was very cold and the icy wind brought a chill wherever one moved on deck. As they do easily, the children befriended other children and soon games were going. More than half way across an iceberg was glimpsed, bringing a certain fear amongst the adults. And then they were in sight of land. Betsy was thankful that this part of the journey was nearing its end and they were still all safely together.

Slowly the land took shape and they were sailing into the river mouth, past shoreline communities and buildings and a multitude of river activity. Then they saw the city and docks. Glasgow was impressive but here, the passengers stood in awe as the liner sailed on past the miles of quays and warehouses. Then the Statue of Liberty was in sight and they knew they were at their destination, Ellis Island. Alex, in his letter, had explained the procedure for new immigrants so Betsy was prepared. But, being marshalled along with hundreds of other immigrants was daunting. It gave her an uncomfortable sense of guilt that she should not be here and was not welcome in the States. All nationalities were in evidence and Betsy felt particularly sorry for those foreigners who had no English. How must they feel when they could not even understand directions and explanations? The waiting was tedious, but at last came their turn at the immigration desk. It was all straight forward- passports, birth certificates, letters of introduction and Alex's letter from Jacksonville to confirm their reception. Jane's adoption papers took a little longer to establish, then they were through and being directed to the station that would link them with the railway to Jacksonville.

It was a long, long journey. Days and nights followed each other and soon the novelty of having their own compartment with bunk beds began to pall. The children felt caged. As they travelled south, state after state, the heat increased, even in this cold season, and Betsy began to wonder, if this was winter, just how hot would Florida be in summer. Occasionally the train stopped and it allowed them to walk on the platform, but not for long. Eventually, they were passing through Georgia and they knew from their map that it would not be long now. Mary Bella had prepared for the journey with a map and the precious, little guidebook, which her teacher had presented to her on her last day at school.

What the children observed from the train windows had now become a confused jumble in their memories and Betsy was not very impressed by what she saw. There seemed to be lots of desolation and poverty in the countryside and so many black people! She knew about the Civil War but now saw the continued results of that conflict. How would it affect them? The cities appeared prosperous and quite beautiful, but out on the land was a different story.

Chapter 18

The now familiar, long drawn out toot of the horn heralded their arrival and the train slowed in to halt at the Jacksonville platform. They were all there to meet them, Jessie, Bill, young Billy and Margaret and, the most important one of all, Father. The children just could not let him go. Betsy stood and laughed and wept, so relieved at last to hand over the responsibility, and Alex smiled across at his remarkable and very beautiful wife who had undertaken and accomplished such a journey on her own. They would have their own time together later and he would tell her so. His heart was overflowing with pride and gratitude for such a wife as Betsy.

They stayed with Jessie and Bill for the first week till they set up their home and registered the children in school. It allowed the travellers to rest and adjust a little to the heat, and also to get to know these relatives whom they had not seen for many years. Betsy and Alex found a house in the same area, just a few streets away from Jessie and Bill and they moved in shortly afterwards.

It was a wooden bungalow with a front stoop opening on to a lawn with some shady trees. Opening directly on to the stoop was a large, living room incorporating a kitchen and dining area, and three bedrooms, toilet and cupboard space completed the house. Being all on one floor, Betsy liked it immensely and the low overhanging roof kept the rooms shaded and cool.

The children settled in to school and found that in most subjects they were well able to match their peers. Friendships were soon formed and the three soon felt at home and happy in their new environment. There seemed to be a relaxed informality in school, which they enjoyed. It made them feel welcome. Once they became accustomed to the new accents and the new timing of school hours, long mornings starting early and finishing early afternoon, their pattern of life was very happy. Every afternoon Mary Bella or Jane collected the milk from the dairy at the end of the road and most days returned with an apron full of oranges or peaches. The maid told them to help themselves from the basket on the porch. This kind of generosity was wonderful to them and they received it from many directions, especially from the church people, once they had established themselves there.

As the months passed into spring and summer, the family suffered greatly from the increasing heat, and the high humidity sapped their energy. Betsy realized that the normal Scottish wardrobe would not work here so she re-clothed them in cotton-dresses, pinafores, trousers, shirts, underwear; even cotton suits for Alex, just to control the constant perspiring.

The humidity accompanied by the sunshine produced such a luscious growth in nature that the spring burgeoning seemed to happen overnight. Suddenly, the little, nearby woods where the children often played, became a scary place with the dark canopy overhead sending down long trailing vines and lianas to catch on their faces and hair. Underfoot too, the ground became damp and soggy and they had to learn to watch out for snakes and other crawling creatures. Mary Bella in particular was fascinated by the whole subject of nature and read all that she could find in the school library. Snakes caught her imagination, especially ones that swallowed things whole, even people. She knew it was true, but could hardly understand how that happened. Nature was so violent and intense here cornpared to the gentle and beautiful arrival of spring in Scotland.

Chapter 19

Right from the start Alex and Bill got on well together. They were about the same age and from similar backgrounds and they enjoyed reminiscing about Fraserburgh and Cairnbulg in their own Doric tongue. It was evident that Bill was a skilled craftsman in carpentry and building work and, in this world of timber, the calls on his services were never ending. It seemed to Alex that Jacksonville was a woodcrafter's heaven, for everything was made of wood; buildings large and small, tools and farm implements, household utensils, even pavements. There was no end to the potential for Bill's business if he wished to expand, and Alex realized where he could work with Bill. He himself had no wood working skills but, having managed a boat, he did know how to run a business. He would have to learn technical terms and timber knowledge of course, but he had no fear of that. Bill needed someone to manage the office work, and also money to invest in wider expansion.

Alex and Betsy discussed the matter over the first two months and, with Betsy's agreement, they decided it would be a good investment to have a substantial interest in the firm. So the money from his share in the Anchor of Hope went into the carpentry business and Bill and Alex were able to expand with new machinery and a proper office for Alex to run that side of the company. Proper advertising was organized and they employed an extra carpenter to help with the increasing workload. It was a happy arrangement, which suited all.

Betsy and Jessie became very close and in time, Betsy began to form her own circle of friends, mainly in the church. She found a lively group of women there, much like the Fraserburgh church, and soon was in the midst of the mission work and finding opportunities to exercise her many talents. Jessie and Bill were Salvationists and, dressed in their uniforms, went regularly to their meeting hall. But Jessie enjoyed the Baptist Women's Meeting and, together with Betsy, they made a formidable pair when it came to getting things done. The congregation was a multiracial company, mainly migrants from Caribbean and Indian backgrounds with a scattering of Europeans. These folks had a more relaxed attitude to church projects and, when Betsy and Jessie exercised their drive and enthusiasm, the other ladies would just laugh, shake their heads and say,

"That is their Scottishness again!"

Week by week they learned to adjust to the heat and this, so relaxed, new way of life. Of course, there were the conventions and the marks of respect paid to people in certain positions, and Sundays were days for rest, worship and quiet pursuits. But, alongside that ran the openness and relaxed attitude to life in general. Clothing was informal, people sat on doorsteps and chatted in the evenings, children ran barefoot, even to school, people smiled more and seemed to have time for each other. Betsy believed it was down to the heat. Alex's view was that they were all strangers in a strange land and, after generations of tradition, they had moved away from the bonds and restrictions they had left behind. Now they were all free to make a new start according to their own desires. Whatever it was, Betsy and Alex and the children were happy, and more and more confident day by day.

The news from home was good. Mary May and all the families were well. When a letter arrived from one or other of the sisters Betsy always felt a little sob of longing rise up into her throat. She wondered when that would cease, but the parting was still raw, even after five months. There was one other little shadow on Betsy's happiness and that was Alex. Now he was forty years old, in the prime of life and just embarking on a new, interesting enterprise and he seemed happy and contented. The only times he referred to the Anchor of Hope and the sea was in a happy, reminiscing way when he chatted with Bill about Fraserburgh and the old days, and he showed no sign of regrets. But Betsy was disturbed by the occasional shadow that would pass over his face, especially in the evenings after the day's work. Was it sadness for the past? Was it financial worry? Was it exhaustion? She did not know, and she could not ask.

Chapter 20

It began like any other day. Betsy and Alex were up early, breakfasted together before the children stirred and then, carrying his lunch box, Alex set out to catch the trolley bus that would take him a few blocks to his office in the carpentry yard. Betsy waved him off and then turned to ready the children for school and assist Norman who still needed a helping hand. It was a good day with, thankfully, some breeze, so the washing dried soon and then after lunch she set out to the Women's Meeting. It was held outside, under the trees in the church garden, while the little ones played nearby. Betsy liked that. The meeting usually closed in time for the mothers to collect their children from school. And that is what happened.

As she stood chatting with the other mothers Betsy watched the girls come down the steps and she felt so proud of them. They were smiling and swinging their satchels and, when they saw her, they ran to be first to have a chance to push Norman in his pram. Despite the heat. they thrived in the air of Florida and seemed to have grown inches, especially Mary Bella. Soon Alex appeared at the boys' entrance, deep in conversation with another boy as they compared their bags of marbles. When he spotted Betsy he waved and rushed over to join the group, and they set off to walk home.

There was a brief stop at the green vegetable stall in the market and then they were home. Mary Bella went off for the milk from the dairy and the rest sat in the shade on the stoop. Betsy was in the rocking chair with Norman asleep in her lap and Jane played marbles with Alex on the path below. Marbles were in vogue these days. Mary Bella returned with the milk and an apron full of peaches, and they debated whether they should eat them now or have one and save the rest for dessert after dinner. They decided on the latter and Betsy went in to prepare the food. Alex would be home by five o'clock and she liked to have the meal ready to serve as soon as he arrived.

As she worked away in the kitchen she hummed to herself and listened to the children's chatter coming through the open door. Yes, they were happy and settled here. She enjoyed the long day to herself with Norman when she could visit, work in the house and garden or dress make, and then prepare a good evening meal for them all after their mid day packed lunches.

The meal was ready, but Alex had not arrived yet, so Betsy fed the children who were ravenous. When six o'clock came she grew concerned and sent MaryBella to Jessie's house to find out if the men had a meeting after work and Alex had forgotten to tell her about it. But Bill was home from work and he immediately accompanied Mary Bella back home.

"Betsy. fan he didna come in this mornin' a jist thocht he wasna feelin' great an' hid decided tae tak a day aff. A niver thocht onything was wrang aboot `at. Far can he be?"

"He gid awa as usual this mornin wi his piece box in his han' an' a hinna hard a word o' him since. Fit can we dee ?"°

They waited till nine o'clock, trying to hide their anxiety from the children. Then they went to the police station to report what had happened. The police said they would make inquiries at hospitals and other police stations but meantime they needed a detailed description of Alex. It was like the nightmare she had always dreaded and Betsy feared the worst.

The long night passed, Norman being the only one who slept. All next day they waited. The children did not go to school and Jessie came round to keep them company and help Betsy with the children. Bill went in to work but, having set the men their tasks, he returned to be on hand if the police arrived. But no reports came and another night passed. By now Betsy was frantic with worry and despair.

Just before lunchtime on the second day two police officers arrived with news. A man had collapsed and died on the pavement. He had no identification on his person and he had been taken to the town morgue. After a close examination, it was discovered from some markings on his watch fob that he was a Free Mason. The Mason Lodge members identified him as Alexander May. The police were now notifying the family and requested that the next of kin should come and identify the body. A post mortem would be held to establish the cause of death and then the body would be released for burial. It was all so cold and factual. Betsy shivered. Could this be really happening here in their home? Alex should be here to deal with it.

Bill accompanied her to the morgue while Jessie stayed to comfort the stunned disbelieving children The three sat silent, not knowing what to say or do, until Jessie sent them to bed where they collapsed, exhausted, now free to weep and deal with their sorrow in private. As she gazed down at her husband, through her tears Betsy could see the young Alex she had married seventeen years before. The worry lines had gone and his face was calm and peaceful. It was hard to believe he would not open his eyes and smile up at her again. She wanted to put her hands under his shoulders and draw him up to her warmth. Instead, she stroked his smooth, black hair and his moustache and, when she felt the cold mouth below, she drew back. This was not her Alex. The warm, loving man she knew had gone. He was only a lifelike shell. Betsy turned away. As she left the morgue she was handed a small cardboard box containing Alex's few possessions from his pockets. Inside was his watch with the chain and heart shaped fob, and the coins, which would have been his return fare from work.

Chapter 21

That night, in the solitude of her room, Betsy suffered her Gethsemane. As she paced the floor, wringing a face towel in her hands, she stifled the choking sobs and the cries of grief and loss. Her agony went on till she collapsed on her bed and slipped exhausted into oblivion. But then, when she roused into realization once more, it began all over again. Alex was too young to die. What would they do without him? And how could she live all these empty years without him? Had they done wrong coming here to Florida? Should she have tried more to persuade him not to come? And how could she manage now that all their money was tied into the business? But always it came back to the loving, the needing, the wanting of her lost lover and friend. Sometimes she tried to pray and think of scripture promises of comfort and reassurance, but always the agony of loss forced its way into her mind. At last, as the dawn light crept into the room, she slept.

Jessie was quietly at the helm. She had spent the night there while Bill looked after their own two children at home. Now they had gone off to school and he appeared at the kitchen door ready to help. He had a plan for the children, to take them away out of the scene, at least for a few hours, to allow Betsy and Jessie some time together to share their sorrow. Betsy had lost a husband but also, Jessie had lost a beloved brother and Bill was conscious of this.

A very composed Betsy helped to get the children ready and Bill departed with them while Betsy and Jessie sat down together to share their thoughts. Betsy could not free herself from the guilt of not dealing with Alex's health sooner. Maybe his death could have been prevented if she had pushed him to see a doctor. But would he have gone? Jessie tried to reason and allay her feelings of guilt.

"Betsy, Alex was a prood man an' aye did things in his ain wye an' in his ain time. Ye dinna ken fit wis wrang wi' him. Maybe naething cud hae been deen for him. Sudden death like 'at needs an explanation so jist wyte an' see whit the autopsy says. But ye maun stop blamin' yersel. The bairns are oor main thocht noo an' ye maun be strong for them."

The knock at the door halted the conversation and Jessie answered it to discover two well-dressed men on the doorstep. The older man spoke.

"Mrs. May?'

"No I'm sorry. I'm her sister in law. Mrs May is not able for visitors today."

"We understand, but it's about her bereavement we have come. We are from the Masonic Lodge where her husband was a member and we really would like to speak with her."

Satisfied by their manner, Jessie ushered them in, hopeful that what they had to tell Betsy would help to ease some pain. After a warm handshake they sat down opposite Betsy and proceeded to tell her what they knew of Alex's death.

"After he stepped down from the bus Alex collapsed on the pavement. A passer by tried to help him but it was already too late. He had died instantly. The police took him to the town morgue where they looked for identification in his clothing, but there was nothing there except some coins, which they laid aside. Then the police removed his watch and chain before his clothing. It was then that one of the staff, himself a Mason, recognized the patterns on the fob and suggested that the Lodge might supply an identity. So, they approached us and we were able to help." He continued,

"Alex would have been identified eventually through your appeals to the police, but it would have taken longer. Many people collapse daily in Jacksonville and many are never identified, so you have been saved that time of fear and worry."

Betsy nodded, grateful at last to have received some facts. Still gripping Jessie's hand, she spoke,

"Thank you for coming to tell us these things. We knew nothing from the police about how he died and why. We just had to go and identify him. It was so hard. This is Jessie Noble, Alex's sister. She has been here all the time. I dinna ken whit I wid hae deen without her."

Betsy lapsed into a sob.

"Now we have something else to discuss with you. Perhaps it's too early, but you need to know what we have to suggest so that you can think it over and come to a decision.

"We have not known Alex May very long but he has already become a valued member of our Lodge. We appreciated his deep Scottish thinking, his wise counsel and his real gentlemanly qualities. To mark our esteem for him we would like to give him a Masonic funeral and undertake the costs of all the funeral expenses. It would all be done with your approval and to your wishes of course."

Betsy sat speechless, gazing at the visitors. It was just dawning on her. What lay ahead? Funeral arrangements? What was she going to do afterwards? What about money? All they had in the bank was the little left over after their fares and setting up the home. The real money was in the business and tied up there. Betsy nodded at last.

"I dinna hae tae think it ower. I thank ye for yir offer and I accept it. We hae very little money at han', an' I cudna gie him a pauper's funeral. So I thank ye frae ma hairt. It seems like charity tae me bit, frae yir words, it is an honour ye are daen him an' he merits that. He wis a fine man. Thank ye."

So it was arranged. Alex was laid to rest in a quiet corner of the churchyard of the local Baptist Church. The coffin, the cortege, the refreshments and all the other accessories were provided for Betsy and she never knew how much it cost. The same two members from the Lodge joined the large gathering of mourners around the grave, but they were just two of the many folks who had come to know and appreciate Alex May during his few months as a businessman in Jacksonville.

Chapter 22

The children went back to school and Betsy resumed her housekeeping routine, always managing to present a courageous attitude for the sake of the children and friends. But at night, in the quiet of her own room, she battled with her overwhelming sorrow and loss, and an ever- increasing worry. How were they going to manage to survive without an income? The half yearly dividend from the business was only minimal at the moment, and she had no skills to offer apart from housekeeping. And who would employ her with four children? Maybe one yes, but not four. For nearly three weeks Betsy struggled with it. There was a decision she knew she had to make but, because it was one she wished to avoid, Betsy refused to give it con- sideration at all. It would negate all that she and Alex had planned and sacrificed for. And yet now, the responsibility was hers alone and she had to carry the load of deciding for the family.

The quandary was settled for her one evening when she had a late call from the two Masonic friends. She was sit- ting on the stoop in the darknes, enjoying the coolness of the evening before going in to light the lamps. They stopped by the gate and came in at her invitation.

Over coffee they inquired how Betsy and the children were getting on. Had they met any problems at school and had she herself had difficulties?

"You see, we were concerned about you being so newly arrived in Jacksonville and without extensive family support. This is all part of our Masonic pastoral work. We gave you a little time for grieving and adjustment and now we need to know if you require any help or advice from counselling. Have you taken any decision about your future? Are you planning to stay on in Jacksonville or have you decided to return to Scotland?"

As she listened to the quiet flow of the calm voice Betsy felt a great sense of relief and reassurance pass through her. Here was someone who understood her problem and was presenting her with that moment of decision, which she had been avoiding. Yes, she must go home to her family in Fraserburgh. How, she did not know, but that is what she must do. For the sake of the bairns. She could work there. But Alex would be here. Betsy knew within what Alex's advice would have been so she nodded her head,

"Yes, we need tae gang back tae Fraserburgh, but I dinna ken hoo we are tae get there."

"That is all we need to know. We can make the arrangements. We shall return very soon for some addresses, dates and other details, but just be encouraged. We do require you however, to say nothing to anyone, especially the children, until all is finalised. As you know, all our work is based on confidentiality and silent help. That is why we have not told you our names and why Mr. May did not reveal his Masonic connection to you, his wife. The Scriptures says, `Do not let your right hand know what your left hand giveth.' And `Do good deeds in secret.' That is what the Masonic rules follow."

That night, for the first time in a long while, Betsy slept soundly. No more wrestling now the decision had been made and voiced. The way ahead seemed clear and she could follow her natural instincts for planning and organizing their departure.

But some days were not so easy. Days when she was drawn back to his grave to sit and wonder how she could ever think of leaving him there alone. Because of her faith, Betsy knew that the real Alex was not there, but always with her in spirit. But here lay the Alex she had touched and loved and laughed and cried with. They had had this dream of their family and life together in Florida. Now it was all shattered, and she wept bitterly. How could God take away such a good man when they all needed him so?

But then, as though Alex had put his hand on her thoughts, she knew he was approving of her decision, encouraging her to go on with her planning and her journeying, and reassuring her of his presence day by day. She felt Alex's strength flow through her and she could turn away from the grave and go home to the children.

True to their promise, the two friends returned to collect addresses in Fraserburgh, check passport details and consult with Betsy about when she would be ready to leave. Within the following month all was organized, goodbyes were said to church and school friends, and they moved in with Jessie and Bill for the last few days. Over the past weeks it had been a very difficult time for them. To some extent they felt responsible for Betsy's financial plight, but could do nothing to ease the difficulty. Their money too was trapped in the business and they had nothing spare to lend. Betsy understood and assured them that she and Alex had faced up to the risks they had willingly incurred. She would be happy if they would dispose of the few pieces of furniture and send whatever share of the dividends was due to her at the end of the year.

The farewells were hard, Betsy remembering all the kindnesses of Jessie and Bill, especially at the time of Alex's death. She had grown so close to her sister-in-law and now, would most likely never see her again. Life had been so full of partings. As the train pulled away and they were still waving, Betsy caught a glimpse of her two Masonic friends standing at the back of the platform. They smiled and raised a hand in farewell and Betsy acknowledged them gladly. 'Caring to the end.' She thought.

The long journey northwards passed slowly. This time there was not the anticipation of meeting Father and the cousins, and of living in Jacksonville. But gradually the children began to remember their old school chums and the cousins in the Broch, and Granny, and the question of where they would stay. Lots of speculation, but it was a comfort to Betsy to hear them talk that way. She just felt that, once she was home again in Fraserburgh, things would work out for them all.

The first reunion would be in New York where, she was sure, after reading her telegram, Maggie Ann would be waiting for them and Betsy could hardly wait to see the familiar face. A long time had passed since Maggie went away. Would she have changed much in the twelve years?

But she need not have been concerned; Betsy spotted her at once pushing her way towards them along the thronging platform and, as she handed Norman into her sister's arms, Betsy for the first time, felt some release from the icy chill of grief, which had held her in its grip since Alex's death. For a little while she could hand over responsibility and leave the next few hours in Maggie Ann's care.

Chapter 23

The crossing was smooth and uneventful. Once they were clear of the sight of land and into the wider ocean, Betsy began to feel a sense of calm and healing for her emotional turmoil. Now that she was free of her commitments to people, she could concentrate only on herself and the children, and what might lie ahead of them. She would have to carry on alone, but Betsy was conscious all the time of her years with Alex and his wise counselling ways. She would go on like that and make a life for them all. These two wonderful days with Maggie Ann in New York had given her a glimpse of the joy that could still be theirs. She would never forget the memories of these hours.

Sometimes in the darkening, after the children were asleep, Betsy would stand at the stern following the wake of the ship and looking back into the glowing sky. There she saw the promise of hope and strength from her God and, always when the first star appeared, she knew she could trust in His faithfulness. And Alex was there with Him, still loving her and reaching out to them.

Day by day, Betsy was conscious of the good behaviour of the children, allowing her peace and time alone. Mary Bella had taken charge and, as Betsy watched her handling them, she realized who would be her major support and strong arm in the life ahead. She remembered Mary May's words when Mary Bella was born, "She'll bring ye baith great joy."

Now they were docking in Glasgow and hanging on the rail searching for George's long, craggy face in the crowd. There he was, smiling and waving and eventually they were in his arms. As he put his arm round her shoulders all he said was,

"Betsy, ma gerl, I'm verra sorry."

And then they set off to catch the train to Aberdeen.

It was late when the engine steamed into Fraserburgh station and the six weary travellers descended to the dark platform. A thick haar pervaded everything giving the dim, gas lamps an eerie glow as the damp wisps filtered by. Janet and Sandy stood waiting beside the guard at the barrier and there were just some silent hugs and handshakes in greeting, everyone too tired and emotional to say much. It was a relief to move freely again and the tramp of their feet as they passed through the echoing, gloomy, station hall excited the children as they ran to the door. There stood Sandy's faithful hurly and it was soon loaded with the hand luggage and then the children. The two men proceeded to push it up the Station Brae and then into Victoria Street while the sisters, arms linked, followed more slowly. As they left the station, Betsy paused momentarily, taking a brief look across at the harbour, and then she turned with Janet to continue their walk. It was so good to be in the cool, damp air and share the silence. Janet, as always, understood. There would be plenty of time to talk later.

All was ready at Ena's house. A meal was on the table and beds prepared. Mary May sat in her chair by the fire, hardly able to believe what was happening. All her life she had disdained to show emotion, but that night tears rolled down her cheeks as she held the children close.

"It's winnerfu. I niver thocht tae see ye aa again."

Talk was about their journey and the two wonderful days in New York with Maggie Ann, how wonderful she had been, and the good news that she would be home for a holiday in the spring. And then it was time for bed and quiet descended on the house. Once again Betsy and her children were in strange beds, but they were only one step away from their next home.

The following forenoon the three sisters and Mary May were round the table again enjoying a cup of tea as Betsy talked and described to them the events of their lives in Jacksonville.

So very much had been good and never to be forgotten, but the last few weeks had passed like a nightmare. As she had promised, Betsy said nothing about the aid from the Freemasons, but went on to describe Alex's funeral and then the decision to come home. Maggie Ann's help in New York had been amazing. She had really gone out of her way to make the day special for them all and Betsy would never forget that.

Once Betsy had ended her story Janet put her hand over hers.

"Betsy, we hiv aa felt for ye an' suffered for yir plicht, sae far awa. But only oor mither could raley ken whit ye hae geen through, an aa on yir ain tae." Mary May nodded and put out her hand,

"Aye lass, ye've lost a gweed man. Time 'll heal, bit ye'll aye be left wi a sair bittie there."

Janet continued,

"Noo, we wid like tae tell ye whit we hae planned for ye for the present. Fan we wrote tae tell Bella whit had happened an' that ye were comin' hame, she wrote back at eence tae say ye could hae their hoose at 21 Charlotte Street. As ye ken, they hae owned it for a curn o' years an' let the upstairs, but kept the doonstairs for thir ain holidays frae Hartlepool. Noo, they want you tae use the rooms, tae mak yir hame there for as lang as ye want. There's twa big rooms doonstairs, a bedroom up, an a sma room aaf the kitchenette at the back. It wad dae ye fine an' it's near han' yir foulk."

Betsy just gazed, overwhelmed at this news, unable to speak. Gratitude could not adequately express her feelings of relief so she just nodded and smiled through her tears.

That afternoon the little group of sisters and the children took the short walk down Charlotte Street and opened the door of No.21. It gave directly on to the pavement, and the well scrubbed stone doorstep and half moon of pavement, gleamed in the sunshine. There was a hallway ahead leading to the rear of the house and to the right, a staircase rose to the upper flat. Everything smelled clean and fresh and the potted aspidistra at the foot of the stairs gave a welcoming effect.

The back room was the sitting room with a fine burning range with ovens, and the front and upstairs rooms were bedrooms with a double bed in each. Everywhere was comfortably but simply furnished, as behoved a holiday home and the extension at the back provided the sink, and oil fuelled cooker, an inside toilet and the little room which Betsy immediately saw as her own. This was her domain and she would have her single bed here where she could work without disturbing anyone. The garden was right there and, as in Barskimming House, she would be able to garden, keep her hens, and come and go by the back gate at the end of the yard. It was all rushing through her head at once. But when she opened the cupboard doors and saw the shelves packed with food, the linen piled neatly in the press, the coal in the scuttle and the flowers in the vase on the table, it was too much for her and Betsy just sat down and wept uncontrollably. The others left her alone and went to make a pot of tea in the scullery while the children went to explore the yard and garden. Later, Janet and Ena told her,

"Fan the news o' Alex cam oot and then that ye were comin hame wi the bairns, a' yir freens were concerned for ye. Mony offered a place tae bide, bit, fan Bella and Willie gied us this hoose, we thocht it best tae keep it in the faimily. It's yours for as lang as ye want it. Kennen you, ye micht want tae mak an arrangement wi Bella, bit for noo, settle doon an' come tae yersel. A' that ye see in the press was gien by yir freens an', I'm sure ye wull hae mair tae come yet. They are jist anxious tae show thir concern for ye. Ye did the same yersel in the auld days on Albert Street; so accept it in the spirit it was meant. Noo, faar is abody gaan tae sleep?"

"We're haen the front room." immediately from Jane.

"Weel, we'll hae tae sort it oot. Norman is three noo so he can share wi Alex upstairs. You gerls can hae the front room bed an' I'll hae the little back room for masel. We'll start awa like that till we see foo things work oot. I maun write Bella at eence an' tell her fu grateful we are. An tae ye aa. Nae words can express whit I feel for ye."

Later, as they walked up Charlotte Street to call in for a moment with Janet at No 51, and then on to Ena's for tea and a second night, there was a new spring in their step. The children laughed again and, as they passed the Central

School, the talk was of going back there tomorrow. Life was beginning again for them. They had a home, a family, school, and what was needed now was work for Betsy. Already her plans were formulating.

Chapter 24

The following weeks were busy. Many visitors called bringing comfort and gifts and one in particular was the Rev. William Farrar from the Baptist Church. He was the pastor who had wished them Godspeed and now he was here to welcome back Betsy and the children and to pass on a gift of money from the Church Fellowship Fund. He alone had the disposal of this fund and it was given in needy cases. Betsy was quite taken aback at this offer and, as graciously as she could, refused the money saying that they would manage, and that there must be many people in more need of it than they were. The old Betsy pride was returning.

She had much on her mind these first weeks at home. For work she had three options. She could go gutting, but that was seasonal and would require Jane to leave school and be at home. She could go out cleaning, but that was too poorly paid for the long hours of work, again away from home. Her third and favourite choice would be to start a shop, here in the house, where she could run the home and make a living at the same time. For that she needed the permission of Bella and Willie, the local authorities, and the neighbours on each side of No.21. The more she thought about it she visualized selling eggs from her own hens, vegetables fresh from the garden, home baked scones and tarts, and all the other goods provided by a small, general store. She felt excited and hopeful and full of purpose for the future. In fact it was the greatest challenge and antidote to the grief and despondency that still overwhelmed her occasionally.

In due course she dealt with all the correspondence and, while she waited for replies, got on with preparing the garden, the hen run, again with Sandy's help, and reorganizing the house.

The children had already happily returned to school, back to their former classes and friends and now they had new friends from the neighbouring families, the Hays on one side and the Stopannis on the other. So it was a good little group going up Charlotte Street together every morning.

One of her first responsibilities was the sad visit to Alex's family, now living in Loch Street in Aberdeen. Betsy took the children to stay overnight and then returned home on the Saturday. Alex's mother now lived with her daughter Mary Ann and, losing her eldest child so soon after his father, had dealt her a second blow. Betsy had dreaded the visit but it was right that they should hear the story from her, even though it opened the wounds again. She was also anxious that the children should know and keep the strong contacts with their Father's people and she promised, all being well, to carry on the New Year's Day visits.

Eventually, the required permissions came back. Bella and Willie were enthusiastic about the shop project and agreed that she should pay them a rent once the business was established. As there were not too many shops in that section of Charlotte Street, the local authorities had no objections as long as Betsy fulfilled the By Laws, and the neighbours were pleased to have a convenient store so nearby

Betsy proceeded to rearrange the house and dispersed the front room furniture throughout the other rooms. The large lined and floored attic was cleaned and became a wonderful room for the boys, and the girls moved up into the bedroom on the first floor, leaving the large front room ready for shelves, a counter and a window display shelf. Sandy did the joinery work; the cost of which Betsy added to her growing list of debts to pay once the shop was functioning properly.

She next visited the wholesale department of Macdonald the grocer on Cross Street. Here was where her Mother had shopped and as children, they had always accompanied her on Saturday afternoons. Betsy too had been a regular customer in the Albert Street days so she was well known and respected, which was important in view of what she was going to require of the shop. Betsy explained her situation, that she had no capital, but if Macdonalds would supply her with a basic stock to start off with, namely dry goods, tinned food varieties, cigarettes and sweets, she would commit to paying back a weekly percentage. However, knowing her story and her reputation for honesty, the firm agreed to supply her needs without her weekly commitment as long as she remained a loyal and regular customer. Again Betsy marvelled at the kindness shown her.

So the shop at No.21, commonly known as 'Betty May's', began and it was to be their mainstay for many years. Every one in the household had a part to play. Jane dealt with the housekeeping and cleaning for the family, Mary Bella helped in the shop, kept the books and arranged the stock, Alex took charge of Norman, worked in the garden and made the occasional delivery while Betsy herself cooked, baked, bottled beetroot, made jam, prepared potted meat, all to sell, and she tended her hens and her precious garden which in coming years, would supply the seasonal vegetables for the shop. No one was ever idle.

There had always to be time for the school homework and even to play a little but after the shop closed on Saturday afternoon, then it was family time and all day Sunday. They were happy together. Their lives now were new, belonging to a totally different way of life. Yes, they were poor, but what they had was due to their own efforts and they made a good team.

All the relatives and neighbours supported the shop with their custom and Betsy was amazed how quickly she got to know the local people of all ages. Being a gregarious person by nature, she enjoyed the camaraderie over the counter, she heard herself laughing again and her busy days allowed her little time to mourn. But in the quiet of the evening, before going to bed, they would sometimes talk together of the old times with Father and Betsy was glad to encourage these moments. They had been privileged to have a very special Father and she wanted them always to keep his memory alive.

Chapter 25

The spring-cleaning was early and very thorough this year. Maggie Ann, true to her word, was arriving soon and the sisters were somewhat in awe of this person who had such a grand job as housekeeper to a Professor. It was so long since they had seen their sister, they really did not know what to expect. Betsy had assured them that she was still the same and very much the old Maggie Ann, but they found that hard to believe, and so were anxious to give her no reason for criticism. All four sisters had comfortable homes but they did wish to make a good impression on this sister who had been adventurous enough to leave the Broch and seek a new world. Her life was so different to theirs and they were just a bit nervous about how she would react to them all, especially the children whom she had never seen.

Maggie Ann had written to say she would be travelling with Jane Cow who was also coming home on holiday to Cairnbulg, so there was no need to meet her at Glasgow. They would arrive at Fraserburgh on the evening train and she was looking forward to seeing them all then. And so, on the first Tuesday in April, they were all there standing waiting for the signal that the train was approaching. They made quite a gathering. Bella and Willie with their two girls had already arrived from Hartlepool for a few days, part of their Easter break, so the family was complete.

Only Alex was missing and Betsy felt that acutely. Tom and Willie, Janet's two sons, towered over the six girls and Alex and the two little boys, Wilfred and Norman, played hide and seek between the legs of the adults until they were caught from the danger of falling off the platform. Mary May was there too, closely supported by Mary Bella, and when Maggie Ann stepped from the train, they were the first to greet her and feel her arms about them.

After all the introductions to the children the gathering moved to Janet's house where Maggie Ann was going to stay. There they ate supper and talked and Mary May sat back, quietly listening, and oh so grateful that she had seen the return of her precious first born. No one would ever know how much Maggie Ann had meant to her in those long ago years of struggle and she was so glad that her daughter had found happiness and fulfilment in her life in Boston.

The month soon passed. Maggie Ann spent most of the time with her sisters, endlessly talking and learning all that had happened in the long interval. She went often to Cairnbulg to visit her aging Aunt Annie and Mary May often accompanied her, enjoying her support on the train journey. Maggie Ann was saddened to see how frail her mother and Aunt had become and was all the more thankful that she had returned now.

Maggie Ann was still concerned about Betsy and the future of her children and so she often dropped into the shop for a chat. She could see that Betsy was handling the whole situation well and, as she had expected, was finding purpose and an outlet for her energy as well as making a livelihood. She was not sure just how well the shop was doing but it was early days yet. What she did observe was the way the children returned from school, changed into their work clothes, and turned to their various tasks. Jane had her cleaning and ironing routine, Mary Bella relieved her Mother in the shop and was responsible also for restacking the shelves and keeping the shop and entrance clean, and Alex found plenty to do with the outside chores, gardening and looking after his small brother Norman. Maggie Ann was impressed by what she saw and wondered if she should interfere at all. However, the opportunity occurred one day and she broached the subject.

"Betsy, when we were together in New York and I met all the bairns, an idea came to me and I want to tell you about it. I wondered if you would allow Jane to come and live with me in Boston and train to be a housekeeper. There is such a great opportunity out there and such wonderful positions to be had amongst the wealthy families. It is very different from here where domestics are regarded as slavies and treated as such. There, you are respected and you become one of the family. The Ripley's home is my home and, as my niece, Jane would be welcomed into the family.

"It would be one less for you to keep and she would have something better to look forward to than the gutting yard or service to the rich folk in the Broch. Just think it over. As long as you know that I am willing for her to come."

Betsy's face was a study, quite shocked at this suggestion. Tears came into her eyes as she shook her head.

"Maggie Ann, she's nae fourteen till August. I cudna lat her gang a' that wye. I jist cudna lat her awa. She wis my first baby an' brocht sae much joy tae Alex an' me. I cudna pairt wi her noo. An' I need her here tae help me in the hoose. I thank ye Maggie Ann for thinking aboot us an' wantin' tae help, an' for that winnerfu' time in New York, but I canna think o' lattin her gang sae far awa yet. Maybe in a year or twa, but nae noo."

Maggie nodded, not surprised at the reply, and just left the idea to germinate. The matter was not referred to again for the rest of Maggie's visit, but at the goodbyes Betsy quietly embraced her whispering,

"Thank you Maggie Ann for athing ye hae deen for us an' I hinna forgotten whit ye said."

So Maggie once more departed, sad at leaving the ones she held most dear. She had a precious family in Fraserburgh and she intended to return to them much sooner next time.

Chapter 26

"Mam, Mam! Ye'll hae tae come. Norman's nae weel. I canna waaken him up an' he's roassin."

When Betsy saw Norman she knew something serious was wrong. For a few days he had been listless and she just thought he had a touch of cold. But now he was in a deep fever and, remembering Alex's illness, she knew she had to get the fever down and send for the doctor.

"Alex, bring me up half a pail o' verra caal watter an' twa clean dish tools fae the press. Be verra quait on the stairs. You gang in ower my bed and syne ye can rin for the doctor fan it's day licht. I'll try an' get doon this fever a bit afore he comes."

And so Betsy worked on Norman with the cold compresses on his head and body, stripping the bed to the sheets, even cutting off his flannel nightshirt. He seemed to be burning up, but gradually he quietened and rested more easily. She could see a flicker of his eyelids and Betsy began to hope she was winning. But there was always the restless turning of the head from side to side as if Norman was in pain so she held on the cold cloths wrapped around and down the sides of his head. It was a relief when Alex arrived about six o'clock, ready to go for Dr. Mc.Laren.

"Mrs. May, you've done a good job here. You may even have saved the boy's life for you have stemmed a deep fever.

He is still very, very ill and I have to tell you he has caught Infantile Paralysis. That can have very serious affects on the body, as you maybe know, and it is also very infectious. Now you could nurse him yourself at home, but with other children in the house and so many round the doors, I strongly advise you to allow him to go to hospital until he is better and the infection gone.

"The house will need to be fumigated and the children kept off school till we see if they are free from infection. You must not let them mix with the other children till they are cleared. We have had a few cases in the town lately and it's worrying how it spreads."

"The cabby arrived for Norman and, wrapped in a red hospital blanket, he was gently carried down stairs and laid on the long seat. The door closed, the horse was whipped up and Norman was away, leaving the family on the doorstep and a crowd of curious neighbours standing around. The arrival of the `cabby' always caused a stir and drew a crowd.

Betsy quietly gathered her children inside and closed the outer door. The shop would not open again till they had the all clear from the health authorities. Deep inside, she wondered what next could befall them. Also she worried about the outcome of Norman's illness. Would he be mentally affected or lose the power of his limbs? She had heard some terrible things about Infantile Paralysis.

In the days that followed the house was fumigated and cleaned as never before. Every article, tin and packet in the shop was dealt with, counter, shelves, windows and doors were washed with chloride of lime and Lysol and all the bedding blew on the lines day after day. At last they had fulfilled the required quarantine and taken all the necessary measures to be declared free of contamination. Not another child on Charlotte Street caught the disease, for which Betsy was very thankful, and now the children could go back to school, Jane reluctantly, but Mary Bella and Alex very gladly, for both enjoyed learning and did well.

Meantime Norman lay in a small isolation ward along with three other children, all suffering at different stages of the same disease. Although they could not touch or speak with him, Betsy and the others could come to a window and wave to him lying in bed. After a time he was taking notice of them and waved back and then one day, he was wheeled to the open window and spoke with them, telling them all about his friends in the ward. But he did want to know when they were coming to take him home. Betsy told him,

"When you are strong again and able to walk."

Betsy felt a huge relief that Norman could speak sensibly and had all his faculties and she considered it just a matter of time till he was fit to come home. However, one day Dr. Mc. Laren called for a private talk with her.

"Mrs. May, I have delayed having this meeting with you for I wanted to be sure about Norman's progress before I presented you with the facts of his condition. As you can see he has made a wonderful recovery and I'm glad to say he has all his mental faculties intact. He is a very bright child, talks well and knows a lot for his age. The fever has not affected him in any way except for a weakness in his right foot and leg. This is caused by an atrophy of the muscle and tendons in his ankle due to the effects of the virus. At the moment he will have to use crutches to get around and he will be limited in his activities. As long as he is growing it will be so but, once he is physically mature, an operation can give him back the use of his foot and ankle. Doctors in America have discovered a way to transplant live sinews and ligaments from behind the knee into the ankle, enabling the foot to operate up and down. But he will have to be sixteen before they will perform that operation. And it can only be done in Boston in the States."

Betsy sat gazing at the doctor, hearing his voice coming and going and all the time thinking,

"Norman needs crutches. My baby is a cripple. How will I be able tae manage wi a' that?"

The doctor stopped speaking, allowing Betsy to take in the heartbreaking news. He knew her story and her already proven courage and strength, but he also knew there was a limit to human endurance and hurt. Would this lady have the strength to face this new challenge? When Betsy began to ask about the crutches and the operation in Boston and what part she could play in strengthening the leg, Dr. Mc. Laren knew she would win through.

"Daily massage is the best advice I can give you. This keeps the circulation moving and the muscles and joints flexing. It prevents the leg from withering and keeps the tissue fresh. I have read that fresh seawater has great healing properties. You have that on your doorstep and it's something the children could help you with. Otherwise, treat Norman as normally as possible. He is a strong boy and should not be regarded as an invalid. I shall keep a regular check on his leg until he is ready for the operation."

So Norman came home complete with his small crutches, which he used with great dexterity. He was quite a hero on the street and showed off a little by climbing the stairs with one crutch. He joined in most of the games on the street but when it came to football, he would retire to his stool by the shop door to watch. Betsy could read the resignation on his face and her heart went out to him. Day by day he was growing so like his father, features, colouring and even the quiet capable manner of handling himself that Alex had. How she missed him. How wonderful if he could only have been here just now.

Chapter 27

Another year and Norman would be school age and Betsy's new dilemma was how to get him to school. It was too far to walk on crutches and uphill for most of the way. He would need to be accompanied which would mean closing the shop at the busy morning time and going with him. She had much on her mind to sort out. Also, since the quarantine, the shop had not picked up so well and Betsy was straining to meet her wholesale bills. There was really no profit for family use. Maggie's offer began to stir in Betsy's mind. At least that would give her one less mouth to feed.

Jane was very keen to leave school. Now that she had moved to the Academy she found it hard to be a small pebble on a wide beach. Always attention seeking, she had enjoyed holding court in her Primary class and currying the teacher's favour, but Secondary school was different and Jane was unhappy. When Betsy eventually told her of Maggie's suggestion Jane's face lit up and, without hesitation, she said she would go. In fact, she began at once to plan clothes and dream of the ship and the fine house she would be working in. But that did not solve Betsy's problems and much had to be arranged such as clothing for Jane, correspondence with Maggie, a passport and booking her passage.

As usual the family rallied and garments were donated, some new and some for make over, and, evening by evening, Betsy and the girls stitched and the little trunk began to fill. Betsy dropped a few tears amongst the garments; saddened that Jane was so anxious to go. And Mary Bella just felt a little pang of jealousy that all this finery was for Jane and never for her. Not that she would go to America. Her mother needed her here and Mary Bella had some ideas of her own about that.

News came back from Maggie that she was delighted that Jane was coming and the Ripley family was happy to welcome her into the household. She would go ahead with booking a passage for Jane as soon as Betsy could have her ready and Maggie would pay for all the extra expenses. The only remaining hurdle was a medical examination, which had to be gone through at the U.S. Immigration Centre at Glasgow. Due to her young age and the fact that she would be unaccompanied by family, this check was obligatory. Betsy had no worries about Jane's health so, when George Noble volunteered to accompany Jane to Glasgow, she waved them off confidently, proud of Jane, so smart in one of her new outfits.

Three days later they returned, very downcast. Jane had not passed the test and would not be going to the States. She refused to discuss the matter, to give any explanation, and firmly stated that she had left school and would work at home and help look after Norman. Betsy was shocked and mystified, even angry, but at the same time, now and again happy that she was not losing Jane. Eventually, George in private related to her all that had happened in Glasgow.

As the journey south progressed he was aware that Jane's excited chatter about Boston grew less and less. It was as though she was becoming aware of the increasing distance from home. Then, when they walked in the city, she was totally silent, overwhelmed by the crowds and noise and the tall buildings. Their short visit to the docks to see the liners produced little response and so, when they received the results of the medical examination, George was not surprised to hear that Jane had failed to pass. She had pleaded pains in her legs, breathlessness, and during the eye tests, had given nonsense readings on the letter board. There was no possible way that she could be a suitable candidate for settlement in the States and the examining board had recognised her deception. To say the least, George had been embarrassed by the whole episode and felt very sad for Betsy as he related the story. They decided that the matter was now closed and would not be referred to again. Betsy would notify Maggie to cancel the sailing and the other details.

The family, for the most part, was not surprised at Jane's rebellion. Over the years they had recognised the ease with which she deceived and told lies, but they also considered it was asking much of a fourteen year old to leave home and travel so far to strangers. Janet and Ena had both voiced their thoughts to Betsy but she had been sure of Jane's desire to go. Mary May, blunt as always,

"Aye, she'll try ye tae the bitter end Betsy. She's the sleekit oolet."

Chapter 28

But the question of the States did not go away. Another letter arrived from Maggie suggesting that perhaps Mary Bella might like to go in place of Jane.

Once again Betsy was faced with the dilemma of parting with a child or saying `No' to Maggie and depriving the child of an opportunity in life. Mary Bella was only thirteen and still at school but already Betsy regarded her as her mainstay and support. She possessed a mature, common sense and lacked nothing in initiative and practical planning. The previous summer she had spent her holiday working hard at all hours in the gutting yard to bring in some money for her mother and now she had returned to school with the firm intention of leaving at fourteen and becoming a wage earner for the home. Jane was helping in the shop so she would earn outside the home. Could Betsy let her go? She knew that Mary Bella, if asked, would accept the proposal. If it was to be a solution to Betsy's difficult situation Mary Bella's sense of duty and responsibility would win and she would go, no matter how much it hurt to leave her family and friends and especially her beloved Granny, Mary May.

Betsy pondered long, unwilling to resurrect the question after the upheaval caused by Jane's refusal to go. Relative calm had descended on the household with Mary Bella and Alex at school, and Jane proving herself a great help in running the home and especially in her handling of Norman. Betsy now had time to concentrate on the shop and making goods to sell. Her baking was widely acclaimed and, at that end of Charlotte Street there seemed to be a growing clientele of young men who frequented her shop for cigarettes and sweets. Things were picking up and Betsy could have now felt more at ease with her life had it not been for worry over Norman and his schooling and now this problem of Maggie's letter.

It was Jane who finally opened the subject of Maggie and the Ripleys. While dusting one day she came on the letter tucked behind the clock on the mantelpiece. Recognising the stamp, and eager to see Maggie's reaction to the change of plan, without a qualm, she read the letter. Jane felt rather piqued that Maggie should express no disappointment over her refusal and had now asked for Mary Bella, so at the first opportunity she could not resist passing on the information to see her sister's reaction. Mary Bella quietly listened then turned away as though the news presented no surprise. For some time she had had the feeling that eventually she would be the one to go and it would happen when she was fourteen. If that was how she could best help the family so be it. Of course she did not want to go and leave them all behind. Norman, Alex, her cousins Nellie and Netta, the aunts and above all, Granny growing so frail; along with the school friends they filled her world and parting from them would be terrible. On the other hand, she remembered the other crossing not so long ago and that day with Maggie in New York. She had been so kind to them and had been such a help to Mother. Mary Bella thought about the work opportunities in Fraserburgh and they did not present a great prospect. So she decided that if her mother asked her to go she would agree without fuss and meantime continue at school.

When Betsy discovered Jane's meddling and mischief making she was furious. For the first time it seemed she acknowledged Jane's deceitful habits and strongly rebuked her for deliberately interfering and going behind her back. After her own performance Mary Bella's future was none of her business and Jane should have had more respect for her mother and her sister. But now the matter was out in the open and Betsy decided to leave the choice to Mary Bella. If her daughter decided to go to Maggie, then Betsy would find a travelling companion for her and there would not be a repeat of the Jane fiasco. Mary Bella was a very different type of young person; there would be no scenes with her.

Mary Bella became fourteen in July and by then preparations were well ahead. The passport was to hand along with a welcoming letter of residence from Professor Ripley, the sailing was booked and the medical examination successfully passed. Betsy had found a travelling companion for Mary Bella in the person of a lady, Margaret White from St. Combs. She was a stranger to them but was sailing to Boston on the same ship and was willing to supervise Mary Bella. Most of the clothing prepared for Jane was altered for the taller Mary Bella and so all was ready for the day of parting.

It took Betsy a very long time to get over the horror of that day. She felt like a criminal. The sisters and her mother could not understand how she would allow her child to undertake such a break from her family and home; and alone, into service in a strange house with a strict maiden aunt she hardly knew. And to go on that journey alone with a stranger. Betsy also knew in her heart that Alex would

never have condoned the action and that hurt her all the more. They could have managed, the five of them together. But once the wheels got rolling she could not seem to halt the process and once Mary Bella had decided to go there was no changing her decision. Betsy knew very well that at that point she had lost the most valuable and responsible of her children. Jane was fickle and Alex and Norman too young, but Mary Bella had shared her every worry and hope.

The day Mary Bella left home Betsy was too confused to really understand how it had all come about. The pain under her ribs was very real. She herself was hurting, but all the more so for the hurt she was causing other people; her mother, the close and wider family, the friends and most of all, Mary Bella herself who must have a sad and strange opinion of a mother who would allow this to happen to her daughter. She would never forget the strained, white face as Mary Bella waved goodbye at the door and walked away with Ena to the station. Would she ever see her again? Somehow Betsy felt another chapter of her life had been closed. She had Norman to deal with and Alex to keep studying to prepare for an apprenticeship, Jane would eventually need to have some sort of occupation; and of course the ongoing shop to provide them with a livelihood. Plenty to work for, but she would so miss the long legged daughter with the freckles and flying, black hair who kept them all organised and positive in their outlook. She had inherited so many of her father's traits.

As long as she was busy in the shop and in the home Betsy managed to keep a cheerful aspect but there were times when her loss was almost too much to bear. It was like a death in the family, the second in two years. An overpowering sense of guilt lay heavy on her mind and she could not free herself of the knowledge that she had let Alex down and had not measured up to the high regard, which he had always felt toward her. Mary Bella was his favourite child and what had she done to her? Yes, it would likely be to her advantage and Maggie and the Ripleys would be good to her, but it was the sending her away so young and on her own.

Betsy struggled with her thoughts and was always glad of her walk to collect the tidal water for Norman's massage. As she slipped out at the back gate and walked down the quiet lane to the Broadsea shore, she could give way to her tears and thus found a certain release and balm. This was when she prayed and asked God to forgive her if her decision had been wrong. Daily she committed Mary Bella and the family to His care and gradually found some peace from her turmoil. She also came to realise that for too long she had left God out of her calculations and now it was time to return to the church family, and the sense of security brought by her faith in God.

At last the long awaited telegram arrived saying all was well. Mary Bella had arrived safely. A long letter followed, partly written by Maggie and by Mary Bella. It had been a good crossing and Mary Bella had enjoyed it. There were lots of children on the ship, mainly from Eastern Europe, and Margaret White had been good company. Mary Bella had spent a very long time going through the immigration barriers and that was where Maggie and Professor Ripley had finally collected her. She had her own room and her household tasks to do, but she had to go to school during the mornings as she was under fifteen, the States' school leaving age. The Professor had to promise this as a condition of her residency in the States. The letter continued with more details of her arrival and her meeting with the

Ripley children and the rest of the household and, to Betsy reading it, Mary Bella seemed to be happy and settled to her new life. The tone of the letter did much to ease Betsy's mind and lift the cloud of guilt.

Betsy, Norman and Jane at Fraserburgh, Scotland c 1918

Chapter 29

The time flew by and, within a few weeks of Mary Bella's departure, another event took place, which submerged all other thoughts. Britain with France and other countries had declared war on Germany. Fraserburgh was in a frenzy of recruitment parades and bands, and parents feared for their sons who were so fired up with patriotism and a desire to be in on the action. Charlotte Street was so well populated by young men, most of them apprentices and `joining up' was all their conversation when they came to the shop. Betsy was thankful that Alex was too young, but Janet's boys, Tom and Willie were the right age and their friends, the three Findlay boys across the street, Jim, Alex and Bobby were also full of enthusiasm. Getting to `the Front' was vital, and as soon as possible, to have a go at the Hun and get the war over with. Remembering the tragic losses during the Boer War and its affect on Broadsea, Betsy cringed when she heard their talk. The Boer War was so far away but this one was so much nearer in France.

Gradually the boys disappeared from the street although some delayed a bit to finish an apprenticeship. Tom went to the Royal Navy, Willie as a qualified chemist joined the Medical Corp, Jim Findlay became a signaller in the Royal Horse Artillery and was in time for the major thrust at the Somme where he was wounded, Alex joined the Gordon Highlanders and unscathed, went over the top from the trenches at Passchendaele and Bobby, only eighteen, enlisted in the Royal Engineers and was in time for the great Battle at Cambrai where he died in the last months of the war. So many went from the street and many returned exhausted, wounded and disillusioned, all the glory gone out of the great adventure. But so many did not return and in this close-knit community the sorrow was shared by all. Every day Betsy heard the latest information in the shop and, in her old habit of supporting the bereaved, she would make a point of going to the family with some sort of aid and comfort.

Things were not easy in the shop. Because of scarcity, wholesalers were allowing only quotas of supplies, especially of tinned and packet goods, Betsy's main merchandise, so she had to rely more and more on her own produce, baking, vegetables and potatoes. She took orders for dried and smoked fish which she cured in the wash house using her mother's methods, and Sandy kept her supplied with bundles of firewood kindling to sell in the shop. They made a living and their home routine was good. Jane was content in the shop and house and Alex was progressing well at the Academy. He had his name already entered in the Consolidated Pneumatic Tool Company to begin an engineering apprenticeship when he became sixteen. Norman continued to improve and, by the time he was five, was strong enough to tackle school. How that was to be achieved had been an on going worry to Betsy but it was resolved in a wonderful way.

For some time Janet and Sandy had been aware of Norman's transport problem and had discussed it with Ena and George. He was not an invalid requiring a wheel chair and, using his crutch, was perfectly mobile. What Norman needed was a means of travel that he could control and power himself without requiring his mother to accompany him to school. A boy had to feel independent, particularly if he had a handicap like Norman. Finally they came up with the idea of an adapted tricycle.

Sandy and George searched second hand shops in Fraserburgh, Peterhead, Aberdeen and many country places until they found a tricycle in good condition and large enough to last Norman for a few years. It was stored in the cooperage where Sandy worked on it cleaning, scraping, painting it a fine blue colour and finally he set about his adaptations. On the right hand side of the upright bar and just clear above the pedals, Sandy fashioned and attached a wooden cradle to support the weak leg. Then he fixed a block to the left pedal to enable Norman to reach on the large tricycle and finally, two brackets were fixed, one under the seat and another at the top of the upright bar just under the handlebars. These would carry his crutch on his journey. Last of all, George had a beautiful, sailcloth bag made and attached behind the seat to carry his books and lunch box. It was a wonderful machine, created with imagination and love and meant to be a total surprise for Betsy and Norman.

A week before he began school Norman and Betsy were called to the front door to find Janet, Sandy, Ena and George on the doorstep. There stood the gleaming, blue tricycle waiting to be mounted and Norman's eyes lit up. Betsy was speechless. After a few adjustments to the seat and the foot pedal Norman was away on his own, steering carefully and learning to control the brake on the right handlebar. The child was totally enthralled, so proud to be moving without the crutch or the limp. It would be another year before his left leg was long enough to propel him along but meantime, family and friends would push Norman.

Sandy had another aid for this and next day he arrived with a sturdy, walking stick. The ferule had been replaced by a neat metal hook, which clipped under the seat and enabled the pusher to work from an upright position. When not in use it would lie alongside the crutch. It made a fine little outfit, which any boy would be proud of.

On enrolment day Betsy followed Norman and his retinue all the way to the top of Charlotte Street and round the Hexagon to the Infant School. She was anxious to discuss his difficulties with the Headmistress and to arrange for the tricycle to be carefully housed while he was in school. She need not have worried for it was all arranged. The janitor, Mr Watson, would meet Norman at the gate every morning and bring the machine into his own shed for safety. And then after school he would see that Norman was safely mounted and one of his friends organized to accompany him home. Betsy was greatly reassured by the thoughtfulness and willingness of the staff and again experienced a lifting of the load of worry she seemed to carry day by day. In her conversations with Miss Tait Betsy related a little of Norman's background and how anxious she was that he did well and enjoyed school. With his handicap he would be unable to have a practical occupation and therefore had to develop his mental skills and become educated in that field. Miss Tait agreed and encouraged Betsy to keep thinking that way. She would be welcome to call at the school any time to discuss Norman's progress and to suggest any further ways they could assist.

There was a spring in Betsy's step as she set out for home taking the longer way round by the Hexagon for she could not yet bring herself to pass Barskimming House, 'their house'. How handy it would have been if they had still lived there on Albert Street, right in the middle of the schools as Alex had planned so long ago.

Now there was just the question of Jane to settle. She had been accepted for nursing training in the Tomas Walker Hospital and would begin the course when she was sixteen. Betsy was not sure whether Jane's desire to become a nurse was real or if it was the attraction of the uniform but watching her patient handling of Norman, Betsy had a hope that Jane would succeed in making this a good career.

Now that all her brood was accounted for Betsy planned to have more time in the shop developing her range of goods and branching out into new 'home made' lines. The fish and baking were doing well and Betsy now planned to try 'potted herring'; easy to make but smelly while cooking. Again the washhouse would be handy but before that she must thoroughly clean it and white wash the walls.

So Betsy's resourcefulness continued. There was no end to her energy and her cheerful courage in tackling difficulties. And in trying to run a shop there occurred plenty of these. Her clientele was suffering from a tragic war. In spite of a war effort unemployment was increasing and money was scarce. Betsy found it hard to redeem debts from those who ran up credit bills. Finally, taking advice from George, Betsy put up a sign saying, "No Credit Given" but, after a few hours, she took it down again. That sign was not the way. Why should she make life more difficult for people already suffering? People should help each other. So Betsy continued to give credit and where she knew there was real need, she would slip in an extra piece of baking or pound of sugar. Some Saturdays a better off customer would settle her bill and most weeks Betsy would count her takings and find herself in profit, narrow but enough.

Eventually the war would end and things would get better. The men would come home and the street would come alive again. Jane would become a nurse, Alex an engineer, Norman would do well in his studies and hopefully walk again, and some day Mary Bella would return from the States. That was Betsy's dream, which she held on to, leaving the future in God's hands for she had learned that His way was best.

Part 3
Mary Bella 1912-1979

Chapter 1

Mary Bella was my mother. I was her second child and I knew and loved her for the last fifty years of her life. Mary Bella never considered her early life to be of interest to anyone and therefore, it was not easy to persuade her to talk about it. However, there were occasions. In the early days she would take me to bed for a rest on Sunday afternoons, hoping I would sleep, but instead I insisted on a story- my favourite being the snakes in Florida. Another time I was recovering from a long, painful illness and she spent many hours in the night telling me stories of her childhood on the Broadsea shore and her visits to Shetland and Aberdeen. The most fruitful time was during her last year in life when she lived in our home and we talked long into the night, almost as if she realized there was not much time left for sharing. I recount these treasured memories in her own words.

"Yes, I had a very happy childhood. I suppose you could say I had two homes. The main one was at School Street with my Mother, Jane and Alex and Father, when he wasn't away at a fishing. It was nice there. Clean and shining and there was always a good smell of baking and cooking. We hadn't a garden but there was a big close and yard where we played with the Taits. Martha and Alex were our age and our best friends. They lived in the front house on to the street and we were in the back house up the stone stairs.

"But my other home was with my Granny in Broadsea and that was my favourite. You see, my Granny was special. I was her favourite granddaughter, the oldest and, though she never told me, I just knew she loved me. I would have done anything for her. I learned to walk with her and, I understand, as soon as I was weaned, she took charge of me so that my Mother could look after Jane and later Alex. Granny carried me until I could walk and then we went on the Braes together and we guddled in the rock pools for crabs and fish or gathered whelks.

"On the Thursdays, when she did her fish round, I was at home with my Mother, but all the other days I was with Granny 'helping' her and all the time copying her in so many ways. When my legs were long enough I accompanied her on her country round. It was shorter now that she was older, but it was still five miles and the creel was as heavy as ever. I carried the basket with the specials covered with a snow-white cloth. I always got a scone and jam at certain farms and sometimes a penny was slipped into my apron pocket, but Granny did not like that. She preferred to exchange her fish for butter and eggs and did not approve of children being given money. She would have nothing to do with charity of any sort.

"My favourite day was Saturday afternoon when we went to the shops to pay her bills at the butcher's and grocer's. They were never big bills as there was just the two of us at home, but she was a person of routine and this had been her Saturday programme all her married life; her weekly excursion into the world outside Broadsea and the fisher folks. I always felt a bit scared in the butcher's because of the two bulls' heads staring down at us from the walls. Their horns were monstrous and they looked so real. But I loved the smells in McDonald the grocer's and the soft sawdust under our feet. Granny always bought me a lollipop and I sucked it slowly to make it last as long as possible. We always came back by the Braes and then I went home to School Street to sleep as we went to Church and Sunday school the next day.

"Apart from Saturday and Sunday, until I was five, I slept with my Granny in the box bed in the kitchen. Friday night was special as the house was all clean; I had a bath by the fire and my hair was washed and pleated; the feather bed had been all taken apart and shaken out fresh and next day was Saturday and our excursion to the shops. We always had fun putting the bedding back in as the bed had three enclosing walls and it was so awkward to tuck the sheet and the blankets down the back. I had always to climb up and stretch over but it was difficult not to flatten the newly puffed up feather mattress. It was wonderful to have a cup of warm, milky cocoa and then climb up into the soft, clean bed, which just closed in round about you as you slipped down. It was when lying in bed with Granny that she told me so much about her five girls and all the antics they got up to. And they thought she didn't know anything about it. She sounded so proud of them and happy for them in their marriages. Maggie Ann had never married but had gone far away to America. I could hear the sadness in her voice and I thought Maggie Ann must have been her favourite. Ena too, her youngest, was special and Granny would never go to bed without Ena's coloured blanket spread on top.

"I remember one night. There had been a fierce storm all day and the seas were mountainous in the wind, and the rain was lashing down. We had not been out all day and went to bed early. Granny and I were just settled down when we heard a loud knock on the door."

"Noo, fa can 'at be on a nicht lik es?" And when she opened the door, there was Tom on the doorstep, dripping wet.

"I thocht ye micht be scared o' the storm so I've come doon tae sleep here for company. Ma mither kens I'm here so dinna worry."

"Noo ma loon, 'at wis gye gweed o' ye tae think o' that. We'll jist get ye dry an then a cup o' cocoa. Then ye can come in ower wi Mary Bella an' me or ye can hae the hurly bed 'at my Alex eased tae sleep in."

"Tom took the hurly bed and soon we were all lying in the darkness talking about the storm, and what had happened at school, and at home in Charlotte Street. Strange how you talk about things in the darkness which you would not share in the daylight. I was thrilled that night for Tom was ten; my big cousin, and I thought he was a hero for coming down to look after Granny. He also was special to her, her oldest and favourite grandson.

"That winter was long talked about for the storm was the worst in memory. Great damage was done to property but the most tragic was the loss at sea. The west coast fishing boats were caught on their way home and had to make shelter in whatever ports they could reach. Some of them did not find safety and the families at home waited in fear of the reports that were so long in coming. I remember the constant visits of my aunts and uncles coming to the house to ask for news and the quiet talk and the serious faces, and then the relief when the shipping office sent up word that the boat was safe in port at Macduff.

"I think that was the first time I became aware of real fear. When I saw the adults frightened and worried my carefree childhood changed a little and I experienced a growing sense of responsibility. We all needed each other.

Chapter 2

"That year 1905 was special for me. It was a milestone in my life. First of all we moved to our new house on Albert Street, then in the summer I became five, and later in August I started school.

"The day of the flitting Aunt Ena took Jane, Alex and me to Granny's in Broadsea out of the way of the steer. We were a bit disappointed not to be in at all the activity and fun, as we thought, but later in the afternoon we walked the length of Albert Street to Barskimming House to see the glories of our new home. And it was beautiful. The new linoleum, and the rugs, and then the furniture, the bedroom with the two beds for Jane and me, and the huge front room with the great wide window; it was all so wonderful. We had an inside toilet and a kitchen separate from the living room and a back and front door with a long curving staircase, very grand.

"When we arrived they were all sitting round the table having tea and pies so we had a chance to go round on our own, opening all the doors and exploring. That was when we discovered the dark, secret staircase and the two rooms in the attic. We loved our new home but these two attic rooms became our haven, our retreat, our den, and the scene of most of our best childhood memories.

"That summer, having my own bed and sharing a girl's bedroom, I began to sleep less at Granny's. She understood that I needed to grow up with my family and it made no difference to our closeness. Often I went down on Friday and helped her with her bed and then just stayed the night with her. But my main reason for staying at home was that my Da was there and I had to be near him. You see, I loved my Da more than anyone. My Granny and my Da were the people I loved most in all the world. He was often away at the fishings but, in the summer, the boat fished out of Fraserburgh and he was on shore sometime every day. So, I had to be there to see him and get a hug. As I was growing older and more knowledgeable about people, I was aware of this strong feeling for my Father. I liked my Mother too but it was more admiring her. She was beautiful and clever and we lived in a nice comfortable home but I could not say I loved her the way I felt for my Father. You see, I always knew she loved Jane more than me. Often I felt in the way and was made aware of my lack of good looks and my boisterous ways; I was a tomboy and Jane was her pretty doll, always clean and tidy. My Granny and my Aunts spoke to her about it, but it made no difference and my Father's love made up for it all. However, we were a happy family. Mam had Jane, my Da had me, and Mother and Father together were very close, and we all loved baby Alex with his comic ways.

"When he chose to build his house on Albert Street my Father indicated that he intended his children to have a good education. The Infant School was almost next-door, the Primary stood across the road and the new Academy was being built at the top of our lane. We were accustomed to hearing bells and seeing children coming and going at certain times and I could not wait to go there too. I can remember standing inside the classroom door looking up at a sea of faces; there must have been more than forty children, all sitting quietly in rows with arms folded. The tiers of desks almost reached the ceiling. The teacher stood against the fireguard facing the class and she was reading a story.

"Come away Mary Bella. You can sit here beside Liza. I think you may know each other."

"We didn't, but I did not say so.

"That was one of the most wonderful days in my life. I met education. I simply loved school, every aspect of it. Because I was tall for my age and very active, I was good at gym and I had an excellent memory for poems, Maths tables, and History and Geography facts. But it was reading that held my greatest interest. Being very practical people neither of my parents could have been called great readers. The ' Peoples' Friend' and the 'Sunday Companion' along with a daily newspaper were the regular reading materials in our house. So I had to search around for books to read. Whenever we were given a new school reader I had read through my one within a week and nearly knew it all by heart. Later on when I went to the Central School, the upper Primary, I was old enough to join our new Library on the Hexagon and I could take out books from the children's section, two or three a week. I used to disappear into the attic room and get lost in the adventures of Robin Hood or some of the history heroes of Scotland or Greece.

"That attic room has so many memories for me. From the bay window, between the Gallows Hill and the roof tops of Broadsea, we could see a good stretch of the Moray Firth, so my Da set up an old telescope on a swivel frame and we could watch the boats coming through the Firth from Wick or the Canal. He tied a large heather bisom on to his masthead so that we could pick out the Anchor of Hope and race to the harbour in time to see them come in.

This was always so wonderful as they had been away on the west coast for weeks. With my long legs I was always first at the pier head and as the boat came close in I took a flying leap on to the deck, knowing that my Da was always there with his arms stretched out to catch me. Then I had a sail round to the landing jetty. I was a favourite with the crew, especially with my Uncle John. They always had tea and hot buttered rolls before going ashore and I sat with them round the galley table and enjoyed mine. The first stop was at Bloomfield's office to sign in the boat's arrival then the hurly was loaded with parcels and gear, with me on top and we were away up the Brae and Commerce Street and home to Albert Street. These were such happy times. The coming homes were always such fun. Just being all together again.

"I had two special friends at that time; Liza Jolly and Mattie Summers. Liza's father was a policeman and they lived across the road from us in a large house next to the school janitor. Mattie was a very clever girl, the best in the class, and we three were always together and shared secrets. One day in school Liza whispered to me that we were all going to die soon as the world was coming to an end. Her father had told her. Something was going to smash into the earth and would kill everything on it. Of course we believed her; her father was the policeman. But soon the rumour was round the school and lots of children were upset until the teacher explained the situation to us. It was a comet that passed by close to the Earth every so many years. It was called Haley's Comet after the man who discovered it, and it could be seen through a telescope or with the naked eye on a clear night. So night after night we used to gather in the attic with the lights out and swing the telescope till we could pick out the comet. As long as it grew brighter and nearer we were very worried, never quite sure that the teacher was telling us the truth, but then it disappeared and we relaxed and talked about the wonder of it all. But that was a scary time and it made me think about God in all this and wonder what part He played in the working of the Universe.

"I only once had the strap in school and it was the year when we had our most favourite teacher, Miss Cockerill. She stayed on Albert Street so we felt we had a personal interest in her. When she forgot things like her spectacles she used to send me across to her lodgings for them and I felt very important. One morning I saw a dead blackbird lying behind the back gate of the sawmill next to the school playground and I told Liza and Mattie. We decided to eat our dinners quickly and go to look at it on the way back to school. The gate was locked so we had to go round the school to the front and run through the mill yard without being seen, for the mill was forbidden to pupils. We found the bird, laid it against the wall and covered the beautiful plumage with stones to keep cats from tearing it apart. Alas, when we got back to the school the lines were all in and the door was shut. We were terrified. The headmaster was very strict and we knew what to expect. We were each given two straps and we had to write out fifty lines about the rule we had broken. But what was worse was the disappointment on Miss Cockerill's face when we went back into our classroom. I really felt so hurt and ashamed that I had let her down. It was a real lesson to me about other peoples' feelings and how we can hurt them through being thoughtless. I did my best to make up for it and worked hard at my lessons, especially my essays, and one day I was so proud when Miss Cockerill called me out to read my essay to the class. It was about a fishwife and I wrote about my Granny."

Chapter 3

"Jane and I were in the Central School when our Father's new boat, the Anchor of Hope, was launched. We were given a day off school and the whole family, Granny included, drove to Sandhaven in a brake, which my Da had hired. We just felt like royalty as we passed through the town and people stood up to watch. We had new red outfits, coats and hats trimmed with fur and muffs to match and our boots were black, patent leather with pearl buttons. We had never had such beautiful clothes before but Mother said it was a most special occasion, particularly for Father. I didn't understand at the time but later I learned just how much the new boat meant to him. That was a great day, feeling so small alongside the towering dock, watching the tall boat slip down and the great wave that rose up, then the feast. It was all like a party and picnic rolled into one. Looking back on that time it seemed all joy and there seemed no end to the good things that were happening.

"When the Anchor of Hope came back from Yarmouth the following year, Uncle John brought Jane and me two beautiful dolls. They were dressed in rich grey and red silk trimmed with gold and white lace and were complete with parasols, white boots and fans. A little girl's dream. Jane's one had long, curly, golden hair and my one had rich, dark brown. They were so perfect we did not dare handle them so they stood in the corner of the sofa in the best room and we went in every now and then to gaze on them. At last, Mother had two glass cases made and the dolls were placed on the wall, one on each side of the fireplace. The only time we handled them was when Jane and I sang a lullaby at the Sunday School Soiree and we rocked our babies.

"Then there was the summer holiday we spent in Bressay. What a beautiful place. I would have liked to have gone back later to see it all again, just to confirm my childhood memories of the wonder of it all. Maybe it was because we were all there doing things together as a family. We had Mother and Father all to ourselves, the freedom to roam, the space, the sea, the sheep to feed, the shepherd's kind wife and the ancient cottage with no water or gas. The month was too short and we promised ourselves we would come back, but we never did. All we had were beautiful memories and a little, orphan lamb to nurse and feed in our field on Albert Street.

"Another thing I looked forward to was our annual trip to Aberdeen to Granny's to bring in the New Year. After Granda died my Granny May moved from Shore Street to live with her daughter Mary Ann on Loch Street in Aberdeen and my Da kept up the tradition of bringing in the New Year with his family. So every Hogmanay Day, laden with parcels of presents, a portmanteau of clothes and a very large clootie dumpling wrapped in an oilskin bag, we boarded the train for Aberdeen and landed in the city in the late afternoon. From the station we climbed the long stairs up to Union Street and stood a moment to get our breath back and take in the scene of hustle, trams, people and noise. It was always the same and we loved to watch it for a moment before we set off for George Street and through into Loch Street and Granny's house. It was an upstairs flat with only a sitting room and two bedrooms, but somehow we all managed to sleep and there was great fun sorting us all out. I slept with Aunt Nellie and Granny in the box bed in the living room. It was a tight squeeze as Nellie was quite big. Mother and Father were in Aunt Mary Ann's room with Jane and Alex on a shakedown and my Aunt and Uncle Charlie were in the other small room in Uncle Doddie's bed. Where he slept I don't know, probably with his chum next door. We were too excited to sleep anyway as we were hanging up our stockings on Hogmanay, for Santa came that night. This was an old North East custom and few people held Christmas for anything other than a church service. In fact most people worked on Christmas day but New Year was the big event with a distinct, holiday atmosphere.

"After a good tea Nellie usually escorted us up Loch Street to the Gallowgate and Broad Street where we stood in awe before the Marischal College, all lit up and shining. It was so beautiful. Hundreds of people seemed to be milling around, many of them drunk with early celebrating and we had to hold on to each other. But all we saw was the miracle of the tall spires gleaming in the street lamps and the clear frosty moonlight. We continued down to the Castlegate where there was a small market all lit up with coloured lanterns, and braziers roasting chestnuts. Musicians were playing fiddles and on the edge of the market a piper played some dance tunes. People tried to dance but there wasn't enough room so they just capered and laughed and hugged each other. Everyone was so jolly and friendly. We wandered slowly up Union Street to the bridge, stopping often to gaze at the wonderful shop windows, especially the toy displays and we wondered if Santa would bring us anything like that. Then Nellie said it was time to go back to Granny's and she would take us on her ghostie walk. She assured us it was quite safe but even the adults were a bit nervous as we descended the steps to Correction Wynd alongside the graveyard of St. Nicholas Church and followed her through the ancient arches and lanes below Union Street. She knew where she was going and eventually, we came out on the Upper Kirkgate and saw George Street ahead. Not far to go now. That walk had been so exciting and now it was time for Santa. I had brought one of my Father's sea boot stockings and was determined to stay awake to see Santa fill it. But I never did manage. Nellie's walk had seen to that.

"New Year's Day was always perfect. All the lovely surprises in the morning; a shining new penny, a sugar pig, an apple or an orange, a pretty tin of caramels and then the big surprise. Santa never brought us clothes- that was too ordinary. It had to be a game or a toy or books or anything we could play with- and he never failed. After the wonderful meal and the clootie dumpling with the little, silver, three-penny bits in it- there was usually one each- the adults elected to have a rest and just talk, but Nellie was for an outing with us children. So, all muffled up against the cold, the four of us set off for Union Street and waited at the tram stop for a No.1 or No.2 tram, whichever one came first. And we hoped it would be a horse drawn one with part of the upstairs open to the outside. No.1 went from the Bridge of Don to the Bridge of Dee and No.2 went from the beach to Hazlehead; both good trips, but we could get off and walk at the beach or at Hazlehead. I always hoped it would be the No.2 as Hazlehead woods were beautiful and on the way we passed all the lovely, mansion houses built on Queens Road. Nellie had a real way with children and it made our trips to Aberdeen so wonderful. When I think back over the years, we must have celebrated only four or five New Years in the city but they were truly splendid."

Chapter 4

"We children were very lucky in having such a wide family of aunts, uncles and cousins. Mother often took us a walk round the harbour and, of course we dropped in on Granny May for a cup of tea and a biscuit. There was always fun in that house with Aunt Nellie and Doddie and Charlie, our young uncles. My Da, the oldest, was a quiet man, but his younger brothers and sisters were very lively and jolly. We had no cousins on Shore Street as they lived in Florida where our Aunt Jessie had settled, but we had some on our Mother's side in Broadsea. and her daughter Nellie, my cousin, was a very bad tempered and jealous child, spoiled by her father and not always easy to live with. Aunt Ena gave in to Nellie for the sake of peace but nothing could cure Nellie's temper and I often felt sorry for my Aunt, although she never complained.

"I would describe my Aunt Janet's house as serene. It was always calm and organized, even though two lively boys and a bouncing, baby girl lived there. Perhaps it was because Uncle Sandy was always present, working away in the cooperage at the top of the yard and Janet could rely on his strength and support where the boys were concerned. But looking back on it now, I think it was their strong faith in God and their belief in the teachings of Jesus about the things that really matter in life, that made their home so welcoming and comfortable to be in. It was clean and simple with very little grandeur but there was an instant feeling of being at home and in the heart of the family.

"Janet and my Mother were so alike. Both were tall and beautiful, good, hardworking, house wives and mothers, very keen and successful gardeners and so generous to the needy. But there the resemblance ended. Where Janet was quite happy in her family circle, Mother needed more of the excitement of life amongst people and was involved in outside family activities like church committees and supporting my Father in his work representing the fishermen on various harbour boards. I used to listen in on their talk about what went on in the development of the harbour. There were always interesting things going on in our house and I think it was due to the kind of parents we had. With our Father being a seaman, we early became aware of far away places, our church life took us into the various mission fields and, of course, we were strongly encouraged to study and read. I suppose ours could have been called an enterprising family."

Chapter 5

"It was at school that I first learned about babies. One day in the playground a girl came up to me and said,

"Your mither's gan te hae a bairn."

"Taken aback I asked,

"An foo dae ye ken 'at?"

"It's true. I heard ma mither tellen ma faither."

"I could not believe it. My Mother was too old. She was thirty- four and women did not have babies after they were thirty, or so I thought. Such an event had never entered my thinking. We had always been the three and, since I was barely two when Alex was born. I could not remember it ever being anything different. Women did not talk openly about being ' in the family way' as they put it and tended to conceal the state as long as possible, only going outside when necessary in the later stages, and well covered up. A sense of modesty was maintained but behind it all was real joy and anticipation.

"I decided to say nothing to Jane and Alex but keep my eyes open and listen to conversations whenever I could. I noticed that Mother had been knitting little garments quite a lot lately, but I just thought it was for the church Missionary Wants Box. And she was getting stouter, but all women did that as they got older. I wanted so much to ask her about it; I was just too shy and uncertain of how my Mam would respond, so I went to Aunt Ena and she confirmed it. I was so excited. We would have a baby in the house and a pram to push and all the other wonderful things that a baby brings. I hoped it would be a boy to match Alex, though the baby would be so much younger than Alex. But I kept all these thoughts to myself. Mam would tell us in her own time. For now I had to think of ways to help.

"Without saying a word, I got up a little earlier in the mornings and carried up the two skuttles of coal from the outside cellar. I also undertook the weekly washing down of the outside back stairs, polishing the hall floor, and cleaning the front and attic stairs. Mother was always so particular about the entrances. Nothing was said but, from her nods and smiles, I know that my Mam was pleased. There was still no mention of the baby until Father came home from the west coast fishing and then, sitting round the tea table, we were told together.

"You never forget such happy times. We were all bursting with excitement asking when the baby would come and did they know what it would be, would it be born in the house, and so on. All Mother could tell us was that it would be some time in April and yes, it would be born in the house, and we were not to go out and speak about it with anyone till after the baby was here.

"So we contained ourselves until one night we three slept at Granny's house while the baby made his arrival, a little, dark haired boy to be called Norman Taylor May. From the start we just loved him. Everything about him was so tiny; hands, feet, ears, but all perfect. And he was so like our Father, more so even than Alex or me. Mother used to say she might have had at least one child like her. The new pram arrived and the cradle stood in the corner of the front bedroom. Visitors called to see the baby and Granny, with Aunt Ena's help came to stay for a week till Mother was on her feet again.

"That was a glorious summer. Jane was eleven and I was ten so we felt really responsible. We walked everywhere in the sunshine, taking turns pushing the pram and, when we arrived home, we made a job of wiping it all down and saw that it was safely in at the front door where it stood at the foot of the stairs. We were so proud of our baby and loved showing him off. We couldn't wait for every new stage-when he would smile, when he would sit up, when he would have teeth and eat food. This was such a new world for us and we were so glad we were older and able to enjoy these things like our Mother. And Norman certainly grew. By the end of his first year he was doing all we had looked for; he had outgrown his cradle and was in his crib and making real attempts to get around. He was a long baby and promised to have the tall, slim build of his Father whom he resembled more and more.

"It seemed there was no end to our cup of joy and, looking back, I think that must have been one of the happiest times of my life. As children we were carefree and worry free, enjoying our little responsibilities in the home and school and so confident of the security and love of our parents and family. We ran and played and worked and it just felt that nothing could ever change to spoil this wonderful time. But life is not like that, as we were so soon to learn. I think that year of 1911 saw the end of my childhood, and my happy, little world changed for ever."

Chapter 6

The summer fishing at Fraserburgh had been very successful and now the boats were at Yarmouth and Lowestoft gathering in a bountiful harvest. Judging by the lists of catches posted on the fish salesman's office window, the Anchor of Hope could be the top boat, or near that level, for the season. So anticipation was high and Betsy was just waiting for the letter saying when the boat would return. The usual preparations had gone on- big cleaning and baking, and patience was stretched to the limit on the part of the children for there was always the 'opening of the presents' ceremony.

One day Betsy was called to Bloomfield's office to receive an urgent message. John had wired them that the Anchor of Hope was returning early as the skipper was ill and they were bringing him home. They would be arriving next day and transport was required at the pier. A doctor would be necessary also. Betsy was shocked at the news and doubly anxious when no mention was made of the form of illness. Alex was young and had always been healthy. Could he have had an accident?

Her questions were finally answered when a very weary and haggard- looking Alex was carried upstairs and laid on his bed. He couldn't speak but his eyes told her that this was the only place he wanted to be- at home with her. Alex was diagnosed as having rheumatic fever and the doctor promised a long hard time of nursing for Betsy and isolation for Alex.

After their initial grief and sense of loss, the children decided they had a role to play in the situation. Mother must be free to nurse Father so they must take on everything else. Jane would deal with Norman and they would move his crib to the girls' room, Mary Bella could handle the cleaning, cooking and shopping and Alex would carry the coal, chop firewood, tend the hens and keep the garden and yard tidy. When they explained their proposals to Betsy she wept at first and said it was too much for them. But Mary Bella insisted that they needed to be busy and wanted so much to help. Maybe Jane could have some time off school to look after Norman but she and Alex would go to school and do their work before and after.

Work was the antidote for Mary Bella's grief. In reality, she was heartbroken. Sometimes she would slip in and stand by the bedroom door gazing at the frail figure in the bed and it was hard to choke back the sobs that rose to her throat. And when she heard the groans of pain coming from her Father's room she covered her ears and ran from the sound, for it was more than she could bear. At times she envied her Mother, even resented her being able to touch and care for her Da. It was what she longed to do. But she covered up her pain and resolved that everything would work out and her Da would get better. Jane was excellent with Norman, a real, capable, little mother, and Alex and she could cope with the rest, now that Aunt Ena and Aunt Janet had taken in hand with the washing and ironing.

Mary Bella was anxious not to miss school as the tests for the Academy would be held in the spring and she was anxious to pass well. Jane could not wait to leave school, but Mary Bella was keen to stay on and some day fulfil her dream of being a teacher or a nurse. She wanted to be another Miss Cockerill. The first step was to pass the tests to the Academy and so, even though it was hard, she rose early for her house keeping and cooking and studied late to do her homework.

This sad time became a pathway of discovery for Mary Bella, both of herself and of other people. She realized her talent for planning and organizing and, in a few days, had the household running smoothly, leaving her Mother to concentrate totally on Father. Mary Bella learned to control her feelings and, no matter how broken and worried she felt, the others must not be aware of it. She had to inspire confidence in Jane and Alex and be firm with them when they grew tired and would give up. No longer had she time to slip away to Granny's or Aunt Ena's to have a shoulder to cry on; but they came to her and most evenings one or the other would call in to inquire about Alex, but also to comfort and encourage the young ones. How grateful Mary Bella was for the family.

Another thing Mary Bella learned was the generosity of friends and neighbours. She made the broth and soup but, most days, their main meal was a gift handed in that morning. It was almost as if the street had come together with a food plan; no two days were the same and they enjoyed the stovies, shepherd's pies, casseroles and fish pies. When Mary Bella asked her Mother about it Betsy simply replied,

"That's the best wye ye can help fowks fan there's a need. Be sure ye pit a twa- three eggs in the empty dish fan ye gie it back."

And Mary Bella remembered the many times she had seen her Mother slip out to deliver a covered dish to someone in need. Now it was their turn and she was grateful.

The days of waiting passed slowly but eventually, the morning came when the fever had reached its climax and Alex was resting peacefully in a real sleep. Betsy was with the children and the sense of relief was palpable. Alex had a long recovery to make, but he was still with them and would get better, and then they would all be together again.

At times Mary Bella slipped into the bedroom and stood gazing at the sleeping face on the pillow, so pale and all the more so against the head of black hair and the dark moustache. She wondered if the time would ever come again when her Da would hold out his strong arms to catch her when she jumped. Mary Bella doubted that time would come back for she was growing too big for that sort of thing. Sometimes she read to him from her library book, especially chosen to interest her Da, and they travelled to far away places as they talked about the great ships now being built and crossing the oceans. Other times they just sat companionably as she related the day's news of school and the goings on in the family, especially baby Norman.

Much happened during Alex' convalescence time; things that puzzled the children but, at the same time, excited them. Father was leaving the sea and Uncle John now owned the Anchor of Hope. Their home was being sold up and they were all going to live in Florida with Aunt Jessie and Uncle Bill. It was a thrilling outlook for any child, but Mary Bella had strong reservations. What about Granny, and leaving the family, and their attic room, and the school, especially at this time? And who would get their beautiful dolls? Why did they have to go so soon? Mary Bella struggled hard with her worries but eventually, events carried her along and she was left with the hardest task of all; saying goodbye to her beloved Granny.

Father went ahead and then, a month later, Betsy followed with the children and they set off on the great adventure. Little did they anticipate the life-changing events that lay before them.

Chapter 7

"If only, if only." That recurring phrase haunted Mary Bella's mind. During the daytime when she was busy, it was not so bad but, as she lay beside the sleeping Jane, her thoughts roamed over the disastrous losses they had suffered in Florida and also at home here. If only her parents had waited another six months and curbed the headlong desire to get away. Father might have been stronger, another occupation might have come to him, and they would have avoided the terrible, fierce heat and humidity of summer in Florida. Her thoughts ranged this way and that but always came back to the same, central fact that her Da was gone, and nothing could assuage this raw grief that gnawed at her heart. She could not speak of it to anyone, the hurt was too deep, and her Mother's grief must be far greater. So Mary Bella quietly mourned and longed for her Father.

If only she had been given the opportunity to sit her tests she would now be in her first year at the Academy along with her friends. Instead, on her return from Florida, Mary Bella had been placed in the Supplementary class in the Primary School, along with the less able pupils, to wait until she was thirteen and permitted to leave school. At her Mother's special appeal Mary Bella was given an exemption from school to assist her widowed Mother in the home. So her hopes for the future were dashed and this, along with the loss of her father, caused Mary Bella to have some bitter thoughts. Jane had been happy to leave school and, as long as she had her Mother and Norman, Jane was content. But Mary Bella was different and, even after Norman's illness, she still felt this sense of loss of direction and defeat. Was this all that remained for her; the gutting yard in summer, domestic service in winter and filling in at the shop when her Mother was busy elsewhere?

When they first returned from Florida Mary Bella had been so supportive of her Mother in all her efforts to make a life for them, but now she was restless and sad within herself. Oh, she worked and played, pushed Norman in his chair, enjoyed her neighbouring friends Nellie Hay and Ethel Stopanni and outwardly was a happy girl. But Mary Bella knew that, if she was going to do anything with her life, she would have to break away. Aunt Maggie's visit the previous year had stimulated her interest in wider horizons and Jane's refusal to go to Boston had opened the door for her opportunity. So, by the time Betsy broached the subject, Mary Bella had it well thought through, had faced the sacrifices of family and friends, and accepted the offer as her chance in life, hard as it would be to carry it through. She was newly fourteen and the journey on her own was daunting, but she had been this route before, not so long ago, and she knew what lay ahead. Her Mother had arranged a travelling companion and Aunt Maggie would meet her at Boston.

Chapter 8

It had been a good crossing, smooth and free of icebergs. Margaret White had proved a lively companion and Mary Bella and she became good friends. Most of the passengers were middle aged with children, few of Mary Bella's age, and so she was glad of Margaret's company, as the latter was of hers. But now she was on her way south to Virginia to domestic work and Mary Bella was alone in the vast immigration hall. It seemed that for hours she had watched hundreds of anxious, weary people shuffling through in an endless queue. Rich and poor were there, of all ages and speaking all kinds of languages. Now, with the last of them gone, Mary Bella was on her own in the echoing hall, which resembled a giant cage with the wire mesh in the windows. She felt terribly alone and worried a bit that her Aunt was so long in coming, but at last she appeared accompanied by a tall, craggy- faced man with kind eyes, Professor Ripley. Because Mary Bella was a minor they had had to face various immigration authorities to vouch for the care, schooling and housing of Mary Bella and each interview had taken so long. But now they were here and ready to set out for home and her new life. The Professor had become her official guardian and, along with Maggie, would supervise her well- being for the next two years. Mary Bella was very happy with that and at last she could relax in the comfort of the automobile ride through Boston to Newton Centre. She felt very tired, exhausted by this day of unknowns, solitariness, fear and worry, but now, as she watched the passing landscape of the beautiful city and suburbs, Mary Bella gave herself up to the unusual luxury of handing over responsibility to others for a little time. Tomorrow she would start work with Aunt Maggie, but not yet.

Chapter 9

As it turned out, their sojourn in Newton Centre was short. The family was in Maine enjoying the summer and Maggie and Professor Ripley had come down to Boston especially to meet Mary Bella. The Professor had used the opportunity to visit his publisher and they planned to return to Maine the following day.

Mary Bella was glad of this little respite before having to meet the family and it also provided her with the chance to get to know her Aunt a little better as they shared news from Fraserburgh, and talked about the Ripley family and their two homes and way of life. This was a completely new world to Mary Bella. It filled her with awe and she was somewhat apprehensive in case she would not fit in to this learned and academic household. Maggie knew what she was feeling and reassured her that they were all very comfortable and happy people who would make her so welcome. Mary Bella listened and decided that this opportunity had provided her with a challenge. She had responsibilities to people now, to Aunt Maggie and to her employers, the Ripleys, and she would do her best to fulfil their requirements. But she also felt there was something special about the whole atmosphere in this home. The paintings, the many books and the piano in the huge sitting room all told of a used elegance, a refinement and culture. True, most of it was under dustsheets, but Mary Bella had never seen anything to match this home. Barskimming House had been wonderful but it did not possess the air of graciousness she could feel here. Of course she kept these thoughts to herself but already, she could feel the stirrings of excitement in her new life and a desire to reach out to every fresh experience.

Next day brought them to Maine, to Toad Hall and the family. Will Poole met them with the buggy at East Edgecomb Landing and, as they came up the drive, Mary Bella could hear the shouts,

"It's Pappa! It's Maggie!"

And soon they were surrounded by children, it seemed of all ages, clambering to hug the new arrivals. But Mary Bella stood back a little till the Professor drew her forward and introduced her.

"Here is Mary Bella from Scotland. She is Maggie's niece and she has come to live with us and assist Maggie. You must help her to settle down for she is a long way from her home. I hope you will be happy with us and feel that this is your home now Mary Bella. Come and let us eat for we are all ravenous."

Chapter 10

Mary Bella was tired and she sighed as she leaned against the bench by the garden wall. It was not a sad sigh. This had been a wonderful two weeks. In a few days the household would be moving back to Newton Centre, full of happy holiday memories, and ready again for school and work. And she looked forward to going with them. Annie and she had just washed up the dinner dishes and Hannah had put them away while Maggie dealt with the breakfast preparations. This was the routine before each one slipped away to her personal ploy. Mary Bella was taking her last glimpse of the river, or sea, as she preferred to think of it, since it rose tidally every day.

Twilight was falling. A light air drifted up from the shore far below and Mary Bella could recognise the tang of the seaweed left by the ebbing tide. So like Broadsea. It brought Granny so close. And behind her, the embers of the dying, barbeque fire added their smoky scents. She would treasure the memories of the fun they had shared that day cooking the fish over the fire.

Day by day Mary Bella had been drawn into the family activities as she accompanied them on outings and picnics. She had developed a role for herself by becoming Betty's companion for the child, so much younger than her siblings, was often left to tag along while Davis and Bill forged ahead. Mary Bella stayed by her and gave her the task of laying out the picnic or some such responsibility. Betty knew all the trails and paths through the woods and the rout to the Cabin and the tree house so, many times, the two were off on their own, Betty teaching Mary Bella the ways of the countryside. It was a good arrangement and the family was grateful for Mary Bella's care of Betty. When she considered her niece's age and the traumatic period she had just experienced, Maggie also approved of these developments. She could see the healing process beginning to show in the more frequent smiles and the lighting up of Mary Bella's eyes. This was a bruised child that only time and change could heal and Maggie felt justified in her desire to bring Mary Bella to be by her side here in this household. But she also knew that once they were back in Boston, she would have to begin the serious training and prepare Mary Bella for a future occupation.

Later, as she lay in the darkness of her little room next to Maggie's one, Mary Bella listened to the silence of the night. A soft breeze stirred the screens at the open window and now and again the hoot of an owl or the cry of the nightjar floated over. She could recognise them now. The peace of this place had soothed her grief and lightened the crushing load that lay on her heart. She would always miss his presence but Mary Bella knew that this was the beginning of her new life and her Father would expect her to live it to the full and to do her best. It seemed a long time since she had felt so peaceful and free.

Chapter 11

Leaving Toad Hall was a revelation to Mary Bella. Moving ten people and closing up a home for the winter was like a military operation and Mary Bella was in complete awe of Maggie. As she helped her to check off her list of 'must does' and carried out her allotted tasks, Mary Bella's admiration for her Aunt knew no bounds and she worked hard to satisfy her standards. The 'mice war' was very real and Maggie used every tactic to defeat the intrusion of this woodland menace. Cupboards, drawers, bookcases, beds, linen chests- everywhere that the tiny creatures might nest was thoroughly cleaned, repacked with a good helping of moth balls, and sealed. Will Poole would make regular checks over the winter months until they returned in June.

As they travelled home to Newton Center Mary Bella relaxed in the pleasure of the journey; the steamer, the train and the magnificent woodland and villages. On their journey north she had been too tired and confused to take in anything. She studied her Aunt Maggie, wondering what aspect of her character she would meet in Newton Center. That day in New York Maggie had been so wonderfully kind and sympathetic, during her month in Fraserburgh she was friendly and very sociable, and Maine had shown a firm lady, very much in charge of household affairs but also relaxed with the children and their activities. What would

Maggie be like in Boston? Mary Bella could see the warm relationship between Maggie and the children, especially Betty and, as her niece, she felt she should be closer still. But, at the moment, she felt very much a stranger on the edge. She wondered how her daily round would turn out in this new environment in the city and Mary Bella felt some apprehension at what lay ahead.

Chapter 12

Maggie's plan for Mary Bella was to attend school until mid-day break then have lunch, change into uniform and do her domestic round until after dinner. The rest of the evening would be her own for school preparation and reading. She would have one afternoon free every weekend. Glad to have an orderly regime planned for her, Mary Bella was happy to cooperate. She could see that Maggie did not permit drudgery amongst her staff and decisions were taken together after discussion, but Mary Bella knew that Maggie had set a high standard of perfection for all and insisted on it both in work and appearance. She was very conscious of the proprieties and considered that, as housekeeper for a Harvard Professor, she could demand nothing less.

So began Mary Bella's life at Ripley's; at times tedious, at other times lonely, but brightened daily by her hours in school. The first morning Maggie accompanied her for enrolment and her subjects were to be mainly English and Maths with some History and Geography as time permitted. She was in High School at last with her peers and Mary Bella felt like singing. As time went on she realized that she could well match the standard of the other pupils and that gave her greater confidence.

One day the English class began a study of Robert Burns and his poems and Miss Sawyer suggested that Mary Bella should read 'The Cottar's Saturday Night' aloud to the class. With her Scottish accent she would best pronounce the words and perhaps be able to explain the meanings of the difficult ones. Mary Bella was thrilled and spent hours memorizing large sections of the poem before approaching Maggie to listen to her reciting it. That was a very happy moment as was the class lesson. But when Mary Bella was chosen to recite it at the end of term concert, Maggie with Betty was there in the audience, proud as any parent.

Mary Bella on stage looked beautiful in her dark, ruby red dress, her cloud of black hair drawn back with a matching bow and her calm, serene confidence as she walked to the front of the platform. In her soft Scottish accent she began to narrate the solemn lines of the wonderful poem and every ear hung on her words. Now and again she referred to her script but then the flow began again and the story went on. Listeners could hear the voice of one who knew this Scotia, this homeland, speaking with such pathos and pride. Tears welled up and the applause confirmed her success. Maggie was very satisfied and very proud.

Another success came to Mary Bella when the class was asked to write an essay on any subject of their own choosing. Mary Bella decided to describe the herring fishing in Britain, using the Anchor of Hope and its crew as her subjects. Of course she knew it intimately but, in the writing, she felt the closeness of her Father. It almost seemed as if he was at her elbow telling her what to write. She could hear his voice. It was as though they were in this together; away to the west coast, to Shetland, to Fraserburgh, to Yarmouth, casting the drift nets and hauling in the crans of herring. The tired crew, the fearful storms, the working of the steam drifters, the coming home to the family- she covered it all. And when Mary Bella asked Maggie to read it before it was handed in her Aunt nodded her approval,

"Yes Mary Bella, that is well done. You have covered it all. I don't think you could improve on that. Mind you, there is a lot more to the herring fishing than the herring boats. Think about it."

Mary Bella received an A grade for her essay and high praise from Miss Sawyer, but it did not stop there. News had passed round the staff and soon she was asked by her Geography teacher to give a short talk on 'Living in Scotland'. Many of the pupils did not know where the country lay and he thought this would be a good exercise for them all. Mary Bella was nervous and very reluctant but Maggie suggested that she treat it like an essay and write it all down as she would tell it. Then she could hold on to that as a support to refer to if she required. So that is what she did and once Mary Bella was out in front with the map of the United Kingdom beside her on the wall, she told her story of the fishing community which had borne her family and hundreds of others who sailed these waters for a livelihood. She also touched on the herring fishing links with other countries like Ireland, Shetland, Norway, France and England which came as a surprise to American born pupils who understood little of the European scene. Others, immigrant children like herself, could share her understanding of different countries and travel and, as far as her knowledge allowed, she did her best to answer their questions.

Such highlights made her year of schooling a joy for Mary Bella. Sadly, it had to come to an end and with June came the final Presentation Day. Maggie sat proudly in the audience and, as she watched Mary Bella go forward to receive her 'Intermediate Certificate with High Commendation in Language and Literature' she would have given so much for her to stay on to attain the Higher

Certificate and Graduation. But it could not be. Maggie could not afford it and Mary Bella, like so many other bright children, had to work for her living. It was a hard wrench for Mary Bella to finish school, but she still harboured thoughts of teaching or nursing and meantime, she would read and learn and wait.

Chapter 13

Other thoughts were occupying her concerns as she read reports of the War in France and she wondered about the folks on Charlotte Street, how it would affect them. Tom and Willie were of age for war as were many others on the street, and would it affect the shop and her family? She waited avidly for the letters from home.

At the beginning the United States was not involved in the Great War and there were no headline reports in the newspapers but, as time went on and European travel was more curtailed, it became a growing concern, especially when trading and markets were affected. Armaments began to be a feature and the steel industries expanded at a tremendous rate. These questions of war and economics were often the subjects of discussion during the frequent dinner parties and Mary Bella listened closely as she went quietly about her waiting at table. Maggie had taught her that she was never to impart any information she overheard on these occasions so Mary Bella kept these things to herself and hoped that America would soon be brought into the War to help Britain and France.

Now that school did not use up so much of her time Mary Bella began her real training with Maggie, a true disciplinarian. Although she had her moments of kindness and gentleness, Maggie showed no favouritism to her niece and Mary Bella, with the other members of staff had to go through the whole regime, taking the rough with the smooth. It meant cleaning fireplaces in the dark winter mornings, marketing by ten o'clock having served family breakfast and then preparing lunch or dinner in addition to all the dusting, polishing and other household tasks. Some days Mary Bella felt she could not tolerate it but then there were times when Maggie gave her personal training in different table settings such as afternoon tea or dinner party, formal or informal, and other refinements of waiting, which was very enjoyable. Best of all, when Maggie began to involve her in cooking, Mary Bella's interest was really sparked and over the years she became skilled and able to relieve Maggie of some of her heavy cooking load.

Winter in Newton Center was a learning time for Mary Bella. But there were diversions of many sorts. She was always included in the skating parties and soon became skilled on the ice. When Maggie attended her Scottish Charitable Society meeting, if the program was suitable, Mary Bella often accompanied her. Together they saw Shakespeare's plays, enjoyed Gilbert and Sullivan, sometimes heard the Boston Symphony Orchestra or an opera and never missed the Burns Night Concert at the Boston Music Hall.

Maggie enjoyed watching the growing development of her niece and her appreciation of the cultural side of life. The shy young girl they had found in the immigration hall was becoming a poised, young woman, still quiet and reserved, but now much more confident and sure of her own place in the world of people. Mary Bella was also quite striking in her appearance. Tall and slim with that wonderful, thick cloud of black hair, she reminded one of a leggy young colt ready to gallope off. Her face too was interesting, fine featured with bright blue eyes and a curving mouth and chin, and covered with a fine dusting of freckles. Usually Mary Bella had a solemn expression, which tempted Davis and Bill to do their best to tease her into laughter. Sometimes they were rewarded when her eyes lit up and she responded with a good chuckle.

Chapter 14

If Newton Center was the work place for the Ripley household, Maine, over the years, had become their haven where they could take time to be really their own persons. The Professor longed for the peace of his Cabin to study and write and Mrs. Ripley always had her planting schemes ready for her garden above the meadow. Ruth, so much older than the other children, had already invited her grown up friends to stay and, with Maggie's help, had organized outings and picnics to entertain them. Being an excellent artist, she also had in her mind her various scenes and models to sketch and paint, but these were not always achieved, as Ruth was not too well organized from day to day.

Davis and Bill always had some ongoing project. Repairs to the old house, maintaining the boat or boathouse, maybe building out the landing pier or cleaning out the massive barn; they were never at a loss. They teased Maggie mercilessly for her cookies, even going the length of raiding her cupboards but, in her room above the kitchen, she heard them and the cookie box was removed to Maggie's room and safely guarded. She could not allow them to ruin their morals by stealing and, unless it was a family picnic, eating between meals was not permitted. Betty just wanted to meet her best friend, Constance Mc.Dougal, and then they would slip into their own world of play and make believe.

Mary Bella's best friend in Maine was Flora Webber who lived on a farm about a mile away from Toad Hall. When there was a large house party, Flora often came to assist Maggie. The Webbers had a large family of six girls and the last child, a boy called Karl, was still just a baby. Flora, Eleanor and Beatrice were about Mary Bella's age and she loved to go down to their farm where there was always fun and laughter. Often the girls came to Toad Hall and joined in the games there. Sometimes on a Saturday evening Will Poole would drive Mary Bella to the village dance in the hall above Burnham's shop, often calling in for Flora on the way. This was wonderful fun, which the girls enjoyed although Maggie always insisted that they were safely home by ten o'clock. That friendship with Flora was to last a very long time.

Books were everywhere at Toad Hall and one day Mary Bella was helping Ruth to clear out some shelves in her room. The books were from her childhood and Ruth wished to use the space for other things. Mary Bella carried them to Maggie who suggested they should be stored on the shelves in the box room at the top of the back stairs.

"You might find something you like there," said Maggie, holding out a copy of 'Little Women'.

So began Mary Bella's love affair with American literature. They were all there and a lot more besides. The March sisters, Anne of Green Gables, Freckles and the Limberlost, Pollyanna, The Scarlet Pimpernel, Mr Toad, The Count of Monte Christo, and so many more, a great array waiting to be read. Maine had many highlights but, for Mary Bella, these books were the best. She read them all, some many times, and all the sequels, leading on to other subjects. None of the books ever came back to Newton Center; they belonged to the summer time and to Toad Hall and, year-by-year, Mary Bella looked forward to them with anticipation. Some day Betty would read them but for now, they were her responsibility.

Mary Bella and Maggie knitting soldiers' comforts WW1

Chapter 15

At last in 1917 the long war of words in Congress came to an end with the tragic sinking of the Lusitania and the United States entered the Great War. Maggie and Mary Bella in their relief could now hope for an end to this terrible conflict that had already cost so much suffering and death. Over the three years letters from home had told the story of sons lost in death, indescribable horror in France and futile battles. The overwhelming death toll was crushing the population at all levels and the country was reeling under it. Food was scarce but hope was still there and now the entry of the United States would bring such encouragement.

Maggie and Mary Bella, through the Scottish Charitable Society, had been knitting garments for the Soldiers' War Wants for quite some time. Groups were set up to roll bandages and create First Aid Kits for the military and there was a real wave of war effort. Davis volunteered for action but was refused on account of his age. However, he drove an ambulance, was wounded and received an award for outstanding bravery. Everyone was so proud of him.

For a little while there was a ripple of excitement at Bracebridge Road. Due to his wide knowledge of transportation and economics Professor Ripley was appointed by the War Department to be Administrator of Labour Standards. This meant frequent meetings in Washington and many journeys to the Capital. For the young ones in the family there was only one solution- they must move to Washington. Sadly that did not materialize as the War came to an end and the last thing the elders wished to do was to upheaval their home life. The boys had lingering thoughts of regret for what might have been.

Janet wrote of their worries for Tom and Willie, both boys in action, Betsy worried about the shop and difficulties in getting food supplies. She was relying more and more on what she could grow and produce herself. Bella from Hartlepool described the bombardment and their decision to move back to Fraserburgh once Willie found work. Ena's letters were more cheerful, all about the children, especially the antics of Wilfred and Norman, but underlying was her concern for Granny who was growing increasingly frail and wandering in mind. Eventually, the letter arrived telling of Granny's passing away peacefully and Maggie and Mary Bella wept together for the loss of this indomitable, little person they had both loved so deeply. With her going the Book of Broadsea had been finally closed though they would treasure the memories forever. As they worked together Maggie and Mary Bella often shared stories of the strong-minded, proud little woman who had shaped their lives so profoundly and they resolved that, once the War was over, they would return to Fraserburgh for a visit.

The months moved on and Mary Bella became eighteen. The War was brought to a conclusion and, after much deliberation and delay, the Treaty of Versailles was signed. The future seemed to open up more clearly now and Mary Bella began to plan ahead for her career. She realized that academically she was not qualified for teaching, but with some extra study she could possibly reach the requirements for nursing. So Mary Bella visited the Massachusetts General

Hospital, had an interview and came away with a pro-
spectus, a schedule of study and the date of the entrance
examinations. It was an awesome outlook but Mary Bella
was a very determined young person and Maggie supported
her all the way. Needless to say she succeeded and was
enrolled to begin her training in the entry for the following
year, 1919. Meantime, Mary Bella was measured for her
uniforms, which she would collect on taking up residence
in the nurses' accommodation. It was all so daunting, but
exciting too and she was so grateful to Maggie and to the
Ripleys for all the support and encouragement they had
been to her since she arrived in their home, a shy, lonely
figure.

Now, in the few months remaining she would arrange
her passage and go home to Fraserburgh to see them all.
That thought gave her a little flutter of uncertainty. Five
years is a long time and much would have changed. How
would she get on with them? Her Mother, Jane, Alex and
Norman, no longer a baby but a schoolboy. And she had
changed too. Now she was a woman with her own life and
somehow she felt more American than Scottish. How would
they receive her?

Mary Bella 1919

Chapter 16

Mary Bella loved the sea. This was her fourth crossing of the Atlantic and she revelled in the luxury of fresh sea air, good food, and peace to relax as she pleased for a few days. Sea- sickness had never been a problem and she often stood in the stern watching the heaving sea lift the white wake of the ship. Its restlessness seemed to suit her mood of excitement. Now that her future was assured Mary Bella could reflect on the past five years with Maggie. So often she had thanked God for the twist of fortune that had brought her to Boston and given her a glimpse into a totally different and wonderful way of life. She wanted these values for herself and for her children if she ever had the good fortune to marry. The secret lay in education. Her Father had realized that and now she had seen it working out in real life.

As the days passed Mary Bella often found a young man walking the deck by her side. He was Iain Hunter, an engineer from Pittsburg and, like herself, he was going home to visit his parents in Duns in the Scottish Borders. Both had arrived in the States raw and lonely young teenagers but now, after five years, they felt grown up, mature and ready to make something of their lives. After the month at home Iain was returning to Boston to study at M.I.T. and Mary Bella likewise was returning to nursing training. So it was that an attraction arose between them and they agreed to write and to meet up again in Boston. Mary Bella was a very happy girl as the ship came in sight of the Irish coast and headed for Glasgow.

Remembering the sad circumstances of her departure Ena, Betsy and Janet stood silent at the barrier waiting for the afternoon train to arrive. They had no idea what to expect when Mary Bella would step off the train. But there she was tall, elegant, smiling broadly and ready to hug them all. As the four walked through the lanes home to Charlotte Street, Mary Bella linked arm in arm with her Mother and Betsy could see there were no feelings of resentment, and she was thankful. The children were all in school so there would be a family gathering in the evening when everyone could be present.

Norman the baby had gone and now the boy stood before her straight and tall and leaning on his crutch. He was so like Father it hurt Mary Bella to look at him and he had little recollection of his big sister, so this was a relationship she would have to work on. Norman was delighted with the little model of the liner she had sailed on and declared confidently,

"I'll sail on her one day when we go to America."

Alex's arrival gave Mary Bella a great sense of pleasure. Here he was a tall, strapping young man nearly seventeen, and half way through his engineering apprenticeship at the Toolworks. A fun loving teenager given to practical jokes and laughter had replaced the quiet, retiring little boy. He resembled both parents with his Father's height and colouring and Betsy's eyes and nose. At once Mary Bella felt the warm tug between them as she wrapped her arms round him.

Jane was not there so Mary Bella presumed that she was on duty at the hospital where she was in training. The cousins arrived and gradually she sorted them out, surprised to find so many near her own age; Nellie, Tina, Maisie, with Netta five years younger. Then Nellie Hay and Ethel Stopanni walked in and the party seemed complete. Just like old times but five years on. Mary Bella felt this was going to be a happy few weeks.

Chapter 17

Once all was tidy again and the dishes washed up, Alex went upstairs to join Norman and Mary Bella was left to enjoy a quiet last cup of tea with her Mother. An uncomfortable silence now lay between them. Mary Bella had an uneasy feeling that something was not right and her Mother did not know how to voice it. To make an opening she asked,

"Mother, when does Jane come off night duty?"

Betsy burst into tears and through her heart- broken sobs the whole story came out.

"Jane is nae at the nursing noo. She wis sent hame and the Matron followed her doon tae tell me that she wis in the family wye an cudna bide on. She didna ken fa the father wis. Jane widna tell her. Since an she has bidden in the garret an winna gang further than the back close. She winna even ait wi us. I'm that worried aboot her. Atween her, an the shop, an Norman I'm at ma wit's end. The family kens aboot the bairn bit naebody else on the street. She jist hides awa, sometimes greetin', sometimes ragin', but maistly sulkin'. Ma hairt is broken Mary Bella. I did ma very best for her a' her life bit there wis nae guiden her. She took her ain wye."

Mary Bella was shocked, totally silenced. This was the last thing she could ever have imagined happening in her family. After a time listening to her Mother's sobs she asked,

"Fan is the baby due?"

"It will be aboot three weeks the doctor says. He has been in eence or twice tae see her and the midwife has been booked for then. Jane is weel enough, jist verra big wi the baby and that micht be a problem as she is sae little herself. Mary Bella, fit am I gan tae dee wi a bairn tae look efter an a'?"

"You adopted Jane. Could you nae hae this baby adopted as weel? Have ye asked Jane what she wants? I'm sure there must be some wye tae find oot aboot these things. Maybe we shud jist gang tae bed and face it a' in the morning. There *will* be a wye bit we are ower tired the nicht. Let's jist leave it till the morning."

It was a long night with Mary Bella's thoughts swinging this way and that, mingled with fleeting dreams in her shallow sleep. A heavy sense of foreboding hung over her, something she had not felt since her Father died. What was to become of Jane? Was she going to ruin all their lives with her selfishness and folly? Her Mother was too close to the situation and numbed with grief and worry so Mary Bella resolved that she would talk to Ena first thing in the morning. Ena, at least, would listen and might come up with some solution.

Mary Bella waited until the children were in school and then she visited Ena, hoping that a quiet talk might help her to understand the situation and maybe find a way out.

"Come awa in ma lass. I can see ye hae heard the news. This has been a sad hame coming for ye efter being awa sae lang."

And sitting together, Ena told her the whole story.

"The shop and the hoose were ower quait for Jane. She wanted tae work oot so yir Mother payed for her tae start the nursing at the Thomas Walker Hospital. Aathin wis fine and then she gied the Matron cheek and wis warned. Then she had tae be warned for playin' up tae the young doctors, and she had ither lads as weel so naebody kens fa has fathered her bairn. I dinna ken if she kens herself. Granny wis recht aboot Jane. 'A sleekit oolet' she eest tae say. She thocht o' naebody bit herself. Bit noo. It's all come back tae roost on hir ain back. Whit has yir Mither been saying aboot it?"

"Ena, she canna think straight and greets when I speak aboot it. She is so disappointed in Jane and has no idea where tae turn. Usually Mother is strong, always has been able tae overcome everything, but I have never seen her sae broken."

"Aye weel lass, that's true, bit jist be carefu'. Eence this is a' past Jane'll bounce back an yir Mither wull recover. Mind, Jane has aye teen first place, an wull again, so stick tae yir ain plans for yir life an' dinna be perswaad itherwise."

"Ena, whit dae ye ken aboot adoption? Is there a chance the baby can be gien tae a couple jist as Jane was?"

"Weel, I ken there's a couple frae the Hielands doon here for the fishin' and they are lookin' for a bairnie tae adopt. The man was in the store speakin' tae George, confidential like, an' telt him his story. They hiv nae family an' wid like a bairn, boy or girl, tae tak hame wi them. George likit the man an' the wye he spoke. I hinna dared tae say onything tae Betsy bit maybe you cud spik her roon, an see fit Jane thinks."

Glad of this ray of hope, Mary Bella nodded.

"I'll try. This may jist be the wye oot."

Chapter 18

Jane just wanted the baby to go away, but Betsy was concerned for its well being and was anxious to meet the couple from the Highlands. George became the go-between and an evening visit was arranged when the two parties met and shared their stories. The couple was in their thirties, quiet fisher folk, and they could hardly hide their excitement. Betsy remembered her own feelings of joy when she and Alex were adopting Jane; the waiting and then the actual day. A satisfactory arrangement was decided and, once the baby was handed over, Jane and Betsy would have no further claim or right to interfere in the child's life. When the baby arrived George would be notified and three days later, if all was well, it would be handed over to the couple at the early morning train to Aberdeen.

A deep sense of relief came over everyone. Day by day they waited and then in the second week Jane's labour began and the midwife was called. The baby was a girl, tiny but perfect and quite beautifully featured. George was notified to inform the couple and he arranged to register the birth immediately. It would have been so easy to love this baby. Jane would not look at her, but Betsy and Mary Bella, even the boys, could not help feeling her innocent attraction. She was registered as Elizabeth May, Mother Jane May, Father unknown, and illegitimate. On the third day Mary Bella carried her to the 7am. train and handed her over to her new parents. She was beautifully dressed and wrapped in a plaid and, as Mary Bella passed over the birth certificate along with a bag of necessities, the lady put her arms round her and tearfully whispered,

"God bless you lass. Thank you."

Anxious to get the ordeal over with she hurried from the station, stood a moment watching the bustle of the harbour, and then turned towards the quiet of the beach road and the Sudan shore. Mary Bella could not go home yet. She needed time to recover from the ordeal she had just experienced and to think through the whole situation.

What could Jane do now? Where could she go? The shop had still not recovered from the War and required money to build up the stock. Alex's board money was the only financial help in the home and her Mother was struggling to manage. Where did she herself stand in all this? Had she some responsibility in the family? How she wished Maggie was here to share her dilemma. Her nursing pay in Boston would be very little but she could send something once a month. Her heart went out to her Mother but in a way she felt detached from the whole situation. Her life was away from here now and she longed to get on with it. Remembering Ena's words of warning Mary Bella was not so sure her Mother *would* forgive Jane for her wayward behaviour; she had been too let down and hurt. Mary Bella sensed that Jane had gone beyond her Mother's forgiveness and a coolness was apparent. Her immediate decision was to telegraph Maggie and ask her to wire £100 from her savings, which Maggie had control over. At least she could do that much to help.

Chapter 19

It was now into her third week and Mary Bella was becoming very conscious of the rapid passing of time. The confinement was past and never referred to. Jane had recovered enough to be about the house but was still dominating all with constant complaining and grumbling. Her jealousy of Mary Bella erupted often in a flow of spite and bitterness making the whole atmosphere explosive when Betsy tried to remonstrate. Mary Bella had seen none of this sort of behaviour for a very long time and she just wished she could escape back to the wholesome discipline of life with Maggie.

Now and again Mary Bella and Betsy worked together over some of Maggie's best recipes, with the possibility that they might sell in the shop; the chocolate cake with the special fudge icing, brown Betty apple pudding and, above all Pinucchi, a wonderful, walnut tablet. These were all new to Betsy and she thought they would sell well. The gift of money from Mary Bella had greatly encouraged her and now she had begun to renew her enthusiasm for the shop. It was during one of these companionable moments that Betsy voiced a thought.

"I wis jist winrin Mary Bella foo ye wid feel aboot bidin wi me a fylie langer an lat Jane gang oot tae Maggie in yir place. Ye hae bin awa sae lang an yir holiday's been spylt wi a' this trouble. It wad be a change for Jane an gie her a new chance in life."

Mary Bella looked into her Mother's face and thought,

"This is it. I've known it was coming all this time. It has been hanging over me like a threat. Now it's out in the open. This can't be happening to me a second time. I can't give up all for Jane again."

Mary Bella turned, ripped off her apron and ran to the back gate into the lane and sought the Braes at Broadsea. She needed to think and sort out her confusion and emotions.

"What makes them think they can use me like this? I have a right to my life. I worked hard and learned to live with Maggie, all on my own. I have a career to go back to and I worked hard for that too. And friends and a new life in Boston. Why should I give it all up for Jane who won't do anything with her life anyway, wherever she might be? It's asking too much, making me pay for Jane's folly. Ena was right. They haven't changed. Mother will ask anything of people if it will help her Jane."

Her grief lasted a long time and then a calmness came over her. The practical, common sense side began to prevail and possible solutions emerged. She *could* stay longer and delay her nursing entry for another year. Remaining here would give her an opportunity to get to know her family; her Mother, Norman, Alex and all the cousins, and maybe without Jane to dominate her, her Mother could get on with her own ambitions and enjoy life a little more. Yes, there would be benefits for all if she stayed. What hurt most was the thought that they felt they could use her without any regard for *her* wishes or feelings. She knew Jane had planted the seeds of the idea in her Mother and it angered

Mary Bella that Betsy could have such little regard for her sensitivity and wishes.

That evening, after tea Mary Bella told the family what she intended to do. Without any show of anger or grief she simply said,

"I have decided tae bide here for anither year and then I'll gang back tae Boston and start my Nursing training. I've left Ripley's already, but I'll wire Maggie and the hospital and cancel the sea passage. That's a' I have tae say."

And with that she rose from the table and ran weeping to Ena's for some comfort.

Chapter 20

Mary Bella was in a hurry. It was five o'clock on Friday. She had finished work for the week, and was now anxious to get home and have an hour with her Mother in the shop before sitting down to dinner with the others. Alex and Norman carried a lunch to save coming all the way home at midday so dining late was their usual procedure. Tonight was the Christian Endeavour Meeting and she had promised to go with Nellie Hay and a few others. This was something new and Mary Bella was curious. As she walked briskly up Mid Street she hummed to herself in time with her footsteps and felt a real sense of exhilaration. Yes, life was good. Things had turned out well and she was enjoying herself.

Strange, how during all these years with Maggie she had never realized the miss of friends her own age, especially in Newton Center. True, she was often included in family events, but there was always that sense of being on the edge and apartness. Maybe Maggie was responsible for that with her strong awareness of 'place'. Now Mary Bella felt young, alive, and full of energy for all that was happening in the group of youth that surrounded her. She was particularly close to Nellie Hay and Tina.

It was now six months since Mary Bella's return from Boston and Jane had been gone almost five. Maggie had written that Jane would be accepted on to the staff in the

Ripleys' home but on the strictest code of best behaviour. Failing that, there would be no second chance. Only Mrs. Ripley and Maggie knew of her history and they were willing to give Jane the opportunity to make good. So she had departed with no fuss and the reports to date had been satisfactory. Mary Bella was only too aware of Maggie's rigid discipline and wondered how long Jane would conform. In the winter Newton Center with Boston nearby would be diversion enough for Jane but Maine, with all the freedom and the wide variety of youth that came and went, was a different agenda. Would she manage to resist temptation? Thankfully, that was not her, Mary Bella's, problem.

To start with Mary Bella had helped Betsy in the shop. With the boys at work and school all day, the two women had a free hand and made a huge difference in the layout, reviewing and widening the variety of stock and working out Betsy's best days for her home products, which were becoming more and more popular. The latter meant many evenings of work in the kitchen, which she was prepared to do with Mary Bella's help. They began to enjoy a new relationship based on mutual respect and admiration for each other's talents. Mary Bella loved her Mother's sense of humour and optimism, which always seemed to see her through. And when she heard Betsy's laughter in the shop or kitchen Mary Bella would smile to herself and think,

"Yes, she's getting over Jane."

Mary Bella's growing concern was her own state of unemployment. She felt there was not enough work to occupy two women in the house and shop all day and she must find a way to bring in some additional income to the home. She answered an advert from a tailoring firm looking for experienced seamstresses. On being invited for an interview, she decided to wear one of her best outfits made under Maggie's tuition. As evidence of her skill this proved successful and Mary Bella was employed to work in the department tailoring for gents' outfitting. Along with fifteen other ladies she was now a member on the staff of Mackay's, a well- known tailor in Fraserburgh and it felt good. Every Friday she brought home her pay and handed over her board money to Betsy who carefully put it away with Alex's contribution, for that day when something special would be required. Now they were more than just making ends meet and it was most satisfying.

James W. Findlay, Royal Artillery WW1 1916

Chapter 21

Mary Bella's arrival at No.21 Charlotte Street had caused quite a stir in the neighbourhood. Many had not known her as a child so that made her all the more intriguing. Her quiet, refined manner, her proper speech and her tall, attractive appearance made her the subject of much discussion and many came to the shop just to see and talk with her.

This was particularly so on the part of the young men on the street. Jim and Alex Findlay, cousin Tom's best friends, were regulars. Like so many others, they had been demobbed after the War and were now back in work following their trades, Alex an engineer in the Toolworks, and Jim a plumber with a local firm, Morrison Stuart. Mary Bella enjoyed their banter over buying their cigarettes and gradually she was drawn into their circle, which was mainly associated with the Baptist Church. Her cousins were also deeply involved with the church activities and so, one way or another, Mary Bella found herself in the midst of youthful rambles, picnics, cycle runs and all the meetings organized for the youth.

The choir played a large part in their weekly activities and, although not particularly musical, Mary Bella was enrolled into the alto section. Serious practice was going on and rehearsals for 'Elijah', to be sung at the church anniversary, were happening twice weekly. The church was not always available for these occasions so the choir gathered in the organist's back shop in High Street.

Nellie Noble and Davie, her brother, lived in the flat above their shop, which was of a general variety. They sold mainly fruit and vegetables, sweets of the old fashioned kind, now and again flowers and bedding plants in season, tins of fruit and, Nellie's speciality, trays of Swiss milk tablet and coconut ice. People came from far and near to buy it. The back and front shops were separated by a glass partition from behind which Nellie could see her customers if she was busy in the back. There she stored her vegetables and fruit, cooked her tablet, made meals for Davie and herself and generally did everything, including having a rest on the old chaise longue standing in the corner. Pride of place was held by a beautiful Bluthner piano, which Nellie often played between customers.

All this activity did not lend itself to careful hygiene and occasionally a heavy odour of decay pervaded the shop. Nellie was not known for regular hand washing but her customers relished the good humour and friendliness, which was always present there. Whatever Nellie and Davie's shortcomings, all was forgotten when she sat at the organ on Sunday and lead the singing. She could make that little pipe organ sing or trumpet forth in voluntary or hymn tune and she inspired the whole congregation to give of their best. Passers by on Victoria Street used to linger a while and listen while the hymns were being sung.

Mary Bella thoroughly enjoyed the informality and camaraderie of these rehearsals and, as the standard improved, the grandeur of the oratorio had its own effect on her. Jim Findlay had the lead tenor part, Jessie Stephen sang the main soprano and Chrissie Ewan, the curer's daughter, had the alto lead. She and Jim often sang duets

443

during the services but their 'Piece de Resistance', which they sang on other occasions, was the 'Crooked Bawbee'. It was good to be part of it all and, after a welcome cup of tea, the choir would all set out together for home, gradually pairing off as they separated. Living across the road from each other, it seemed natural that Jim should see Mary Bella to her door, and that was the beginning of their relationship.

Chapter 22

As the weeks and months of summer moved into autumn Jim was becoming more and more captivated by this girl who was so different from the other young women in the Broch. During their long walks, taking the long way home, they discussed so many subjects ranging from the War, to travel, to labour conditions, to the poverty that so cruelly pursued their own class and the many other situations, which had influenced their lives. He loved to listen to her descriptions of life in the States, especially the summers in Maine and life with Maggie. She did not often speak of Florida; that was a memory still too sore. Jim was so intrigued with this girl who could have a firm opinion and confidently state her views. In addition, he enjoyed her quiet sense of humour, which bubbled up to the surface and lit up a twinkle in her blue eyes. Mary Bella was good to be with and Jim felt so proud that this beautiful, stylish girl should be willing to become his close friend.

Mary Bella, on her part, was very happy that it was Jim who had singled her out and, as their relationship progressed, she liked what she was learning about him. Though he was by profession a practical man, Jim had also an intellectual leaning, judging by the books he read. He was a visionary and had dreams of what the future might hold. The War had brought home to him the fragility and brevity of life and now Jim longed to develop his skills, to travel and to widen his horizons, and to achieve something with his life. As she listened, Mary Bella felt she had found a kindred soul but what gave her deeper gratification, was the fact that Jim had chosen to share his dreams with *her*. At last, she had met someone who really valued her for her own sake and not just for her usefulness.

Aberdour Beach was deserted that beautiful Saturday in September. In the whole bay, from the grassy cliff towering away on the left to the brooding, red sandstone arches at the end of the mile long shingled shore not a soul was to be seen. Only the wheeling gulls and the foraging birds broke the silence while the constant sough of the crystal clear water breaking on the pebbled shore provided a soothing accompaniment to the screech of the birds. Here time seemed to have stood still since the first missionaries were sent out by St. Columba, and St Modan founded his tiny, community church tucked into the cliff side. All gone now, but people still think about him and remember his name. The stone encircled spring and the well trodden, narrow, cliff path leading over the arched promontory to the hidden bay and beach tell of generations of visitors who have found the peace of this place. Tranquil on such a day as this, but also raging and storm ridden when the blast roared up the Firth from the north.

Into the quiet broke the laughter of Mary Bella and Jim as they slowed their bicycles to a halt beside the well. After the long pull uphill from Rosehearty they had enjoyed the quick zigzag descent to the shore and were now ready to rest and enjoy their picnic somewhere on the rocks. They had been here before with the church group but, this time, Jim had insisted they would enjoy exploring on their own. Since the tide was out, he led Mary Bella through the arches and caves to the second beach and they paddled on the soft sandy shore and then lay in the sun. Later they climbed the rocky outcrop above the arches and sat together, silently enjoying the wonderful view. Suddenly Jim reached out his hand to Mary Bella and, grasping her one, held it aloft and declared,

"Listen you birds. This is Bella. She's my lass and I want you all to know that. I love her and I think she loves me. Div ye love me Bella?"

Mary Bella was so amazed at this outburst she could only turn and look into his face. But what he saw there was his answer. He drew her into his arms and softly kissed her. Then she drew back and, holding his face between her hands, she looked earnestly at him and replied,

"Aye Jim. I'm your lass. I div love ye and I always wull."

Then she returned his kiss like a seal to her promise.

These were precious moments. Later, as they strolled hand in hand back to their bicycles by the well, their happiness was so complete. They wished this day would go on forever. If a heart could sing Mary Bella felt that her one was singing now. At last she had found some one who loved her selflessly like Father and Granny, and Maggie too but, she had always felt there was a little element of duty there.

As they flew, free wheeling down hill into the wind, their laughter made a glad sound and, although they approached Charlotte Street in a more decorous manner, the joy remained. Now they could stand together and let the world know that they loved each other.

Chapter 23

The remaining months of 1920 were exciting and busy. Living so close, Mary Bella knew Jim's family well, Jeannie and John still at school and Alex, nearer to Jim in age. When she visited their home Mary Bella sensed they were still grieving for Bobby who had not returned from France. He had been the middle one of the children and a person of great fun and laughter, making his loss all the more acute. There was always a sadness in his voice when Jim spoke of 'my brother Bobby'.

Then there were his many Aunts, some in Fraserburgh and more in Aberdeen. Mary Bella could not remember them all. She too had a host of relatives- Aunts and Uncles in Fraserburgh and Aberdeen. So they decided to follow the tradition and spend Hogmanay and New Year in Aberdeen, Jim staying with his young Aunt Jamesina and her husband Alex Wood, a very close wartime friend of Jim, and Mary Bella with her Granny, now a frail old lady. During the two days they would visit as many as possible and bring in the New Year together.

This was a very nostalgic time for Mary Bella as she recalled the annual visits with her parents and shared her memories with Jim. Listening, he realized that when circumstances had weakened the bonds Mary Bella had not only lost her Father but that whole side of her family. As a child she had loved them and now for her Father's sake, she wanted to keep the closeness. Jim resolved to do his best to enable her.

The crowning moment of that New Year was the presentation of the engagement ring. Jim had planned a cosy tearoom setting but, since everything was closed on New Year's Day, he chose a quiet bench in Union Terrace Gardens and brought out the little grey box from his vest pocket. He laid it into Mary Bella's hands and before she could open it he wrapped his arms round her and held her so close.

"I love ye with all ma hairt an' I jist want us tae be aye thegither." He whispered.

Mary Bella rested in his arms, her heart overflowing with her love for him. All she could do was nod and whisper,

"Aye Jim always."

As she lifted the ring from its red velvet nest tears came into her eyes. Here was something wonderful. A diamond and ruby ring chosen and engraved inside, MBM, JWF, 1/1/21, all prepared in love for her. It was hard to believe. But it was true and when she held out her hand for him to slip it on her finger she whispered,

"It's beautiful. I jist think it's wonderful. I cudna hae wished for better Jim."

Now that things were official, wedding plans became the topic of family conversation but Mary Bella refused to be drawn in. Other things concerning their future were on her mind.

Chapter 24

It was about this time that dramatic reports filtered up north from Yarmouth. Towards the end of the yearly fishing in that port a religious revival had broken out and there had been a great stirring of the Holy Spirit amongst the fisher and town communities alike. The main evangelist was a young cooper named Jock Troup whose preaching had been so inspirational that the tide of conversions and recommitment to God and Jesus Christ was unstoppable. Eventually, it spread north with the fishing fleet and Jock Troup with his helper, Bill Bruce, came to Fraserburgh to lead the Gospel Campaign there.

There was an amazing atmosphere in the town. People were caught up in the message of reconciliation with God and wherever groups gathered in shops, at street corners or round kitchen tables, the topic was the same, the need to repent. It affected both rich and poor, people of high esteem, or the humble herring gutter at the farlan. What was also significant was the number of worthy dignitaries in the various churches who bent the knee and confessed their sins. The Revival belonged to no particular church but, as the weeks went by, the Baptist and the Congregational Churches became the centres of activity and the converts tended to go there.

Of course Mary Bella, Jim and the young folks in the Baptist Church were deeply involved in the Crusade and they spent many hours together facing the truth of the message and examining their own position in relation to the question of salvation and Christian living. Finally Mary Bella and Jim along with others took the decision and went forward as converts. It brought them great happiness and peace, and an understanding of many things. What had been the habit of conforming to church life had now become a deep reassurance and hope in God and, for Mary Bella especially, she could now look on all the grief and hurt of the past with the eyes of love and forgiveness. They were glad that all this had come about at the beginning of their life together and now they could go forward into the future with this reassurance of their deep bond in Christ.

The conversions led to baptisms and, in due course, Mary Bella, Jim and Alex along with many others went through the waters of baptism and became active members of the Church. Jim became a keen Bible student and occasionally led study groups, which became essential locally as the Revival moved on to Buckie and the coastal towns along the Moray Firth.

Chapter 25

'Betty May's' at 21 was always a cheery and popular place and customers enjoyed going there. Betsy loved people and, whatever their purchase, she always had a personal word of interest in their well being and progress. For all that good will, the shop still struggled week by week to make a profit and clear expenses. The after effects of the War, men returning to no employment, a country almost bankrupt and a distinct lack of financial resources had made the clients either restrict their shopping or run up accounts which they never seemed to fully clear. This had been an increasing problem for some time and, had it not been for Mary Bella and Alex's contributions to the housekeeping, Betsy would have had to close her shop. But she struggled on, always looking ahead to better times when she would have more money in her hand and not have to rely on Mary Bella for her book keeping skills and all the extra tasks in the home which she had made her responsibility. Being all too aware of the situation Mary Bella pondered the question of her wedding. She knew that her Mother's pride would wish it to be a proper occasion; church, reception and all the trimmings, but the pragmatist in her realized the impossibility of that. Rather than hurt Betsy's feelings, Mary Bella decided on a radical alternative, which she proposed to Jim.

They had thought and talked about their wedding for a long time, trying to find a simple and inexpensive solution to their problem. Both had large families who would expect an invitation and Jim's work, with the present economic climate, was in a doubtful situation. Although he was a fully experienced journeyman, he could be paid off at any time. Mary Bella's small savings from her American years had been used up to clear the shop debts and Jane's travelling expenses to Ripley's. So she suggested to Jim that on the local June holiday they should go off to Aberdeen for the day and come back married. They could have a special licence and it would cause no fuss or extra expense. At first he was doubtful. Mary Bella deserved a proper wedding and he longed to see her, a bride in all her beauty. But she was very adamant that the finery was not the problem; it was the costliness of the expectations of the two families and all that a wedding reception would involve. At last he agreed and began making enquiries about marriage licences and their requirements.

Before he had made much headway the matter was settled for them. Jim was given a week's notice of dismissal and, along with many other skilled men, he became unemployed. But it did not last long. He applied for work available in Glasgow and within a few weeks was working in the Gourock dockyards, fitting out the last orders of vessels on the Clyde. He found lodgings in the town and Mary Bella, although she was heart broken at his departure, was relieved that their plan had been interrupted. She had a better idea. This was still early spring and Jim's contract was for three months at least, which would give her sufficient time to prepare.

Having been employed by MacKay's for over a year Mary Bella was entitled to a week's holiday so she booked the third week in July, when she would become twenty-one. She then purchased a length of fine cream silk from the fabric department, receiving her discount as an employee, and proceeded to plan her wedding dress. Every free moment at home she worked on it, Betsy presuming it was an order from the shop, and as it began to take shape Mary Bella, like any other bride, began to feel the thrill and excitement at what lay ahead.

It was a very simple design. The rolled collar came to a deep V at the front and the hip line sash accentuated her slim figure. The over dress reached below the sash and met the full pleated skirt which hung to calf length. The fine pleating was continued in the elbow length sleeves and, just to make it more wedding like, Mary Bella added a little cream lace to the cuffs and collar edging. Once finished, she was very satisfied with her creation and hung it away at the back of her wardrobe, covered with a sheet. Every now and again as she made ready for bed, Mary Bella would peep at it and give a little smile of anticipation. Cream shoes and stockings came eventually and she was ready. To complete the outfit she treated herself to a short, silk brocade jacket with a matching little hat in a deep apricot shade, which made a beautiful contrast to the dress. Now Mary Bella was ready to put her plan into action.

Chapter 26

Mary Bella smiled. She had to give herself a little hug to contain her excitement. Here she was in the Aberdeen train, a bride on her way to be married and no one in Fraserburgh knew a thing about it. A momentary sense of guilt flashed over her conscience but was short lived as her thoughts turned to Jim. He had been so keen to agree with her plan, especially its simplicity. It meant that their wedding day would be for them alone. Jim had made all the arrangements about the licence and the minister. Already the banns had been called twice and they would hear the third declaration on Sunday when they attended church. His best man was to be his friend Tom Sim, now married to Kitty and conducting buses on the Glasgow routs. Her friend, Ethel Stopanni, was at present nursing in Glasgow Royal Infirmary so Mary Bella invited her to be bridesmaid. Both would travel to Gourock on Monday morning and come to Mary Bella's lodgings.

It was a glad reunion when she stepped off the train into Jim's arms. How free they felt in this place where no one knew them or could make demands on them. Their time was their own and Jim had the week off work too- a wonderful surprise at the last moment. He had booked Mary Bella into the boarding house next door to his lodgings and, after the wedding he would join her there for the week. His own landlady, Mrs. Kelly was very excited about the event and insisted that on her arrival Mary Bella should come home with him for a meal. It was all so hearty and jovial and, as Mary Bella was to learn, typical of the Glasgow generosity.

Now they stood together watching the fast flow and the widening sweep of the great river, changing course to the south, and they felt such joy in each other. The summer evening was darkening as the sun set over behind the Kyles of Bute and they just wished to hold on to every moment. In the distance to the right the clatter of the night shift at the dockyard echoed across the water and below them the occasional liner changed course as it headed into the wider Clyde estuary and the Irish Sea. This brought their thoughts to the future and the uncertainty of Jim's work. His dream was eventually to set up his own plumbing business but that required financial backing and, in the present depressed atmosphere of work, there was no future in that aspiration. And things were becoming worse. So they talked as they walked, turning over possibilities, but allowing nothing to mar the happiness of the coming days. Tomorrow they would hear their names proclaimed together and then the next day they would be one. As he kissed her goodnight, Jim held her so close and whispered,

"Not long now. There'll be nae mair goodnights on the doorstep."

Sunday was the usual quiet Scottish Sabbath. After the service Mary Bella was introduced to the minister and they went over the wedding arrangements before setting out for lunch and a long walk to the famous Cloch Lighthouse high on the hill behind Gourock. The vistas were magnificent. As they sat in the sun looking away across the wonderful surrounding seascapes Mary Bella began to tell Jim what it felt like to be on one of these huge liners passing through the waters and leaving your family and country behind. Her lips trembled and her voice grew husky as she spoke. His arm resting on her shoulder gripped her tightly as he responded,

"Ye'll niver dae it again on yir ain Bella. Bit, wad ye gang tae America again wi me?"

She sat, silent at his words, and then turned, her face lit up.

"Jim. I loved America, every minute, once I got there. I never wanted to come back tae the Broch. But now, I wud gang back in a minute if you wad gang an aa. Hae ye been thinking along these lines?"

Jim nodded, saying no more on the matter. But it had triggered Mary Bella's thinking. If the matter arose again she would have some proposal to make.

Chapter 27

"I'll get up when that sunbeam reaches the dress."

Mary Bella had been awake for a long time lying musing as she watched the sunbeam steal slowly round the room. It looked a good day and it was her birthday too. And she was twenty-one. As she thought back over these years it seemed that she had lived a lifetime already and today was another huge step in her life. But this was a glad one and she had no qualms. Jim was steadfast and hard working and he had his romantic side too, which gave her a little thrill of pleasure. What would it be like being married and living closely with some one? She had only ever shared a bed with Jane. Would Jim take up a lot of the bed, would he kick or snore in his sleep? Mary Bella giggled. She would know soon. And what about tonight? She hoped Jim would know because no one had ever told her what to expect in marriage. In the fisher circle mothers did not talk openly about that sort of thing, but Mary Bella had learned something of the technicalities of procreation from Jane. She felt somehow that their love for each other would see them through any difficulties and she had no fears for what lay ahead. In fact she could not wait for this wonderful day to begin.

By midmorning Ethel and Tom arrived followed soon after by the delivery of a posy of beautiful cream roses from Jim, the romantic. Tom was closeted for an hour with him next door and then returned for a hearty lunch with Ethel and Mary Bella. Her landlady, Mrs. Davis insisted that they ate well.

"It'll be a long time afore ye hae yir wedding tea." She reminded them.

As she descended the stairs dressed in her finery and carrying her roses Mary Bella was reassured by the smiles of approval on their faces.

"My, ye look bonny. Just the right colour. It brings out the pink in yir cheeks. Jim'll be a prood man the day."

Tom, playing dual role as best man and also as a relative giving away the bride, travelled with Mary Bella and Ethel in the taxi to the church where Jim was already waiting. The news of a wedding spread and a little crowd had gathered round the door. But Tom was prepared and when the car drove away he leaned out and threw the expected scatter of coins for the children to scramble after.

The organ playing softly in the background was a wonderful surprise and as she walked down the aisle on Tom's arm and saw Jim standing before the communion table waiting for her, Mary Bella felt her throat choking with tears of happiness. The sun streaming in through the stained glass had placed him in a circle of light and as she stepped into it beside him and he took her hand and smiled, Mary Bella knew the happiest moment of her life.

Chapter 28

The days were passing all too quickly. But oh such happy days! After their wedding tea in the restaurant Mary Bella and Jim had accompanied Ethel and Tom to their bus. He was returning to a late shift and Ethel to night duty. As they said farewell Jim handed each of them a little parcel,

"Just a little minder of today and a thank you for helping to make it so perfect. Bella and myself, we canna thank you enough. Give oor love to Kitty and tell her all aboot the day. We will maybe visit ye soon, efter yir baby is born."

Reluctant to give up their first moments of aloneness they strolled very slowly back to Mrs. Davis' house while Jim explained the parcels. Tom's contained an enamelled cigarette case and Ethel's a plain silver bracelet, both inscribed with their names and the date.

"I jist thocht it wad be good tae gie them something tae remind them o' oor wedding day. Did I dae the recht thing Bella?"

"Aye Jim. It was good tae think like that. I'm sure they will appreciate yir kindness jist as I feel aboot my roses." And smiling up at him, she held them up close to her face.

They had hardly shut the door before Mrs. Davis appeared at the foot of the stairs.

"Here you are at last. Come away in and have something to eat."

With that she opened the sitting room door and they were confronted by a sea of faces, all smiling and calling,

"Congratulations! The bride and groom!"

All the Kellys and Davises were there holding up their glasses and enjoying the surprise on the faces of Jim and Mary Bella. What a party it was. The beautiful square wedding cake had to be cut and Jim made a speech in reply to the toast, shyly referring to his 'wife' and almost breaking down when he tried to express their thanks for this wonderful hospitality and wedding reception. It had just completed a most wonderful day.

"Na, na man. It's no ower yet." came a Glasgow voice amid much laughter and blushes, and the fun went on all through the meal. At last, after a few songs and some story telling, exhaustion took over and Mrs. Davis declared,

"Now you young folks have had quite a day. We'll just see you on your way upstairs." And with that the whole company rose and escorted Mary Bella and Jim to the foot of the stairs and stood watching while they mounted and turned to smile their thanks from the landing.

"Now ye *will* carry her over the threshold Jim?" and with that Mary Bella was lifted aloft over the doorway and the door firmly closed behind them. The night enfolded them as they entered a little world of joy and adventure, which was theirs alone.

Their week was not without mishap. One morning Jim hired a rowing boat and they planned to go down the coast away from the shipyards and have a picnic on the sandy shore. All went well until the afternoon brought clouds and a rising wind, which made them quickly embark for the return trip. But the rising tide had created cross currents and Jim found the little boat impossible to handle. All they could do was land again and wait for a change in the weather. Meantime they had to find shelter.

This was a particularly desolate length of the Ayrshire coast. As far as the eye could see mainly moorland stretched ahead, dotted here and there with grazing sheep but no signs of even a shepherd's cottage. Jim and Mary Bella followed the sheep tracks for a while, always keeping the shore in sight, and eventually came on a low, lean-to shed used for storing winter fodder for the sheep. Here they could be dry and warm amongst the bales of straw and just wait out the night. They still had picnic food. Their only concern was the worry they would be causing Mrs. Davis, but there was nothing they could do about that. So they settled to rest, to talk, to love, to dream, to love again and in the morning to rise, new people after a night of discovery and pleasure. Their honeymoon had many peaks but this night must be the summit of their joy and the memory of it never faded.

All too soon it was Saturday and, after a heart-breaking farewell, Mary Bella was once again on the train heading for Aberdeen and home. Now she had to face her Mother and the two families. She had no regrets or shame in what she had done. Her motives had been for the best, but she knew there would be an atmosphere of criticism on both sides.

Chapter 29

Of course they did not understand. Why had Mary Bella and Jim eloped? All sorts of questions were asked and there was some real speculation. But Mary Bella ignored them all, went back to her tailoring, and was determined that, now they were a unit, she and Jim were not going to be swayed one way or the other by any family remarks.

In due course, Jim's work in Gourock came to an end and by September he was back in Fraserburgh unemployed, and feeling very despondent about his future. So many were like him. It was then that the subject of emigration again came into their conversation and the decision to go ahead brought a ray of hope and excitement. The only problem was finance. They had managed to save very little. But Mary Bella had been pondering and felt she had a prospective source which she could contact with Jim's approval.

Aunt Bella and Uncle Willie had moved north again when he had retired at the end of the War. They were comfortably off due to Willie's large income from war work and were living in a beautiful cottage in the new Alexandra Terrace on the south side of Fraserburgh. Willie was now a shareholder in George Noble's ship chandlery and the couple enjoyed life with their gardening hobby, renewing old friendships and making new ones amongst their upper class neighbours. Having been away from Fraserburgh for so long Bella understood the parochialism that her niece was facing and supported Mary Bella wholeheartedly in their quiet wedding arrangements.

When they finally came to request a loan of £25 Bella and Willie agreed to lend them the money for Jim's passage to Boston. He promised that it would be repaid as soon as he found employment and then Mary Bella would follow once he had saved up her fare. But Bella interrupted,

"No Jim. Get out there yourself and then bring Mary Bella as soon as possible. Two will work together better than your being in lodgings. Our money can wait till you are both settled. We trust you and admire your initiative. We moved away from Fraserburgh ourselves and know exactly how you feel. We wish you all the very best in your adventure and God bless you."

The opposition to their move was very strong. Jim's Mother Betsy was grief stricken. Having lost one son in the War, now she was losing another. Alex, John and Jeannie were still at home but that made no difference. She felt that Mary Bella had persuaded Jim into this move and, despite the fact that they were married, Betsy resented her influence.

Mary Bella's Mother Betsy argued from a different point of view, again laying the guilt on Mary Bella.

"I dinna ken foo I'm gan tae manage without ye Balla. Rinnen the shop an' looking efter Norman an' the hoose, forby Alex, is mair than I can dae on ma ain."

"Well Mother, ye'll jist hae tae get somebody in tae help ye in the shop. It's rinnen fine noo and bringing in a fair profit so ye could afford somebody for a few hours a week. My first thocht is for Jim noo and I hiv tae support him in his plans, jist as you did my Father. He canna gang idle like this. It's nae in his nature. He's only joining hundreds of others daen the same thing and fan he's settled I'll gang an aa. That may be a few months but I *wull* gang."

No more was said and Jim quietly went ahead with his arrangements-passport, references, addresses, medical, passage booked and sailing date fixed- all without hindrance, and finally it was time for him to go; too soon for Mary Bella's feelings but, for Betsy and Jimmie Findlay, it seemed goodbye forever. To them America was the other end of the earth and they would never see their son again. Jim sailed from Glasgow on the SS Metagama and, along with many other young Scots, arrived in Boston full of hope and determination to make a good life for Mary Bella and himself.

Chapter 30

With Jim away Mary Bella settled down to her old routine of work, shop and home and the halcyon days of her engagement, marriage and honeymoon became a wonderful memory which she relived in the quiet of her own room at night. Sometimes, when the longing for Jim overcame her, she shed tears but generally Mary Bella kept a brave front and waited patiently for his first letter. Frequent visits across the road to the Findlay home improved the relationship with Jim's parents, but Mary Bella soon realized that she would always be regarded as Jim's wife, a daughter in law, but nothing closer.

At last the letter arrived. Jim had landed safely after an excellent crossing. A few other North East men were on the ship so they befriended each other during the week and enjoyed the company. Once they landed in Boston, all strangers from home, they parted, heading for different destinations and Jim made his way to Jamaica Plain to Teenie Stephen's home. On Maggie's advice, Mary Bella had prearranged this and Teenie had it all organized. Now in her retirement years she no longer kept boarders but still maintained the 'Welcome' role for newcomers. She had found good lodgings for Jim quite near in Jamaica Plain and, after a hearty meal, Teenie escorted him to meet his landlady, Mrs. Buchan, originally from St. Combs.

Now happily settled, Jim set out next day to find employment and by afternoon had found work with a plumbing business in Jamaica Plain. Jim's references and his Journeyman's Certificate stood him in good stead and the boss was very keen to have Scottish workers. With many more details about the North East folks he had met at Teenie's and the comfort of his lodgings and some private words for her eyes alone, Mary Bella was so happy with the letter. Her first call was across the road to read relevant parts to Betsy and Jimmie, which pleased them. Their letter would be following.

These letters became the focal point of their week. Jim had a good flowing command of English and his descriptions of American life opened their eyes to a whole new world. When he told them about the number of bathrooms he had to install in ordinary homes, and central heating being the standard everywhere, his parents began to realize that maybe his move had been for the better after all. Mary Bella, who had lived with these amenities and had sorely missed them when she came back nearly four years previously, was pleased to see this change in their attitude.

Now Mary Bella was faced with a new quandary. For some weeks, and even before Jim's departure, she had noticed some changes in herself, but said nothing at the time. It was too important that he should sail and make a beginning to their new life so Mary Bella kept quiet about her suspicions, knowing he would not go and leave her.

Yes, she was pregnant. The doctor had confirmed it and the baby was due in April. But she decided to keep it a secret as long as possible for she needed to work and save. MacKay's had been generous in keeping her employed after her marriage, for having married, female staff was not their rule. But pregnant staff was not acceptable. So Mary Bella said nothing to anyone and carried on with her normal life. Fortunately, she kept well and the weeks passed until the fifth month when she could conceal her pregnancy no longer. It was with a great deal of sadness that she handed in her notice for she had enjoyed working with her colleagues and had learned so much. They held a little party for Mary Bella and presented her with a beautiful amethyst ring in a thistle setting to remind her of Scotland when she went to the States.

Chapter 31

Now that she was at home all day, Mary Bella enjoyed preparing for her baby. Jim's letters continued to be positive and, once he recovered from the initial realization of approaching parenthood, he shared Mary Bella's joy in the prospect. Of course he would have preferred to be at hand with Mary Bella, even contemplated returning to Fraserburgh, but she was adamant that he should stay and prepare at that side.

"Babies are women's work Jim and there's plenty here looking after me. I'm surrounded by advice, especially from your Mother with all her experience. So just stay there Jim and wait. I'm fine and healthy and so is the baby and you would only have to wait and watch. You will get a wire as soon as the baby's here. I can feel it kicking now, very lively, feels like it could be a footballer. Not long to go now. Keep your letters coming. I live for them week by week. I've kept them all and now and again reread them. The Christmas ones were wonderful. Just think, next Christmas we will be three of us together in our own place."

And so the letters became the life line keeping their love alive and, in a strange way, deepening their knowledge of and respect for each other. Both were able correspondents and expressed their inner thoughts far more easily in writing than orally. The pen became their communication mainstay and recorded everything – family, local news, church affairs, opinions, sad moments, joys, worries, hopes and plans.

Jim had done well in sending money. Bella had been repaid and now Mary Bella was building up the bank account for her own fare. No unnecessary expense was to be lavished on the baby, as they would be travelling as soon as the child was able for the journey. Janet still had Netta's pram so that was brought out of the cooperage to be cleaned and polished and Jim's Mother produced the cradle that had rocked so many of her thirteen children, Jim included. Mary Bella treasured these offerings and quietly sewed the tiny garments while all the Aunts knitted. This was already a much- loved baby- the first great grandchild for Jim's Broadsea Granny. Often in the darkness Mary Bella would slip out on her own to visit one or another of the older folks and she especially enjoyed a ' news' with Jim's Granny who had known her own Granny, Mary May.

Chapter 32

Elizabeth Duthie Carle Findlay was born on 14th. April, 1922 and was so called after both Grandmothers-Jim's Mother, Elizabeth Carle and Mary Bella's Mother, Elizabeth Duthie. Both ladies were delighted.

It had been a long, agonizing labour going on all day and into the night but the midwife, strongly traditional, would not consider calling on the Doctor to administer a pain killer or assist Mary Bella in any way. The baby was healthy and it would come in its own time and the Mother must just play her part. Bearing a child was never an easy process and that was how the Good Book said it had to be. When eventually the baby emerged she left an exhausted, haemorrhaging Mary Bella whose only thought was,

"Never again. There will be no more if this is what it is like."

However, Mary Bella was young and strong and she had a great incentive to recover from her ordeal. The baby was thriving and Jim was waiting on the other side. The proceeding few weeks were spent enjoying the baby, now called Betty, and slowly preparing herself for the journey and her new life.

One major problem was her teeth for, during the pregnancy, they had deteriorated badly. The dentist recommended that they should all be removed and he would provide her with a good set of false teeth. But that was going to eat into her precious savings causing a delay in her departure. Finally, a compromise was reached when Mr. Buchan created two plates, the upper and lower, each with the four incisor teeth, and space was left for the canines and molars to be added at a later date when she could afford to do so.

The weeks were speeding by and Mary Bella was having to contend with real psychological harassment from both sides. It was cruel to be depriving them of their only grandchild. When would they see her again? It was too long a journey for her to tackle on her own with so young a baby. Betty would grow up better in the Broch with her folk around her than in a foreign land amongst strangers. Jim should just come home and settle down here and, in time, work would come. So it went on endlessly and Mary Bella felt she could hardly bear the innuendos being thrust at her. The only moments of encouragement and advice she experienced was when carrying Betty, she slipped out unobserved at the back gate and went down the lane to visit Jim's Granny

"Noo ma lass, niver mind whit they say. Gang tae yir man. The bairnie an him are the only eens that maitter an ye maan pit them first. The foulk here wull git ower it an settle doon eence ye're awa. The langer ye wyte the sairer it'll be tae loss ye baith so dinna linger ower lang. Jim's got himself a gweed wife and mither for his bairnie an' he's needin ye sair Mary Bella. Gang tae him. Ye hae my blessing. A'm gan tae miss ye an aa ye ken."

So Mary Bella made her arrangements, booking her own passage as Betty, under six months, would travel free, and finding a fellow traveller from Inverallochy who would be company on the crossing. This lady, Liza Stephen, was going to the States to join her fiancé and to be married so she would make cheerful company.

During the last week and wishing to avoid tearful good-byes at the station, Mary Bella with the baby visited each of the relatives in their own homes to say her farewells. Only Alex accompanied her to the station and, as he helped her on to the train he whispered,

"I'll be following you as soon as my time is out. So keep a bed for me."

And with that he slammed the carriage door and was gone.

Chapter 33

The SS Alba had been sailing up the Charles River for some time and within the hour it would be dockside and the disembarkation would begin. Mary Bella had found a shady corner under the deck canopy and there she sat, cradling Betty, watching the frantic busyness prior to the ship's arrival in port. It had been a good crossing and the third class, shared cabin, which she had opted to book, had proved comfortable. The two other passengers were friendly and enjoyed Betty, always offering to guard her while Mary Bella was having a meal or had to leave the cabin. Liza, also travelling third for economic reasons, was good company and, in her turn, appreciated having Mary Bella, young and newly married, to share her dreams and fears.

The week had flown past and her excitement was almost choking her. The nine months had seemed like an eternity but now, it was all behind and she would have Jim's hug and see his face when she put Betty into his arms. How different from her last arrival in Boston eight years ago, a lonely, frightened, grieving child waiting in an endless queue. Little did she know then how much the following six years would mean to her in establishing her values and forming her ambitions. She would always be grateful to Maggie and the Ripleys and looked forward so much to introducing them to Jim and Betty. Maggie's letters had kept her informed of changes in their homes and amongst the family, but Mary Bella just longed to sit down with Maggie and share news face to face.

At last the hawsers were thrown and the gangways rumbled down. Passengers were already stationed at the rails frantically searching in the crowds below to pick out a familiar face. It took Mary Bella a little time to find Jim but there he was waving a straw hat and laughing up at her. But what was amazingly wonderful was the figure of Maggie alongside Jim. There she was in a bright summer dress with white hat and gloves, waving and smiling up at Mary Bella. That just made her arrival perfect.

Their reunion was beautiful and emotional. Tears were shed as Jim enfolded his wife and child in his arms and then cuddled his daughter. Maggie, always correct and reserved, would have shared a handshake and a kiss on the cheek, but Mary Bella wrapped her arms round her and hugged her hard, so glad to have this special woman back in her life and so appreciative that she had come to Boston to meet her again.

At last, immigration preliminaries all behind, they were settled in a comfortable taxi bringing them to Jamaica Plain. Considering the baby and the luggage involved, this was arranged on the instructions of Mrs. Ripley who thought it would be more comfortable for all.

They found Teenie waiting and the meal on the table was so welcome. The baby, fed and changed, now lay sound asleep in a huge oval washing basket lined with a folded pink flannelette sheet. This was to be her cot until they could purchase her own real one. At last they could sit at leisure and catch up on the news of the two families and the friends in the Broch and the villages. Teenie had been away so long she had outlived many of her contemporaries but she still enjoyed hearing about the folks 'ower the waatter' and listening to the dialect and the cadences of the 'hame' voices.

"Afore Maggie Ann has tae gang awa I want tae tell ye Mary Bella whit we hae planned for ye. It's nae time sin Betty's birth an ye've hin tae arreenge a' the journey and packin', forby the traivelin' itsel. We feel it's time ye had a rest so, I want the three o' ye tae bide here wi me for a week or twa . It wad be winnerfu for me haen the bairn and you and Jim cud set up the apartment he has rented on Sheridan Street. It wad gie ye time tae look aroon second hand shops and syne yir ain kist wad be here. Fit say ye tae that Mary Bella?"

Much as she longed to be in their own place, Mary Bella saw the sense in Teenie's arrangement and, it was true. Now that she had arrived, she realized just how exhausting the strain of leaving Fraserburgh had been. Here she had Jim and that made all the difference. And these loving friends who cared. With tears in her eyes and a smile on her face Mary Bella expressed her appreciation and the matter was settled. Maggie nodded her approval and accepted Jim's escort to the subway taking her to Newton Center. Before leaving Maggie answered Mary Bella's query about why she was still at Bracebridge Road in July. Why was she not in Maine?

"Ruth, Betty and the boys went on ahead to open up Toad Hall. They are old enough now to do that and Will Poole is there to keep an eye on them. The Professor, Mrs. Ripley and I will travel up in the automobile at the weekend. It will be a nice quiet journey. They both had affairs to attend to and it gave me an opportunity to see you."

The warmth of the smile and the loving expression in her Aunt's eyes gladdened Mary Bella.

"I shall write Mrs. Ripley and thank her for the taxi. It was so thoughtful of her. Maggie, you will come and see us when you come back from Maine? We will be settled by then."

Chapter 34

Knowing that he had worked many hours of overtime in the preceding weeks, his employer granted Jim a week's holiday to enable him to settle his family. An old house on Sheridan Street had been divided into apartments and Jim rented two rooms on the second floor. They were to share the bathroom with the opposite tenant but its great advantage was the low rental. It would do as a start off place. The whole area and the houses looked run down but Mary Bella was full of optimism about what they could do with their rooms.

Jim had already bought a table and two chairs and the large bedroom contained a bed. The rest of the furnishings he left for Mary Bella's choosing so the first few days were happily spent in second hand shops purchasing just what they required and making their precious money stretch as far as possible. Betty's baby carriage was first on the list and, in the meantime, it would also serve as a cot. Two easy chairs were added and contacts made with the fuel supplier and the iceman.

In due course the kist was delivered and revealed the wisdom of Mary Bella's preparation. It contained very little clothing but a good supply of bed and table linen, blankets and curtain materials, some ready to hem and hang. One or two very heavy, woven covers were spread on the wood floor, as rugs for Betty to crawl over and some of the heavier materials, Mary Bella decided, would make good armchair covers. What a pity she had not been able to bring her sewing machine. She felt bereft without it but she would find a second hand one soon.

Thanks to the generosity of her Aunts the kitchen was almost fully equipped with pans and enamelware and all Jim and Mary Bella had to purchase was some crockery.

By the end of the week they felt ready to move in and take up residence in their first home, now almost a year after their marriage. That made it all the more wonderful. At last they could live their own lives, plan their future and be responsible to no one but each other. Mary Bella, in particular, felt she had waited a long time for this.

It did not take Mary Bella long to fall back into the American way of life which she had loved. The ensuing weeks developed a routine. Always a morning person, she was up early with Jim and, pushing Betty in her carriage, accompanied him part of the way to work before heading for the market and her shopping. The summer heat of Boston affected Mary Bella badly and so she always aimed to be back home into the shade before mid morning. The rest of her day was spent in cooking and house keeping, sewing, once she had acquired her sewing machine, and attending to Betty. Sometimes in the severe heat Mary Bella longed for a breath of the cold, fresh North Sea wind but she was happy with her life for the present.

She got to know her neighbours and visited with a few, always amazed at the variety of nationalities represented in Jamaica Plain. By far Scots outnumbered the others but, coming from Fraserburgh, this was a very cosmopolitan scene for Mary Bella. Mr. And Mrs. Bonnet, the owners, were French, speaking with a strong accent and they lived on the bottom floor. Once a month when Mary Bella paid the rent, she visited briefly and, from the many statues and candles burning everywhere, she realized that they were staunch Roman Catholics. Her immediate neighbours she never really knew as they left early and returned late causing Mary Bella to surmise that they travelled far to work.

Weekends were the highlight of the week. This was when Jim and Mary Bella explored Jamaica Plain and then, further afield, Boston City. A picnic lunch was packed into the pram along with Betty and somewhere, perhaps on Boston Common, Quincy Market or Franklin Park, they would sit and enjoy their meal. Mary Bella knew Boston and so loved sharing with Jim some of her happy memories. It was an exciting time for them both, discovering each other again in this new environment and responding to their varied reactions to every new situation. Jim was inclined to over react but Mary Bella kept calm and matter of fact as the occasion demanded.

Strong contacts were held with Teenie and other 'Brochers' in Jamaica Plain and, one Sunday in October, Mary Bella took Jim and Betty to visit Maggie in Newton Center. Jim was very impressed with the house and felt very privileged to meet Professor and Mrs. Ripley. They were so pleased to meet him and to see Mary Bella grown up, married and a Mother herself now. Betty Ripley walked off with the baby so the adults had a little time for conversation before Maggie served tea. Jim felt slightly in awe of Maggie but, as the three of them shared news, he eased a little and began to observe where Mary Bella had acquired some of her strong characteristics. Maggie, for her part, was very pleased with Mary Bella's husband. He appeared a very personable young man who seemed knowledgeable and spoke well, and Maggie felt reassured about her niece's future happiness.

Mary Bella with brother Alex. Jamaica Plain, 1924

Chapter 35

Letters came and went regularly and Mary Bella wrote faithfully to each family on alternate weeks. Answers did not come as frequently but she was firm in keeping her promise, and there was so much to write about in these early days. Not all the Fraserburgh letters came from family. Many of Jim's young friends were contemplating following his move and wrote for information concerning work opportunities and life in the States. One or two had already decided and asked Jim if they could use his name and address as reference for admission on immigration.

Remembering how essential Teenie had been to their own arrival, Jim and Mary Bella were anxious to help and debated long over the matter. Accommodation was the problem. They had one bedroom. Fortunately, just at that time, their neighbours moved away nearer their work and the rest of the floor became vacant; two large rooms and a small one over the downstairs vestibule. Mary Bella at once applied for the rooms and the whole floor became their own. Now they had five rooms, a bathroom, a veranda and an outside entrance stairway all for themselves. It would mean a higher rental but Mary Bella had a plan and, once Jim thought it through, he agreed.

Mary Bella and Jim would provide a welcome house for newcomers from the North East who could lodge there until they found work and their own accommodation. Mary Bella would charge board and lodging and run the house from that income and it would give them a chance to build up a little nest egg from Jim's salary. Furnishing the rooms would mean an initial outlay but they could manage that. Mary Bella was very excited about the whole idea, gratified that she had found a way to contribute to the family's future comfort and also to help others from home.

The first arrivals were two brothers, Robert and John Stephen, old friends from the Baptist Church, and both trained engineers. John's girlfriend Mary Duthie, and Bobby's girl Nellie Hay, would follow as soon as the men were settled and then they would get married. Mary Bella was delighted that her chum Nellie would be joining them. Soon brother Alex arrived, his apprenticeship completed, ready for a new life. Uncle George had wished to encourage and finance Alex to attend college and further his engineering career but the young man had his hopes pinned on the States. Alex was allocated the small bedroom for himself while the others were happy to share the larger rooms. Then followed Sandy Stephen, engaged to Nellie, Mary Bella's cousin, and a succession of short-term visitors who stayed briefly until they passed on to various locations and work.

Life was very enjoyable with their large household. Busy yes for Mary Bella but, once the men were off to work with their packed lunches, she could concentrate on Betty, shopping, cooking and laundry, even manage some sewing and visiting, before they all gathered for dinner in the evening. They were young and enthusiastic about so many things and the discussions ranged over huge areas of interest. John and Bobby had an irrepressible sense of humour and kept the laughter going while the quieter Sandy and Alex put in their view - point. Jim and Mary Bella found the company stimulating and, although it was a large household to supervise, they all worked together in the kitchen and bedrooms keeping things in order. There was always a baby sitter for Betty or someone to fetch an errand from Levine's shop at the corner, and Mary Bella and Jim could have an occasional evening out on their own.

The lodgers very much appreciated the role that Mary Bella and Jim were playing in their new life. The home from home atmosphere eased their sense of loss and homesickness and encouraged them to be purposeful in planning ahead. Gradually they moved away and settled near their work places and new arrivals filled the rooms. Bobby moved to Malden and when Nellie came out the bride stayed with Mary Bella. There was a wonderful reunion when the friends all met up at the wedding. John and Mary followed suite but Sandy could not persuade Nellie to leave home so, after a year, he returned to Fraserburgh and joined George Noble in the ship chandler's business. Two other memorable lodgers were James 'Hammie' Duthie and 'Shimmen' Strachan. Once they settled in they did not wish to move out despite all Mary Bella's encouraging. They found work in Jamaica Plain and life was very comfortable with Mary Bella so they became permanent lodgers. Because of their patient ways, Betty became very attached to them and it was 'Hammie' who eventually coaxed her to take her first steps at the age of two and a half. She was quite a plump child and it was all too easy to just sit and be waited on.

Another exciting event was the arrival of Flora on the scene. Ever since their teenage friendship during the summers in Maine Mary Bella and Flora Webber had kept up an occasional correspondence. Now that she was back in Boston Mary Bella renewed contact and invited Flora to visit. Alex very gallantly gave up his little room for the visitor and found Flora much to his liking. Within days the quiet young man became her escort and a strong bond developed between them. As time went on, Alex, now well established at Reidville's Engineering, was invited to visit the Webber family on the farm in Maine and eventually, another very happy wedding took place. Mary Bella was delighted with the match and more so when they set up home just a short distance away on Wyman Street.

These were good years for Mary Bella and Jim. Memorable for the way they struggled to succeed over poverty and hardship, for the exciting experiences in adapting to a new style of living, and for the various personalities who passed through their home. They achieved much together and their marriage was happy and fulfilled.

Chapter 36

As usual on the first Saturday of the month Mary Bella called on her landlady to pay the month's rent in advance. Occasionally Mrs. Bonnet invited her in for a cup of coffee while she signed the rent book and they enjoyed a chat, often about the children, the two daughters Ivette and Julie. This particular Saturday Mrs. Bonnet was very excited as Ivette was to have her first Holy Communion the following day and Mary Bella must see her white dress and veil. During the happy conversation Mrs. Bonnet voiced a worry and request,

"Mrs. Findlay, I have one problem about tomorrow. We need someone to supervise the house while we attend the ceremonies at St. Joseph's. You know we have a still in the basement, which requires regular checking for temperature levels and pressure. We don't know how long we shall be absent but I wish to ask you to look after the still for us. We shall leave instructions----."

Mary Bella's shocked expression must have made Mrs. Bonnet hesitate. Here lay the explanation for the scented candles. This was totally breaking the law of prohibition and Mary Bella wondered if her landlady realized that.

"I shall have to discuss this with my husband but I shall let you know later today." And quickly Mary Bella made her escape.

Suddenly, they were brought to the realization that their three happy years had been spent on top of a time bomb. The prohibition laws against illegal distilling were severe and now, having knowledge of the still, as immigrants, they could be deported back to Scotland. Should they report the Bonnets and stay on the safe side of the law or find another apartment and move as soon as possible? They decided on the latter and during Sunday forenoon Mary Bella visited the still twice to check the levels. When she saw the rainbow coloured chemicals floating on the surface of the raw alcohol Mary Bella was repelled and amazed that anyone would drink such poison. She had also heard of the vast profits gained from its illicit manufacture and sale. Evil exists under many disguises. Within the week, Mary Bella gave Mrs. Bonnet their notice of departure.

Now it was all change. Jim and Mary Bella acquired an apartment at 174 Chestnut Avenue in a more residential and salubrious area of Jamaica Plain. Nearby was a park and a school and the Mission Hall which Jim and Mary Bella with the lodgers had attended occasionally. Trees luxuriated and the whole area appeared pleasant and peaceful.

Their apartment was the middle one of the three storeys. It consisted of a kitchen, living room, three bedrooms and bathroom and, as with the previous apartment, it was entered from an outside staircase landing at the side of the house. Mary Bella and Jim were very delighted with their new home and were now looking forward to having it for themselves. They wished to be their own little family again but, meantime, Hammie and Shimmen would come with them to Chestnut Avenue.

Chapter 37

"Betty May's" was closed. New tenants lived in 21 Charlotte Street and Betsy's long promised journey to Boston took place. After Norman's fifteenth birthday she had set wheels in motion for their forthcoming departure and gradually the plans came together. The Doctor, always so encouraging about the success of the operation, made all the arrangements with the Boston hospital and Norman was booked in for preliminary tests. Betsy gradually ran down the shop and made final arrangements for Mc.Donald the grocer to take over the residue of her stock. Their fares were booked and paid for, thanks to the generosity of Jim, and the final farewells were made.

This was difficult. Betsy never forgot her sisters' support and encouragement when she returned from Florida, widowed with four young children. Here she was again leaving them all, but she had no other course to take if Norman was to walk again. He, on his part, was excited but also very loath to leave his cousin and close friend Wilfred. They were soul mates and all their lives Wilfred had been Norman's greatest support both physically and mentally.

Now they were settled in their middle floor apartment in Springpark Avenue, just round the corner from Mary Bella in Chestnut Avenue. She and Jim had furnished it with the basic requirements and a few excursions to the second hand shops with Betsy had completed it to her taste. This was the first time in many years that Betsy had had the pleasure of setting up her own home and she was enjoying it. With three bedrooms she was able to take over Mary Bella's two boarders, which would provide a little income until Norman was well again and she could find some light employment.

Of course Betty was a source of endless delight. Now Betsy could enjoy her grandchild. Norman passed more hours in Mary Bella's house than in his own and Alex and Flora were just round the corner. At last, they were a family again and Betsy, always forceful and dominant, had to learn that her children were now adults in their own right and heads of their own households where she should not interfere.

A very successful series of tests had proved positive and Norman's operation went ahead without any problem. The surgeons were very impressed by the excellent condition of his paralysed leg and, when Betsy explained her procedure of daily massage with fresh seawater, they were most interested. Ligaments were removed from behind the knee and implanted in the ankle to give the foot strength and lift and then a cast was placed on the whole leg. Norman was informed that he should expect to walk normally again, possibly with a slight limp, and he may have to rely on a walking stick, but nothing more.

During the long wearisome weeks of waiting he spent many hours with Mary Bella and the baby discussing life in the States and what he might do with his future. Norman read widely and had left Fraserburgh Academy with a fine collection of Merit certificates and references. Once walking, he hoped to enter high school and qualify for college but what to aim for as a career, he was unsure. Mary Bella loved discussing with this young brother whom she was just really getting to know for the first time. Her advice was to take it in stages, leg recovery first, high school next and then would be time enough to decide about career. Meantime, read widely, learn about America, and enjoy his convalescence time.

Chapter 38

Mary Bella and Jim had done well in their first few years in Jamaica Plain. Thanks to the boarders, Mary Bella had built up their bank balance, and Jim had gained promotion in his work. They were now comfortable and, provided they remained healthy, they enjoyed a pretty good prospect. Their circle of friends was mainly the family and church folks but they kept up with the North East immigrants like themselves and had regular get- together times. Jim and Alex sang in the church choir and Mary Bella often joined the other young mothers in the church garden where they worked and talked while the children played safely. Often Nellie 'Hay' Stephen visited with Billy and, when her second baby Marjorie was born, Billy came to stay with Mary Bella for the confinement period. When Flora had her second child, also called Marjorie, Bobby aged two came to Mary Bella. There was a warm atmosphere amongst the friends and a great sense of caring for each other.

Another event, which gave Mary Bella great delight, was the discovery that her Father's sister Mary Ann and her husband Charlie were now living in Boston. She had such happy memories of them in Aberdeen. Mary Bella made contact and they became frequent visitors to Jamaica Plain, giving her a greater sense of completeness in having a few of her Father's people there beside her. Norman his double, and Mary Ann his sister, brought her Father so much closer. Mary Morrison, Charlie's older sister, often came with them and she and Jim enjoyed long discussions, sometimes arguments, over politics, religion, cars, literature and other subjects. They relished a battle of words and then Charlie's humour would cut across and the climax would resolve itself in laughter.

These were the days of the miracles of crystal radios, motorcars, talkie cinema and electricity and Mary Bella and Jim were enthusiastic users. Jim along with a few friends had set up a crystal set and the rows of valves glistened on the shelves in the corner of the sitting room. Here they would sit, earphones in place, and listen to the boxing and football commentaries. Often the car engine was taken apart on the kitchen table, much to Mary Bella's disgust, and gaskets cleaned or some other maintenance completed. Their little four seater Ford stood at the sidewalk and every Saturday evening they would do the weekly shop and then drive round the blocks looking for the greatest bargain in petrol or gas, as they learned to say. The car took them far afield and gave greater freedom in visiting Maggie and other friends who lived outside Jamaica Plain. Franklin Park Zoo was a great favourite and long Saturday trips to the beach at Lyn or Boston Common, Cape Cod and Plymouth Rock.

Generally Norman was included and, once his operation and convalescence was successfully completed, the long promised camping holiday was undertaken. Jim had two weeks and the plan was to follow the Mohawk Trail and hopefully reach the Detroit area where his Uncle Robert lived with his family. This was the adventure of a lifetime to set out on such an undertaking with no experience. But they did and survived. Betty met her first coloured baby while camping by the river and registered great puzzlement.

When the Trail took them high over the mountains, they came face to face with a large brown bear. As they stood staring petrified, he studied them for a few moments then turned and trundled away, much to their relief. Niagara was stupendous as was the drive along the Great Lakes, but when they reached industrial Detroit and finally located Uncle Robert, there was a sad disappointment. The jolly, optimistic man that Jim remembered was now scratching a living on a poor, dirt farm in the mid west. He had left Fraserburgh with his wife Jessie to make a fortune in the gold fields, but he never reached there and, without any skills, had settled down to this existence. Their home was a wooden shack and Jessie struggled to keep house in primitive conditions. Robert, the teenage son, worked the land with his Father, but there was no sign of any up to date equipment other than a weary horse.

The visit being the main object of the trip, Jim was so disappointed. Robert was Jim's Mother's only brother and he had always been a favourite in the family and spoken highly of. Jim decided when next he wrote he would say as little as possible about Uncle Robert. But the holiday had been two weeks of amazing sight seeing, camping and adventure, and the car had behaved wonderfully. It was a memory they would carry always

Chapter 39

Jim and Mary Bella with Betty on Jamaica Pond, 1924

Life was good in Jamaica Plain and Mary Bella was very happy there. She had a fine home, her family close by, Betty developing into a healthy little girl, Jim doing well and enjoying his church life and his hobbies, friends visiting often, and they as a family enjoyed many things together-outings, picnicking in summer and skating in winter. Mary Bella had taught Jim to skate on Jamaica Pond. She was always busy but sometime every day, mainly in the evening, Mary

Bella took time to read and indulge in her imaginary world of travel.

Her elderly neighbour upstairs interested her very much. He was Mr. Yehzer, a German immigrant, whose wife had died a few days after Mary Bella and Jim moved in. They saw the mortuary basket with the remains being carried down stairs and felt concerned about the old man who spoke very little English and seemed rather reclusive. However, Betty bridged the gap and the child found a warm place in his heart. They spent hours together in the yard sitting on the circular bench in the shade under the old apple tree. They seemed to communicate in a language of their own and Mary Bella felt glad for the old man in his loneliness. He would never accept an invitation to visit for supper, but was always glad to receive an offering of soup or home baking.

If there was one shadow on their lives in Jamaica Plain it lay in the occasional letters from Jim's family in Fraserburgh. Contrary to all the good reports that Mary Bella sent detailing their lives, their home, work and friends, and every development in Betty, the Findlays still considered the American period as a temporary episode and it was time for Mary Bella and Jim to return home to Fraserburgh.

"Do you not think it's time you came home again? Things are better here now and there's more work to be had. Mother and Father are getting older and think long to see the bairn again. They feel they are missing so much of her childhood."

This tone of letter often arrived and Mary Bella developed a strong sense of guilt about the separation. But Jim just laughed at her worries and reminded her that they were already doing much for his parents in sending their rent every month. They could not do that without remaining in the States, but of course, that point was never remembered in these letters. So Mary Bella held her peace and quietly thought through a plan that would suit everyone. Finally, she explained her idea to Jim who disagreed immediately. She suggested that he take leave from work for the month of April and take Betty to Fraserburgh for a month's holiday. It would be spring in Scotland then and it would give his folks a good length of time with them both.

"Bella, I canna gang without you. Whit wad we dee without ye? And we canna afford it onywye."

"Aye we could. And I'll find a job while ye are awa. It's only for the month and that'll sine pass. I'll miss ye baith but it's you twa they want tae see and it'll maybe put a stop tae these letters."

Finally, after much persuasion, Mary Bella had her way and the arrangements were made. With a heavy heart she prepared sets of outfits for Betty on the journey, one for every day, and wrote down instructions for Jim to deal with the clothing. As the departure time drew near Mary Bella began to have doubts about the wisdom of her plan but she was resolute, believing it was the right thing to do considering all her family was right here beside her in Jamaica Plain. Once they were away Jim and Betty would be fine and she could set about finding temporary work.

As she looked up at the ship's rail and Jim holding Betty high in his arms to wave, she could hardly make them out through her tears. The old feeling of hurt came back.

"I should be up there with them an' a. Why should I always hae tae stand aside tae please ithers? I've lost my man and my bairn for a hale month, across an ocean, tae please ither folk. But I ken it wis the recht thing tae dee."

Then she joined the crowd dispersing into the city and made her way to the Ritz Carlton Hotel to take up her new role as chambermaid. The previous week her appointment had been confirmed after the personnel manager had interviewed Mary Bella and read her excellent references from Mrs. Ripley and from Mr. Mackay in Fraserburgh. The fact that she was Scottish was an additional asset.

Once she received the telegram saying Jim and Betty had arrived safely Mary Bella settled down to concentrate on her new work. She rather enjoyed the feeling of being on her own and responsible to no one but her employer and herself. She was determined to make the most of this opportunity both financially and experientially.

Chapter 40

Ever since the Florida days Mary Bella felt she had lived on the edge of poverty and the constant need to economise and make do with 'second hand'. True, the Ripley time was more luxurious, but Maggie was always there, emphasising economy and the need to save. Even now, in their own home, their small luxuries had been bought only after long consideration, all the more treasured because of that. Both she and Jim had inherited nothing from their families, rather the reverse, but they had the satisfaction of knowing that all they had achieved had been by their own efforts and there was always a little surplus available for the needy. More than a few North East folks had been helped in their efforts to reach America, not all of it paid back. The tragedy of her Father's death and its repercussions had laid on Mary Bella an overwhelming need for security and it was only in the last few years in Chestnut Avenue that, at last, she felt some relaxation from that worry. Mary Bella and Jim enjoyed their little luxuries and considered they were very blessed.

The Ritz Carlton was a breathtaking experience for Mary Bella. Her letters to Jim could hardly deal with the grandeur and opulence displayed there. It pleased and excited her to be employed in such surroundings with such a gracious staff and she was determined to enjoy and make the most of her month.

After studying the rest of the staff Mary Bella had her hair cut and styled in fashion and, with her tall, slim figure, once fitted with her uniform, she knew she looked good. Her week consisted of five days working in shifts and then the weekends were free for Jamaica Plain. As home was some distance away from the city Mary Bella stayed in the hotel Monday to Thursday and then travelled to the suburbs late on Friday. The hotel provided accommodation for such members of staff. Her role was to work as chamber- maid for the occupants of four suites on the second floor of the hotel. She had no cleaning or laundry duties. She was to be at the disposal of the occupants, dealing with clothing, food ordering, personal needs, flowers, even listening to their stories and concerns. Having guests in all four rooms kept Mary Bella busy and the almost regular change over of clientele meant a constant mental readjustment to their requirements.

Many guests were high society young ladies enjoying a few days shopping in the city. Others were couples, some honeymooners, and others film stars. All were rich and their demands and excesses astounded Mary Bella. She had never seen such prodigal waste. Food, drinks, cigars and cigarettes were called for and hardly ever completely used. A lavish lifestyle seemed to be their order of the day and Mary Bella fulfilled their wishes, keeping her opinion to herself.

But there was another side to the guests, their generosity. Some weeks she almost doubled her wage in tips and received many gifts of clothing and fruit from the grateful clients. The male guests presented the money but the ladies gave away the dresses and under wear which they wished to discard. There was no official rule restricting the receiving of gifts so many weekends Mary Bella returned to

Jamaica Plain with a parcel of beautiful dresses and clothing to share with Betsy and Flora, whichever best fitted them. The close fitting styles of the twenties suited Mary Bella's slim figure and for many years she treasured these beautiful dresses and wore them on special occasions.

The whole atmosphere of the Ritz Carlton excited Mary Bella. Her encounter with such mirrored and carpeted grandeur, the discrete and refined manners of the staff, and the constant passage of beautifully clad people fulfilled much of what she had read, but never expected to experience. It was a time for which she would always be grateful and never forget. April was passing very quickly and, although counting the days till Jim and Betty would step off the gangway, Mary Bella did have a twinge of regret that her lovely job would be coming to an end.

Chapter 41

It was the end of her third week and Mary Bella was sitting in the train returning to Jamaica Plain. She was a little weary, but looking forward to finding a letter from Jim awaiting her. Sometimes Betty included her little drawing or scrawling letter and Mary Bella laid these away safely in her treasure box. How she longed to see them both again.

Now she sat white faced, staring at the pages, not quite believing what she was reading. The kettle steamed away in the background but Mary Bella was oblivious to everything but the old, overwhelming hurt that had once again descended on her mind and feelings. How could Jim do this to her; how could his parents even ask it of her?

Jim had written suggesting that he leave Betty with her Grandparents for a year and then Mary Bella could come to Fraserburgh and have a holiday before bringing Betty home again. Betty could start school in Fraserburgh and Jeannie, his sister, would help to look after her. It would give his folks a share of Betty, but he could not make that decision himself without her opinion. Would she send word by return and let him know what she thought?

Mary Bella knew exactly what she thought. A child should be with her parents always, unless there was a legitimate reason otherwise. And a whole year! How could Jim consider such a length of time? What would happen if Betty became ill? They were fully ten days and an ocean crossing away. How could he allow himself to be swayed in this way by their talk and persuasion? She knew so well the subtlety of suggestion, which she had suffered and now Jim seemed powerless against it. Mary Bella was at times so angry, and then her anger turned to sympathy for Jim, and then fear for Betty and her homesickness, which she was bound to feel. Mary Bella resented that someone else should be escorting Betty on her first day at school; that was the Mother's prerogative. Then there was the enforced expense of her own holiday in Fraserburgh to collect Betty.

So she wrestled with her thoughts and tears for the rest of the night, knowing finally that she had to acquiesce and give Jim her agreement. Once again, against her better judgement, she had to give in to the persuasion of others. Jim was Betty's Father and had some responsibility in the decision, but Mary Bella was hurt that so little consideration had been given to her feelings and what it would mean to be separated from her only child for a whole year. She knew Betty would be well looked after, probably spoilt too, but she herself would be so lost and empty in that long time. In the morning she wired him, very briefly,

"Betty can stay in Fr." hoping he would realize from the brevity of the message, that she was angry. Her first instinct was to sit down and write a furious letter to Jim pouring out all her anger and frustration, her disappointment at his lack of thought for her, and her worry for Betty, so far away, and for so long. But she resisted the temptation and refrained from writing words she knew she would regret later. Jim was a victim too. She just wished he could have been stronger willed and not allowed Betty to become a pawn.

When Mary Bella told Betsy and Flora that Betty would not be returning with Jim, they could hardly believe it.

"What a thing to happen. After going all that way to please them. For them to ask to keep the child for a whole year!"

"It will not be a whole year. I have taken that decision myself and will go for her when I feel it's the right time, regardless of what has been said."

Mary Bella was quite adamant on that score. She had cooperated but, with reservations. Betty must come first and Mary Bella as her Mother, claimed the right to make these decisions.

During her last week at the Ritz Carlton Mary Bella applied for a further six months extension to her employment. On the strength of her excellent service, already noted, this was granted and, when Mary Bella set off to meet Jim at the gangway, she knew her life in Jamaica Plain would be on a part time basis and Jim must accept that.

It was a glad but also sad reunion. That little all-so-important person was not there. Mary Bella's arms felt empty and her longing to see her child almost crushed her. If only some miraculous change of mind had brought Betty home. But it was not so. Jim was alone.

Life settled down for them again. Jim went back to work and lived a bachelor life until he and Mary Bella were reunited at the weekend. Their relationship was restored also and often they met in the city on Friday evening and enjoyed an outing in Boston before returning home for the weekend. In some ways it resembled their early years of marriage, just the two of them, but always thoughts of Betty kept recurring to concern them.

Jim was glad Mary Bella had her work at the hotel. He could see that she enjoyed her association with the glamour and opulence of the rich and her experiences and anecdotes helped to divert her thoughts from the miss of Betty. He also enjoyed the new, modern Mary Bella, well groomed and stylish, and was glad that perhaps she was finding some advantage in her respite from housekeeping and motherhood. But he did miss his little family circle.

Chapter 42

Once again she stood at the rail watching the approaching Irish coast. This was her fourth crossing on her own and Mary Bella wondered how many of her companions were as well seasoned travellers as she. The September crossing had been good but Mary Bella was glad she had not waited longer to make the journey. Already the signs of autumn were there in the earlier darkness and the changeable weather moods. She would be happy when October came and they could make the return journey before the real winter Atlantic storms arrived.

Many letters had been exchanged during the past six months and Betty seemed to have enjoyed her stay in Fraserburgh. She had settled in at school and, of course, there was the remark that it was a pity to interrupt her first year when she was so happy there. But Mary Bella left the Grandparents in no doubt that she would be arriving in six months to take Betty home before the winter crossing became hazardous.

As the train sped northwards and she allowed her thoughts to linger on the past six months, Mary Bella acknowledged that she and Jim had enjoyed the time on their own. It was like the honeymoon that they had not been able to afford, and her work at the hotel had enhanced their security and financed their holidays. But nothing could compensate for the empty arms and the aching longing for her child. Jim felt it too but Mary Bella was the mother and Betty her only child and so precious. However, that was nearly over. There would be no recriminations or bitterness and, as far as Mary Bella was concerned, the month would pass as pleasantly as possible.

Slowly the train pulled into Fraserburgh station and Mary Bella descended to the platform. Nothing had changed. The ticket collector stood by the barrier at the end of the platform and behind the railings friends and relatives patiently waited. Just as she handed over her ticket, above the hiss of the steam, a scream sounded, 'Mammy!' and a little body hurled itself into Mary Bella's arms and clung there.

"Oh Mammy, Mammy," she repeated over and over while Mary Bella buried her face in the child's neck. The pent up tears of all the months overflowed and she could hardly control them as she turned away for a few moments with Betty still in her arms.

Betsy and Jeannie watched silently, perhaps realizing just a little of what their request had cost Mary Bella. But soon they gathered together for warm greetings. Ena and George were there along with Bella and Willie, Netta and Nellie, and they were a happy crowd as they made their way up Station Brae.

The weeks sped by and every day was enjoyable visiting relatives and friends, joining in the young church group, now that bit older, and always having the comfort at the end of the day of sharing Betsy's front room bed with Betty. Many changes had taken place during her five-year absence, some sad and others joyful and Mary Bella was anxious to visit all and hear their stories.

Aunt Bella and Uncle Willie in their lovely, fairy tale cottage on Alexandra Terrace were anxious to hear how things had worked out for them in Boston. Also Bella wished to have first hand news of Maggie who was now in her late fifties. Mary Bella was happy to hear that Tina and Maisie, her cousins, were courting, Tina with John Noble, an up and coming accountant on the Town Council, and Maisie with a teacher friend from early days in West Hartlepool.

When returning from escorting Betty to school Mary Bella often dropped in on Ena who, as ever, made her feel so at home. Nellie from her flat upstairs would join them over a cup of tea and they would sort out all the events of the past years. Nellie had eventually married Sandy Stephen but she was anxious to hear about Boston life as she felt Sandy still had a hankering to go back there. Mary Bella assured her that it was a very good life for a couple to share but one had to adopt it in a positive way and keep looking forward. The North East immigrant community was very supportive and the Church fellowship was like a caring family.

Ena also told Mary Bella the sad story of Janet's lingering death from cancer. She was nursed at home, all of them helping where they could and supporting Netta and Sandy, but it was hard for them to come to terms with why such a sweet, gentle, Godly woman like Janet should suffer so and die so young. She was only forty-eight. Netta had grown up during that sad time and was now a grand little housewife, looking after her Father Sandy, who was still toiling in the cooperage but looking significantly older. Netta was walking out with Bob Stephen, brother of Nellie's Sandy, so Nellie expected one day to be Netta's sister in law. Mary Bella remembered Bob as a very tall, young man in the church group and a wonderful musician who sometimes played the organ. So Mary Bella hungrily gathered up all the news to take back to Jim.

But Mary Bella herself engendered much interest. Many remembered the girl from America who had stayed to help her Mother in the shop, had eloped with Jim Findlay and then set off on her own with her young baby to join him in America. This poised, young woman, beautifully dressed and confident, made a good impression. Her friendliness and obvious interest in her past drew people to invite her out. She visited them all, the Hays, Stopanis, Nellie and Davie Noble, (the piano still in the back shop), Jim's Aunts, and many people, relatives of Jamaica Plain Brochers, who had sent messages to their loved ones. It was a busy time and the days sped past but she still managed a few walks along the Braes with Betty. That was when she told her the stories of her own early days with her Granny, Mary May and how good life had been doing things with her Granny.

"It's my Granda who does things with me. He takes me along the shore and up to the lighthouse and round by the boats at the harbour. He shows me lots of things. I saw him making a barrel one day. I liked the smell of the wood. He promised to make me a washtub like Granny's, but smaller. Do you think he will manage it before we go back to Daddy?"

Mary Bella visited Jim's Aunt Helen Ann, and Aunt Maggie made a special trip from Aberdeen by bus to visit Jim's wife and 'bairnie'. Jamesina and Alex Wood came from Aberdeen in their new automobile and, parked outside Betsy's door, caused a great stir at the bottom of Charlotte Street. Betsy preened as though the Queen herself had visited her. Alex was doing well and now owned a butcher's shop as well as three trawlers, and they had bought a bungalow on Queens Road opposite Rubislaw Quarry. Lots of news to take home to Jamaica Plain but Mary Bella was most happy that a relationship had been restored with Jim's family. She understood Betsy and Jimmie better, realizing that they meant well, and Jeannie had gone out of her way to make Betty feel loved and at home. Brother Alex, still at home and still the easy going young man, was holding a long courtship with Mary Duthie and the family was patiently awaiting the date of the wedding. John was still an apprenticed draughtsman in the Toolworks but his time would be out soon. He hoped to go to work for Ford's in the States so he might join them soon.

Chapter 43

How wonderful to be back. As she stepped down the gangway, firmly holding on to Betty, Mary Bella saw the smiling faces of her loved ones and thought,

"Yes, this is home for us now."

Waiting to greet them was a laughing Jim reaching out his arms to Betty, and there was Betsy, tears rolling down her cheeks, arm in arm with Maggie, and tall, handsome Norman alongside. How good to see them all.

Back in Chestnut Avenue as they shared the meal, Mary Bella related all the news from both families. Maggie and Betsy wept over Janet's passing but were cheered by the developments in the younger generation. Tom and Kitty in Glasgow now had three children, Alex, Nancy and Jessie, Ena's Nellie was expecting soon, and the only unattached ones were Wilfred, apprenticed as a draper to Benzie and Miller's, and Jeannie, although Mary Bella suspected there was a young man called John West on the horizon. John Findlay was career minded and would likely be joining them soon.

Jim laughed and shook his head as Mary Bella described the visits with his Aunts and the effect on his Mother when Jamesina arrived from Aberdeen. He knew Betsy's weakness and understood her proud reaction to the Bentley at the door. Jim always sympathised with his Father who was a humble, patient man and suffered somewhat from Betsy's pride and extravagance. Jim was glad to hear Betty's loving praise for her Granda.

At last they were on their own again, Betty tucked up in her own little room and, as Mary Bella kissed her goodnight, she put her arms round her Mother's neck and whispered,

"I liked the Broch and all the folk there but I'm so glad to be home with my own bed in my own room. We won't be going away again will we Mammy?"

"No Betty. We won't ever be separated again. I promise you that. Just cuddle down now and think of meeting your old friends tomorrow."

Jim and Mary Bella talked long into the night, discussing the more private details of their two families. Betsy was at last free of her boarders, Shimmen and Hammie having returned to their families in Fraserburgh, and she had found employment as companion and maid to Mrs. Cornell, a wealthy widow in Jamaica Plain. It was easy work and would take Betsy out of the house more, now that Norman had graduated from High School and had taken on work as a linotype operator with the Boston Globe. He was just awaiting his acceptance into Harvard Law School. Mary Bella felt so proud of him. But she also admired her Mother's will power that had brought about his success. Without her fortitude and optimism he might not even be alive today. It was so good to have her there with her buoyant laughter.

Living on Charlotte Street had not been all that easy. Conditions were very primitive compared to what they enjoyed in Jamaica Plain; outside shared toilets, no hot water on tap and people crammed into just a few rooms. The lack of privacy led to arguments and tempers flared so that sometimes Mary Bella was glad to slip out with Betty and have a walk on the Braes. Once the young folks married it would be much better but at the moment, there was a strained atmosphere. Staying the month was long enough for them all.

Later, lying close, drowsy after their deepest reunion, Jim and Mary Bella rested in each other's arms, grateful that their separations were over and glad to be here where they could freely love and laugh and care for each other again.

Chapter 44

Events rapidly followed each other. Betty restarted school on Chestnut Avenue, happily joining up again with her old friends, Kathleen and Mary Ryan. Unfortunately, on her way to school one day, Betty was knocked down by a van and suffered a fractured skull, which brought her into hospital and caused a very worried Jim and Bella. However, she recovered well but within weeks Betty, having fallen out of a tree, was back in hospital suffering from a broken leg and elbow. Betty was a tomboy and very accident-prone. She became well known in the accident department of Massachusetts General Hospital.

Some time after her return from Fraserburgh Mary Bella realized she was pregnant. Seven years was a long time and it was hard to take in. She did not know if she was happy or disappointed. Life was good with just the three of them and also, Mary Bella had horrendous memories of Betty's birth in Fraserburgh. Could she go through all that again? However, Jim encouraged her and accompanied her to the doctor who listened to her story and her fears. He took copious notes and then referred her to the Maternity wing of the Massachusetts General Hospital in Boston, which would take over her case. Such was their care Mary Bella learned how to relax, how to eat the correct food, especially to build up her iron reserves and, above all, to have confidence in their ability to see her through. She began to look forward to this baby and sewed and knitted as before.

When the delivery date arrived Betty went to Granny's at Spring Park Avenue and Jim took Mary Bella into hospital for the birth. It was wonderful to rest and relax in the days waiting for the baby. Would it be a boy or another girl? For Jim's sake Mary Bella hoped for a boy but she would just be glad for either, safely delivered.

As expected, the birth was not easy and in the process Mary Bella suffered much pain and loss of blood. But the nurses knew their job well and administered gas and pain-killers, allowing her to slip into semi consciousness during the worst of the ordeal. When she woke up it was to find herself freshly dressed, the foot of her bed raised on blocks to assist the blood flow and her little, fair- haired baby daughter by her side. She was such a bonny baby. Mary Bella could hardly express her gratitude. Now she had nothing to worry about. She could lie back and be cared for while she recovered and learned to nurse her baby. Mary Bella and Jean were in hospital for three wonderful weeks, almost like a holiday, Mary Bella recalled, and then they returned to Jamaica Plain, refreshed and strengthened, ready to take on normal life again.

But things were different now. They had a baby to consider and more than once the three sat into the car and then remembered the baby lying on the bed, all wrapped up and ready to go. Betty too had to learn to share her parents and relatives, not easy after being the centre of attraction for seven years. As time went on however, and Jean grew into a sunny little person, the family adjusted and once again enjoyed the jaunts, picnics and skating adventures; Jean cosily wrapped up and pulled behind in a box fixed to a sledge. She became the family pet, much loved, especially by Betsy and Norman.

Chapter 45

In the summer of 1929 Mary Bella and Jim moved house to Mozart Street. This was a good change as it still kept the family close and brought them within walking distance of their church, First Baptist Church, and of the Mary Curley Elementary School which Betty, having become seven, was due to start in September. Chestnut Avenue had become an increasingly busy thoroughfare and, with Betty's propensity for accidents, a quieter location was deemed advisable.

The new apartment presented many advantages with large bright rooms; a lounge, a dining room, two bedrooms and a smaller bedroom, which became Betty's own, a bathroom and a kitchenette. Electric fans kept the rooms cool and Mary Bella could at last have an electric fridge in the separate kitchenette. Jim and Mary Bella launched out with some new carpet rugs for the wood floors, occasional tables and brass reading lamps and finally, a piano for Betty who was anxious to join her friends having music lessons. They took great pleasure in their beautiful home and, although Mary Bella and Jim had always enjoyed giving hospitality, they could now take greater pleasure in entertaining round their dining room table in an atmosphere of space and comfort. Many came to their home where there was always a warm welcome and a bed if required.

The piano remained popular for a few months but soon the tedium of practice became too much and, during her practising time, Betty began to move forward the hands of the clock. Eventually the lessons ceased but the piano remained, hopefully for Jean when she was older.

Betty enjoyed school and proved herself a quick learner. Mary Bella was delighted that Betty had inherited her own passion for books and enjoyed guiding her in her choice of reading. She remembered her own hunger for books during the Albert Street days.

Church activities also played a large part in Betty's life and, because she was such an energetic and imaginative girl, she was often at the centre of concerts, plays and outings. The little white church at the top of Mozart Street played a large part in their lives. Mary Bella worked in a practical way with the young mothers, helping new settlers to feel at home and find their way around Jamaica Plain. Every Friday evening the congregation gathered to share a supper, which the women provided, and this is where Mary Bella did so much of her work in holding out the hand of friendship to strangers. The church was always open and the women gathered with their children to work in the garden, to talk about many things, and to form relationships. Language was never a problem; friendship broke down barriers.

Jim led the weekly Bible Study group and revelled in being so near Boston where he had access to so many great teachers and evangelists. He often spoke of hearing and seeing the drama of Amy Macpherson preaching in Tremont Temple and the teaching enthralled him during the wonderful series of lectures on the New Testament Churches given by Campbell Morgan in the same church. These were fulfilling times for both Jim and Mary Bella and, with their own family and the wider circle of family and friends, they shared many common interests.

Jim's young brother John was now in Detroit working as a draughtsman with Ford Motors so at last Jim had one of his own family near him. And he had hoped that soon Alex would join them. Mary and Alex were not long married and work opportunities were very scarce in Fraserburgh but it was a huge wrench to leave all you have known, family and friends, to go into the unknown. That was a step Mary and Alex were finding very hard to take.

Chapter 46

But all was not well in Jamaica Plain and in the wider world of industrial USA. A growing cloud of insecurity was hovering over the financial world and permeating the lives of all from the high financiers to the ordinary worker. The Promised Land to which so many had sailed, full of hope, had now become a scene of fear and disaster. Terrible hardship ensued leading to crime and violence, and it became a climate of real suffering in many areas. Qualified men such as Alex and Jim felt secure in work but the unskilled were the first to go. Businesses failed, payoffs became widespread and people, unable to pay bills, insurances and rent, found themselves homeless on the street. The spare bedroom frequently housed a destitute family when Mary Bella and Jim gave them shelter until they could find a way out of their problem. One Fraserburgh family, parents with four children, came in literally off the street and stayed for several weeks till Jim loaned them money for their fares and eventually passage was arranged for them to return to Scotland.

Church premises were opened up to provide shelter and a rota of women from the congregations produced meals. This was a lifeline, particularly for new immigrants who had not yet built up their own wall of security. It was also a rich time spiritually for Christians who were now actually sharing in the teaching of Jesus when He said, "Love one another."

The climax came when the banks crashed and began closing doors to clients who had queued to withdraw their money. Riots and panic disturbed the normally peaceful streets of Boston and other cities. Fortunately, Mary Bella and Jim anticipated this and a few weeks earlier had quietly withdrawn their hard earned savings from the First National Bank. It was not a comfortable atmosphere to be experiencing. The uncertainty of the situation dominated peoples' lives, especially Mary Bella and Jim, and led to long discussions about their future.

The eight years spent in Jamaica Plain had fulfilled all they ever wished for; a little family in a good home, relatives and friends nearby, a good church and school, and a way of life which gave contentment and peace. Mary Bella especially rejoiced in it and felt truly at home in the American way. But she always felt Jim had certain reservations. Earlier, when her brothers Alex and Norman, with a view to the future, took out US citizenship, she would have joined them but Jim held back, unwilling to give up his Scottish citizenship. Mary Bella teased him about being a sentimental Scot but did not pursue the matter, content to let events take their course.

As the depression went into months and eventually, another year, the question of citizenship had to be faced again. Unemployment was steadily increasing and Jim observed that, in dismissals, non-citizens had now joined the ranks of the unemployed. If he was to feel safe in work he would have to become a US citizen and he found that decision very hard to make. He knew several Scots who had returned home but conditions were little better over there. John had asked for a transfer to Fords at Dagenham,

London and he would soon be setting off. Jim was torn both ways. Finally, one evening Mary Bella broached the subject,

"Jim, it's time we sorted this out and made a decision. I ken whit's going on in yir mind and I understand yir feelings, but we hae te settle this. Are ye gan te become a citizen?"

"Bella, I find that a very hard step. I canna get awa from the fact that I belong te Scotland, and I fought for it in the War. A big bit o' my life lies ower there. I think I'll aye want te be tied to it and my folks. I ken you are different wi a' yir ain family here around you and ye've had a lang association with the American way of life. I ken ye feel at hame here an' I've weighed up a' we would hae te gie up if we left Jamaica Plain, but I canna bring mysel' te tak oot citizenship papers."

Mary Bella listened but did not argue. Again the old hurt ached around her heart as she realized just how little Jim understood her feelings for their life here and how finally she had found that peace and security, which her youth had denied her. Her family ties had become very precious and the last five years had brought Mary Bella and Betsy closer than ever before. She had a deep sense that, if they left Jamaica Plain, she would again be saying goodbye to all her nearest and dearest, possibly forever.

The day came when Jim returned from work to report that the plumbing firm was forced to close. It could not meet its financial commitments. He and all the other workers would be without work at the end of the month.

In the following search for employment Jim realized the value of US citizenship when he was regularly turned away on that score. Finally, he decided they would have to return to Scotland. He would go first, find work and set up a home as he had done all these years before, but Mary Bella firmly refused that suggestion.

"No, never again. I promised Betty we would never be apart again, and I meant it. We will sort things out here, write to yir folks and book our passages, and try to be as orderly as possible. Bit, we must gang thegither."

And so it happened. Within a few weeks the new carpet, the brass lamps and occasional tables were crated and sent on ahead, the piano went to Alex and Flora's and the rest of the older furnishings went to members of the family or to whoever had need of them. A separate crate held crockery packed inside bedding along with Betty's precious, pink goldfish bowl, a birthday present from Alex and Flora, and her tiny brass candlesticks and thistle shaped crystal vase from Mr. Yazer, her very old friend. A new family passport photo was taken; their passage was booked on the SS Cameronia sailing to Glasgow on 2nd. June 1932, and during the final week they moved to Betsy's on Spring Park Avenue for final goodbyes to family, friends and church.

That was particularly hard for Mary Bella. All her family was here in Jamaica Plain and she had become closer to them now than ever before. Betsy was well and enjoyed her work with Mrs. Cornell, Norman was studying hard and working for the newspaper, Alex and Flora were happy, safe in work and they had three lovely children Bob, Marjorie and Richard aged between Betty and Jean. Then there was Maggie, now in her sixties, not far away in Newton Center, and the host of friends they had made over the ten years. During a goodbye social evening in the church, amid emotional farewells, Jim was presented with an inscribed Schofield Bible and Mary Bella with a beautiful red fox fur. But nothing could compensate for the loss of such wonderful friends.

Betsy, Norman and John saw them off and lingered a while on board for photographs. The ship had provided for child passengers and a young sailor had set up a game of deck volleyball, which soon drew Betty. Jean took possession of a small, green, basket doll's carriage standing nearby and it became her property for the whole voyage. She wheeled her baby doll everywhere.

After the final handshakes and hugs, as they left, Betsy whispered to Mary Bella,

"Once Norman has finished his studies and is ready to work, I'll retire and come hame to the Broch beside ye. It'll nae be ower lang noo. Jist be patient an' things will work oot for ye. Ye've had te mak big decisions a' yir life, ower mony for een sae young, so jist be strong and patient and God 'll gie ye wisdom."

And with that they turned away to the gangway and stood waving on the quay till the ship swung out into the river.

That evening in the quietness of their cabin, after the children were asleep, Jim presented Mary Bella with an official looking envelope. Inside she found an Immigration Service Permit allowing Jim to return to the States within a year of his departure date. There was his photo and full description and the official stamps.

"If it disna work oot Bella we'll come back. A lot can happen in a year. We'll gie it a good try and then mak oor minds up in the spring."

Tears rolled down Mary Bella's cheeks. How she had misjudged him. He had understood her feelings and prepared this door of opportunity for them to come back.

Somehow she felt they would not return, but now they could legally do so if need be.

"Thank you Jim. That maks a' the difference." as she put her arms round him and laid her head on his shoulder.

Chapter 47

The sun felt comfortingly warm on her back and a soft gentle breeze crept in from the sea. The sweet, woody drift of smoking fish filtered down from the kilns on the Braes. Little had changed here. Yes, Mary Bella was back in Broadsea, sitting on the grass just below her Granny's house where she had passed so much of her childhood. She felt like a bridge in time.

As she watched the two little, fair-haired girls, Mary and Jean, playing in the sand with their spades and buckets, Mary Bella smiled, remembering their arrival at the station. When the two children met they looked at each other and then turned to walk away down the platform hand in hand. And when she saw Betty walk off arm in arm with Jeannie, and all the loving, smiling faces welcoming them, Mary Bella began to feel that maybe, after all, it had been a good decision to come back. Time would tell.

Today was a lovely day and they were all in their favourite places. Betty was engrossed in the rock pools trying to float the delicate seaweed on to sheets of paper, as Uncle Alex had taught her. He had a special way with children. And Mary Bella could just now and again catch a glimpse of the two men as they made their way along the Braes, weaving in and out of the kilns, and the horses and carts trundling to and from the gutting yards. Alex and Jim were heading for the quieter slopes around the lighthouse where they could discuss in peace some finer point of doctrine. Both men were keen Bible students and this was one of the joys in their reunion after ten years.

The two women, Mary Bella and her new sister- in- law, Mary, sat companionably on the grass, chatting and knitting as they kept an eye on the children. Mary Bella liked Mary. She was about her own age and had a warm compassionate nature crowned with a sparkling sense of humour. Mary Bella also took some comfort and strength from the knowledge that Mary, like herself, was on the edge of the Findlay family and she could appreciate some of the present difficulties Mary Bella was experiencing in living so closely with them. Mary understood and Mary Bella felt comforted when she spoke,

"It'll be a' recht fan ye hae yir ain hoose an' can come an' gang. There's jist nae room there at Charlotte Street for ye a'."

"That's true Mary bit I hae an idea that might jist work oot, an' nae cause offence. It wasna fair te land on them a' like this, and Jeannie needs some place te tak her lad, John. Jist wyte a day or twa an' ye'll hear fit I hae in mind."

Once again Mary Bella took the initiative and, without any family consultation or debate, she made a call on Louky, Granny's neighbour, who lived in the other half of the ground floor in identical accommodation. The front room or parlour was for visitors and most summers Louky let it out on a weekly basis. Louky and her niece, Maggie Bella, shared the box bed in the kitchen and Lewis and John, her nephews, slept in the tiny bedroom off the kitchen. They made a quiet little household and Louky was a kindly, elderly lady. She understood Mary Bella's problem as she listened to her request, nodding in sympathy.

In view of the overcrowding and Jeannie's approaching wedding would Louky rent Mary Bella her front room for a while until they could find their own accommodation? Louky agreed on condition that Maggie Bella and the boys approved and the arrangement was settled without any problem. Mary Bella insisted on paying Louky ten shillings a month and her share of the gas bill.

When Mary Bella explained to Jim what she had arranged, he was rather taken aback, concerned how his folks would feel and how they would all manage to live in one room.

"Jim we dinna even hae one room here. And it's nae fair on Betsy and Jimmy nae kennan foo lang this is gan on. Jeannie needs the front room for the weddin' an we're needin' a place o' oor ain for some privacy. And I need te ken fit I'm daen wi the shopping an' hoose keeping; I seem te be buying a' the time. I'll explain te yir Mother an' I'm sure she'll understand and even be pleased. We'll jist be ben the hoose."

And so it turned out. Betsy adopted a little air of being offended but, when Mary Bella spoke of the coming wedding, she relented and agreed that it would be a help.

"Ye'll nae be far awa an' we'll see the bairns a' the time."

Within two days Mary Bella had Louky's front room set out with the double bed in the alcove behind the door and a single bed in the opposite corner. A table and four chairs stood in front of the window, two armchairs were beside the fireplace and the wall press by the fireside held their foodstuffs, crockery and utensils. The small wardrobe held the hanging clothes and, by the hearth, a low cabin trunk covered with a blanket and cushions, provided a seat for the children and contained the family underwear. Mary Bella visited Sandy's cooperage where the American crates were stored and brought away the necessary dishes, pots and pans and utensils, and Betty rescued her pink goldfish bowl, still intact. Jim connected up a gas ring burner, which stood inside the hearth and, along with the fire, gave Mary Bella extra cooking facility. Lastly, two enamel pails with lids were purchased, one to hold fresh water and the other for slops, both placed safely out of sight behind the press door. Now they were ready.

They moved in amid great excitement from the children. Jean, fast losing her American accent, kept saying,

"Come and see oor little hoosie!"

But Betty wasn't so sure about sharing her single bed with Jean.

Chapter 48

At the time, Mary Bella and Jim never anticipated that they would live there for over eighteen months. Steady work continued to be difficult to find and hopes rose and fell. Occasionally Jim was employed for a week by local plumbing firms and he even considered working in Aberdeen. In the present climate, his dream of starting his own business was out of the question. Never having been a very patient man, Jim suffered much from the indignity of unemployment and Mary Bella was sorely tried at times to keep him occupied.

Often he and Alex would cycle out to the country with Mary and Jean perched behind them on their child seats. Their favourite rout was by Loch Pots Road to the Watermill Dam where Alex would sail his model yacht. They examined the corn and barley ears, the wild flowers, collected brambles, spoke to the travelling tinkers who usually camped in the "Whun Dutch" – the whin ditch, and frequently passed an afternoon at Alex's allotment behind the fever hospital. For the little girls it was all adventure and education, which they never forgot.

In July Betty started school and, being ten, was placed in Primary six with Miss Wood. This was a very happy liaison and Betty responded to the patient kindness of her teacher. She felt competent in all her subjects but maths, especially the monetary values, became a real worry. However, Miss

Wood arranged a few visits to her home in the Hexagon and together they sorted out Betty's problems. Amongst all her teachers Betty regarded Miss Wood as special and long after she had moved on to Secondary she continued their friendship.

Day by day Jean made her happy presence known in the area round No22. Sometimes when she disappeared from sight Mary Bella would find her in Jamieson's Dairy across the road, watching the cows being milked. She knew them all by name and learned the time of day by the arrival of the herd from the fields at Watermill. Other favourite haunts were Carle's bake house, also on the other side of the road, when the smells of newly baked bread and fruit cake drew her over; and the joinery business just down the road from Granny's close kept Jean supplied with small off cuts and trimmings of wood. The work- men did not know what she used them for but they enjoyed the child's company and en- couraged her to talk, just to hear her accent. Unfortunately, that soon disappeared but Jean was always welcome, as she was with all the neighbours. During that year, amongst the whole family, Jean was probably the happiest and most carefree member, welcome everywhere and secure in the knowledge that she was loved.

One outstanding memory she carried with her all her life was the net mending afternoons beside the washhouse in the cobbled back yard. Jessie and Annie Bella from up- stairs, and Louky and Maggie Bella were all fishermen's wives or sisters and, on a fine day they would hook up the nets to the wall and work in pairs filling in the torn sec- tions. Jean had her little net as well and she learned to operate the needle to make that special knot. Often there was a tea party treat or lemonade and at night, as a bed- time story, Mary Bella would tell Jean about helping her

Granny and her Mother to mend the nets in her Granny's close or in the cosy, attic room at Albert Street. It all seemed so very long ago now.

Chapter 49

The months sped by and Mary Bella and her little family adapted to their new way of life. They were warm and cosy in their one room and, although at times in the evenings they felt overcrowded, the children often disappeared through to Granny's where Granda always had a story to tell, or there was a kitten from the cooperage to be nursed.

Several highlights occurred during that time, beginning with the New Years Day party. John, home from London for the holiday, and Jeannie had organized it in Granny's house and all the family was present. Having the grandchildren there made it all so meaningful for Betsy and Jimmy as they sat smiling in their armchairs. They sang all the old songs and hymns, John at the piano and Jim with his old violin, rescued from under the kitchen bed. They played games and surprise parcels kept arriving with presents for everyone. The children were awestruck when they saw Santa's sooty footprint on the top of the kitchen range. But the climax came when the sofa leg went through a weak floorboard causing a hole in the linoleum and tipping the occupants on to the floor. There was great teasing and laughter and in future parties the children always hoped it would happen again; but it never did. Finally, Jimmy drew everyone together with a Bible reading and prayer and then it was time to go home.

The next major event would be Jeannie's wedding in June. Betty was to be flower girl and, for everyone's sake, Mary Bella and Jim did so want to attend. No one knew of the Re-entry Permit and they spent many agonizing hours discussing what they should do. Work was still the major problem and if they decided to return, they would have to begin making arrangements in April. Could they disappoint everyone by leaving before the wedding? That would really give cause for offence. Would Jeannie bring the wedding forward to May? Or should they forget the Permit and wait to see how events worked out?

The dilemma was taken out of their hands and settled for them. Jim had a few weeks' work and, during a repair job when he was in a trench jointing two pipes, hot solder shot up into his face and sprayed across his eyes. With his lids sealed closed by the hardened solder Jim was blinded. A taxi brought him home; the doctor was called, and there began a week of worry and waiting. The eyelids had been burned and the solder would have to be taken off quickly to prevent infection setting in and causing damage inside the eye. Jim was in severe pain but the sedative injection calmed him down and enabled him to endure the removable of the solder. As the doctor gently handled the tweezers and lifted the tiny particles bit by bit, Jean watched closely as they dropped on to the dish with a tinkle. She thought she must take them through to let Granny see them. The eyes were rinsed with disinfectant and pads with healing ointment laid on each eye under a bandage.

At the end of a week Jim was very relieved when the bandage was removed and he realized he could see. He had lived through a week of pain and torment, realizing his folly in not wearing a mask, and worry about their future if he was blind. But Mary Bella was strong and, as best she could, she maintained normality and calm in the situation. Once Jim was on his feet again there was no more discussion about America and they decided to put it in abeyance until April when final decisions would have to be made.

One day while out walking during his convalescence, Jim was hailed by a friend, Mr. Wiseman, who ran his own plumbing business and Jim had worked occasionally for him on a temporary basis. There was a good rapport between them

"I heard you had a nasty accident Jim. How are you?"

"Oh, I'm fine. Just thankful I have my sight. It could have been worse. My biggest worry is finding work. Nothing seems to be changing here in the Broch."

"Well now, I have some news. I've had a word with one of the Town Councillors who is a good friend and he tells me something is coming up which might interest you. In fact I think you could be just the right man. There's to be a huge town expansion of houses for rental, stretching away beyond Finlayson Street and over the Gallow Hill. They are looking for a man who would work with the Burgh Surveyor in planning water supply and sewerage piping; someone with practical knowledge. I think there will be a house along with the appointment. The job will be advertised so get in there quick and I'll put in a word for you."

Jim could hardly wait to tell Mary Bella. In due course he applied, was called for an interview and at the beginning of April Jim was appointed Fraserburgh Water Inspector. The only problem was that the first housing allocation had already been made and his one would have to be in the second phase. But they would have the first choice in the street, Gray Street. Nothing could worry Mary Bella and Jim now. They had work, the promise of a brand new home, and their health. They would happily stay as they were in Louky's room and wait. Their thankfulness knew no bounds. They could now enjoy the wedding.

It was a beautiful day for the event, held in the Bellslea Hotel and, Jeannie and John both being popular and well known in their work places, many spectators came to see the wedding. There was a little gasp of admiration when the taxi drew up with Mary Bella, Jim and Jean; Mary Bella, tall, slim and very elegant in one of her American dresses, black chiffon with a red poppy pattern, and her black picture hat; and Jean like a fairy in a full skirted shell pink, angel skin dress trimmed with pink rosebuds. Wilfred had sent away for the special material and Mary Bella had so much pleasure in sewing it. It all caused quite a stir. Betty, pretty in blue, arrived with the wedding party and Jeannie was one of the most beautiful brides in Fraserburgh that year. It was a very memorable occasion, relatives meeting up again and Betsy, so proud of her daughter, and of the guest list, which included some of the head personnel of the Tool Company where John worked.

The glorious summer days of 1934 slipped by so quickly. Jeannie and John moved into their flat further up Charlotte Street and Betty and Jean were frequent visitors. During the school holidays every good day Mary Bella and the girls joined Nellie, Netta and Tina at their regular rendezvous on the beach beside the Kessock Burn. Quite a little gathering of cousins had developed and the children happily played in the stream while the mothers talked and knitted and enjoyed tea from the flasks. The bond between Mary Bella and her cousins was very strong; so close they might have been sisters. Now that she had left her immediate family in America, Mary Bella found great comfort and strengthening in being included in this group of her relatives. The very deep affection they had for each other continued all their lives.

Chapter 50

As the weeks passed by Saturday afternoons saw regular walks to the new Gray Street to study the progress of 'their house'. Jim and Mary Bella had already decided on which would be their flat. They chose the one, which would catch the morning, afternoon and evening sun, facing south, and upstairs to be lighter and warmer. Gray Street was a short street of four granite blocks of flats, sixteen in all, and their number would be No.8. It comprised a sitting room and two bedrooms requiring furnishing and everywhere, including kitchen, bathroom, hallway and staircase, would have to be carpeted or linoed. Eventually, they were able to measure for flooring and curtaining.

Much as they had loved their homes in Jamaica Plain, the furnishings had been mainly a collection of second hand and 'make do'. Only latterly in Mozart Street had they indulged in the few luxuries which awaited unpacking in Sandy's cooperage. Jim and Mary Bella decided that, since this was to be their permanent home, they would indulge in new furnishings and take time to look around and choose what appealed to their taste. Finally, they settled on what Benzie and Miller had to offer; flooring, carpeting, a mouquette three piece suite, an oak table and chairs, an oak writing bureau for Jim and a most beautiful, hand made oak sideboard, Mary Bella's delight. The bedroom requirements came from Maitland's store and every now and again Mary Bella would take a stroll round the shops to enjoy another glimpse of her furnishings. It gave her such a thrill to see the label 'Sold' attached to them. They were really hers.

At the end of August their flat was ready for them to move in. The excitement of the preparation, the scrubbing and cleaning, the carpet and lino laying, unpacking the crates from Sandy's cooperage and finally, the arrival of the new furniture and the difficult manoeuvring to bring the larger items round the stair landing. Another day saw the curtains hung and the roller blinds fitted in the windows and through all this, Mary Bella was always drawn to the kitchen to marvel at the two sinks, one deeper as a wash tub, the hot and cold brass taps, in the corner the gas cooker with three burners and an oven, the vented larder in the other corner, and the hot water tank above the cooker keeping the whole place warm. Best of all was the wide double window facing the street where they could sit and eat and watch the world go by. Mary Bella had never experienced such household luxuries, not even in the States, and she could not wait to move in.

Eventually all was ready and, at last, they slept in their own rooms, Betty and Jean in the smaller bedroom adjoining the sitting room and Mary Bella and Jim in the main one off the hall. Their sense of freedom was indescribable; just to walk around from one room to another, to be alone in a room, to use the toilet any time, to turn on the tap and feel hot water, have a bath, talk freely without the fear of being overheard and to be obliged to no one but themselves. It all came together in joy and wonder and it did not take the little family long to feel comfortably at home.

Getting to know their neighbours was interesting too. Amongst the sixteen homes was a mixture of people from all walks of life, and size of families varied from no children to six or seven. Of course, in some cases, there was overcrowding but, in 1934, sharing rooms, even beds, and sleeping in the living room was quite accepted and common in most working class homes. Here were fishermen, grocers, a cooper, several tool workers, a blacksmith, the town road surveyor and one or two widow and spinster families. One huge and rather disconcerting surprise was the presence in No.6 of people from Jamaica Plain days; the very family they had taken in and housed before helping them home to Scotland. At first there was some embarrassment but after a few months, when the father found work in London, the family moved away. Betty and Jean revelled in the company of so many children and the freedom to play in the quiet street.

Gradually the gardens took shape, divided out into allocated areas. Drying greens were laid and the summer evenings saw families out clearing the ground and planning vegetable and flower patches. Mary Bella wished to have a rockery in front of the front door so, one day Jim borrowed a horse and cart from the council yard and caused quite a stir on Gray Street when the horse clip clopped up to the gate and a pile of large white stones was deposited on the pavement. They had come from a field by the Federate water works near Pitsligo. The gathering of children carried them in and eventually Mary Bella had her beautiful rockery, which she planted out with cuttings from Aunt Bella's wonderful garden. She also set a red rambler rose by the doorway and a sweet smelling white rose on the trellis at the end of the rockery. That first year the rest of the garden was planted out in potatoes to 'clear the ground' and Alex and Jimmy had a little input in advice as Jim was a complete novice where gardening was concerned.

Rather than have coal carried upstairs, everyone had a coal bunker built and placed in the back garden This provided an extra spacious cupboard in the hall and comfortable garden seats against the wall of the house, in the full afternoon and evening sun. Here was a favourite gathering place for the women folk and neighbourliness really developed here as they shared their stories.

When school took up again after Easter Betty had only a short walk for her first day at the Academy, and Jean, a little further on, was enrolled at the Infant School. Mary Bella recalled her own enrolment day. Things had not changed except that it all looked so much smaller than she remembered. Even some of the teachers were still there. As she left Jean with Miss Will at the classroom door Mary Bella felt a little pang,

"That's my baby awa. Now I'm gan hame tae an empty hoose." But instead she turned in the opposite direction and went to Ena's for a cup of tea.

Chapter 51

Now that she had more hours in the day at her disposal, Mary Bella set out to rebuild her relationships amongst the Church folks and the relatives, especially her Father's people who were living mostly in Aberdeen. She renewed her association with the Women's Auxiliary and continued working for the Hall Fund, set up so long ago by her Mother Betsy, and others. Their target had not yet been achieved but the church leaders expected to lay the foundation stone during this present generation. Mary Bella enjoyed the friendliness of the women and admired their enthusiastic industry in working for the mission field. This was where she contributed her skills in sewing garments for the Wants Box and articles for the annual Hall Fund sale. Jim became a deacon and again took up leadership in Bible Study amongst the youth. Betty joined the choir and Jean entered the Sunday school.

So Sundays became busy days for the family and ever increasingly, the Baptist Church played a large part in their lives. Betty found her new friends there and it was not long before Jean knew every corner of the church and the small hall behind the pulpit. She was Mary Bella's constant companion at the meetings and, whatever her Mother or Father was busy with in the church, Jean was there keeping them company.

Ever since her conversion during the '21 Revival, Mary Bella's faith had been strong and constant. She was not an up-front person taking the leadership chair; she preferred rather to work practically and hand out 'the cup of cold water'. Mary Bella had a deep concern for people and their needs, but, as she had learned from her Mother, one performed these kindnesses quietly. This firm, church family connection gave Mary Bella deep satisfaction. It gave a sense of stability and structure to their lives, which she hoped, would become the values of her two girls as they found faith in God for themselves. Many changes were to take place in the years ahead but nothing could shake Mary Bella's loyalty to this fellowship and the Christian beliefs she shared here with so many dear friends.

It was during these early months in Gray Street that the family needed Mary Bella. Uncle Willie had died very suddenly leaving Aunt Bella bereft. They had been such a devoted couple; Bella was in charge, setting the tone, knowing the right people, deciding where one should live, having the correct neighbours; but always she deferred to Willie and his quiet wisdom. Mary Bella remembered their first visit to the cottage after their return from America when they found Bella and Willie on their knees laying crazy paving under the long archway of rambling roses. The beautiful garden was their hobby. Now Bella was on her own without her helpmeet. Every afternoon for a few weeks Mary Bella collected Jean from school and walked up Queens Road to the Terrace to visit Bella and then came home through the fields in time for tea. It brought a little sunshine into the older lady's life and she enjoyed having the child there. So far Bella had not been blessed with grandchildren.

It was on one of these visits that the subject of Maggie came up. Now that she was approaching sixty- five Maggie

in her letter had referred to retiring and Bella was specu-
lating about what Maggie would do. Would she come home
or stay in America?

"It's more than fifteen years since I saw Maggie. We were
in West Hartlepool the last time she was here. You would
know more about her than anyone Mary Bella when you
saw her regularly in Boston. Is she still the same, so strict
and disciplined?"

"Yes, still the same; firm and a disciplinarian. She had
to be like that, carrying all the responsibility for the household and four children. But she did mellow a bit. After the
children grew up and gradually left home life became a
bit easier for her and, as Maggie grew older, Mrs. Ripley
saw that she had plenty of assistance. Maggie had high
standards and won the respect of all. You know, the whole
household stood in awe of her and, at the same time loved
her deeply. She was like a Mother to Betty Ripley and I
treasure the memory of the years I spent in her care. It will
be a very hard wrench for her if she decides to come back
here and leave so many loved ones there. Yet she always
spoke of you all and called the Broch 'home'."

Mary Bella could see that her Aunt was pondering over
Maggie but said nothing more. In time events would take
their course, whatever Maggie decided to do. Mary Bella felt
a little thrill of excitement at the thought of Maggie coming
to stay in Fraserburgh. She realized that over the years she
had come to love this Aunt who had been her Mother for
six important years of her life.

For the spring holiday weekend in April Mary Bella and
Jim with the girls went to stay with Jim's Aunt Maggie in
Torry, Aberdeen. The plan was to visit as many relatives as
possible in the time, which they did and the number of new
cousins he did not realize he possessed overwhelmed Jim.

Aunt Kirsten had a large family of five daughters and one son, Robert and Aunt Jamesina's two daughters, Jean and Ina, were nearer Betty's age. Alex and Jamesina had really prospered and lived in a most beautiful home on Queen's Road. The welcome was warm and wholehearted and Jim enjoyed renewing his friendship with Alex. For Mary Bella the highlight was finding her Aunt Mary Ann living on Walker Road in Torry, just round the corner from Maggie. Like so many other Scots, Mary Ann and her husband Charlie had returned from Boston and he was now employed in a fish selling company. The old sense of humour was still there and they had a wonderful visit recalling happy times in Jamaica Plain, and even before that, at New Year time in Aberdeen. Mary Bella learned that Nellie now lived with her son on North Street in Fraserburgh, Jessie was still in Florida and George, (Doddie) was married and had a daughter Sarah. They lived in Mallaig. Doddie visited the North East every year at the end of the fishing and he would surely visit Mary Bella now she was there.

In the opinion of all it had been a worthwhile and enjoyable weekend but, for Betty and Jean, the best part was the sail on the Dee when Daddy took them out in a rowing boat and they went from bridge to bridge. They promised each other they would come back again for another good time.

Chapter 52

But events control the smooth planning of our lives and things do not always work out as intended. Shortly after their holiday Mary Bella realized that she was expecting and, at first, the shock filled her with dismay. Somehow, she had always felt this would not happen again. Their family was just fine; the four of them together and she had visualized it always being so. Now this had happened to interrupt the peace they had so lately achieved and Mary Bella dreaded what the event would mean for her. She shuddered at the memories of the hours of labour before Betty's birth; this time she was thirteen years older and there was no maternity hospital to aid or advise. Mrs. Wilson was still the local midwife with her traditional ways. So Mary Bella struggled with her fears until at last she began to think positively and came round to remembering what she had learned in the Boston hospital before Jean's birth; how to eat properly, to relax regularly, to keep active and, above all, to look forward to the baby. Mary Bella felt rather ashamed of her original attitude. After all, if the baby was a boy it would be special for Jim. But one thing she would firmly request was that Dr. Webster should be present at the birth. Since she had seen him handle Jim's eye accident Mary Bella had great confidence in his skills.

After she had sorted out her fears Mary Bella at last told Jim her news. Of course he was delighted, but worried also about Mary Bella and what it would mean for her. He had not been present when Betty and Jean were born so Jim had no real understanding of Mary Bella's dread. But he was anxious for her safety and for the remaining months did all he could to ease things for her.

Jean was too young to notice any changes in her Mother and Betty at twelve was too shy to ask about it. Girls did not discuss these things with their Mothers but from her friends on Gray Street Betty had plenty of advice. During the autumn months, as the winter drew in, she watched her Mother sewing and knitting baby clothes and Betty just knew that these would not be going to the missionary box. She felt very excited about the whole mystery and eventually plucked up courage to ask her Aunt Jeannie.

"Auntie Jeannie, is my Mother gan tae hae a baby?"

Jeannie laughed,

"Yes. Has she nae said onything aboot it tae ye yet? The baby's due aboot New Year time so it'll be a fine present for ye."

Betty was satisfied and hugged her excitement to herself. Now that she had the knowledge she pondered on how such a wonderful thing should need to be kept secret. Adults were strange. She would want to tell everyone. But she didn't, just her closest friends.

When Mary Bella opened her eyes on New Years Day morning she felt at once that something was going to happen that day. The baby lay differently and she told Jim. As usual the Santa stockings were opened and it was wonderful to see the joy and delight on the girls' faces. Jean loved her doll's cradle (secretly made in Jim's workshop) and snuggling inside the blankets lay the little, black, baby doll she had particularly asked for. Betty, now nearly a teenager, was more interested in clothes and was thrilled with her new twin set and an Academy scarf. There were also the new books, the sugary pigs, fancy tins of caramels, fruit, and shiny pennies and all the other parcels, which had arrived from friends and had been kept till New Years day.

Mary Bella never forgot that morning. It was such a happy time; all four of them in the one bed laughing and talking and sharing goodies. It never happened again for, after that day, things changed dramatically for them all.

Chapter 53

That first day of January 1935 was a quiet day. Being so near her time, Mary Bella wished everything to be as calm as possible for the family's sake, but mainly for her own sense of relaxation. She had to stay calm.

Jim kept a good fire going in the sitting room and came and went to the kitchen where he was supervising the New Years Day dinner, already prepared well in advance. Mary Bella with the girls played their new games; Ludo and Happy Families, and read their books. Both girls were avid readers and Betty at the moment was into the Alcott books; this New Year it was "Little Men". After hearing Nelson's story in school, Jean had developed a love for history and her new book was "Heroes of Long Ago", beautifully illustrated, and with her name artistically inscribed by Jim on the flyleaf.

Dinner was wonderful; the roast hen, the plum pudding with the tiny, silver threepenny pieces and the sugar sauce, and the trifle. Replete, they sat for a little while to digest and Mary Bella lay down to rest for an hour. Then it was time to tidy up and prepare for Granny's party. This meant party dresses and ribbons, more food and fun and a walk in the dark to Charlotte Street where all the family would be gathered. Jim was concerned for Mary Bella but she was determined to act normally and insisted on being there for five o'clock.

" The walk'll do me good and it'll help me if onything happens the nicht."

There was quite a gathering round Granny's kitchen table; nine adults, and the three children, Betty Jean and Mary had a little, separate table alongside. During the meal Mary Bella knew they would have to leave early and, once they were assembled in the front room, she quietly told Jim. John West, Jeannie's husband, owned a small Ford car and Jim had alerted him about what might happen and to be ready to give Mary Bella a lift home. Lastly, he told his Mother and Betsy was very anxious to accompany them to keep Mary Bella company while Jim went for the Doctor. Jeannie would look after the children and keep the party going with the rest of the grownups.

Such was the fun the adults were not missed until bed-time when Jean asked for her Mother. But then it was exciting all going to bed together in the front room bed- Betty, Jean and Jeannie while the two Johns slept in Jeannie's house further up Charlotte Street. Late into the night Betty and Jeannie sat making clothes for the little, black dolly and keeping Jean busy until she fell asleep. But at last all was quiet and Betty and Jeannie lay whispering and wondering how things were going at Gray Street. There was worry and apprehension but also deep excitement; would it be a boy or a girl and would Mary Bella be all right? Neither slept much that night.

Dawn was breaking when Mary Bella roused from a deeply sedated sleep. As expected, the birth had been hard but, to avoid too much haemorrhaging for Mary Bella and stress for the fairly large baby, Dr. Webster had applied forceps and brought the child more quickly. Just before midnight the delivery was over but the doctor lingered into the early hours to keep an eye on Mary Bella in case of complications. Now it was morning and Mrs. Wilson was in charge.

Jim and his Mother Betsy had kept vigil all through the night and were now sat by her bedside watching the pale sleeping face. Jim had gone through a night of fear and shock at what childbirth had meant for Mary Bella and now he understood her dread.

"Jim, I brocht thirteen bairns into this world bit niver gaed through whit she did last nicht. She's jist nae built for that. She's a gye brave woman."

As he heard his Mother's words Jim prayed his gratitude to God for his wife and her amazing qualities and for the fine little boy lying in the cradle by the fireside. True, his head was temporarily scarred by the forceps but he was so perfect in every way. Jim could hardly contain his tears of joy and thankfulness.

When Mrs. Wilson at last laid the baby into Mary Bella's arms tears overflowed as she laid her cheek on his head and whispered,

"Ye're jist my Father ower again. If only he could hae seen ye."

Shortly after dinner excited voices and running foot-steps came from the staircase and the bedroom door burst open. Jean and Betty drew up sharply at the sight of Mary Bella in bed.

"Mammie, are ye sick?"

"No, no, jist having a rest. Come and see your baby brother."

They gazed, silent, delight and wonder on their faces and then Betty whispered,

"He's so little. Look at his fingers. And all that dark hair! When can I hold him?"

Meanwhile Jean ran from the room and Jim followed to discover her lugging the doll's cradle out of her bedroom. Soon, complete with the black dolly, it was set up alongside the baby's one and Jean set herself the task of carefully rocking the two cradles simultaneously. The larger cradle was an heirloom which had come on loan from Mary's attic; a beautiful cradle made from polished oak, complete with two china knobs on each side to attach the criss cross webbing holding the baby secure. Soon he would be too big for it but now, he looked very content.

Jeannie and Granda arrived behind the girls and, once they were settled with a cup of tea, Jeannie broached the subject,

"He's real bonnie. It's fine ye got a loonie efter the twa girls. Hiv ye decided on a name for him yet? Is he gan tae be anither James Watt Findlay?"

Before Mary Bella could answer Jim broke in,

"Yes, he'll be called James, but nae Watt. We thocht that since Betty was called Elizabeth efter you Mother and Jean efter Jeannie, the boy should hae his ain name and Mary Bella wanted her Father's name in it. So he'll be James Alexander May Findlay and we'll call him Alastair, the Gaelic for Alexander."

Weel, weel, that will be a change. Ye ken, so far he's the only een tae cairry on the faimly name."

Jim could see by her expression that his Mother was not pleased and Mary Bella was relieved that Jim had undertaken the task of explaining the name. But no more was said while the baby was passed round for every one to enjoy a hold. Granda especially was proud to cradle his

first grandson and to say a prayer of blessing on the baby
and the family.

Chapter 54

It was some time before Mary Bella felt restored to her former health. A hungry baby caused sleepless nights and all day nursing until, eventually, she took Betsy's experienced advice and began to bottle feed Alastair with Cow and Gate baby food. He thrived and at last Mary Bella could concentrate on her own needs. Persistent tiredness and weakness were her problems until she was finally forced into accepting assistance in the home and with the baby.

After the second week Betsy went home to Charlotte Street so Mary Bella now had freedom to work out a plan. In a few weeks her own Mother would be arriving from Boston but, until then, she needed help and found it in the person of Jessie Stephen, the daughter of her next door neighbour. Jessie had left school and was looking for work so this part time occupation of six hours weekly suited her fine. She came from a large family and knew how to work so Mary Bella passed over the housework and ironing to Jessie, leaving her free to concentrated on the baby and the family needs. In the evening when Jim was home to assist, she prepared the food for next day and Betty took care of the shopping. The home began to be orderly and, best of all; Mary Bella rediscovered her old zest for life.

It was so exciting when Granny arrived from America. Only three years had passed since they had last been together but so much had happened in that time it seemed much longer. The sleeping arrangements were changed round setting out the larger bedroom with three single beds for the girls and Betsy, while Mary Bella, Jim and the baby had the smaller room.

Her arrival caused some upheaval as she had returned with the intention of staying permanently and thus had brought home all her possessions; boxes of china, glassware, favourite household things and, of course, her clothes of which she had many. To accommodate all these put pressure on Mary Bella until the large walk in cupboard in the bedroom was given over entirely to Betsy and her belongings. But it was good to have her there.

Betsy had always been a cheerful, people- loving person and now she was enjoying her grandchildren and her own sisters and their families. It seemed to be the season of new babies; Netta already had Sandy and Ray, and Nellie, Tina, and Jim's sister Jeannie were all waiting for new arrivals. But there was sadness too. Bella had lost Willie and Ena was sorely grieving over the death of her granddaughter, Margaret, Nellie's only child who had died a few months ago from the after affects of measles. It had been a devastating blow and George and Ena found the child a terrible miss in their lives. Perhaps the new baby would help them to some recovery.

As she spent time with her sisters Betsy was aware in them of a sense of aging. There appeared very little optimism and very little purpose in going on from day to day. She too had known deep grief, but always the motivation to get on with living had helped her to survive. Perhaps poverty had been her salvation. All their married lives both Bella and Ena had enjoyed the advantages of well- to- do husbands and had never experienced the impossible problems and decisions she had had to face on her own. Strength through adversity. She had never examined that statement before but felt sure there was some truth in it. Now, again she had another decision to make.

When Betsy agreed to retire and come back to Fraserburgh at Mary Bella's request she felt gratified to be needed and welcomed. Leaving Norman had been hard but now he was self sufficient, working and in his own apartment. The final goodbyes to Alex, Flora and the three children had been heart rending. But, once she was on her way, Betsy could be honest with herself and confess that it was time to go home, time to find her own folk again. Time to stop being at Mrs. Cornell's beck and call, kind though she had been, time to be her own person and, at last, to follow out what she wanted to do with the remainder of her life. Yes, Mary Bella needed her now but, knowing her daughter, Betsy felt that would be only a temporary arrangement. She was wise enough to know that two women in one kitchen did not work out and she was certainly not the person who could be a lady of leisure and sit with her hands folded in her lap. She would enjoy this first experience of living in Mary Bella's home but, when the right time came, she would have her plans sorted out and know when to leave. Two factors would control that; Mary Bella's progress and her own financial situation. And she was only sixty years old.

The summer days were here, Mary Bella and Alastair were well and the trips to the beach and the Broadsea Shore had resumed. Now the time had come to make the move and one evening at the tea table Betsy broached the subject,

"Balla and Jim, I've something tae tell ye. Noo that Balla is sae much better and managing fine, I've been thinking I need something tae dee wi' ma time. I canna sit idle, an' I need tae mak an income for masel. There's a little general shoppie tae let on Denmark Street and I've offered tae tak it on for a year till I see foo I can manage. I'll bide on here if it's a' richt wi you and maybe find some place nearer afore the winter. I ken ye wanted me tae retire an' bide here wi you bit I need tae be independent an' mak my ain wye. It's jist the wye I am. I hope ye understand."

Mary Bella and Jim were not surprised at this news. They had watched the signs in Betsy and also understood her feelings. She was still an able bodied woman, young at heart for her age and immensely interested in people and in helping them. So they gave their whole- hearted support and suggested that they should all go together now and have a look at Granny's shoppie. Since it had stood empty for quite a while Mary Bella would help her to clean it out and Jim would assist with any shelving and alterations required. Setting it up became a family enterprise and Jim gave Betsy a substantial boost in purchasing stock. She would have no perishables apart from a few vegetables, and tinned goods, confectionary and cigarettes would comprise her main stock. Betsy renewed association with McDonalds, her wholesale company from Charlotte Street days, and they were very helpful in suggesting how she should set up her goods in such a small space. And it was a very small space; but large enough for Betsy to comfortably manage.

The wider family gave her full support but her main clientele came from the passing trade of the fish workers employed in the yards and cooperages on Denmark Street and the Braes. She soon became known as Betty May, famous for her cheeriness and her obliging ways. She provided freshly made sandwiches for the workers at lunchtime; neighbours would leave house keys with her if they expected deliveries while they were at work; and it wasn't unusual for her during the quiet time to put a 'Back- 30min.' notice on the door and go and sit with a sick neighbour for half an hour. Betsy was in her element. She was back with her roots. Broadsea was just behind her shop, Charlotte Street was round the corner and she was in amongst the people she understood and loved; the fisher folk. These were some of the happiest days in Betsy's life.

At the end of a day's work Betsy found the long, uphill walk to Gray Street very hard. But fortunately, it did not last long. She soon heard of a room for let in Jameson's Dairy house at the lower end of Charlotte Street, only a few doors down from no. 21. It felt like going home. It was a very small room but with a fireplace, and a window facing to the back of the house. Once the bed settee, armchair, wardrobe, washstand, china cabinet and small gate legged table were in place, it was full, but very cosy. Betsy had known her landlady, Maggie, for years and she appreciated the small rent she charged. Also, on the cold nights when she came home tired from the shop, to find the fire lit and on the table, a jug of milk fresh from the dairy was wonderful.

Chapter 55

The children came to know Betsy as 'Shoppie Granny' while their other Granny became 'Charlotte Street Granny', although they both lived almost opposite each other on the same street. A happy little routine developed. Usually after church on Sunday Betsy came home to Gray Street for dinner and then, later, some of the family accompanied her home to share a cup of tea round her little table. Granny and Granda at no. 22 were usually visited after the evening service when often others in the family were there and keen theological discussions took place amongst the men. In April Jeannie had given birth to a daughter Betty, so now Betsy and Jimmy had even more joy in their lives with two infants, Betty and Alastair, two little girls Mary and Jean, and Betty, a teenager who was not quite sure where she belonged but tended to feel very grown up beside the others.

During the summer Nellie, Tina and Netta all had baby boys- George, John and Allan and Mary Bella rejoiced with them, especially with Nellie and Tina who had already lost children. The summer gatherings at the beach resumed and now there was a little collection of prams drawn across the sand nearby the Kethock Burn. Very often Mary Bella and the children lingered later and met Jim after work on the grassy slopes of the Links where they had a picnic tea and then some ball games before going home to bed tired, sunburned and happy.

Mary Bella felt very blessed that first summer after Alastair's birth. He was thriving well, she had rediscovered her own strength, the girls were happy and busy at school, Jim was becoming more and more interested and immersed in his work and all their families and relatives were close and harmonious. Perhaps one day they would be reunited with the missing ones in Boston, but meantime, life was fulfilling. Sometimes, when she sat beside her Mother in church Mary Bella would offer up a silent prayer of thankfulness that the hurts of the past were gone, that once more she had been able to support and encourage her Mother. Whatever lay ahead of them she prayed that this peace and harmony would continue amongst them all.

But that was not to be. At the end of the summer an epidemic of Scarlet fever struck Fraserburgh and Jim became a victim. During visitation as Water Inspector he had caught the fever and the result was six weeks' confinement in the isolation hospital not far away on Loch Pots road. There was such excitement on Gray Street when the horse and cab drew up at no.8 and Cab Jimmy drove away with Jim wrapped in a red blanket. The family was shocked by the suddenness of it all and Jean wept sorely to see her Daddy driven away.

The house had to be fumigated and all the bedding washed in disinfectant and then there was nothing left for Mary Bella and the children to do except wait for medical reports. Eleven other men were in hospital with Jim and all were totally segregated from the outside world. Mostly they were mild cases and before long they were up and walking about, able to come to the windows and wave to their families looking over the boundary wall. There was a regular evening pilgrimage on the hospital road to climb on to the banking and wave over the parapet.

At last Jim was well and came home. He quietly admitted that, after the first week or two, he had enjoyed the hospital life. Not like his war experience. It had been a privilege to know his fellow patients and they would keep in touch. Now he had to catch up on the many hours of work neglected during his illness.

Chapter 56

Fraserburgh continued to expand, spreading away over the top of Gallow Hill to the old bowling green and sweeping downwards in a series of levels to the main Watermill Road. A new town boundary, the very broad Hamilton Road/Union Grove thoroughfare, looked as though it may have been planned as a major trunk bypass for the town of the future and, at the moment, was the limit of this first phase. The town population was excited by the huge housing development and grateful for the slum clearance and the rehousing of the deprived and overcrowded areas of the harbour and town centre. Of course, everyone did not understand the use of a bathroom and, in his work as Water Inspector, Jim came across a few families who kept coal in their bath. Hard to believe, but true.

This town expansion was the inspiration of the Burgh Surveyor, Mr. Hamilton, who visualized Fraserburgh as a major centre for fishing, shipbuilding, a seaport, tool and engineering works, farming and fish processing. All these occupations were already there; it only required the town authorities to provide modern housing and facilities to attract more people to the town and increase its wealth and standard of living. Jim was so very enthusiastic and Mary Bella spent many hours listening to him describing what was still to come on the agenda and the limits to which the town would eventually extend.

She was not so sure that she was such a devotee of all this change. The longing for the simplicity of the Broadsea days with her Granny filled her being. And then she remembered the long chain of events, which had shaped her still young life, and Mary Bella knew that change could not be halted, it was inevitable, and one had to adapt.

So the table in the sitting room was extended to its limits and Jim spent hours tracing out the plans for his water supply and drainage piping. The original drawings were drafted under the scrutiny of Mr. Hamilton and then Jim used these to trace his copy on to linen tracing cloth. He used three inks, green, red and black, and his special drawing pens became Jean's responsibility to keep them clean and dried, ready to use in the evenings. The operation fascinated her. The copy was coded and marked with the area reference and then, when the ink was dry, the linen tracing was trimmed and stored in a cardboard cylinder, ready for Jim's office. The operation took a long time to complete and, even then, in view of the anticipated town growth in the coming years, they knew that it was unfinished. Little did the Burgh Surveyor and Jim realize then just how invaluable these drawings would prove in the nearer future.

Chapter 57

The first day of January in the year 1936 was memorable for a few events. It was Alastair's first birthday and, to mark the occasion, Alex and Jamesina had ordered a New Years Day turkey to be sent from their butcher's shop in Aberdeen. It arrived by special delivery and when Mary Bella opened the container and saw the huge bird, all cleaned and trussed, ready to cook, she exclaimed,

"Oh, Maggie, whit can I dee wi this? It wad need a spit! Naebody has an oven that big!"

True, the turkey weighed many pounds, and few ordinary folks had ever seen a cooked turkey far less one that size. But, after a bit of thought, Mary Bella approached Thompson the baker, who was delighted to oblige and the beautifully cooked turkey was delivered on New Years Eve.

It was indeed a wonderful birthday dinner. The three Grandparents, Uncle John, Jeannie's family and themselves all sat round the spread and it was such a time of fun and enjoyment. The two babies, Alastair and Betty, nibbled at their own tasty bits while the adults relished the piece de resistance taking pride of place in the centre of the table. It was a leisurely meal, everyone enjoying the traditional fare and happy conversation until at last they all sat back to have some respite before Betsy and Jeannie departed to prepare for the later party at Charlotte Street. True to her style, Mary Bella shared out the remains of the turkey and Jeannie carried away a large portion to add to the party fare. Another helping was set aside for Mary's family who had shared dinner with her relatives but they would be at the evening function. So the turkey fed a multitude and went down well in family history. Of course, Alastair had no recollection of the event but his first birthday was always remembered for 'The Turkey'.

Later that evening at Granny and Granda's house, the usual excitement flowed. The two little ones held centre stage and Santa delighted everyone with his gifts but managed to cause a brief consternation when his beard caught fire on a candle. John had to make a hasty retreat before Jean and Mary discovered who Santa was.

Mary Bella recalled the previous New Year party night and gave a sigh of relief that it was all in the past. Now was a good time. She was well, Jim had recovered from the fever, and Alastair was a great wee boy, she could not wish for better girls and her Mother, Betsy, was settled and happy. As she looked around the circle of happy faces Mary Bella felt so thankful but, at the same time, felt a pang of loss, when she remembered her very own family so far away in Boston. A few hours from now they would be celebrating too. Would they be thinking of her and their Mother? As she mused Mary Bella became aware that she was being asked a question.

"Bella, what aboot a trip tae London this summer. Would ye gang?"

And so the great adventure began.

John was the motivator and organizer of the holiday. His boss at Fords was taking his family to Detroit for the month of July and he offered his home in Upminster, rent free, for John to accommodate his family for two weeks. Travel was also arranged for them to sail overnight from Aberdeen to London, much to the delight of Mary Bella who loved sea travel. This was much easier for the two babies than going by train, it was cheaper and added an extra day to their holiday.

Sadly, Betty and Jean were left behind because the house was not large enough to accommodate them all, but it was only for a week, and they were promised good presents; a new tennis racket for Betty and a doll's pram for Jean, whose strict instructions were that it had to be a leather, folding down one and not a push chair! During the day the girls were to be at Charlotte Street Granny's and then in the evening they would accompany Shoppie Granny home to Gray Street to sleep. She did not mind taking the long evening walk for the week and it was good to have the girls to herself for a while.

Since they had just one week Mary Bella and Jim made the most of every day; up in the morning and, as soon as breakfast was over, the push chair was packed with baby, lunch, nappies and necessities for the day, and they were off to the underground for the city centre. Jeannie and John West, with two weeks' holiday, could take a more leisurely time and left most of their sight seeing for their second week when John hired a car. But for Mary Bella and Jim, it was like their early days in Boston with Betty in the pram. How they revelled in their freedom and the magnificence of the city. There was so much to see; St. Paul's, the Houses of Parliament, Westminster Abbey, the River, the Tower. Day by day they planned their area so that they would miss as little as possible. In all probability they would never be back again to London.

They sailed north again on the Sunday evening and dis-embarked to do a little shopping in Aberdeen before catch-ing the Fraserburgh train. The Rubber Shop on George Street was their destination and there they found the per-fect racket in a protecting frame, and a doll's pram, grey in colour and exactly to Jean's specifications. Triumphantly, they arrived on Gray Street to see the two anxious faces at the kitchen window. What a reunion, and such delight in the presents. Many times round the fire in the evenings the story was told of the wonders of that ancient city. The tennis racket was treasured and used for years and Jean pushed her little grey pram for miles, sometimes nursing her doll Doris, or Julianna, her cat, all wrapped up in a shawl and content to lie warmly under the hood.

Chapter 58

It was nearing the end of the summer and Aunt Bella was in her front garden trimming back some of the rockery plants and weeding at the same time. Willie and she had built the rockery thinking it would suit the appearance of the cottage and be easier to handle. But it had not turned out that way. Some plants flourished lavishly and needed controlling while some survived only a season and then disappeared. That Snow in Summer looked beautiful in full bloom but was a rampant tyrant. She must get rid of it and rethink the whole rockery. Thus Bella mused and every now and then rose from her knees to stretch and look around for a passer by, but, being at the end of the cull de sac, and virtually in the country, not many people passed the cottage. So the arrival of the postman with a letter was a welcome interlude. Bella knew him from away back and they had a good exchange of news before he rode off down the hill on his bicycle and Bella looked at her letter. The American stamp and Maggie's handwriting excited her at once and the gardening ceased. She quickly tidied up her tools into the shed, set the kettle on the gas to boil and opened the letter.

Yes it was the news she had been waiting for so long. Maggie was coming home. She had made the decision on her birthday in July when she became sixty-seven and, now that Betty Ripley was married, Maggie felt she had fulfilled her responsibilities and could return to her family. If Bella still felt favourable about their living together in the cottage, she would be very grateful for the arrangement. Other wise, Maggie would find a place for herself.

Bella could not hold back the tears. Since Willie died no one could know how lonely she had been; the silent house, the missing companion in the wide empty garden, no one to share thoughts or argue with. O yes, she would welcome Maggie. But how would they get on? From what she knew, Maggie was strong willed and rather dictatorial, accustomed to being in control, in fact, quite like herself. Would they clash? She needed some one to talk it over with. Balla would know.

Hoping to find Mary Bella at home Bella set off for Gray Street after lunch and found a warm welcome there. The cup of tea was soon brewed and as the two women sat down to chat Bella handed the letter to her niece. Tears rolled down Mary Bella's cheeks as she read of Maggie's plans. She understood the soul searching that had taken place before Maggie would thus put pen to paper. Here was a brave woman who had come to terms with the reality of her age, questioning on one hand her continuing usefulness, her responsibilities, her possible failing competence and her future dependence on other people. On the other hand, she was sacrificing the years of love and respect of a family she had known and treasured for nearly forty years. Over that time deep bonds had formed and Maggie had found a firm place in the lives of both adults and children alike. Her strong Scottish honesty, wisdom, practical skills, loyalty and discretion brought her dignity and deep affectionate respect. Betty Ripley was virtually Maggie's child and, now that she was married, Maggie could hand over the reins but keep all her treasured memories.

Mary Bella tried to explain these things to her Aunt. Her tears were for Maggie and the heartrending decisions she had had to make. But Mary Bella was sure that Maggie had done the right thing and, with Bella, would settle down and enjoy the last years of her life.

"I'm sure you have nothing to worry about. Yes, Maggie can be bossy, but you are very much alike and you are both intelligent women. If you set up her bed sitting room, and have your own separate space, then both will have freedom and enjoy the times you are together; like meal times or evenings when you choose each other's company. Just give it time and it will all fall into place. Maggie has to learn what it means to be retired, just as you had to adjust to a new life after Uncle Willie died. When you are older that is not easy. I know how it was when Mother was here with us. But you have a roomy house and space to be apart, or together, as you choose. When do you expect Maggie to arrive?"

"I think maybe about September."

"Yes, that will be after summer in Maine. Maggie would want to complete that time at East Edgecomb, which she loved so much. It will be so good to see her again."

The weeks sped by and here they were, all together at the station, waiting for the train to pull in. Mary Bella could not help but reflect on the times this station had dominated events in her life; huge, life changing departures and arrivals, some happy, others tragic. She wondered how it would be for Maggie. Tina's husband, John Noble, had gone to Aberdeen to meet Maggie and escort her home and, as she stood with Jim and the children looking around at her Mother, at Bella, Ena and George and the array of nieces and their husbands and children, Mary Bella wondered how Maggie would react to it all.

But she need not have worried. Maggie stepped down from the train, a little, elderly lady, straight backed and dignified, and walked forward to hand over her ticket at the barrier. Then she turned with a smile to meet the family. A discreet kiss on the cheek for her three sisters and handshakes all round brought Maggie close to the new nephews- in- law and the babies she had not met. Amid all the talk and laughter Maggie gave Betty and Jean a special smile,

"You've grown into a fine young lady Betty, and Jean, you were a baby when I saw you last!"

So, Maggie came home to Fraserburgh- a very different town to the one she had left so long ago. Her Mother, Mary May and her beloved Janet were gone but she could feel the warmth of the family and, before long, realized that Mary Bella was the pivotal force behind the bonding. Possibly, as the oldest of the five cousins, she felt a responsibility to look after them all, but Maggie could observe that caring characteristic, which was part of Mary Bella's personality.

Some weeks passed before Mary Bella had the opportunity to hear news of the Ripley family. In the interim, Maggie had settled in, arranged her room and filled her bookshelves and small china shelf with the personal treasures she had retained from the long years of service. She and Bella found they had much in common; both spoke English with a very occasional Doric word dropped in, both were keen readers and kept abreast of local and national events and they shared a strong dislike of dirt and extravagance in the home. Bella took great pleasure in introducing Maggie to her friends and neighbours in that area of the town as,

"My Sister, Miss Duthie, who has just returned from America. She was housekeeper to Professor Ripley of

Harvard University in Boston. She has come to stay with me."

Certain things were important to Bella. But the two accommodated each other very well and shared many pleasant hours together. The down stairs drawing room was beautiful and bright but their favourite haunt was the little sun room built out from the mid stair landing. When the kitchen had been extended this room was built above and the panorama windows from floor to ceiling provided a view stretching from the North Sea in the East to the setting sun in the West. Because the house stood on a hilltop they had an uninterrupted view of the bay, the long curving beech to Cairnbulg and Inverallochy, the cemetery, the golf course, the trees at Philorth, places which conjured up so many memories; and all the comings and goings on the Aberdeen and Strichen Roads. Even in winter, they pulled the long curtains and enjoyed the heat from the little fireplace in the corner, which was in keeping with their joint views on good house keeping economics.

Chapter 59

It was here one afternoon that Mary Bella found Maggie alone as Bella had gone to her VAD class in the Library. Now the two could freely share news of America. Mary Bella wanted to hear about the house in Maine and the one in Newton Center. What had happened amongst the Ripleys and the others at East Edgecomb; the Webbers, Will Poole, the servants; who had taken on Maggie's work? And all the people who came to Toad Hall during the summer months. Mary Bella realized that Maggie would not want to close the door entirely on her past life and that she, Mary Bella, was the only one who would understand and share her reminiscing and news.

So they talked and Maggie appreciated having a willing and knowledgeable listener. The full story would take much telling and many afternoons, but there would be plenty of time for that. The Professor and Mrs. Ripley were still active and busy, he mainly with writing and she with reform for Women's Rights and conditions of work; so much suffering had followed the Depression; and now there were several grandchildren to take up their time. Ruth had married Emmet Carver, Davis' wife was called Miriam, Bill had married a very sweet girl called Lydia, of Dutch origin and, just before Maggie left, Betty married Joseph Nicholson. The wedding was held in the sitting room at Toad Hall and had been wonderful. Flowers were everywhere in the dining/sitting room area and, as so many people were there for the ceremony every one stood and then spilled out into the garden till the buffet was laid out. Guests occupied every corner of the house and the cabin and even some neighbours gave hospitality.

"We were preparing for weeks but we had extra help. Veula, who took over my place at Toad Hall, was a real tower of strength. I was glad to see Betty so happily married to a good man. He is of Quaker stock."

That was the first of many afternoons when Maggie and Mary Bella allowed themselves the treat of reminiscing over happy times in Boston and Maine. Since Alastair was still a baby and Mary Bella's freedom was restricted, most often Maggie came to Gray Street, enjoying the walk down Queens Road and the welcome awaiting her. She also called on her other nieces and her sisters Ena and Betsy, but most often it was to Mary Bella's that Maggie found her way. Such a strong bond had been established so long ago when an adolescent Mary Bella needed a Mother and Maggie had been there for her. Now Maggie needed a daughter and Mary Bella, realizing that, felt grateful she in some measure could fulfil that role and be there for her Aunt, especially when she was going through this time of transition.

Most of the relatives felt a little in awe of Maggie, mainly due to the years of separation and to a lack of understanding her personality. She looked severe, her dress was extremely plain and she had very frank views on certain subjects. Jim and Betty treated Maggie with great respect but Jean was different. To her Maggie was like another Granny and she freely chatted away asking endless questions of the old lady. When she was eight Jean suffered quite a severe illness extending over three months and during that time

Maggie was an almost daily visitor. She sat with the child reading to her or telling endless stories of the places she had visited in America, and the things the Ripley children got up to when they holidayed in Maine. Maps were studied, cardboard boxes were made into a doll's house and the dolls were dressed from clippings from Mary Bella's dressmaking bag. As she came and went to replenish the fire or bring tea Mary Bella could hear the murmur of the voices in conversation and she marvelled that the innocence of childhood could break through the barriers, which adults had created for themselves. Jean remained a favourite with Maggie and Bella and, as she grew older, played many roles in helping the old ladies.

Chapter 60

Mary Bella was troubled. She knew she should not feel this way. Jim was happy and satisfied in his work, especially the housing project, which was nearing completion. The children were healthy and had recovered from all the usual childhood infections. With a little help the Grandparents continued to manage on their own and Maggie was home, and content to be so with Bella. As a firm believer Mary Bella felt she should have faith to surmount all her worries and trust in God's strong hand, but she could not shake off the dark cloud.

It began with the insidious rumours of the King and Mrs. Simpson, leading to the unbelievable announcement of the abdication. A shocked nation reeled, and many feared war over the state of the royal institution, which, up till now, had been rocklike. How could the King desert his inheritance and country for such a liaison? Affairs in Europe also concerned Mary Bella as she read reports of Germany's aggressive expansion and how the British government continued to vacillate and show a fearful lack of direction. Mary Bella dreaded war. The twenty years since the last one seemed no time at all and, although she was then in America, there remained vivid memories of the sadness of her Mother's letters, telling of the wounded and lost sons, many of whom she knew.

Closer to home was concern over their financial situation. When he commenced his employment with the Council Jim's salary had been more than adequate for their needs, but now their family had increased and Betty and Jean as they grew older required more. Furthermore, the two sets of Grandparents needed some support with rents and when customers ran up unpaid bills Shoppie Granny relied on Mary Bella to help pay the wholesale account. All these had become a burden and Mary Bella was compelled to constantly economise and work out ways to meet their expenses, making all the clothes for the girls and herself, even Alastair's little suits, and shopping wisely. She was determined not to break into the little pot of savings, which had been so carefully rescued from the Depression. That was for their old age and retirement and Jim would have no employment pension.

But Mary Bella's greatest disappointment was Betty's anxiety to leave school and go to work. So much for dreams of educating her children. Mary Bella believed that all her children were clever but, of the three, Betty was the brightest and could do well in education. Her English was an excellent grade A and, apart from Maths, Betty earned good grades in all her subjects. However, nothing would persuade her to stay on at school for her Higher examinations and she left in the fourth year to become a shop assistant in Benzie and Miller's haberdashery department, earning five shillings a week. Mary Bella wept as Betty went off to work on that first Monday morning. If only she would take advice. But Betty was headstrong and insisted on her own way.

Mary Bella's fears were confirmed on 3rd. Sept. when war was declared on Germany; that beautiful Sunday morning when they stayed at home from church to listen to the grave voice announcing that the country was now at war. The tears flowed as she whispered,

"Nae again. Nae sae seen efter the last war. Div ye think ye'll hae te gang Jim?"

He shook his head as he held her close.

"Maybe no. We'll jist hae te wyte and see. Maybe I'm ower auld or maybe I'll be needed mair here in the toon."

So, World War Two began and the next five years were to change lives forever. The pace of life increased. The worriers still worried, but were so busy they hardly noticed their personal cares. Everyone, from the youngest to the oldest, became involved in the massive war effort and many found themselves accomplishing deeds they could never have imagined.

Chapter 61

Over the first few weeks there was a deep sense of waiting. No one knew what to expect of this war and those who were aware of the true situation did not wish to reveal how unprepared the country was. For many, memories of the Great War were too real and the fears of bombardment and invasion were uppermost. So, almost immediately, strict total blackout was enforced and beach defences were built all the way along the bay to Cairnbulg. Gun emplacements were set up at various strategic points in the town and gradually there was an increased military presence. Local men went off to the services; some volunteering, others conscripted, and their jobs were taken over by all the women available to fill the vacancies. Grandparents came into their own when the mothers went out to undertake their part in the war effort and to meet their own challenge.

As she pedalled away at her sewing machine Mary Bella wondered how many yards of heavy black sateen she had sewed in the last few days. Once her own curtains were complete she had helped out her neighbours. But now the job was almost done and she could get on with the gas mask bags. The girls wanted leather cases but that was an unnecessary expense and she could make them nice, washable ones.

Mary Bella was pleased with her girls. Betty had left Benzie and Miller's and was now working as a tracer in the drawing office of the Toolworks. She was enjoying the work and was thrilled to be involved in the real war effort. Although they were on half-day education, Jean was doing well at school and coming home most weeks wearing the 'Top of the Class' medal. She had also commenced violin lessons, which were gradually making more pleasant listening and the practice did not seem to be a hardship for her. Alastair would be starting school at the Christmas enrolment and that would be good for him. He was ready for school.

The military had commandeered the Annex part of the Academy, which meant that some secondary pupils had to be accommodated in the eight upstairs classrooms of the Central School. The primary classes shared the remaining downstairs rooms and attended school morning or afternoon on alternate weeks. This was particularly hard on Primary 6 and Primary 7 pupils preparing for the Qualifying Exam. which would dictate their level of entry into Secondary Education and indeed, their future opportunities of further education. As she mused Mary Bella felt that, judging by her weekly reports, Jean would manage well.

And so, the winter weeks passed and Mary Bella was always busy. Rationing brought its own problems as the scarcities manifested themselves and she had to use her ingenuity to improvise satisfying meals. Betsy in the shop was having difficulties sorting out her Points quotas for reordering and needed Mary Bella's help. Jim was now a warden and a member of the Fire Brigade, and he had also joined the Home Guard as a signals instructor, using his signalling knowledge from the Great War. This latter involved his going on training manoeuvres in the Grampians. That first time he had a grand send off when, in full uniform, pack on back and rifle across his shoulder, he set off on his motor bike. Jim loved the camaraderie of the men and Mary Bella was sure he revelled in the importance of his role and feeling young again.

But at home Mary Bella felt a heavy load of responsibility. She worried for her children coming and going to school, for Jim out in all sorts of dangers, her Mother on her own in that little wooden shop. What would happen if they suffered a bombing raid, as was happening in other places? Once the concrete shelter was constructed in the garden she felt much more assured.

The real war came to Fraserburgh in July 1940 on a beautiful summer afternoon. Schools were on holiday and people were out and about enjoying the sun. Mary Bella, Jean and Alastair were at Betsy's shop for a brief visit before going to the Broadsea shore and, while they waited for their Mother, Jean stood for a little time at the corner of the main road watching the passing traffic, while Alastair, a little further back on Denmark Street, was absorbed watching the blacksmith shoeing a big black horse. Mary Bella called the children in for a drink and the door of the shop was hardly closed when the air was filled with the most terrible, strident screaming sound and then a great 'garuuumph' followed. Mary Bella caught the children close and covered their heads in her lap; Betsy was somewhere on the floor behind the counter. For a short time the pandemonium of noise was deafening and then a terrible quiet fell. It was eerie. Finally Mary Bella opened the door and they emerged into a scene of utter chaos. Debris; boulders, mud, telephone and electric cables were ankle deep, and the telegraph pole which Jean had been leaning against at the corner, lay across the doorway with its concrete base still attached. Without warning, the bomb had landed in open ground just across from the shop, which was so near that the erupting material had gone over the shop and landed behind. In later times, when they recalled that experience, their lasting memory was of the total silence. When they left the shop and made their way to the shelter behind the Alexandra Hotel, there was not a whisper; no birds called, no buses, no people, and no wind even; it was as though the world had come to an end and they were the only people alive.

Later, in the evening, they returned and wondered at the miracle that had preserved intact that little wooden shop when all around were blasted windows and doors. Mary Bella also took comfort in God's timing when a cup of juice was ready at exactly the right moment.

That day four bombs landed across the town creating much devastation and mess but, thankfully, no one died. However, it was a taster for what was to follow in the next three years. Again and again the German bombers returned, trying hard for strategic targets, but also just jettisoning their loads before returning home. On most occasions they came and went without warning, causing great fear and anxiety amongst the population. Many who could do so evacuated to the country to find relief from the sleepless nights and bombing raids. Jeannie and John took Betsy and Jimmy to live in a cottar house near Rosehearty where they remained for two years. When the petrol ration allowed the men travelled to work in John's little Ford, otherwise, they had to walk a mile to catch the bus at the road end. It was wonderful in summer but the winters were stark when they were snowed in and had to break the ice to find their water supply.

Chapter 62

Can one live in two worlds? Mary Bella often thought of herself as doing just that. The war, the relatives, the shop, the church and the hospitality given so frequently, seemed to absorb one life. But the other, most precious one was her home and family. She strove so hard to protect them from the dangers and influences of the war and to encourage the three children to seek the worthwhile values in living. Mary Bella still had her dreams of a good education, culture and professionalism. It was too late for her, but not for her family, and she did all in her power to foster these ideals.

Alastair, still an infant pupil, was reading well but, at the moment, was happiest with his Meccano set and crane, sharing an imaginary world with his pals. It was Jean, now in the early years of Secondary, who was responding best to Mary Bella's efforts. They had always been close, both in nature and interests and, whatever Mary Bella was involved in, Jean was there nearby, sharing in her efforts. Now that Jean was in a wider field of study, Mary Bella was ever at hand to listen to memory work or check over notes and spelling. Music also played a large part in Jean's schedule and since she was advanced enough, she was often asked to play violin solos at various events in the church and in the town. Mary Bella regularly accompanied her and often stretched the clothing coupons to obtain material for the occasional new dress. It was a happy companionship, each enjoying the trust and understanding of the other. Jean knew what Mary Bella expected of her and applied that criterion in most decisions throughout her life.

It was Betty's age group, which most concerned Mary Bella. She felt the war had robbed them of a carefree, teenage youth and they had been made to grow up too soon. There was an atmosphere of impermanence and teenagers were rushing into hasty liaisons, which they were not mature enough to maintain. This became real to Mary Bella when Betty brought home a young English airman whom she had met while out walking with her friend Margaret on the Rosehearty shore. He was a nice young man, handsome, but five years older than Betty, now just seventeen, and Mary Bella was concerned. The relationship continued until Tom was posted to Northern Ireland and Mary Bella hoped that would be the end of the friendship. However, she was wrong. Betty and Tom corresponded almost daily and, on his first leave, he arrived at Gray Street and presented Betty with a diamond engagement ring.

It was difficult to rejoice and share in the young couple's happiness. Both Mary Bella and Jim felt it was really an occasion for sadness. Their bright, attractive, young daughter, full of so much potential, was binding herself to a virtual stranger before she had any real understanding of what adult commitment meant or entailed. She had still to visit Tom's home and meet his family. Other complications involved his employment; Tom had no official training or job to return to in civilian life, and there was the age difference; Betty was too young. However, the engagement held. Betty visited Southport and met Tom's sisters Peggy and Betty, and his parents who gave her a warm welcome. Tom returned to Ireland and Betty settled down to the round of long hours of work, writing letters and occasionally socializing with her girl friends. Her parents quietly hoped that time would settle the matter when a lively Betty would get weary of the separation and seek more youthful, male company of her own age.

But time did not allow for that. Within a few weeks the telegraph boy delivered an envelope and Mary Bella read,

"Arriving Thurs. Overseas leave. Can we get married? Tom"

Instant panic gripped her. How could she deal with this? Choking tears overwhelmed her. Betty was too young for marriage but Mary Bella knew exactly what Betty would decide. There would be no reasoning with her once the idea of marriage had been sown.

When Jim arrived for dinner at midday, after he had recovered from shock, and some anger at Tom's presumption, they had an opportunity to discuss the matter. At heart they realized that they could do little except appeal to the young couple's wisdom and common sense. But in that climate of fleeting assignations the urge for permanency was strong, requiring deeper, longer lasting promises. Betty at eighteen would bode no interference with her wishes and Mary Bella and Jim knew they could only appeal to the couple and try calmly to lead them into being engaged only, and to wait for a proper wedding when Tom came home.

As expected, Betty refused to consider that suggestion and set off after work to buy her wedding outfit; no white wedding dress and veil but a wartime blue coat with brown accessories. Jean, the bridesmaid, would wear her newish, blue, Sunday coat with a fawn hat and gloves. Tom and his best man would be in uniform. So, when Tom arrived all was ready for them to visit the registrar on Friday. Once the residency requirements were fulfilled and the Banns called three times from the steps of the Parish church, Betty and Tom could approach the Minister to arrange for the Wedding Ceremony. When they returned from church on Sunday evening it was to announce that their wedding would take place on Monday at 11am. which would give them time for three days' honeymoon in Aberdeen.

Mary Bella was shocked. How could she create a wedding lunch overnight? The Grandparents would have to be notified. Jean stayed home from school and was sent off with a note for the two Grannies, and one for the butcher Charles West, explaining the situation and requesting two weeks' ration of meat in the form of lamb chops. She returned with a heavy parcel of sixteen chops, Mr. West had added a few extra, and a bag of carrots and sprouts. By midday the meal was ready; broth left over from Sunday, chops, vegetables and mashed potatoes for the main course and the dessert was a jelly prepared the previous evening from limeade and gelatine served with sponge cake and fruit salad, the latter prized possession from Granny's shop.

Mary Bella put every effort into creating some sort of wedding spread for Betty but, all the time, she felt such a mixture of emotions; disappointment, anger at the thoughtlessness of Betty and Tom, the unnecessary haste and an underlying worry over the suitability of the match. When the wedding party returned from the manse where the ceremony was performed, Mary Bella and Jim met Betty and Tom at the top of the stairs and Mary Bella quietly whispered sadly,

"Well, it's done now."

Tom returned to his company in Ireland, awaiting embarkation, and Betty was not to see him again for the three and a half years he spent serving in Egypt.

Chapter 63

Mary Bella's hopes of returning to some sort of family routine did not last very long. For the past few weeks she had felt concern for her Mother's health and so, one morning, was not surprised to find the shop closed and Betsy at home in bed. It seemed like flu symptoms, but Mary Bella was alarmed at her Mother's slurring speech and drowsiness and insisted on calling the doctor. Betsy had suffered a very slight stroke but should recover with a few days' rest and quiet.

Mary Bella was relieved but, at the same time, she had to face this new situation. Betsy had not really recovered from the shock of that first bombing and it was obvious that she would have to give up the worry and responsibility of the shop. There was also the question of her being on her own. Could they have her to stay in their home? Mary Bella and Jim discussed the situation, finding it hard to make the decision, but knowing all the time that there was only one solution. Betsy would come to them. But, knowing her personality, it was going to require lots of patience and forbearance. Their happy home life was going to be tested.

Once she was sufficiently recovered Betsy was brought by taxi to Gray Street and settled with her belongings into the big bedroom as her own little home. The bed settee was placed in the living room for Mary Bella and Jim while the three young ones shared the small bedroom. It was not an ideal arrangement but it would run on trial for a while before deciding to apply for an exchange to a larger house. This they were reluctant to do as Gray Street and the neighbours had become their life and having their excellent air raid shelter was vital. But Betsy seemed happy, enjoying the company of the family and the visits of Ena, Bella and Maggie and, now and again, some of her old friends from Broadsea would call. She could move around the house but, most of all, enjoyed sitting by her little fireplace reading the Peoples' Friend or one of Annie S Swan's novels from the library.

Once again life took up some sort of order for Mary Bella. But only briefly. A knock at the door one day shook her into a deep dilemma. Before her stood Jane. Mary Bella recognised her immediately. Still the same perky, petite, little person, beautifully turned out and smiling. The twenty-three years rolled back as though they had never been and Mary Bella experienced that old dread of fear and confusion that seemed to follow Jane.

"Hello Mary Bella. I was visiting Aunt Ena and I thought I would just call and see how Mother was since her stroke. Ena told me about it and gave me your address."

Mary Bella was taken aback at the cold, matter of fact tone but she held herself in hand and quietly replied,

"Jane, I'm surprised to see you after all this time. I'm sorry I can't invite you in as Mother is here and I don't want to run the risk of upsetting her. She has recovered quite well but will always have to live with us. You know, after you went away to Ripleys' she vowed she did not want to ever see you again. You broke her heart. I think it would be wiser if you didn't come back. Keep in touch with Ena if you like, but not with us."

And with that Mary Bella withdrew and quietly closed the door. She sat down on the bottom of the stairs, trembling and silently sobbing. Here she was again, in the middle of a conflict, not her own. Being forced to turn away a family member from her door was an act completely against her nature. But she knew she had done the only sensible thing. By her manner, Jane had not changed and Mary Bella, above all, had to protect the peace and equilibrium of her home.

Later she discovered that Jane had visited the ship chandler's shop and contacted George who sent her home to Ena on Charlotte Street. There Jane had gleaned news of Betsy and insisted on having her address. Ena was torn but felt bound to pass on the information, trusting that Mary Bella would know best how to handle the situation.

So the episode of Jane passed and life settled again to the wartime harassment of air raids and the occasional bombing. Night raids were a problem for Mary Bella having to shuttle between the children in the shelter and her Mother asleep in the house. Being very deaf, Betsy seldom knew there was a raid but Mary Bella had to check on her every so often in case she woke up. This meant running the gauntlet from shelter to house between bombings and the threatening drone of the planes. She always maintained that during the war God had given a special dispensation of strength to mothers who had to play so many roles and still show courage.

Chapter 64

So many things happened during that third year of the war; first Betsy's stroke, then Jane's visit, and now the news one morning that Maggie was in hospital. She had tripped on the bedroom carpet and fallen, breaking her left hip. Mary Bella was quite affected when she saw her Aunt lying in bed. Somehow, she had always regarded Maggie as a strong able- bodied woman, not the little frail person resting there under the yellow covering. The prognosis was not good. The hip had been reset but her bones were fragile and the years of hard work since childhood had taken their toll. Maggie would possibly walk again if she had good nursing and convalescence but, at her age, no one would promise anything.

To ensure that she would receive the best possible nursing care Maggie was transferred to Kepplestone Nursing Home, a private hospital in Aberdeen. There she would remain until she was mobile again and then Bella, with her nursing skills, would take over at home. At first Maggie had been agreeable to the arrangement but, as the weeks went by and she was still unable to walk, she began to fret for home. Visits from the family were rare, mainly due to the distance; trains were erratic, often crowded with military and, to spend one hour with Maggie meant a whole day in Aberdeen travelling to and from the hospital. Maggie was also concerned about the growing hospital bills and, at last, requested that she be taken home to the Fraserburgh hospital where she would be cared for near her family. So, after six weeks, Maggie returned to the Thomas Walker Hospital on Charlotte Street, just across the road from Ena's home, and settled in to a ward of five ladies in a similar condition as herself.

Visiting times became special occasions and seldom passed without one or other of the sisters or nieces arriving to spend an hour. Mary Bella came mainly in the evening when Jim was at home to supervise Betsy and Alastair and she often took Jean with her for Maggie enjoyed hearing the child's news of school and her music lessons. Sometimes they just sat quiet while Maggie rested, eyes closed but not asleep.

One afternoon Mary Bella came late to visit and found Bella there on her own. As they watched the pale, worn face on the pillow Bella whispered,

"I see a change. She has hardly opened her eyes this afternoon. What do you think Balla?"

"I can see that, but her hand has a firm grip. Maggie has a strong will. You take a rest tonight and I'll come back for the evening visit. I'll let you know if there is any change."

Mary Bella returned with Jean for the evening hour and found Maggie resting in a semiconscious state. She did not respond to their voices but occasionally a flicker crossed her eyelids and her lips moved. Mary Bella sat pondering over this wonderful woman who had meant so much in her young life; all the quiet love and wisdom she had implanted in those she was responsible for. Mary Bella just wished it could have been possible for Maggie to have lived out her last days in her home with Jim and her family. Jean, on the other hand, was looking on death for the first time and pondering over the change that had taken place in Maggie, the lovely, storytelling, game lady who had been so kind during her illness. She had observed the change in Granny since her stroke and is this what had happened to her handsome Grandfather whose photo hung above Granny's fireplace? Was this how people died and what happened after that? She had many questions but knew that this was not the time to ask them. Mother was too upset. Some day she must ask Mam about her life with Aunt Maggie. Maggie slipped quietly away that evening, never regaining consciousness.

A private funeral for family only was decided and Tina's husband, John, made all the arrangements. A taxi brought Betsy, Jim, Mary Bella and Jean to the service in Bella's large sitting room and all members of the family who could attend were present. At Maggie's specific request she was to be buried in the cheapest possible coffin and she wished to wear her blue, velvet dress with the diamond clasp. As Mary Bella gazed at the figure in the open coffin, she saw again the stately woman, the firm mouth, the slightly pinched nose and the true honesty and integrity shining out from the face and eyes, now closed. She thanked God for having known her.

While the men attended the graveside service the women had a light meal and during that time Bella brought Mary Bella and Jean to Maggie's room to see if they would like any of her possessions; books, china, jewellery. Mary Bella chose the blue tea set with 'A Present from Shetland' decoration, part of Maggie's wedding preparations, while Jean, picking over the scant jewellery, chose a little gold ring with coral and seed pearls inset. Aunt Bella told her,

"That was Maggie's engagement ring. I remember the night Jim Strachan gave it to her. She always kept it. She would be so pleased for you to have it."

Once the men returned, the company gathered round the lawyer for the reading of Maggie's Will. It was simple. After all funeral costs were disposed of all debts incurred in the past by several nephews were cancelled, a special bequest of £500 was to go to Betsy who had no income and was disabled, and the rest of the estate was to be divided equally amongst the sisters Bella, Ena, Betsy and Janet (deceased), the latter's share to become the inheritance of her three children. At the end of the reading was a simple statement

"The gold and ruby ring made from the wedding rings of our Mother Mary May and our Grandmother Belsie, is to go to my next sister."

No name was mentioned and immediately Betsy spoke,

"That'll be me. I'm the allest here noo."

No comment was made and the ring box was handed over. But, Mary Bella was upset at her Mother's forwardness. Janet was next in line to Maggie and, although she was no longer there, she had a daughter Netta who should have inherited the ring. Mary Bella resolved that, once her Mother was no longer with them, she would make matters right and hand the ring over to Netta. Before the funeral party dispersed she had a quiet word with Netta and the matter of the ring was settled.

Chapter 65

Dawn was just breaking and Mary Bella lay awake allowing her thoughts to roam as she listened for the first movements in the house. She had always been an early awakener and enjoyed the moments of quiet as her mind drifted around until eventually, she planned her day. Things were a little calmer now with Jean and Alastair at school and only Betsy to attend to during the day. She had become a handful after that second stroke and Mary Bella wondered just how long she could carry on nursing her Mother. They had moved Betsy to the smaller bedroom off the living room where they could keep an eye on her. It was a night and day process now. Jim's Mother Betsy had died last year after a lingering, weakening illness, which had been quiet to handle but sad for Jeannie and Granda. But her Mother Betsy was a big physically strong woman, almost totally disabled down the left side and mentally quite aggressive at times. Jim during the night and Jean between school times were Mary Bella's stalwarts and somehow, they managed.

Mary Bella wondered how things were working out for Betty and Tom now that they were back with Tom's people in Southport. His not having employment was worrying and with the baby, Betty could not go out to work. Mary Bella hoped that they were keeping hold of the nice sum of savings Betty had earned during the war. They would need it for setting up a home once Tom found a job. Mary

Bella felt concerned. But how they missed Baby Anne. She was such a beautiful child. She had become the centre of their lives during the months before and after her birth. It had been an exciting year with Tom's demob and the baby's arrival. It was good for them to be away on their own to make a life together.

Now Mary Bella felt the house was hers again and Jean and Alastair could share the big bedroom. There was also a smaller household to feed. Rationing would go on for a long time yet but the war was over, that was the main thing. She smiled as her eyes rested on the flag standing in the blue jug on the sideboard. Alastair had carried it down town on VE night when Jim took the young ones to see the town lit up. It was an amazing sight. Every house, shop, pub and building had switched on anything that would light up and the town was ablaze. People laughed and spoke and forgot themselves in the infectious rejoicing. But, it was not so for those grieving. For a moment Mary Bella relived the most terrible night of the war; far worse for her than the night of the great fire raid when Benzie's burned. Mary Bella shuddered as she remembered Jim in that hole on the hospital road, up to his knees in water, working under arc lights, to repair a burst water main. And all the time an unexploded bomb was lying in the base of the pit. As head of the water department, Jim insisted on performing the repair himself and it took many hours before the pipe was sealed satisfactorily to allow the Bomb Disposal Engineer to go in to dismantle the bomb. It was a 1000lb.and one slip could have detonated it and blown Jim away. He was one of the unsung heroes of the war.

Mary Bella reflected that there was still so much to be enjoyed in life. Jean and Alastair were very settled and appeared to be keen to go on studying. Music was holding an increasing place in Jean's life taking her into all sorts of occasions, the latest being Gilbert and Sullivan's operas. Iolanthe was this year's show; it had been quite wonderful. And Alastair was now in the Academy and showing signs of ability. He was so like her Father. At times, when he turned round quickly, her heart turned over at the likeness. Now, if they could have a little peace and orderliness in their lives for a time it would be wonderful.

She could hear Betsy stirring so Mary Bella slipped quietly from bed and began her new day.

Chapter 66

Jean was tired. Higher History was happening in four days' time and she had been trying to study for it all evening. Not easy with so much activity going on in the next room. Now she was lying in the dark on top of her bed watching the last flickerings of the fire on the ceiling and listening to Alastair's deep breathing from the bed by the window. Granny had been very ill for the past week and Jean did not think her Mother had been to bed in all that time. Because Betsy was so violent in her reactions, Mary Bella was frightened to leave anyone else alone with her Mother and insisted that she and Jim would manage between them. It could not go on much longer.

Suddenly, all was quiet for a time then Jean heard her Father's footsteps on the stairs. That was her cue and she quietly slipped through to the kitchen to find her Mother in tears.

"Has Granny gone?"

"Aye. Your Father has just gone for the Doctor and the Nurse. They'll be here in half an oor. Ye shud gang back tae bed. There's naething mair tae dee here."

"No. I want tae see Granny first an' then I'll mak some tea if you wad jist gang ben and sit doon in the room and rest till they come. I'm nae gan tae school the morn. It's only revision an' I can dae that here."

As she was speaking Jean could see her Mother's tension lessening and together they went to look on Betsy. Even in dying, her passing had been one more, long struggle, but now, she was at peace. Already the care worn lines were smoothing out and Mary Bella was happy that at last, after nearly forty years, her Mother was reunited with her wonderful husband, Alex May. She had travelled a hard, lonely road in that time.

Jean found it difficult to grieve for her Granny. All she could feel was relief for her Mother and Father. A sense of lightness and freedom seemed now to pervade the house. Many people came to share in the mourning but Jean kept to her room to study. Unfortunately, the Higher History exam was to take place on the funeral day but Mary Bella insisted that she sit her exam.

"Ye did a' ye could for Granny fan she wis here. I cudna hae managed without ye. Ye must sit yir exam. It's ower important and Granny wad hae wanted ye tae dae that. There'll be plenty folk here tae help wi the tea."

So, Jean missed the funeral but, next day, she cycled to the graveyard to see where Betsy had been laid alongside Maggie in front of the red, granite stone in the shape of a cross. Since Alex was buried in Florida, Maggie had provided for Betsy to be with her in the grave. Mary Bella was so thankful that the two most important women in her life were now together in death.

Chapter 67

During almost thirty years of marriage Mary Bella and Jim had shared a firm faith in God. It had sustained them during some very difficult times and had eventually brought them through, still facing life with hope and purpose. The Baptist Church featured largely in their lives and they served God faithfully in the spiritual life of the Church and worked for the fellowship in all sorts of practical ways.

As happens in most churches, there are high times and low times and, after the war, when people were experiencing continuing austerity, lack of work, grief for broken homes and lost members, change in all sorts of ways, the church was failing to meet their needs. The movement of population, and the wider horizons of the returning service men and women, caused a restlessness, especially among the young people, and 'settling down' to the old regime was for some, an utter impossibility.

As church attendance fell Sunday by Sunday the concerned leadership prayed and considered deeply where God's will was taking them. An evangelical out reach seemed to be the answer and a well-known evangelist, Rev. J Mc.Kendrick, was called from Ayr to lead it. He came for a week but, so great was the response, he stayed for two. Every evening the congregation increased as men and women sought an answer to their needs. They found the pure and simple Gospel preaching satisfying to their souls and a release from the tensions and burdens of modern living. Many had their faith restored and many found faith for the first time, amongst them Alastair and Tina's son John, along with their friends. It was a wonderful time of spiritual refreshing and all the joy and fellowship, which accompany such an experience. Many baptisms followed and once again, the Baptist Church became a place of worship and song and rejoicing. Rev. Mc.Kendrick returned the following year for a further campaign and to consolidate much of what had taken place during the first outreach, particularly amongst the young people.

Mary Bella and Jim were very satisfied. Now their family was complete. Betty had professed her faith in America, Jean when she was fourteen and now Alastair, a young teenager, and Mary Bella and Jim were thankful that, whatever happened in the lives of these three, God's hand would always be on them, guiding and responding to their call when they reached out to Him.

The months following the Revival were joyful and peaceful. With Jean at university in Aberdeen, the household now comprised of three and at last, Mary Bella felt she had space and time to engage in some of her own interests. She spent a day in Aberdeen with Jean enjoying a tour of the university and meeting her friends. The garden was her therapeutic friend and the hours passed there satisfied Mary Bella's creative outlet and brought her close to her neighbours, many of them long standing. Then there was the sewing machine, the Aunts and Cousins, the Women's Meeting preparations, home decorating; all occupying her time pleasurably and gratifyingly. It was a long time since Mary Bella had felt so liberated and her own person. It was into this scene that an unsettling realization came to her.

From his upbringing Jim had always felt a deep affinity for the Brethren Assembly. He enjoyed the quiet worship-fulness of the morning meeting and the deep discussions when members came together on Sunday afternoons for the Bible studies. It was not uncommon for Alex and Jim to go together to the Bible study and occasionally Mary Bella joined them. Other highlights were the Brethren Conferences held annually in the towns and villages along the Moray Coast. The ministry was always outstanding and Jim frequently went with his friend Andrew Duthie in the family car, driven by his son Andy. Jean often accompanied them. Over the years they had made friends amongst the Meeting folk, especially Andrew and Lizzie Duthie, and Sandy and Jessie Watt. In fact the Duthie relationship went back another generation to Betsy and Jimmie who were on visiting terms with George and Kirsten Duthie.

Jim sang enthusiastically in the Gospel Male Voice Choir and was in the heart of the church outreach endeavours. He was quite thrilled with the wonderful response. Now in his middle age, Jim seemed to be enjoying his Christian life; music, evangelism and deeper spiritual study, and Mary Bella and he shared a warm sense of satisfaction and peace concerning their Christian walk.

That is what made the change in Jim so puzzling for Mary Bella. It all happened so suddenly. One week he was in the heart of organizing the Choir Festival of Song and the next he announced his resignation. Now Mary Bella and Alastair went to church on their own while Jim stayed at home and studied his Bible. The long silent evenings were hard to endure but Mary Bella realized that Jim had a problem and needed time to sort it out. So she was patient and waited.

The blow fell one Saturday evening when Jim returned from a conference in Macduff and announced that he was resigning from membership of the Baptist Church and joining the Brethren. He had already approached the Oversight.

"I feel it's the right place to be and I hope Mary Bella that ye see yir wye tae come with me."

Mary Bella was shocked into silence. No discussion. No warning. True, she had seen the signs; she ought to have realized. But the suddenness of the decision, and the imperious statement from Jim expecting her to join him, riled Mary Bella. For a few moments she gazed at him in silence then rose and went to the kitchen. The tears flowed. She just felt the foundations of her life had gone. They had always been one, thought and planned as one, trusted each other completely, found strength in each other's wisdom. But now? This was like a physical blow.

Mary Bella sat a while at the kitchen table. As she allowed her confusion to subside her mind began to adjust to the situation and she could think more clearly. This was one more hurt but, from her deep experience, the grief passes and one can go on. It was not as though Jim was leaving the home. Maybe it was a passing notion and he would get over it once the thrill had gone. Time would prove that. But she had to tell Jim what her thoughts were on the matter. So Mary Bella quietly sat down beside him in the living room.

"Jim, if ye feel so strongly, ye must dee what ye believe to be recht. But ye wull gang on yir ain. Aa my life I've worshiped as a Baptist, wherever I 've been, and sharing in the fellowship is important tae me and my faith. Brethren women tak nae part in the meeting and I cudna be like that. Also, Alastair has jist become a member and I widna want tae walk awa from him at this time. So you gang your wye and we'll cairry on at the kirk."

No more was said and on Sunday morning Jim went up Gray Street and Mary Bella and Alastair went down, each to their own place of worship. As time went on Church folks ceased casting questioning looks and no references were made to Jim's absence from his usual place in the pew. But, Mary and Alex moved forward to the family pew and never allowed Mary Bella to sit on her own.

Chapter 68

After the heartbreak at the start of the decade, the following years of the fifties brought Mary Bella and Jim increasing satisfaction and joy. Jean graduated and was now following her career in the Borders teaching English and History in Sanquhar Academy. Alastair entered Aberdeen University to study Medicine and Betty and Tom were settled in Yorkshire where Tom worked as a TV engineer and they now had Roger, a brother for Anne.

The arrival of their Grandchildren brought immense pleasure, and annual holidays to Northallerton became the norm. At the end of their two weeks Mary Bella and Jim brought Anne and Roger back to Fraserburgh for the rest of the summer. Later Betty and Tom came for their vacation and took the children home in time for school. This was a magical time for Mary Bella and Jim. Many, many picnics were held at the beach but, more frequently at the Broadsea Shore, where Alex and Mary often joined them in their explorations. Alex had a special way with children and he became Roger's hero. Alex knew how to build boats from tin cans, how to make a harbour by damming up the water on the sandy shore, how to fly the kite which Grandad had made for them, even how to make a boggy from an old set of pram wheels and a wooden box. There was no end to the fun, which the two men enjoyed as much as the children.

Although she remained in her own Church Mary Bella supported Jim in his social relations with the Brethren. A few close friendships had developed and, on Sunday evenings, after-meeting suppers became a regular event, particularly in the homes of the Duthies, the Watts and the Findlays. Jim continually made an effort to persuade Mary Bella to join him in membership, which irritated her and offended her self-respect. But she stood firm, although she felt very embarrassed when he did it in public. On one occasion Mrs. Duthie observed this and felt concerned. The two women had become close friends and often shared private thoughts, so Mrs. Duthie, Lizzie May, felt she could express her opinion on the matter.

"Bella, I can see whit Jim is trying tae dee. Bit dinna mak a move till ye are sure ye are deein it for yersel. I wis brocht up a Baptist along wi Andra, my breether, an I only gid intae the Brethren fin I mairrit Ora (Andrew). It wis fit ye did in those days. Bit, I missed my kirk, my freens and the meetings an, if Ora wisna here noo I wid gang back tae the Baptist Kirk far I cud really hae a pairt tae play."

Mary Bella was comforted to hear this from her friend, Lizzie, and appreciated her confidence. Sometimes, sitting around the supper table when the men were deeply debating a point, the two women would catch each other's eye and give a wry smile. It was good to know she had a friend who understood.

There was a happy family gathering for the wedding of Ora's daughter, Liz to James Buchan in the Mission Hall. Both Jean and Alastair managed to arrive home on the Friday evening and so had some real time with their parents. It was difficult not to sense the strain in the home; Jean was concerned for her Mother's loneliness, living under such constant criticism, but Alastair was angry about the situation. He deeply loved his Mother. She had been a rock and support for all three children and he abhorred his Father's attitude of superiority and self-righteousness. How dared he treat her like this? Where was the kindly, amusing, interesting Father they remembered from childhood? Alastair would have wished to voice his opinion to Jim before he returned to Uni. but, he feared it would only make matters worse, so he kept silent.

Jean quietly observed and, during her return journey to Sanquhar, made up her mind where she would help. Her two years' probationary teaching would be completed in July and, much as she had loved the job, the staff and the friends she had made in Sanquhar, she missed the life in the North East. It would be good to return home. She would be company for her Mother and a buffer against the onslaught of her Father's persistence. She would apply to the Aberdeenshire Council for a teaching post in or around Fraserburgh and have it all settled before she told anyone.

Chapter 69

Mary Bella just kept on smiling. Every now and again she would touch her apron pocket or bring out the letter and read it again. Something she never expected to happen was coming about and she could hardly believe it. Jean was coming home to teach in Inverallochy School. Now that there was just Jim and herself at home it would be so good to have Jean there bringing in all the interest and activity that always seemed to follow her. For Mary Bella personally these had been two frustrating years and many times she had longed for the companionship and understanding, which they had enjoyed together during the Academy years. Tears of thankfulness came to her eyes as the realization sank in and already, the loneliness was lightening. She hoped Jim would feel as happy as she did when he read the letter at dinnertime.

Of course Jim was delighted, and together they began to plan a room for Jean. She would have the large bedroom with the fireplace and they would remain in the bedroom off the living room, which they liked for the warmth in winter. One thing led to another; a new carpet square, an extra armchair and a dressing table with a mirror. Mary Bella made a new bedspread to match the curtains and the large walk in cupboard would provide plenty of storage room for books and the extra teaching equipment. Mary Bella and Jim enjoyed the planning. It was like old times and helped to reduce the feelings of resentment they each were aware of. Perhaps this was the beginning of the reconciliation. Time would tell.

At last July came and Jean stepped off the train, complete with violin, cases, her bicycle from the guard's van, and the cabin trunk to be delivered by lorry the next day. The deep gladness they felt to be together again shone on their faces as they walked up Victoria Street and home to Gray Street. As was their way in the North East, nothing was said, but each understood how the others felt. When she saw her room Jean was delighted, but had to express her thoughts,

"It's wonderful. You've gone to so much work and expense. But you two should be in here and I should hae the little bedroom. It would dee me fine."

"No. We've been using the little bedroom nearly a' the time since Alastair gid tae Aberdeen. It's fine and warm and this has become a spare room. Fan Alastair comes hame for a weekend he'll hae oor bed and we will sleep on the settee. Ye need a place tae tak yir freens and it's the best arrangement for us aa. Noo come. Supper's ready and we can hear yir news."

So they heard all about Sanquhar and her farewell from the school when she was presented with a travelling clock. The Congregational Church where Jean had been organist for the two years, gave her a bound Reference Bible, and so many of the children in school had shyly given her perfume, chocolates and various other little gifts. It had been quite an emotional time and it was obvious from her voice that Jean was sorry to leave Sanquhar and the friends there. When she came to talk about Effie and John Mitchell, her home from home, Jean had tears in her eyes as she told Mary Bella and Jim about the early weeks of terrible homesickness and how Effie had rescued her and given her a shoulder to cry on. She also put laughter back into Jean's life and provided an ever-open door. She could never forget that kindness.

"But Effie says that they are coming tae the Broch for a holiday so maybe ye'll hae visitors soon enough."

So began one of the happiest years in Mary Bella's memory. Jean soon settled in at Inverallochy and always had stories to tell of the quaint old building, the very strong characters amongst the staff, and the children who were so well behaved and from a strong Christian background. Jean felt a deep satisfaction teaching there and, all through the rest of her long life, she carried memories of events in that little classroom above the front door; the wide window overlooking the sea; the herring boats returning from Yarmouth, each with its own horn signal as they passed the window so that the children would know that Father was home; the share of rock and chocolate brought for the teacher when the kist was opened; the day the Girl Ann was reported lost on the West coast with all hands and James was absent from his desk because his Father was one of the crew, such a deep sharing of grief and loss; and the happy outdoor activities on the rocky shore and on the disused air strip behind the school where PE was carried out on a good day.

All these events and many more were shared at home and Mary Bella was an avid listener. But above all, she enjoyed having Jean with her in Church, hearing her play the organ occasionally when the organist was on holiday, seeing her in the choir and having her company at the Women's Meeting. Jean fitted back into Church as though she had never been away and Mary Bella gradually was aware of that feeling of restoration and healing of spirit, which came from having a kindred soul.

There was also a firming of the relationship with the Duthie household. Jean was often present at the Sunday supper evenings and frequently was the fourth member in the car when Andy drove the Fathers to a Conference. As many activities brought them together a friendship developed and they became close. One day, a chance remark about the scarcity of PE teachers brought Andy into the teaching world. Inverallochy had no PE teacher. From his Scouting experience with children Jean encouraged him to apply and the result was a month's trial with a trained PE teacher in the Central School. Andy came through with flying colours and was allocated an itinerary of several schools to visit in the week, among them Inverallochy. Andy was in his element and, for the next two years, he put his whole heart into the work.

But, Andy was always aware that he required a full teaching qualification. He knew now, above all, that he wished to be involved in teaching but, although he was highly qualified with Higher National Certificates in Building and Technical Subjects, he required some academic subjects for entry into Teaching College. So, for the winter months, Jean tutored him in English, which he passed at Higher level and Andy was accepted by the Aberdeen Teacher Training College to start the following October.

During all these activities Mary Bella and Jim, and Ora and Lizzie May quietly observed and wondered. Jean and Andy accompanied both sets of parents to Stirling for their first camping holiday, which was a great experience in glorious weather and they toured all the way to the West coast. They also accompanied Liz and James on a long camping trip to Keswick and Yarmouth, again causing some speculation about their relationship. Mary Bella watched and waited and hoped that something would come of it. The last thing she wished for was that Jean should be disappointed when she seemed so happy with Andy. However, all was settled when the pair returned from Christmas shopping in Aberdeen and, before the two sets of parents, Andy presented Jean with a diamond and ruby engagement ring. It was such a wonderful family occasion and, knowing Andy, Mary Bella and Jim were totally satisfied with their future son-in-law.

A summer wedding was planned before the couple settled in Aberdeen for Andy to enrol at College in October. But again, events took another turn and Mary Bella was faced with another new challenge.

Chapter 70

Summer days in the Broch were special. Mary Bella and Jim loved them because they brought the Grandchildren. For Anne and Roger, being by the sea was the high time of their year. Betty treasured the time with her family and all the old friends from Church and Toolworks days. But, the one who found the two weeks most rewarding was Tom. As a city boy he relished the small town life where people knew most every one and felt free to 'drop in' any time. He enjoyed the impromptu conversations with the old fishermen at street corners and, above all, he loved roaming around the piers and quays looking at the various boats and occasionally being invited aboard to see the modern, radio, sonar equipment now being implemented in the fishing industry. Such an advance on his wartime experience of Radar. Tom could see himself feeling very at home working with the fishermen and he often talked enthusiastically about it.

In her weekly letter to Betty, Mary Bella chanced to remark that Marconi was advertising for an engineer to service the fishing boats at Fraserburgh. Nothing more was said until Tom was called for an interview, which proved successful, and he would take up employment in June when the boats would all be fishing at home, then preparing for Yarmouth and Lowestoft.

Of course the family had mixed feelings about leaving Northallerton. After almost ten years they were leaving close friends both from work and school. Betty especially, regretted having to leave her nice home and the sense of freedom they had enjoyed being on their own. She had not always found it easy to be in the middle of the family enclave and subject to interference, no matter how well intended.

Mary Bella's concern was where would they live in Fraserburgh? Even though the war had been over for ten years the Council Housing Agenda had not yet met the requirements of public demand. The list was long and it would mean waiting over a year. So Mary Bella researched private accommodation to rent but again, that was unsatisfactory; nothing being offered that would house the family and their belongings. Finally, together Mary Bella, Jim and Jean decided they would rearrange and, when Tom arrived in advance, leaving Betty and the children to finish the school year and finalise the removal, he would be offered the large bedroom while Jean moved to the smaller one and Mary Bella and Jim would sleep on the bed settee. So, it was all change and once again Mary Bella's organizational skills came into operation.

In due course their furniture was put into storage and Betty's family set up home in the bedroom. Much patience and forbearance had to be exerted but, on the whole, the arrangement succeeded. Betty found work as a library assistant, the children adjusted to school and Tom was happy. Jean was at school all day and meal times were staggered so that there was never confusion in the kitchen. Evenings were usually quiet, the men reading by their own firesides, the children doing homework at the kitchen table, and the women folk preparing for the next day or reading, which was the favourite household pastime. Mary Bella was happy with them all around her. Having the children there brought back into her life a lightness and joy, which she had missed in the past few years, and she laughed again. She knew the situation would last only a few months for , living in overcrowded accommodation had brought Betty and Tom away up the waiting list, and new houses were steadily being built. Meantime, a wedding had to be arranged and preparations and logistics thought through.

Jean and Andy took care of the administration and catering, Betty set up her sewing machine in Jean's room and, following a day in Aberdeen shopping for materials, the whirr of the machine went on most evenings. The bridal and two bridesmaids' gowns were soon on hangers under a white sheet hanging from the picture rail. Cousin Mary, the chief bridesmaid, would be in a soft rosy pink and Anne, the flower girl, in pale apple green and the combination with the ivory satin of the bride's dress was quite beautiful. Once the major items were completed, Mary Bella set to with a thorough cleaning and the final three weeks were spent entertaining, as guests and friends visited bringing gifts, and enjoying the social occasion. Aunt Mary arrived each morning with an offering of newly baked pancakes and neighbours handed in contributions of home bakes, sometimes lingering to help washing up when Mary Bella was talking with the guests. Looking back, these three pre-wedding weeks were as enjoyable , even more so , than the wedding itself. There was so much fun and good will expressed. Everyone was exhausted but that good feeling prevailed and carried the women folk along. Lizzie May and Liz were there most days but the men kept quietly in the background until later in the evening, when all was quiet, Andy, Tom and Jim would appear for a taste of the goodies and have a look at the latest gift arrivals. Tom was amazed. He had never witnessed such a wedding custom and so many gifts! Her bedroom became so crowded that Jean could no longer sleep there and during the last week she slept in Liz's spare room.

It was a fine wedding; the ceremony firmly based on Christian principles, and the reception very convivial with good food, speeches and socializing. Later, Jean and Andy set off for a honeymoon in Ireland and gradually, the guests dispersed. The Findlays and the Duthies went home happy with what had been accomplished that day and looking forward to what the years ahead would hold.

Chapter 71

A quietness had fallen on 8 Gray Street. It was like an anticlimax after the excitement of the wedding. But this hiatus was necessary for tired people living in such restricted accommodation. It allowed them to sort out personal attitudes and problems. Sometimes Mary Bella wondered if ever the time would come when she and Jim would have the house to themselves. In the past months pouring oil on troubled waters had been her role when she listened to Betty's slightly jealous remarks comparing her own wedding to that of Jean, or when the cooped up children quarrelled, or Tom complained that he had nowhere to study or research his new job, or Jim saying that he had no place where he could think or prepare for the Meeting. It all came at her too forcefully at times and she had to escape to Aunt Ena's for a little while. But, even there, Mary Bella was saddened to see her 'young' Aunt aging so, and she realized that soon her own generation would be the 'old' one.

Jim was Mary Bella's chief worry. The previous year, after being severely ill with kidney stones, Jim had been strongly advised to lose weight as the doctors suspected some heart problems, which would only become more serious. This Jim refused to accept and made no effort to discipline himself. Now Mary Bella could detect moments when he showed chest discomfort and complained of indigestion.

But, she feared something else and longed for the peace of their own home for themselves.

Mary Bella was alone in the house when the letter arrived. As soon as she saw the Fraserburgh Town Council envelop heading she knew she had to deliver it at once and set off to the library for Betty to open it. Yes, at last, it was a request for them to call at the office to accept the key to No.21 Williams Crescent. Mary Bella and Betty could hardly control their tears of relief. During her lunch break Betty collected the key and, as soon as Tom came home from work, they set out to find ' their house'. Such excitement and relief! To allow them the first moments on their own Mary Bella and Jim followed a little later and rejoiced with them. It had been worth waiting for; a new semidetached villa with three bedrooms, a large sitting room and all the additional facilities which comprise a modern house. The huge cupboard space and wonderful garden area were amazing and at once the imaginings and planning began. Within the week the house was cleaned, the carpets and lino laid, the furniture brought out of storage, new sitting room curtains sewn and the family moved in to a sort of ordered chaos which would take a little time to resolve. But they were in residence and that was all that mattered.

Mary Bella and Jim could now relax in their own space and have their bedroom back. However, having decided to repaper the room and lay a new carpet, they took a little time over that. But at last, it was ready and their pleasure was real. They hoped the bed settee had borne its final occupants.

How wrong they were. Although the home was again their own Mary Bella and Jim were not left alone for long. Alastair frequently came home at weekends; on alternate months Jean and Andy visited for a weekend sharing between Gray Street and Strichen Road where his parents lived, but they insisted on using the bed settee as that was their usual mode of sleeping in their own small accommodation; Betty and Tom dropped in any time, especially on Sundays, and the children had their own visiting time on Saturday evening when they knew Granny would be on her own while Granda was at the Prayer meeting. The special attraction was the regular bottle of Hay's Ice Cream Soda and the home- made ice cream from Marionni's shop at the corner. Granny was famous for her Saturday treats, which never failed.

The months flew in and then it was Christmas again. This time Betty insisted on holding the family gathering in their new home, just the way they had celebrated in Northallerton. In Fraserburgh the gatherings were always held at New Year time but now, Betty decided they would have it the English way on the real Christmas Day. Tom, being English, appreciated that and, as he sat at the head of his table facing Betty, he made a little speech of welcome and heartfelt thanks to all who had helped them through the past year. Then he said Grace and the wonderful meal began. Mary Bella in particular enjoyed that day. Here was one occasion when she had no responsibility but could sit back in total relaxation. She felt blessed indeed with all her family round her and, as she looked at the precious faces, she silently prayed in her heart that they would all be kept safe and well to meet another time.

Christmas Day at Williams Crescent became a tradition, which continued over many years and they were always memorable occasions. Through time the gathering changed as the older generations slipped away and the new were added. Here it was always open house and there was no question about the welcome.

Chapter 72

The sky was deep blue with, here and there, a scattering of feathery white clouds. The early sunrise was now in full glow, shattering the drifting, morning mists and lighting a silver pathway from the Beacon to the sandy shore of the beach. The horizon was clearly defined and, all the way to the tide line, the surface of the water lay calm with hardly a ripple. Only now and again, away out, a lazy wave would rouse itself and then make its gentle progress to break on the beach with a delicate edging of white lacy foam. No wind ruffled the glittering surface; no boat to be seen; only the searching gulls, swooping and calling, disturbed the early calm. Although the real winter storms had not yet struck the shore, already small eddies of sand, thrown up by the breakers, had formed on the promenade and, further along, where it was more exposed, great mounds had accumulated, blown down from the dunes. But today was a scene of peace with a promise of a good day.

Mary Bella cowered in the corner seat of the public shelter, facing the sea. She needed this solitude but, now she was here, it was difficult to sort out the fears and emotions, which were overwhelming her beyond bearing. Jim was gone. How could she go on without him? All these years ahead? He was only sixty-two. What was left for her to do? Now she was alone, empty.

She was glad to be alone though; she needed to be away on her own. The family had gathered so well after that first heart attack; Betty and Tom, Jean and Andy and Alastair, Mary and Alex, and Jeannie and John from Aberdeen; all came in turn to help with the nursing. But, looking back, right from the start Mary Bella had realized it was a loosing battle. The lack of blood supply to the brain had affected Jim and he had some bad, stormy moments, which, Dr. Webster had explained, would be irreversible and would continue. Nevertheless, between times, her Jim was there and Mary Bella longed for some miracle of recovery. But, over the three long weeks, it did not come.

Mary and she were on duty that night. Jim was resting quietly and the two women kept each other company by the fire. They expected the Doctor to call back around 9.30 so, before that, Mary Bella went through to the kitchen to make a cup of tea. A sudden call from Mary brought her running back to the bedroom to find Mary holding Jim in her arms, but he was gone. There was nothing they could do. He had turned over, given a little cough as he opened his eyes, and stopped breathing. Mary Bella could not take it in. If only she had not gone to the kitchen but stayed, she would have been there with him. How she blamed herself. However, Dr. Webster allayed her troubled thoughts when he explained that Jim would not have recovered, but would have remained an invalid, subject to these unruly spasms, which she would never have been able to handle on her own.

"I'm sure you would not have wished him to suffer such a life, Mrs. Findlay. You did well. He had the best of care and he died at home amidst his family. Now, you must think to yourself."

The next few days passed like a confused and troubled dream. Alastair, Andy and Tom arranged everything with the undertaker and Betty, Jean, Mary and Lizzie May dealt with the catering and hospitality for all the visitors who called in an endless stream. They came from the Meeting, the Church, the Council, Jim's employers and friends and neighbours and, even in the days after the funeral, they still kept coming to inquire for her welfare. Mary Bella was deeply touched by their concern but her extreme weariness and sense of loss was sending her into a state of near collapse. However, thanks to the constant presence of Betty and Jean, she held on, managing to keep a degree of calm and put on a brave face. The children coming about the house was wonderful and Baby Ruth, Jean and Andy's little girl, just four months old, brought such comfort as Mary Bella held her close and felt the new, young life stirring under her hands. But again the sorrow welled up as she realized that Jim would miss all the joy of being Grandfather to these three and all the others who were still to come. If only he could have stayed a little longer.

Now here she was; able at last to give way to her thoughts without interruption. She was so glad that the family had lingered on for the two weeks after the funeral so that they could have Christmas at Betty's again and try to recover some quiet normality. Mary Bella also joined Jean and Andy for New Year at Ora's home where the babies, Ruth and little James were the main attractions. It had been so good and how she appreciated them all in their love and thoughtfulness.

But now they had all dispersed; Betty and Tom back to work, Jean and Andy with Ruth to Aberdeen for College and Alastair restarted University, much against his will as he felt he should stay longer at home to keep his Mother company. But Mary Bella was adamant; he must go back and tackle his next exams or he would lose a year. So he had gone off yesterday and she had passed her first night on her own.

The troubled, restless hours passed slowly. Mary Bella lay drifting in and out of a shallow sleep, aware of every creak and rustle in the cooling house, waiting patiently for the first greyness of the dawn to come through the curtains. She pondered on her day ahead. She knew she must leave the house and take herself somewhere alone. But where? The sea. She must go to the sea. It had always been Mary Bella's refuge when things became too hard to sort out. Somehow, the magnitude of its expanse and the everlasting restlessness quelled her worries and brought them into perspective. The rise and fall of the waves had always soothed and calmed her fears and the tensions receded. Her first thought was to the Broadsea Shore where she could commune with her memories of Mary May and her wisdom. But then again, going there and returning would involve meeting too many folks she knew and she wished to avoid people today. So then, she decided on the beach and, as soon as it was daylight, Mary Bella rose and set off in the raw dawn to reach the promenade shelter by all the quiet roads- Queens Road, Alexandra Terrace and the Links.

As Mary Bella sat watching the glorious panorama of the early day with the colours changing in the increasing light, and the faint warmth of the wintry sun, she felt soothed. The numbness gradually eased and she began to feel the stirring of strength in her limbs. All these weeks Mary Bella had known that God was with her in her grief but now, in this peace and solitary beauty, she believed it in her heart. She would be able to go on. She did not know how, but He would give her the strength to find the way. Mary Bella remembered her own Mother in her extremity of grief and how she had found her solace in hard work to maintain her family but still found time in her busy life for God and service for Him. The words of Scripture came to her,

"They that wait upon the Lord will renew their strength."

She would wait upon Him, and for Him, to show her the way.

Suddenly, in her reverie, Mary Bella was aware of a horn sounding in the distance and footsteps on the road behind. The Tool Works day shift was beginning and she no longer had the place to herself. She waited till the movement subsided and then she slowly rose, straightened her back, and resolutely stepped out on to the promenade. By now the tide was far out, exposing the long, sandy bay and the towering sweep of the majestic sand dunes crowned with the tall grasses, all lying golden in the brilliance of the sun. Remembering Maggie's stories of their childhood, afternoon walks along the beach to visit Granny in Cairnbulg, Mary Bella wondered at their stamina, and smiled as she lovingly remembered her Aunt. Refreshed, Mary Bella turned to cross the railway bridge and walk over the Links to Strichen Road and Lizzie May's where she knew there would be a cup of tea and a warm welcome. No questions would be asked, just a normal conversation about everyday things. That was what she needed and her friend understood. Mary Bella was ready to begin her life again.

Chapter 73

A few evenings after her early morning walk, Mary Bella had just finished her tea and was listening to the wireless news when there was a knock on the door. She wondered who it could be at that time. Betty would just open the door and walk in. Mary Bella hoped it was not one of the Brethren men, a few of whom had already visited, showing care for the widow. But they had been awkward and embarrassing occasions. She opened the door to find her Uncle George standing on the doorstep, looking very distraught.

"Balla, can I come in for a fylie? I need te spik wi ye."

As they sat together at the kitchen table over a cup of tea Mary Bella waited for George to recover his composure and begin his story.

"Ena hasna been weel for a fylie now and this mornin' she collapsed fan she got up. Nellie sent word te the shop and we called Doctor Webster. Fan he cam an' examined her he shook his heid and said she was verra bad an' it wis jist a maitter o' time. It wis her hairt; she's jist worn oot. I canna believe it. Balla, I'm needin yir help. Since her stroke Nellie isna able; she disna ken fit te dee aboot nursin'. Balla, div ye think ye cud help and come and nurse Ena?"

As she looked across at her Uncle, Mary Bella remembered the many times this man had been at her Mother's side, supporting and encouraging. And she remembered the hours of patient listening and advice her beloved Aunt Ena had given her. She reached across the table and laid her hand on his arm,

"Aye George, I'll come. Jist gie me a few minutes te gaither some things thegither and wee'll gang."

George just gripped her hand and said,

"God bless ye Balla. I kent ye wid."

What Mary Bella found appalled her. Over the past weeks she had been so absorbed with Jim and her own situation that she had been unaware of the state of affairs with her Aunt Ena. After the stroke, her cousin Nellie had never recovered her old standard of housekeeping and needed to employ Barbara Noble to come on a daily basis to clean and cook for her household. She had not realized her Mother's increasing frailty and need. George, now an old man but still running his ship chandler's business, came and went in his routine without really noticing anything amiss with Ena, or with the state of their home; not an uncommon trait in North East men of his generation. Mary Bella realized that she was undertaking more than just her Aunt's nursing. But these matters would have to wait till tomorrow; Ena needed her now.

Ena must rest so that first night Mary Bella did as little as possible to disturb her. After washing her face and hands and changing her pillowcase, Mary Bella helped Ena to eat a little toast and honey with a cup of tea and then sat quietly beside her until she fell into a doze. She would have to remove her Aunt from this crowded, dark bedroom. Ena needed more fresh air and light where she could feel she was part of the world and see people. Mary Bella decided that later she would have a talk with George and hear what he thought of her ideas.

"Ena's asleep now George and I wid like te mak some suggestions. It looks as though we micht hae te tak turns sitting up wi her if she gets worse. I wid like te move her into the front room far there's mair air and licht and it's cheerier. I ken it's aye been the best room but noo, it's Ena's turn te hae the eese o't. Ye wid need te licht a fire an' open the windaes te air the room. And could ye bring doon a single bed if there is een upstairs? That wid leave the bedroom clear for you te sleep in, or me, if we were sharing the nicht watches. One mair thing. Wid ye ask Barbara te come doon here an' gie the hoose a good clean. If Nellie and Barbara dealt wi the cleaning and cooking that wid leave us free te look efter Ena and you could manage te look in on Wilfred and Sandy in the shop. Whit div ye think George?"

When Doctor Webster arrived the next afternoon he found Ena where George had carried her, esconced in her single bed in the corner facing the window. Mary Bella had given her a bed bath and now she was refreshed and resting between the immaculate, white sheets with Mary May's crochet blanket across her feet. A bright fire crackled in the hearth and the room felt warm and homely. As he stood a moment and looked around he smiled,

"Now this is just fine. Mrs. Noble will do well here. I believe she is your Aunt, Mrs. Findlay? She couldn't have a better nurse."

After he had attended to Ena he continued,

"Is there anything for the patient that I could organize? You understand about the medicine I prescribed and you will see that she has no visitors for the first week anyway? Mrs. Noble must have total rest and simple meals, easy to digest."

"It would save disturbing her Doctor if we had a bed pan, and she is so frail, something soft for her to lie on would prevent a bed sore; maybe a fleece?"

"I'll see to that. And if you require anything else go across the road to the Thomas Walker Hospital. I'll leave word there that you might need their help. I shall call again in a day or two but don't hesitate to call on me if you are worried."

Within the hour a nurse arrived with the articles carefully wrapped in a sterilized sheet, along with a bottle of the hospital antiseptic fluid. She assured Mary Bella of any assistance she required and promised to look in from day to day to see how things were progressing. This greatly encouraged Mary Bella's confidence.

The long nursing ran into weeks and during that time a routine developed. Mary Bella concentrated totally on Ena and Nellie, with Barbara's help, kept the domestic affairs of both houses running smoothly. Everywhere was clean and orderly and a lovely relationship developed between the three women as each played her role in caring for Ena and George. Some times, if Ena was having a good day, they would all sit together at the window and enjoy a cup of tea and share news. Barbara had always plenty of that. Other times, on a bad day, one would come in and relieve Mary Bella for a spell.

During the first week or two when Ena was at her worst Mary Bella insisted on sleeping in the same room with her Aunt. She made up a bed on the couch and rested very well, knowing that she was at hand if Ena needed attention. But, after the worst was past, George decide that he would take a share of the night watches, and sent Mary Bella home to her own bed for a real rest. So it developed that they shared the nights until, after ten weeks, the end became apparent and Ena slipped into unconsciousness and died, as she had lived, quietly and much loved by all. A bright star had gone over the horizon.

Once the funeral was past and Ena laid to rest beside her beloved Granddaughter, Margaret, Mary Bella settled down at home. During her absence Betty had looked in and kept everything dusted and fresh but now, Mary Bella felt the urge to make changes. She would like to rearrange the furniture, here and there the house needed redecorating, all Jim's books and papers had to be sorted and, hardest of all, his clothes disposed of. Jean and Andy with the baby would be coming for Easter, Alastair for his holiday, and she needed to make sleeping arrangements. Betty and Tom would help move the furniture and so on.

One day, shortly after Mary Bella returned home, she received a large cardboard box from Maitland's delivery boy. Inside, to her surprise and absolute delight, she found a complete, bone china tea set. The delicate floral pattern with the gold edging was so beautiful. Such a thing she had never possessed. Underneath was another package containing a fawn, woollen jacket with a letter attached. Mary Bella was overwhelmed as she sat and read,

"Dear Balla, It's hard to find the words to express what I am feeling just now. I know you will understand because you are going through the same experience. Words are not enough to say Thank You and there is nothing we can do to recompense you for what you have done in the last two months. I know you nursed Ena because you have always loved her deeply but you did much more when you sorted out our families and made our homes clean and comfortable again. Nellie will always be grateful for your support and she joins me now in this letter.

Because you share your life with so many people we thought you would enjoy using this tea set, and the jacket is something personal. They are only tokens of our gratitude; the real thanks lies deep in our hearts and God knows about that. Bless you Balla. Your grateful and loving Uncle George."

Tears flowed as Mary Bella read the letter. She wept for George in his grief, for her own loss of Ena, for Nellie in her fecklessness, for Wilfred who had so loved his Mother, for herself, now alone and missing Jim sorely. It all came out in a paroxysm of choking tears and sobbing, which went on for some time until she fell back in the chair exhausted. Finally, she was calm and, in the usual, practical Mary Bella way, she lay quietly and considered the reason for the storm. Mary Bella felt a deep sense of relief, of cleansing, of release from the load of sorrow that had weighed heavily for so long. She knew she would go on missing Jim and Ena for a very long time; that would always be a real hurt; but these two were in the past now. What lay ahead was for her to deal with; life would go on for whatever time was left to her and she must make something of it. She had to hang on to God's promises. That was her resolve as she rose and began to lay out the beautiful china on the sideboard.

Chapter 74

After the initial burst of energy and all the decorating, cleaning and sorting were completed, Mary Bella searched around for another ploy to fill her days. She visited many of the older Church folks and of course, Nellie, Netta and Tina were a never failing support. The weekly ironing at Betty's house and the various meetings at the Church took up much of her time. But it was the long, silent evenings. As the winter darkness fell earlier, the evening walks and visits, which she had enjoyed so much, became a problem and, many times she returned to the house, put her key in the lock and could not turn it to face the dark, silent house on her own. Instead, Mary Bella turned about and walked away to spend an hour at Betty's house before the two returned together and Betty waited to see her Mother into bed.

The adjustment was hard and sometimes, when it became too painful, Mary Bella caught the bus to Aberdeen to pass some time at Jean and Andy's little house. It was not unusual for Jean to find her Mother standing on the doorstep with a slightly guilty look on her face,

"I jist thocht I wid come in for a fylie te see ye a'. Jist for a change."

And, as she drew her Mother in, Jean understood. Although their home was tiny Jean and Andy had provided for guests and, for a few nights, Andy would occupy the

Zed bed in the kitchen while Mary Bella shared with Jean on the living room bed settee. During the few days Mary Bella enjoyed pushing Ruth in her pram; sometimes with Jean, sometimes on her own; as she walked all around the area, usually ending up on the promenade of Aberdeen beach. The company of the baby and the sea air refreshed her and then, Mary Bella was ready to take the bus back home again.

All through that first year Mary Bella dealt with her personal grief. Relying gratefully on the company of the family and friends, she struggled on and found a way to a renewed purpose for living. How glad she was that she had remained in the Baptist Church. Now, in this testing time, she had discovered the true meaning of Christian love and friendship where the roots went deep through many years of fellowship and proving God's strength and love.

Chapter 75

During that first winter after Jim's death two significant events took place. After much soul searching, Mary Bella purchased a television set, something as a member of the Brethren, Jim would not have countenanced. But, circumstances for Mary Bella were different now and the family strongly encouraged her. It took pride of place in the corner of the living room by the window and solved the problem of the silent house. It also provided Mary Bella with a renewed interest in politics, drama, and world news and eventually, she had her favourite programs. The children Anne, Roger and Peter were often there for treats and snacks and shared her Saturday evening viewing; happy times which Mary Bella treasured.

The second event was a surprise visit from John Noble, Tina's husband. One day, during a confidential conversation with Tina, Mary Bella had described her satisfaction with her widow's pension and the pension from Jim's superannuation settlement. He had been superannuated for only a few years but had paid in quite highly and now she was finding the benefit. She had never felt so well off. But she still did not know what to do about the quite large amount of Saving Certificates in the bank; money she and Jim had planned for their retirement and had kept intact through all the years of ups and downs.

Tina had passed on the facts of their conversation to her husband, John and now, here he was, ready to render his services as an accountant and resolve her problem. John described how he could invest the money in safe shares, which would bring her a regular dividend and increase her income; and he would keep an eye on the state of the share market for her. Once she understood how it worked Mary Bella agreed but stipulated that she wanted no shares in the tobacco or alcohol world. So, most of the money was invested in real estate in London and in the Hawker Siddley Aero firm, with a few smaller amounts here and there. Mary Bella was delighted and, for the rest of her life, found immense pleasure in these dividends, which she often spent liberally on gifts for family and friends. Her simple lifestyle was amply covered by her pensions but, this extra income gave her such a sense of security and freedom and she never ceased to voice her gratitude to John for his thoughtfulness and care for her well being.

Chapter 76

The greatest satisfaction in life for Mary Bella was the sense of being needed. Now that she was on her own with only one to cater for and keep house, Mary Bella found herself ready to go farther afield. Jean and Andy were moving to the Borders for Andy to take up his first teaching post in Galashiels Academy so Mary Bella was at hand to assist in the packing up.

During two years of Alastair's medical studies she kept house for him in Aberdeen during term time; not all to his liking but in having her there, he felt he was helping his Mother. It was in the last few weeks of the final term when Alastair was seriously ill with a haematemesis that Mary Bella was torn between his need of her presence and Jean's need in Galashiels. The baby expected at the beginning of June had arrived prematurely and an emergency caesarean was performed in Edinburgh. Andy called on his Mother, Lizzie May, to help with Ruth who was brought to Fraserburgh for a month while Jean was in hospital with baby David. He was a very ill little boy who struggled hard to survive in the first two weeks of his life. But, he won through and the little family was reunited.

As soon as Alastair was fit again Mary Bella and he arrived in Galashiels and she took over the housekeeping allowing Jean to concentrate on the children. 1959 was a glorious summer of sunshine, which brought healing to all, physically and spiritually, as they spent hours in the beauty of the Border hills and rivers. That same summer Alastair graduated MBCHB and Mary Bella, accompanied by Betty, proudly attended the ceremony, quietly sorrowing that Jim was not with her to share her joy.

Since Mary Bella and Jim had waited long intervals between having their children, Mary Bella was now able to look forward to a prolonged period of weddings, babies arriving, helping to set up new homes and generally being available for whoever required her assistance.

The early years of the sixties saw some sad events for Mary Bella. Netta, the youngest of the five cousins, died of cancer after a lingering struggle and the circle was broken. She was only forty-eight, the same age as her Mother, Janet when she died, also from cancer and Netta's passing left a deeply sorrowing household. Sandy, now well into his eighties, found his loss hard to comprehend and treasured long conversations with Mary Bella. Then they would go back into the old times when Janet and Betsy were there working together in the garden with the children playing round and about and running out and in to the cooperage. More and more, Sandy retreated into the past and Mary Bella relished these shared moments recalling a golden time in her own youth.

Shortly after Netta's death, Jim's brother Alex died after a protracted and painful illness. Mary was devastated for a long time as she and Alex had been a very devoted couple and Alex and young Mary were the focus of her life. Mary Bella, still raw from her own loss, understood best what Mary was suffering and supported and encouraged her through the long time of adjustment.

But there were many happy events following on in the sixties. Over the years a seasonal pattern evolved for Mary

Bella. Jean and Andy usually came North to celebrate alternate New Years with the Grandparents and then Mary Bella returned with them to Galashiels for two or three months. This was a benefit for every one. It gave Betty a break from her constant sense of responsibility for her Mother's welfare, it enabled Jean to take up occasional teaching supply during the winter months when she was most needed, Mary Bella was meaningfully occupied about the house and Ruth and David loved coming home for lunch to enjoy Granny's cooking.

These were very happy times. Over the years Mary Bella became friends with many of the Galashiels folks, especially in the Church and amongst the neighbours; it always felt like coming home when it was time for her annual winter trip south. But, once March came in, Mary Bella would begin to comment on her garden in Gray Street and then Jean knew that her Mother was thinking about going home.

The first spring after Jim died Mary Bella decided that she would redesign the garden, which became a very important factor in her life. She specialized in the spring bulbs, roses and chrysanthemums, giving her a long flowering season and, along the back fence, Mary Bella gradually created a most varied and colourful herbaceous border. The wartime shelter mound became the strawberry bed and, wherever she could, Mary Bella sowed flower seeds, just for the extra colour. She found such satisfaction working there. In the morning she would rise fresh, keen to fulfil her plan of work for that day. Here at last Mary Bella was creating something for her own pleasure and satisfaction and nothing gave her greater happiness than when another gardener dropped in to see her display and discuss their shared experiences and ideas.

Chapter 77

Alastair was courting and Mary Bella was very glad to hear about it. Now that he was approaching thirty Mary Bella was concerned that his enthusiasm for work and his ambition to reach the top of his profession might have hindered Alastair's thoughts of marriage and family life. She longed to see him settled with a good wife and some children before her own demise. Betty and Jean were happily established with their families and she could relinquish responsibility for them but Alastair, the boy and youngest, continued to be her concern. He was like herself in so many ways; determined, focused, very diligent and unsparing in personal effort. She had heard reports of his work in the various hospital wards where he had served, especially his after- care concern, and it made her very proud. Alastair had decided to specialize in Orthopaedics and was aiming eventually to be a surgeon in that field. But Mary Bella was anxious that he should not lose sight of his potential as a husband and father.

But, she need not have worried. Alastair brought Mary Wright home to visit and it was a great success. Mary was an anaesthetist in the Glasgow hospital where Alastair was working and, as he described it, after looking at her for a long time, he plucked up courage and asked her out. Mary Bella was very satisfied. She approved of his choice and, in all the years ahead, this close Mother and Daughter-in-law relationship held and proved itself over and over.

The following year their wedding took place in Hamilton; a quiet event as Mary's Mother, also a doctor, had been killed in a road accident a few weeks previously. But the wedding was remarkable in so many ways. Such a gathering of friends, doctors and teachers mainly, and relatives from far and near. Some Fraserburgh guests came by plane from Aberdeen to Glasgow, returning home the same day. Aunt Mary was thrilled by the flight saying,

"It wis jist like sitten in a bus!"

Uncle John travelled from Brighton to Galashiels and joined Mary Bella to motor across to Hamilton with Jean and Andy in their roomy, old car. Everyone made a huge effort to support Mary and Alastair; Mr.Wright, still crippled and grieving from the terrible accident, and Mary Bella, missing Jim who would have been so proud. Who would ever have imagined that Betsy and Jimmy Findlay would have a grandson marrying in such illustrious circumstances? Mary Bella in these later years often pondered on the reactions of her in-laws to the academic prowess of Jim's children. She was sure they would have been proud.

In preparation for his Primary Alastair continued his studies and this took him to various locations as he sought experience in surgical methods and research. Within their first year of marriage Baby Kevin arrived and they enjoyed living in Dumfries for a period. But then there was a move to Glasgow and during that time Baby Rachel was born. Mary Bella came and went regularly, always taking advantage of a run in a car going south, and having a round of visits to Bearsden and Galashiels before returning home again. These were mainly winter visits and then, when June came in, she was all prepared for the arrival of the families on holiday from the south. Mary came early with the children and Alastair followed later for two or three weeks before taking the family home again.

Jean and Andy holidayed in Fraserburgh and usually spent a month shared between the two Grandparents, but very often they camped at the beach site in their trailer tent, and later in the caravan. Sometimes the holidays overlapped and the campsite became the rendezvous for all the grandchildren and parents. Mary Bella would sit and watch the children, revelling in the company and treasuring every moment. Often Andy and Alastair would take the four children away for a ramble along the beach and sand dunes, Ruth and David taking the little ones by the hand, while the women folk enjoyed their cup of tea in peace and very often Lizzie May, Betty and Mary would join them, always adding to the enjoyment and laughter.

Betty's three children were older and at work but often in the evening Anne, Roger and Peter would drop by the camp and then there would be another time of fun and sharing before Mary Bella at last decided it was time to go home and one or other of the cars would take her to Gray Street. These were halcyon days for Mary Bella when she could have all the family around her and she often wished that time would stand still for a little so that she could savour these moments for longer.

Chapter 78

Apart from the traumatic births of her three children Mary Bella had always enjoyed good health. She jokingly avowed that it was due to 'hard work and modest living' but at heart, she was ever grateful for her early upbringing and the attitudes she had learned from her Grandmother and her Mother. 'Others first, self last' had been their principles in life so that self-pity and selfishness were never allowed to influence their relationships.

However, as she approached her seventies, Mary Bella was aware of gynaecological problems and the result was a short time in Aberdeen Royal Infirmary when the fault was corrected. She returned home feeling a new person and full of praise for the hospital care. But after a few weeks of convalescence Mary Bella began to suffer chest discomfort and Angina was diagnosed. The occasional attacks of pain were very severe and exhausting until the medication, 'the little pink pill' took effect. The family was concerned about Mary Bella being on her own. They felt that she should come and stay with one or the other on a more permanent basis. But Mary Bella firmly refused.

"No, I'm nae moving fae here. I'll get the phone in and we can spick te each ither, bit I'm nae leaving ma hame. I'll come and visit as usual, maybe afener, bit young folk need te hae their hame te themselves."

No more was said on the matter but Betty, Jean and Alastair realized that Mary Bella had considered the situation and had made a wise decision. At the moment, none of the three was in a position to house Mary Bella. Betty's daughter Anne had moved to Oban with her husband George and baby Michael, Roger had followed and now, Betty and Tom were facing a move to join them when Tom took up his new appointment in the Oban branch of the Royal Mission to Deep Sea Fishermen. Alastair and Mary were still without a permanent home as long as he was studying and moving around the hospitals. Jean and Andy were in the process of buying a larger and more convenient house nearer the schools for Ruth and David and things were a little unsettled there. However, it was decided that Mary Bella would go and stay with Jean and Andy for the summer and help with the preparation leading up to the removal in July. She would feel needed and Jean would be able to keep a watchful eye on her.

As it turned out, Mary Bella was a tower of strength in the packing up and organizing and she virtually took over the removal, directing the arranging of the furniture in the large rooms and taking great delight in the guest room, which would become her room. The large bay window facing into the garden became her favourite place and remained so for many years. Between her sojourns frequent guests used that room but always, throughout Jean and Andy's almost forty years residence in that home, the room was lovingly called 'Granny's Room'.

Chapter 79

By the approach of the seventies Mary Bella found herself in a very changed situation in Fraserburgh. Betty and Tom were now settled in Oban and happily managing the Deep Sea Mission Institute by the harbour, Jean and Andy were enjoying their roomy old Victorian home and toiling to establish the garden, which had been left uncultivated for years and, in order to give Alastair further experience in surgical techniques, Alastair and Mary had gone to Canada for a one year's residency exchange in an Ottawa hospital. This last departure had been hard for Mary Bella but, all had converged on Galashiels and farewells were said in unison amid tears and laughter. Mary Bella told herself,

"They are only deen fit Jim and I did. It's only for a year and that seen passes." And then she looked forward to the letters arriving.

But, back in Fraserburgh, Mary Bella missed her close family. Of all the aunts and cousins only Tina remained, Nellie having died a few years previously. There was only her sister- in- law Mary, and Lizzie May, now suffering severe heart problems, and Ora who had retired early to help look after her. Along with a few old friends in the Church and one or two good neighbours these were the ever-open doors where a welcome was assured. And she did miss

Betty and her family dropping in with all their news and fun.

Gradually, Mary Bella tended to stay away longer on her travels and make a circuit of her visits. Occasionally, Anne's Father –in-law, Jim Bruce would give her a lift to Oban when he went to help George with jobs about the house. There she stayed with Anne and visited Betty and Tom at the Mission. After a few weeks they would run her over to Galashiels where she remained until Jean and Andy made one of their frequent visits to Lizzie May and Ora and then Mary Bella came home to Fraserburgh again. So she passed the winter months, almost as if waiting for the spring to come again and her gardening work to begin. But at heart she knew that she was counting the weeks until Alastair and Mary would return from Canada with their two little children.

Unknown to Mary Bella, Betty and Jean had planned to take their Mother on a surprise holiday to Boston and Maine to revisit all her old haunts and then go over into Canada to reunite with Alastair and Mary in Ottawa. But that plan did not materialise as, once their year was completed, they decided to return to the United Kingdom. The work experience had been invaluable but Alastair decided that he needed to return to complete his studies for the final exam. The fierce Canadian winter was another factor, an experience they did not wish to repeat. So once again there was a joyful reunion at Galashiels.

Alastair and Mary began the final preparation for his exam; first in a Leeds hospital and later in Dundee and then came the wonderful day when Mary Bella accompanied Mary to the Surgeons Hall in Edinburgh to attend the graduation ceremony. Alastair, still only thirty-six, had achieved his ambition and was now an Orthopaedic

Surgeon. She was so proud of him, and of Mary who had been his rock of support all the way. This day was another high light in her life and she gave a quiet word of thanksgiving to God for the way He had blessed her in her children.

Chapter 80

Mary Bella had always loved the outdoors. In summer time, and even in winter as she walked or worked in her garden, she relished the clean fresh air and the sun on her face. As spring became summer the sprinkling of freckles on her face and arms spread and darkened until her complexion became a deep nut-brown and, coupled with the bright blue eyes and smiling mouth, Mary Bella presented a most attractive appearance. She had a smile for everyone and most people responded to it, sometimes stopping for a word or nodding in the passing. One day Rachel asked,

"Granny, do you know everyone in Fraserburgh? They all say Hello to you."

With a laugh Mary Bella replied,

"No Rachel, I don't know everyone in Fraserburgh but I've lived here a long time and it doesn't hurt to give everyone a smile."

So, when first Jean and Andy and later, Alastair and Mary invited her to go on holiday with them in a trailer tent she was thrilled to say 'yes'. And so began a series of wonderful holidays in Scotland travelling from John o' Groats to the Mull of Kintyre and all down the west coast, opening up new horizons of such scenic beauty she had never imagined.

Usually there was a rendezvous in Oban for a few days when all three families met at the campsite and then there would be barbeques, visiting, and picnics in favourite haunts. It was important that the families should be together at times, for cousins to get to know each other and for Mary Bella to enjoy the moments of being the matriarch with all her grandchildren and by now, even a few great grandchildren, round about her. As the years flew past, memories of these holidays were treasured by all; highlights in time; the golden age when the children were all young and the adults were strong and energetic. Mary Bella was grateful that she had lived to see it all happen.

It was on one of these camping holidays that Alastair received notification of his appointment to the post of Orthopaedic Surgeon at the Royal Alexandra Hospital at Paisley. Their joy knew no bounds for, at last, they could now settle down in a permanent home and have some structure in their lives as the children, Kevin and Rachel were approaching school age. Baby Elspeth, born while Alastair worked in Dundee, was still a toddler.

Mary Bella was so happy to be with them that week camping at Findhorn and joining in the discussions on where to look for a house. Finding the best area round about Paisley and a good school were very important. So they decided to pack up camp and move to Galashiels for their second week and there Alastair and Mary would leave Mary Bella and the children in the care of Jean and Andy while they set off on their own to do some research. The children enjoyed the freedom and space of the house and garden and the many hill climbs with Andy and David; picnics by the Tweed featured largely and Mary Bella was happy, helping where she could and enjoying whatever ploy had been arranged for the day.

Finally, Mary and Alastair returned with news of a suitably large bungalow in Giffnock within a few miles of Paisley and Hamilton; the infant school and church were nearby and behind the house was Eastwood Park with beautiful trees and space to walk and play. After a review of their resources, Alastair and Mary offered for the house, which was accepted and at last, they had their own home where they could bring up their three children with some sort of permanency.

Alastair's long road of study had been the cause of some concern for Mary Bella but now, she felt very satisfied. Here he was, her youngest, settled with an excellent, supportive wife in Mary, three lovely children, a wonderful home and work which was both fulfilling and beneficial to mankind. She could not wish for more.

The triangle was complete; Oban, Giffnock and Galashiels, and Mary Bella made many journeys between the three as family events took place; weddings, funerals, new babies, new homes. Betty's three children had all married and, between them, had given Mary Bella nine great grandchildren. Jean's two were now approaching university years and Alastair's three were still at the infant level. Thus with such a range Mary Bella's life was full of interest and she kept in close touch with all their development and activities. She was so proud of her little clan and so thankful that they were all healthy and intelligent.

Chapter 81

But things were not all rosy for Mary Bella. Back in Fraserburgh she could see many changes. She became aware of how many of her contemporaries were no longer there, and of those who remained, so many had become frail and housebound. Nellie's death had broken Mary Bella's close ties with the past and she missed her sorely; Tina was virtually a recluse, shut in with her memories of John who had died so suddenly and, as she looked around, Mary Bella realized that many of her old neighbours had one by one disappeared. Of the originals only two really close ones remained, May and Jean, who lived next door. May she had known since Sunday school days and their links went deep into the past.

When she attended Church or any related special event Mary Bella had the distinct feeling of being set aside with the 'old' ones. This offended her deeply as she certainly did not feel 'old' or that she was beyond making a practical contribution to the work. Her loyalty to the work of the Church had been lifelong and her Mother had been one of the founder members of the Hall Fund so, when the opening of the new hall was arranged, Mary Bella felt she had some part to play. On the afternoon of the social preparations she carried along her home bakes, which were warmly received and then she was told to go and sit down and some one would bring her a cup of tea.

"Na, na. I didna come te drink tea. I cam te lay tables and help bit if ye dinna need me I'll jist gang."

With that she turned away, the tears choking in her throat, and sadly she made her way to the beach. Doors seemed to be closing all the time and the young certainly knew how to make one feel old and put in one's place. Mary Bella resented that attitude. One should be respected and valued as long as one was able to play a part. As she walked gradually her anger faded and she rebuked herself for having such a bad reaction. Maybe they did consider her as an old lady, which in years she was, but they could have been more diplomatic about it. Once more Mary Bella was realizing that Fraserburgh, Albert Street, Gray Street, Broadsea and all the rest, belonged to the past; her future lay ahead with the family, wherever they were, and she must think that way when a final move was to be made. She was just so thankful for her wonderful memories and the awareness of a constant God who would be with her in all places and circumstances.

Chapter 82

A wonderful aroma of steak pie cooking in the oven filled the house. The oil for the chips was ready and the table was laid for six. Mary Bella sat by the kitchen window watching for the car arriving, and then the moment when the door would open and the three children spilled out followed by Sally, the black Labrador, and then the rush on the stairs to be first to the top to claim the bed by the window. Mary Bella loved the fun and excitement of it all.

This summer Mary and Alastair had decided on a Fraserburgh holiday, just relaxing and enjoying the beach. Jean and Andy were going to be on the campsite so they would have a good time all together and maybe a joint trip for a picnic at Aberdour Beach could be arranged.

At last the car was there and the children did their usual but, as she watched Mary and Alastair unloading the luggage, Mary Bella thought how tired and pale they looked; sorely in need of a holiday; working too hard. Later, after a good meal, the children finally settled down to sleep and Alastair took himself off to bed leaving Mary with Mary Bella in the kitchen sorting out the children's clothing and preparing for tomorrow. Now that they were on their own Mary closed the door and drew Mary Bella to a seat at the table,

"Granny, come and sit down. I have something to tell you and it's not going to be easy to explain. ------- For the past two months Alastair has not been well. He has felt terribly tired and in quite a lot of pain. The doctor put him through all the tests and he had second opinions at the hospital to confirm what he had found. Alastair has been diagnosed as having rheumatoid arthritis. It's a form of rheumatism, which attacks the muscle tissue causing inflammation, pain and swelling, and severe fatigue. It's a chronic disease and, so far, no cure has been found. But, there is medication, which can help once the doctor finds the one which best suits Alastair's case. He is in the care of one of the best rheumatologists in the country who is very positive in his outlook."

Mary Bella sat as if turned to stone, seeing and hearing nothing. The word 'rheumatoid' had hit her like an arrow and thereafter Mary's voice had receded into the background. This could not be happening again. First her Grandfather, then her Father and now her son; all young men in their early forties. What was wrong with her family? As she gradually focused again Mary Bella began to hear Mary's reassurances that Alastair would be fine once his medication was adjusted to his needs.

"It's not a fatal illness and one can work and live to an old age with it. There can be periods of long remissions when life becomes normal, and then it can return for a time. But, he isn't going to die from it. It's just something he has to take on board and live with."

"Where did this illness come from Mary? My Father had rheumatic fever which was the cause of his death; would it be inherited?"

"No Granny. Alastair probably caught it in hospital. At the moment he is feeling very low. All he sees is himself crippled in a wheel chair, not able to be an active Father for the children, and having to leave work causing all the difficulties of financial problems. Of course that is not going to happen but he has to come to realize that himself and, at the moment, he is struggling. I know this has been a shock for you but you had to know right away and not kept wondering about his weary appearance. He just needs peace and understanding and not too much talk and coddling. He's a man who has achieved a lot and he'll come through this too."

"Mary, I appreciate what you are saying. But I also see what it has taken out of you. Alastair has his Father's temperament and can be a difficult patient. I know something of what you are going through and, rest assured, whatever happens, I'll be there for you and support you in any way I can. You *will* work it out together I know, but always you must trust me when you need help or some one to talk to."

"Granny, I appreciate that. I will admit it has been a hard time but we have made some good decisions. After the holidays the children will all be in school and I found a lady in the church who will come in daily and be in the house when they come home. She is a minister's widow called Betty and I think she will be fine. I've found employment as a GP in a medical centre not far away, part time to start with to see how it goes, and Alastair will go on as usual at the hospital, still operating and teaching. So you see, we will be fine. I'm just hoping this holiday will allay Alastair's fears and help him to see things clearly. You must not worry about us Granny. I will keep you informed about all our doings and I'll take you up on your offer of help when we could do with you there in Giffnock. And remember, you can come any time to stay with us. Your room is there."

"I know Mary. You are very good. When you were all so well settled I just wish this hadn't happened. Life presents some difficult mountains to climb but we do get the strength and just have to take one day at a time. And that's what we'll do this holiday. Make it a good time for the bairns and allow Alastair to join in as he wishes. Now it's time for bed, it's been a long day for you and they will all be up and on the go early. Thank you for telling me everything."

Mary Bella was not a demonstrative person but, as she rose she put her arm round Mary's shoulder and gave her a firm, reassuring hug; comforting for both women who, although full of brave thoughts, were still confronted with an uncertain future.

Sleep eluded Mary Bella for many hours that night. Her thoughts churned over and over until she finally rose and took refuge in the kitchen where she could give vent to her tears and work through her sorrow in private. Although he was a husband and father Alastair was still her child and Mary Bella suffered a mother's grief for him. Dawn was breaking when at last she returned to bed and slept.

During the weeks that followed there were many picnics, and outings to villages round the coast, Andy took the children fishing at the harbour and they held family barbeques at the campsite. To begin with, on most of these occasions Alastair chose to stay at home resting but then, one day he appeared, walking steadily across the Links and joined them sitting by the swings.

"Any tea left in that flask for me?" And that was the turning point. Day by day his attitude changed and the cloud dispersed. The old Alastair was back. No doubt he would feel down again but he had learned that life was worth living and he had much to live for.

That day no comment was passed on his sudden appearance, but the joy and relief was plainly visible on the faces of the women folk and Mary Bella in particular as she strove to contain her tears.

Chapter 83

Now well into her seventies, the years were beginning to weigh more heavily on Mary Bella. The shock of Alastair's illness had had a deep affect on her. All his life she had felt a strong sense of protectiveness towards him; possibly because he was her youngest, so much junior to the girls, and so dependant on her after Jim's death. Through all these years of study Mary Bella had been his rock and he had been so reliant on her support and encouragement. Now again he needed that reassurance, but he was no longer her responsibility; she could only stand on the side and watch while her desire was to be close looking after him. Mary Bella understood very well what Mary meant when she said Alastair was not to be coddled and Mary was right; but it was very hard being so far away from Giffnock and not seeing him regularly. The old worrying temperament returned and that, along with the increasing years, gave her face a careworn, sad expression.

Other events, which contributed to that was the sudden death in Oban of Betty's husband Tom who died from a heart attack. Ora, Jean's Father- in- law, and long standing friend of Jim and Mary Bella, also died of coronary failure and his passing meant the closing of yet another door in Mary Bella's circle. A deep sense of loneliness seemed to overwhelm her at times but still Mary Bella persisted in clinging to her resolve to remain in her own home for as long as possible. Not even when she severely scalded her leg while filling her hot water bottle would Mary Bella concede that she should not be doing that sort of thing. At last she agreed to use an electric blanket. Her strong determination did not make it easy for the family as they sought to find a way round the situation. Much as they loved her and sought to do their best for her well-being, Granny's strong will was a wall they found hard to surmount.

More frequent visiting at weekends and a bedtime phone call from one or other each evening provided some solution. Anne and George often came north to visit his parents and brought Betty to stay with Mary Bella for the two days. It was more difficult for Mary and Alastair with the three young children but, as his condition improved, now and again Alastair came on his own for a weekend. Ruth was now studying at Aberdeen University so Jean and Andy had a good reason for a monthly visit to Granny in Fraserburgh, and calling in on Ruth for an hour before their Sunday afternoon return journey. Both Mary Bella and Ruth enjoyed the home bakes, which Jean brought to replenish their cake boxes, and Mary Bella the little tubs of cooked meals for her freezer compartment. Although Meals on Wheels had been set up for Mary Bella, she enjoyed the variety. Another support was her Home Help lady who called twice a week for an hour, bringing in the news, sharing a cup of tea and giving a once over where necessary. Mary Bella looked forward to her visits and these arrangements, coupled with her annual visits to Oban, Giffnock and Galashiels, sustained her over the next two years.

Some memorable events took place during that time. Betty, now on her own, had made her home in a lovely, two bedroom flat and Mary Bella enjoyed staying with her there when she visited Oban. Once again there was a summer gathering of the whole family when the campers united with all Betty's children and grandchildren at Oban and celebrated together with picnics and excursions. Granny was now the 'old lady' who was to be treated gently. But she did not mind that, content to sit back and let the young ones take over.

Christmas was another gathering occasion. Betty came from Oban and Jean, Andy and the family brought Mary Bella from Galashiels to celebrate Christmas with Mary and Alastair in their home at Giffnock. That was a very special day for Mary Bella. Alastair was well and the three children were still at the magical age of Santa Claus; Kevin and Rachel still pretending to believe for the sake of Elspeth. Mary had surpassed herself with the Christmas dinner and, as she sat back and watched the interplay of personalities, all so different, Mary Bella felt very content. Maybe now things were going to work out well. Betty seemed so happy in her new home and was enjoying her work in the dental surgery, Jean and Andy were happy and secure in their marriage and work, and Ruth and David were progressing steadily in education. Here in Giffnock, Alastair and Mary had adjusted to his health issues and had achieved a stable life style which enabled the children to attend a good school and develop their talents, particularly in music. 'Time is a great healer' thought Mary Bella as she reviewed the traumas they had experienced during the past two years.

Chapter 84

It was in the spring of her seventy- seventh year that the family began to notice changes in Mary Bella. For some time she had been free of angina and felt good, but now, a persistent cough along with slight fever troubled her and caused fatigue and weakness. The doctor was treating her for flu symptoms but Alastair was concerned that something more serious was causing the illness. Eventually he persuaded Mary Bella to go back with them to Giffnock when their holiday ended and he would arrange for her to be examined in the hospital there.

After many tests and waiting for results Mary Bella was diagnosed as having a pulmonary condition, which was slowly destroying the alveoli cells supplying oxygen to the blood. How Mary Bella came to suffer from the disease was a mystery and the doctors took a long time to confirm their verdict but eventually, Mary Bella came home to Mary and Alastair's house to recuperate before returning to Fraserburgh.

She was determined to go home and was adamant that she could manage to live on her own now that she knew what her illness was and she had her medication. And she did try. The family had to allow her to prove it for herself. But the stairs was a big problem and gradually Mary Bella came to realize that she was becoming a prisoner in her own home, and having to rely more and more on the help of her neighbours. As they came and went the family could see this and they worried at their Mother's stubbornness. But eventually she conceded and, when Jean and Andy came north at the end of the summer, Mary Bella returned to Galashiels with them for a trial period before making a decision to give up her home.

The following months in Galashiels brought Mary Bella great happiness. The family came from Oban and Giffnock on frequent weekend visits, Jean kept her busy with small household tasks and, on an occasional fine afternoon after school, they shopped together and enjoyed a coffee shop treat. David, now a college student, was often about the house when Jean and Andy were at school but, just in case Mary Bella was too much on her own, Jean engaged Mrs. Kerr to come for an hour in the forenoon to make her Mother's coffee and do light tasks such as ironing and dusting. Mary Bella insisted on using her pension money to pay for Mrs. Kerr's visits and, just to encourage her Mother's sense of independence, Jean agreed.

On the October mid term weekend Jean and Andy drove Mary Bella north to Gray Street and they had an enjoyable few days working in the house and garden but when Mary Bella was asked if she had decided to stay there she replied,

"No, no. I'm coming back with ye te Gala. It's fine doon there, and there's little for me here."

So it was arranged for a few of her favourite things to be brought by carrier to Galashiels; her arm- chair, the dressing table, her television and some photographs, and Mary Bella travelled south again to set up her room and begin a new life.

Having her own place meant much to Mary Bella. She did not wish to intrude into the family life and yet, she was part of it. She always felt at liberty if she wished to spend an evening at her own fireside with her favourite TV programs. The garden was a great delight for her. To open the front door and step out into it was wonderful and Mary Bella passed many hours there, pottering or just sitting watching the birds or reading. Neighbours dropped in and very often ladies from the Church called to keep her company for an hour. It was a pleasant, quiet way of life. And then of course, the weekend visits when a car would arrive from Giffnock or Oban.

It was during their companionship in these months that Mary Bella shared so many memories with Jean. Sometimes it was her childhood, or the Ripley years, Charlotte Street days, the Baptist Church in Boston, Aunt Maggie; whatever she had been thinking about that day. Jean encouraged her Mother to talk. It gave her a deeper glimpse into the life of Mary Bella and a fuller appreciation of this person she had been privileged to call Mother. As she listened to Mary Bella reminiscing about Jamaica Plain, Jean realized how lonely her Mother had been in the years after leaving to come back to Fraserburgh. The close ties with Alex and Norman had been broken and, over time, only a tenuous correspondence had been continued with Flora. True, Betsy had also come back to Fraserburgh, but their relationship had not been easy, overshadowed as it was by the War and Betsy's long and difficult illness.

These shared moments made Jean realize what a sacrificial life her Mother had lived; how many times Mary Bella had set aside her own dreams and aspirations for the sake of others. It also gave an insight into the qualities of humility and caring which had governed Mary Bella's life and made her the woman she had become. Her greatest achievement had been her family, of whom she was justly proud, but in the wider world, she was deeply respected as 'a fine woman'.

Chapter85

Mary Bella was not well. Despite all the precautions taken, she caught a cold, which went straight to her weak spot, her lungs. It was hard to watch her struggling for breath during one of her exhausting bouts of coughing. After a few days the doctor diagnosed a collapsed lung, which meant hospital in Edinburgh where an operation would inflate the lung and Oxygen would ease her breathing. So began another memorable episode in Mary Bella's life.

At first all went well. Mary Bella adapted to the hospital regime and looked forward to her visitors in the evenings. The lung was restored and she experience two wonderful days of unrestricted breathing, which made her optimistic about her early return to Galashiels in time for Christmas.

But the doctors were not so hopeful. During the family consultation, they explained that the condition had severely affected both lungs and it was unlikely that Mrs. Findlay would ever breathe freely again without the assistance of oxygen. In the event of further lung collapse, did the family wish to put her through another such stressful operation? This information caused deep distress to Betty, Jean and Alastair. It brought home to them the reality of the unthinkable; they were losing their Mother. Very hard to come to terms with as they sat in that bare, hospital interview room. But without hesitation, they agreed that further distress was to be avoided; the doctors would make her comfortable and, as soon as she was ready, Mrs. Findlay would be brought home to Galashiels by ambulance.

Mary Bella was still there in hospital when Jean and Andy visited on Christmas Eve. Alastair had visited during the afternoon and Betty planned on coming next day along with Anne and George. Later in the week Ruth would be arriving from Aberdeen with her boyfriend, Iain McDiarmid, and Mary Bella was full of good spirits as she chatted about the coming days. Of course she was disappointed about missing Christmas at home but the hospital had a good day planned and she would enjoy that. Before they left for home Jean hung a Santa pillowcase on the end of her bed with strict instructions that Mary Bella was not to look in it till morning. Then, with a hug and smiles they departed, promising to be back next day to join in the festivities.

Alas for their optimism. Overnight a heavy blizzard covered the south of Scotland and all roads into Edinburgh from the south and west were impassable. Snowploughs could not keep up with the demands for clearance and snow gates were closed on Middleton Moor and on Soutra Hill. The beautiful countryside was gripped in all its wintry perfection; totally changed overnight into a scene of pristine white, which sparkled in the occasional sunbursts between blizzards. In the garden the branches of the trees bowed low under their weight of snow and long icicles formed on railings close to the warmth of the house. The silent falling of the snow was only part of a silent world; all traffic had ceased, footsteps were muffled, the busy, noisy world had been brought to a halt. It was as though nature had provided an opportunity for people to reflect on the true meaning of Christmas, a moment of quiescence in a usually hectic world.

It was frustrating for the family although they had the comfort of knowing that Mary Bella was safe in hospital. Jean and Andy had to wait five days before the rout to Edinburgh was open and their bus travelled slowly behind a snowplough. A city bus drivers' strike added a further complication forcing them to walk all the way across Edinburgh in deep slush to reach the hospital on Ferry Road. Mary Bella was surprised and delighted to see them and assured them that she had enjoyed her Christmas in hospital, especially her pillowcase. Gradually things came back to normal and arrangements were made for Mary Bella to come home.

Realizing that most of Mary Bella's days would be spent in bed, Jean and Andy rearranged her room positioning her bed to enable her to see the garden and the bird feeders; her favourite chair was set in the bay window corner and the TV was angled to suit both. Andy fixed up an electric bell from her bedside and a very attractive white basket chair commode stood in the corner by the bed. With the fireplace and her other pieces of furniture and photographs the room looked welcoming and very much 'Mary Bella's place'.

A week later an ambulance brought Mary Bella home to Galashiels, complete with oxygen cylinder and trolley. As the nurse made her comfortable in bed Jean was grieved to see how frail her Mother had become. The old framework was there but the covering was thin and it made Mary Bella quite fragile to handle. Because of her difficulty in breathing she had to lie in a semi sitting position, which was hard on the back and hips, so a fleece and a foam air cushion were obtained and that eased her greatly. Gradually everything for her comfort came together and Mary Bella adapted to her new life style. She seemed to realize that these were to be the limits of her existence and she did not resist. Her only worry was the continuing snowstorm, which could close the road to Carlisle and hinder the daily delivery of the oxygen cylinder. That did not happen however, thanks to the diligence of Mr. Holmes, the local chemist who knew that the oxygen was her lifeline.

Chapter 86

A quiet daily routine ensued. Just before seven o'clock when Jean went through with her early cup of tea, Mary Bella was always awake, greeting her with a smile and ready for a new day. After a change of position on the basket chair while Jean remade the bed, Mary Bella had a refreshing wash and returned to bed for a rest before breakfast; a small plate of porridge, tea and toast, which she always seemed to thoroughly enjoy, despite the inconvenience of the oxygen mask.

Before leaving for school Jean brought through the newspaper, checked the gas cylinder level and saw her Mother settled for another sleep before Mrs. Kerr arrived for the forenoon. Then it was coffee time and Mrs. Kerr chatting while she dusted and tidied the room. In between times Mary Bella read or listened to her bedside wireless but, most often, she dozed quietly in a light sleep. It was almost as if her body dictated the need for sleep and rest in its battle with the virulence of the disease.

Jean returned for the lunch hour and they ate their soup and sandwiches together in Granny's room. Occasionally David was there with his lively company but generally it was quiet with Jean doing the talking about her morning in school while Mary Bella enjoyed listening. Then it was time to return to school and Jean departed after seeing her Mother settled for her afternoon nap.

During the winter term most of David's lectures were in the morning so he was able to study at home in the afternoons and be at hand if his Grandmother required assistance. Quite a bond developed between the two and Mary Bella enjoyed his quiet companionship as he sat and studied beside her. Then Jean returned before four o'clock and Mary Bella got up to sit in the chair for a change of position and to enjoy the afternoon cup of tea and a cake. Very often about this time her doctor arrived to check on Mary Bella and sat chatting for a little while before going home. He lived nearby and, over the weeks, Dr. Sands became a friend. Mary Bella looked forward to his visits.

Before the evening meal there was the ceremony of the small glass of sherry, strictly on doctor's orders, to encourage Mary Bella's appetite. Then Jean brought in her meal on a tray and stayed to supervise. Mary Bella enjoyed her food; she refused nothing as long as it came in small quantities; fish in particular was a favourite and simple, easy-to-eat dishes such as shepherd's pie or macaroni and cheese. Afterwards, while Jean returned to her own meal with Andy and David, Mary Bella watched the News on her TV.

She kept abreast of events and world affairs and had certain favourite programs such as Coronation St., Flambards, the Onedin Line and the Beechgrove Garden. She loved a good film or play and followed the political changes closely. When the Conservative Government came in, although a staunch Liberal voter, Mary Bella was pleased because now her shares would increase in value. A pragmatist to the end. It all seemed such a tragedy; this keen, alert mind in a body growing frailer by the day.

But the old willpower was still there, keen as ever. To enable the household to lead their normal lives and have a good night's sleep, Mary Bella was determined to be as self sufficient as possible. Within a few days of coming home from hospital she had mastered the skill of moving from bed to commode, manoeuvring the oxygen cables, and having chairs strategically placed to hold on to. Once a wheel chair had been acquired, Andy fitted a bracket on the back to hold the oxygen cylinder and, on a good day, Mary Bella enjoyed the luxury of being wheeled to the real toilet. Occasionally she joined the family having a meal in the kitchen, or in the sitting room where the change of scene was refreshing. She seldom took part in conversation but enjoyed listening.

Her insistence that Jean kept on her work in school was another condition of her staying with them; otherwise Mary Bella would have remained in hospital or some other care institution. This laid an increased load of work and responsibility on Jean's shoulders but she would not have had it otherwise. The close family was supportive in every way, her Headmaster, Mr. Macdonald, understood the position and was always ready to stand in for her if the need arose; Betty and Alastair kept in close touch and always, Jean and Andy felt the warm, prayerful support of friends who came and went to visit Mary Bella. A great deal of love and caring was engendered at this time and the memories of such remained with Jean always. As she tackled her daily routine, what could have been a burden became a privilege and she was very aware of that special source of strength and courage.

Chapter 87

Towards the end of March Mary Bella's condition began to deteriorate. Her colour changed and the weariness in her eyes became more marked. Although she still seemed to enjoy a light meal and watch her favourite programs, an air of detachment had increased and Mary Bella seemed to live in her own world of thought. The doctor was concerned about her low blood pressure and warned that unless it could be raised it would mark the end. He suggested that perhaps now was the time to call in the family members.

It was on Friday afternoon that David noticed a sudden greyness come over his Grandmother's face. He called Jean from the kitchen and they watched together as Mary Bella seemed to sleep and slowly returned to normal. Dr. Sands would be calling later and he would inform them about what was happening and what to expect. Jean was glad that Betty and Alastair were on their way and would arrive soon.

Following the evening procedure of the commode and having her back massaged, Mary Bella enjoyed a cup of tea and settled down in her nest of pillows warm, relaxed and very at ease. Jean also prepared for the night with a sleeping bag, a comfortable chair and a book and, as she watched the proceedings, a little smile crossed Mary Bella's face,

"Ye're afa good te me." She whispered, giving Jean's hand a little squeeze. And with that she fell into a doze.

The night closed in, the silence broken only by the hiss of the oxygen and Mary Bella's softly laboured breathing. The lamp on the floor and the glow of the fire spread a cosy atmosphere in the room and , as she watched her Mother, Jean found it hard to accept that this could be her last night on earth. It was an agony to let her go. Every so often Andy came to take over the vigil and it was a relief to give vent to her choking emotions in the kitchen.

In the early hours of the morning Mary Bella seemed to rouse from the deep sleep. Her eyelids flickered and she began to whisper indistinctly through the mask. At one point she pulled down her mask and, as though having a conversation, Mary Bella said quite audibly,

"Aye. I wid have liked te see the bairns growe up."

Then Jean replaced the mask. She had been thinking about Alastair's children.

Later, she asked Jean to take her hand and they lay close together in the darkness while Mary Bella whispered intermittently. It did not matter that Jean, too choked with tears, could not speak in reply. Mary Bella was already away in her thoughts. As time went by she sank down deeper into the pillows and the mask slipped down below her chin but Jean did not disturb her, as her breathing seemed stronger and easier. Suddenly she gripped Jean's hand.

"I'm nae feart ye ken. An' I'll see my Granny an' my Father." These were her last words. Gradually her breathing grew shallower and by dawn she was resting, warm and relaxed, almost as if in a normal sleep. But Dr.Sands, when he arrived, shook his head.

"I'm sorry. Mrs. Findlay will not grow better. This will go on until she slips away. It's the body closing down in its own time. She looks very comfortable and I promise there will be no struggle. She is probably aware of what is going on round about so talk to her. You may get a response. Don't hesitate to call me if you are worried. I'll be at home all day."

Betty and Alastair were already there sitting one on each side of the bed. Both were silent, too shocked at the sudden change and at the reality of what was happening to their Mother. Jean spoke to Mary Bella as she stroked her forehead,

"Mam, here's Betty and Alastair. They've come te see ye. Will ye speak te them?"

At that she opened her eyes slowly, looked at them all and smiled. Then with a soft sigh she sank back into semi consciousness.

They made a silent trio as they sat, each overwhelmed by a deep sense of loss and sorrow. Mary Bella had been the king pin who had always rallied them together and on whom, at some time in life, each had leaned for support. She had never failed them, in fact had done the opposite in encouragement and example. Now they were losing her, and all that was left were the memories.

As her life had been, so was her demise; without fuss or drama and, when Dr. Sands returned at ten, he confirmed that she had already gone.

They took her back to Fraserburgh, back to the home on Gray Street where Mary Bella had lived for over forty years. And then on the following Thursday, family and friends gathered for the funeral. In Kirkton Cemetery she was laid to rest alongside Jim, together again after twenty- two years. And, just a little way along the path, marked by the red granite tombstone, were the graves of Maggie and Betsy. Here they lay reunited, close to the sound of the sea, which they had loved; three lives given in faithful service to God and to mankind.

GLOSSARY

Aalest; oldest.

Afener; oftener.

Affgo; the beginning.

Affront; embarrass.

Airms; arms.

Airt; direction.

Aneuch; enough.

Barking; treating the nets in bark solution to preserve the cotton.

Baudlies; outcrops of rocks off Broadsea shore.

Belger; native of Cairnbulg.

Benn; main living quarters in a But an' Ben

Bidden; invited.

Bidden; resided.

Bide; stay.

Bielded; sheltered.

Bigsie; conceited.

Bocht; bought.

Brocher; resident of Fraserburgh.

Cam; came.

Chiel; man.

Chik; cheek.

Cloot; cloth.

Clootie- dumpling; dumpling cooked in a cloth.

Closs; passage; alley; yard.

Clyes; clothes.

Cooperage; building where barrels are made.

Curn; a few.

Didie; Granda

Drappies; small amounts.

Drifter; drift net fishing boat.

Dylt; weary.

Eence; once.

Efter; after.

Faa; who; fall.

Family wye; pregnant.

Fan; when.

Farlan; wooden trough containing herring for gutting

Farrer; further.

Feetwashen; prenuptial ceremony of joint feet washing for bride and groom.

Fermen; farming.

Filie; a little while.

Foo; how.

Forby; besides; in addition to.

Fortnet; fortunate.

Fower; four.

Fowk; people.

Garret; attic.

Glaikit; foolish.

Go-ashore; second best clothes, worn by fishermen ashore during a fishing.

Goon; dress.

Gryte; great.

Gumption; common sense

Gweed; good.

Haar; sea mist.

Hail; heal.

Hallie; the Broadsea Hall.

Hurlie; hand barrow.

Huts; living accommodation for gutters.

Ken; know.

Kent; knew.

Kist; trunk

Kit; open barrel for transporting herring.

Lippen; rely on.

Loonie; young boy.

Mairrit; married.

Mairry; marry.

Neest; next.

Oolet; brat, pest.

Oonerstan; understand.

Ootlins; strangers.

Orra; Andrew.

Ower the waater; Cairnbulg.

Perswaad; persuade.

Plicht; plight.

Prood; proud.

Quait; quiet.

Quinie; little girl.

Quite; petticoat; oilskin gutting skirt.

Redding; tidying, sorting the nets.

Roassin; burning up.

Roost; rest; turbulent area of seas on rout to Shetland Isles.

Sair heedie; small cake heavily encrusted with sugar.

Sairer; worse.

Seen; soon.

Settling-up; end of season sharing out of profits.

Shakky-doon; makeshift bed on floor.

Sheath; straw- filled leather pouch worn under arm to support long knitting needles.

Skull; shallow wooden sledge for carrying baited lines.

Sleekit; sly, sneaky.

Softie; plain bun.

Souch; low whistling sound; sigh.

Spoot holes; drainage carrying brine from the farlans

Spylt; spoiled.

Stey; support.

Stone pig; stone hot- water bottle.

Stoonin; painful, aching.

Strapping; well built.

Sudan; area on south side of Fraserburgh harbour.

Surree; soiree, evening social.

Thole; endure; put up with.

Thrang; busy.

Traivelin, travelling

Twa; two.

Ull; badness, harm.

Umman; Woman.

Voe; long narrow inlet between islands, usually in Northern Isles.

Vrecht; work

Vrocht; worked.

Waens, children

Walken oot; courting.

War; worse.

Warld's End. 16th. Cent. Historic house in Fraserburgh.

Wasten; rocks on the west shore of Broadsea.

Whaup; curlew.

Wid; would.

Wirt; worth.

Wonner; wonder.

Wyte; blame.

Wyte; wait.

APPENDIX

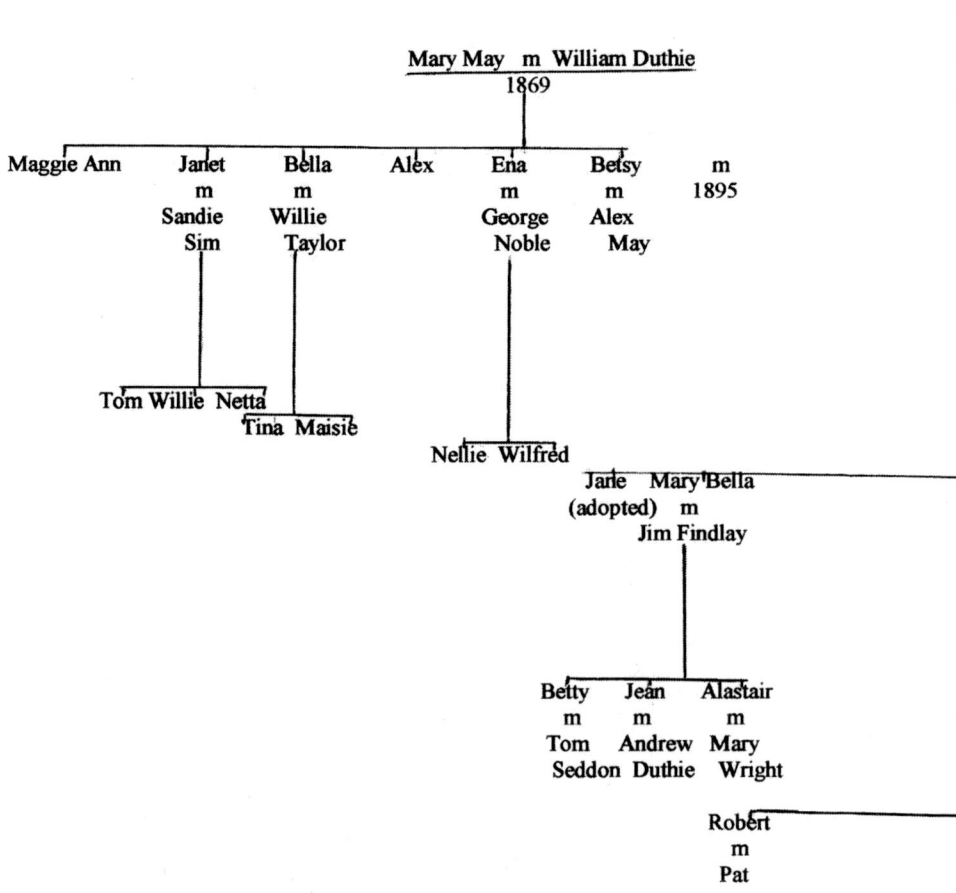

Mary May   m   William Duthie
1869

Maggie Ann   Janet   Bella   Alex   Ena   Betsy   m
  m   m   m   m   1895
Sandie   Willie   George   Alex
Sim   Taylor   Noble   May

Tom Willie Netta
Tina Maisie

Nellie Wilfred

Jane   Mary Bella
(adopted)   m
Jim Findlay

Betty   Jean   Alastair
m   m   m
Tom   Andrew   Mary
Seddon Duthie   Wright

Robert
m
Pat

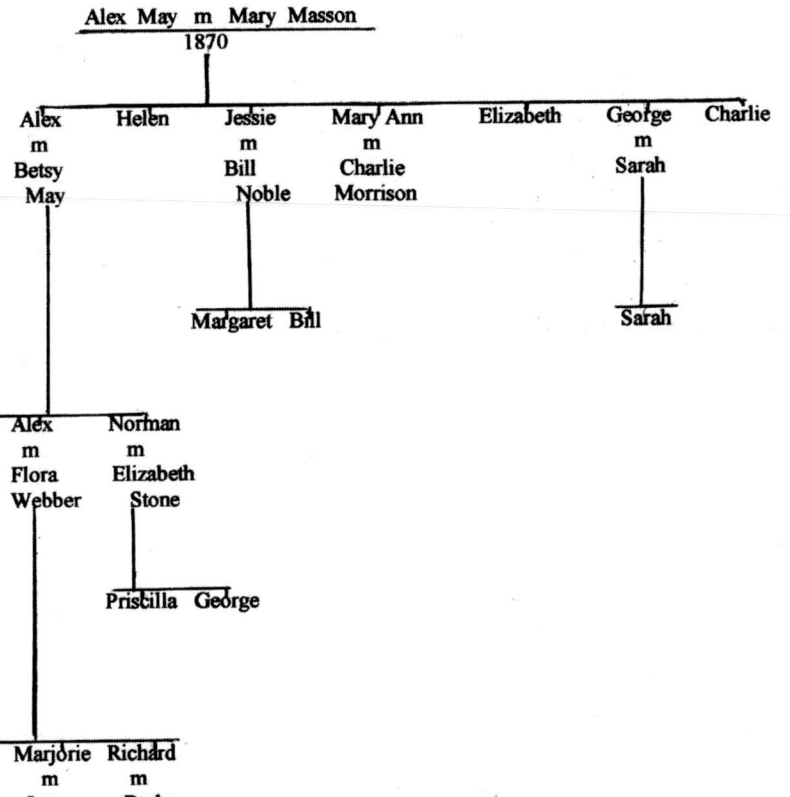

THINGS TO BE THANKFUL FOR

The good, green earth beneath our feet,

The air we breathe, the food we eat,

Some work to do, a goal to win,

A hidden longing deep within

That spurs us on to bigger things

And helps us meet what each day brings,

All these things and many more

Are things we should be thankful for ...

And most of all our thankful prayers

Should rise to God because He cares!

Lightning Source UK Ltd.
Milton Keynes UK
177540UK00001B/21/P